Skagit Gardens
Library Book
Return to Sales
Thanks!!!

The Looking-Glass Garden

The Looking-Glass

Garden

Plants and Gardens of
the Southern Hemisphere

by Peter Thompson

Timber Press
Portland, Oregon

Title pages: Peter Brady's garden, Auckland, New Zealand.

Characters described in the case studies in Chapters 15 and 16 are fictional. Resemblances to persons living or dead are coincidental.

Published in 2001 by
Timber Press, Inc.
The Haseltine Building
133 S.W. Second Avenue, Suite 450
Portland, Oregon 97204, U.S.A.

Designed by Susan Applegate
Printed in Hong Kong

Library of Congress Cataloging-in-Publication Data

Thompson, Peter, 1931–
    The looking-glass garden: plants and gardens of the Southern Hemi-
        sphere/Peter Thompson.
        p.   cm.
    Includes bibliographical references (p.   ).
    ISBN 0-88192-499-7
    1. Plants, Ornamental—Southern Hemisphere. 2. Gardens—Southern
        Hemisphere. I. Title.

SB408.3.S645 T56 2001
635.9′09181′4—dc21

                                                        00-061556

To my mother, Eileen,
who accompanied me
on several adventures
through the Looking-Glass

Contents

Acknowledgements

M Y STORY of the Looking-Glass Garden is based on visits to more than 350 gardens and places where wildflowers grow. Space simply does not allow me to thank everyone who took the time and trouble to show me round gardens, and for the generous hospitality and encouragement that I received. Many of my hosts are introduced in the pages of this book, or are acknowledged in the captions that accompany the photographs, and with few exceptions their names are not repeated here.

I owe a particular debt to the gardeners and curatorial staff of the many botanic gardens that I visited, especially: the gardens of the National Botanical Institute of South Africa at Kirstenbosch, Worcester and Betty's Bay; the Regional Botanic Garden at Manurewa near Auckland, and the Otari Native Plant Museum in Wellington, New Zealand; the Australian National Botanic Garden at Canberra, and Mount Annan Botanic Garden at Campbelltown; and the Royal Botanic Garden in Edinburgh and its outlying garden at Logan in south-west Scotland.

Whenever I came to Melbourne during visits to Australia, Marg and Geoff Harrison and their family most kindly provided me with a base. Jill and Colin Roberts not only welcomed me to their house, but made arrangements for me to see gardens around Devonport in Tasmania. Paul Thompson, undeterred by a morning of drenching rain, introduced me to the magnificent displays of Australian native plants on the campus of Monash University. Biz Nicolson met me with a baby wombat in her arms, and she and her husband, Lindsay, showed me round their serenely beautiful garden of Australian natives at Bonneys Plains in Tasmania. Rodger Elliot gave me the benefit of his vast experience of Australian plants during a tour of the Karwarra Native Garden at Kalorama, Victoria.

My visits to New Zealand would have been much less rewarding without the encouragement and hospitality of Alison McRae and her husband, Doug, and the help of her invaluable book *Gardens to Visit in New Zealand*. Similarly, Rusty and Biddy Barrett at their nursery at Tututawa near Stratford, and John and Fiona Wills at Trellinoe Park near Napier went out of their way to ensure my visits were successful. Help and advice from Esme Dean of Omahanui Native Plants near Tauranga; Jack Hobbs, curator of the Regional Botanic Garden at Manurewa; Wayne and Lynn Clarke of Parikiori Gardens near Whangarei; and Betty and Charles Moore at Doctors Point near Dunedin made crucial contributions to my understanding of gardening in New Zealand. Gill Smith of Northcote Point responded nobly to a request to introduce me to the work of contemporary garden designers around Auckland.

Anne and Angus Bean most kindly put me up in their home in Cape Town, and elsewhere in South Africa Fay Fenn and Nancy Gardiner introduced me to a number of beautiful gardens in the Natal Midlands. Lettie Myburgh gave up her time during a most instructive morning observing the plants on the limestone formations around Cape Agulhas.

People whose gardens in one way or another made a particular contribution to my understanding of the gardens of the Southern Hemisphere include Hans Schmidt in Australia and his compatriots Lysbeth and Bill Allison, Dick Burns, Lindsay and Christine Campbell, Linda Floyd, Ron and Margaret Lambert, David McIntyre, Stephen Ryan, and Anne and Ron Stewart. In New Zealand Diane and Peter Arthur, Gael Blaymires, Sir Thomas and Lady Clark, Geoff Genge, Lois and Wynne Going, Peter and Pamela Keddell, Bev and Ken Loader, Shirley and Peter Lowes, Sandra van der Mast, Jill Maunsell, Wendy and Cam McDonald, Bob and Joe Munro, Peter and Elizabeth Ormond, Stewart Preston, Ted Smythe, Etienne Truter and John and Susan Wallace. And finally, in South Africa Marianne Alexander, Glen Ashton, Pam Barlow, Anne Dew, Felicity Flint, Richard and Hanneke Jamieson, Eve Palmer and Geoffrey Jenkins, Richard King, Elizabeth van Rensburgh, Leslie Rigall and Mollie Viljoen.

Finally, a heartfelt "thank you" to taxonomists throughout the world who have made it possible for me to become acquainted with these plants at all. Working in conditions that I could not endure for a week, on points of detail and minutiae that would drive me to distraction in a day, these taxonomists offered patience and dedication to elucidate the relationships and provide identities for a host of plants, which would otherwise have remained inextricably confused in a bewildering muddle of vernacular names bestowed on them by Zulus and Xhosas in South Africa, Mapuches in Chile, Australian Aborigines and New Zealand Maoris, and subsequently overlaid, transmuted or changed entirely by English, Afrikaans or Spanish colonists. Confronted by the prospect of such a Tower of Babel, I give thanks for simple Latin binomials.

Lewis Carroll's Duchess is featured in stone at Margaret Barker's garden at Larnach Castle near Dunedin, New Zealand.

CHAPTER 1

Through the Looking-Glass

AS CORNWALLIS'S army marched out of Yorktown to surrender to George Washington's Continental Army, the band played "The World Turned Upside Down." The American War of Independence was virtually over, and some wag, so the story goes, chose this West Country air to express the bitter irony of the overturn of the old order by the new. Things would never be the same again. In the world of gardening, the plants we grow, the ways we do things and how we like gardens to look are as solidly entrenched in western European traditions as ever the old colonial powers appeared to be in the New World. But now plants of the Southern Hemisphere are being used in gardens to create effects that look nothing like those to which we have grown accustomed. This book tells of the challenge from south of the equator to these entrenched and long-accepted ideas, a challenge that one day we will look back on and recognise as the start of another revolution—after which, as they say, things will never be the same again.

The foundations of western gardening were laid at a time when few adventured through the tropics, and scarcely any plants were brought back from the temperate lands beyond them. Even during the eighteenth and nineteenth centuries, when an awakening interest in plants from strange places stimulated a broader awareness of their value to gardeners, the Southern Hemisphere provided curiosities for botanists and exotic collections rather than regular plants for the garden. Glimpses of the Cape flora and, after the invention of the Wardian case (a portable glass case used to transport living plants) around 1840, the arrival of a trickle of novelties from Australia, New Zealand and South America were eclipsed by the excitement caused by the discovery of the secret gardens of China and Japan. While

13

Asian plants were enthusiastically integrated into the gardens of western Europe, the southern flora remained a minority interest restricted to a tiny proportion of the plants found there. Pelargoniums and Cape heaths might rule in conservatories, gladioli brightened summer bedding schemes, and gardeners made free with the muted charms of hebes, but otherwise the great plant families of the north dominated the gardens. It was as though a gigantic one-way mirror encircled the globe around the equator. From the north the gardens reflected on the surface of this looking-glass were filled with roses, campanulas, daffodils and tulips, lilacs, camellias, geraniums, rhododendrons, lupins, columbines, cypresses and firs, birches, oaks and other Northern Hemisphere plants. From the south it was a window through which to look back nostalgically at familiar plants in the home-lands left behind. The native wildflowers were disregarded in favour of Old World plants in gardens that faithfully followed Old World patterns.

Today it is easy to pass through the looking-glass and explore the gardens that lie beyond it, gardens that are both natural and man-made. The magic carpets of British Airways, United Airlines or Qantas transport us overnight from one side of the world to the other. We discover variations on familiar themes: countless versions of heathers, pelargoniums, hebes and eucalypts; an unbelievably colourful profusion of South African bulbs; proteas, banksias and innumerable other shrubs with strangely formed flowers; and exotic evergreen trees. We discover, as Alice did when she ventured through the looking-glass, that things we take for granted do not happen—the outlandish becomes commonplace and the impossible is not unusual. Surprises include eucalypts, kauris and other trees that shed their bark not their leaves; a tree known succinctly to Tasmanians as "horizontal" because that is the way it grows; trees in Australia that look like grasses but are lilies; and others in New Zealand that start life in the air but end with their roots in the ground. Most of the trees we refer to as conifers never produce a cone, and the trunks of tree ferns are constructed from their roots. This is a world where Phoenix plants are destroyed by fire, yet cannot survive without it; a place where succulent plants may be almost indistinguishable from the stones amongst which they grow, or live a subterranean existence obtaining sunlight through skylights in the tips of their leaves. Lilies and rhododendrons perch in the trees; flowers hang down and are pollinated by birds;

and clovers grow from corms the size of nine-pin bowling balls. A New Zealand fern produces a leaf that can grow a hundred feet long, and a plant in the deserts of Namibia produces no more than a single pair of leaves which can survive and grow for hundreds of years.

Eurasia and North America, united in the distant past by direct contact, have kept in touch since by recurring land bridges. The southern continents, and even fragments like Madagascar and New Zealand, were once part of a single "supercontinent" known as Gondwanaland, but have long been isolated from one another since the break up of the large land mass a hundred million years ago. Ferns, cycads and conifers were long-established residents, and flowering plants had already appeared when Gondwanaland was torn apart, and each drifting fragment carried its own inheritance of an ancient common stock. This explains the seemingly astonishing fact that closely related plants grow in Australia and South Africa, New Zealand and Chile and even India, even though these places are now separated by thousands of miles of ocean. The implications of these similarities are fascinat-

Few would think of *Welwitschia mirabilis* as a garden plant, though it has fascinating possibilities for gardeners in arid, well-drained situations. Offering one of the most bizarre of all plant forms, it depends on a single pair of leaves throughout a life that may last a thousand years or more. University Botanic Garden, Stellenbosch, Western Cape Province, South Africa.

ing, but for gardeners the plants of the Southern Hemisphere are most exciting and rewarding for the wide variations that occur from one region to another—far greater differences than can be seen in the Northern Hemisphere. New Zealand, western Tasmania and southern Chile reach down into the moist and boisterous regions of the Roaring Forties, and steep mountain slopes create the conditions that produce rain and nourish luxuriant evergreen forests. (The "Roaring Forties" is the area of ocean between 40° and 50° latitude in the Southern Hemisphere, where gale-force winds are commonplace.) The western Cape and Western Australia lie farther north, where air currents create drier conditions, and comparatively modest mountains are less effective rain makers, resulting in drought-adapted floras in conditions very similar to those around the Mediterranean Sea. Even in places with similar climates and topography, however, the plants can be extraordinarily different. Bulbs and succulents grow everywhere in the western Cape, but practically none grow naturally in Western Australia, not because the conditions there are unfavourable for them—immigrants from South Africa thrive in the place—but for some reason they just never happened there. Tree ferns fill the forests of New Zealand with their distinctive forms, but you will look for them in vain amongst the southern beeches, laurels and podocarps of Chile.

Hidcote, Sissinghurst, Filoli and other classic twentieth-century gardens are often described as gardens of rooms, and the Looking-Glass Garden might be said to be the same—on a gigantic scale. As I move from one room to another, the plants I encounter and their atmospheres and ambiences conjure effects that play no part in the orthodox gardening styles of the north. They suggest alternative approaches that are in tune with natural and cultural identities very different to those of north-western Europe and North America. In many parts of the world there is a growing sentiment for embracing indigenous, rather than imported, arts and traditions, and this trend is often accompanied by greater acknowledgement of the value and distinctiveness of the native flora. The "weeds" of the bush or veld, for example, which generations of settlers struggled against to establish farm and range lands, are increasingly being recognised as beautiful in their own right, and valued as garden plants.

This book is about my discovery of the Looking-Glass Garden, a world rooted in nature and expressed in gardens. One hundred and fifty years ago it might have been entitled *An Introduction to the Plants of the Southern Hemisphere; with a Brief Review of Some of the Gardens,* presented in twenty-five volumes, with supplements. Today that sort of prolixity belongs only to the Internet, and ninety thousand words and some colourful pictures mark the limits of readers' patience and time. There is no room here to be comprehensive, or even representative. This is a personal account of places and people I visited, plants I have seen and the glimpses I have had of opportunities to do new and exciting things in gardens—often in places where more congenial conditions for outdoor living encourage us to enjoy our gardens in ways that are substantially different to those that are appropriate to traditional gardens in less favoured climates.

My exploration of the Looking-Glass Garden started after my aunt, Margaret Jones, left me a legacy. She had spent many years in South Africa, and I longed to see the wildflowers that grow in this country of changing, rolling landscapes, dramatic mountains and turbulent coasts. Nelson Mandela had been released from jail, apartheid had ceased to be state policy, and this was an opportunity to do what I had dreamt about for so long. The result was the revelation of a world of plants previously barely perceived. It was a severe shock to the system of someone brought up on the conventional belief that cottage gardens and the tastefully modulated fabrications of Gertrude Jekyll, Vita Sackville-West and Rosemary Verey were the epitome of garden style. I had grown to know and love the familiar, tried-and-tested plants that were long the foundation of gardening throughout Britain, North America and elsewhere; plants that filled my gardens and those of friends and neighbours; plants that I had stocked and sold as a nurseryman. It had never occurred to me to look beyond them, or to suppose that even their enormous variety might be less than sufficient.

Confronted by so many kinds and shapes and forms of plants—beyond, or almost beyond, the reach of gardeners in the cool grey north—I could scarcely say whether I had gone to Heaven or to Hell. But what forcibly struck me was the realisation that those who had persuaded me that the climate of Britain provides an earthly paradise for plants were wrong. We may kid ourselves that we have an exceptional range of plants at our disposal, and that our imaginative use of them, guided, never let us forget, by impeccable taste, has enabled us to create the world's most beautiful gardens, worthy models for gardeners wherever they may be. We might, and indeed have managed to persuade gardeners elsewhere that our gardens are inferior to none, and superior to most, and that a pilgrimage to Britain represents the discovery of the gardener's grail without which none can die happy or fulfilled.

A flight through the mirror into the Looking-Glass Garden south of the equator provides a different impression, projecting us into a world where shape and texture appear in multitudes of different forms, so much so that these plants can appear ill at ease, contrived and out of place in our gardens. Their shapes seem too pronounced and emphatic—too foreign— amongst the understated, muted forms to which we have grown accustomed. That is a criticism of the ways we use the plants rather than of the

The gardens at the Palace of the Lost City in South Africa are a land of fantasy where strange and exotic plants grow amongst the ruins, and wild animals emerge from sandstone cliffs to gaze on the gardens below. The Palace of the Lost City, Pilanesberg, North-West Province, South Africa.

plants themselves. Most of us have had little experience of plants that are so individual and so forceful in their impact, and we need time to get to know them, and practise to assimilate them in ways that not only create agreeable impressions, but introduce us to fresh and innovative styles of gardening. Only a minority may yet recognise it, but the gardeners of South Africa, New Zealand, Australia, southern Europe and California, amongst other places, are the true inheritors of so much more than is dreamt of in orthodox philosophy.

In this small garden in the suburbs of Pretoria, great rocks and small trees are enlivened by a variety of plants with sharply contrasting forms. Taking its inspiration from the bushveld, the appearance of the garden belies its small size, and its serenity provides a soothing alternative to the busy planting often seen in gardens in similar situations. Pieter de Jager's garden, Monument Park, Gauteng Province, South Africa.

CHAPTER 2

Reflections of Nature

PORTLAND, Oregon, may not seem an obvious starting place for an exploration of the Looking-Glass Garden, but in a garden in the northeast of the city, amongst comfortable turn-of-the-century timber houses, I encountered an eye-opening example of the impact of southern plants. Sean Hogan's yard is small, much too small to satisfy his appetite for growing plants, and he has neatly solved the problem by persuading neighbours to let him do their gardening for them. Sean's individuality produces a style of planting all its own, including many plants that are nowhere to be seen in the decorously conventional gardens in the surrounding streets. Eucalypts, grevilleas, leptospermums and cordylines make dramatic entrances amongst the flowering cherries, roses, azaleas and lawns, in crowded communities of shrubs and perennials that threaten to link shoots across the street and engulf the houses behind them. Winters here are wet and chilly, and the presence of these southern natives is testimony to their ability to thrive where less adventurous gardeners would not even consider them.

The flowering cherries, roses and azaleas in the surrounding gardens are the living—and highly attractive—expressions of gardening orthodoxy, to be glimpsed over fences and hedges in precisely similar gardens all over the temperate world. This inheritance from western Europe dominates gardening throughout the New World and in the Southern Hemisphere to such an extent that the editor of the South African magazine *Garden and Home*, to whom I wrote asking for suggestions about gardens to visit in which South African plants prevailed, replied that she doubted if I would find many. *Gardening Australia*'s editor, faced with a similar enquiry, evidently thought it such a forlorn hope that it was months before she could muster a response at all. Fortunately, further enquiries showed that both had underestimated the imagination and spirit of innovation of gardeners in their countries.

The reasons for this dominance are historical, and have little or nothing to do with logic, the ways plants grow naturally or the kinds of gardens that suit the lifestyles of people in these countries. Plants that thrive in England do not necessarily transplant well to other parts of the world, and many potentially excellent garden plants play no part in our gardens at all. By global standards, western Europe is an outlandish place in which to garden, and gardeners there start where the rest of the world gives up. The Isles of Scilly south-west of Land's End lie in the same latitude as the northern tip of Vancouver Island, and the bleak storm-driven landscapes of Tierra del Fuego and remote islands between New Zealand and Antarctica occupy similar positions in the Southern Hemisphere as the south of England does in the north. Gardening is possible in western Europe only because warm ocean currents ameliorate the climate, and the conditions in which gardens exist, and the ways gardens are used, are very different to those encountered elsewhere.

Garden-making Brits learnt to cope with exceptionally low light combined with sporadic periods of moderately severe, but seldom intense, frosts during long winters. They depend on plants able to survive each winter's switchback sequences of mild weather, which encourages growth, followed by cold, which exposes young shoots to killing frosts. During the summer they enjoy normally good rainfall, fertile, humus-rich soils, and exceptionally lengthy days, when sunlight is usually abundant but seldom excessive.

The orthodox gardener's creed that I imbibed in the earliest days of my gardening apprenticeship makes the most of these blessings and minimises the problems.

> I believe in the turning of the soil and the incorporation of humus;
>
> As a virtuous gardener I will frequently and repeatedly sprinkle fertilisers so that my plants shall not lack for nutrients. And, my hand will be ready ever to reach out to separate seedlings, space plants and eliminate all forms of earthly competition.
>
> I shall rest not from hoeing nor weeding by hand, so that no weed may be seen amongst my plants. Nor refrain from pesticidal sprays and the scattering of slug pellets;

Neither shall I abstain from frequent watering, during dry days and in fine, so that each plant may receive an abundance of its life-giving powers;

In the dark days of winter I will raise up plants in houses of glass, or within the comfort of frames. Nor plant them in the earth till all danger of frost be past;

Through the sure and certain knowledge that all has been done and nothing left undone, so that every plant shall grow bigger and better, lies the salvation of my garden.

These are the duties that orthodox gardening imposes on its devotees — and very effective they can be. Eliminating competition and providing protection and a fair share of light, nutrients and water for every plant enables us to grow the widest possible variety with very few thoughts about the conditions in which the plants grow naturally. But to suggest that they are equally applicable to all types of gardens, or acceptable to all kinds of gardeners, is absurd. In many parts of the Southern Hemisphere, in southern Europe and in California, winter cold and short, dark days are not major problems; seasonal, periodic or chronically acute shortages of water are more likely than year-round rainfall; far from being fertile and richly endowed with humus, soils are often the impoverished, mineral dregs of long-decayed rocks. Summer can be a period of endurance rather than plenty, and winter the main growing season. Elsewhere, year-long warmth and humidity enable plants to grow continuously, but encourage weed growth, pests and diseases to a degree unimaginable by the orthodox. In other places and other lands people who follow the creed with its emphasis on deep digging, soil enrichment and ample water find themselves in continual conflict with natural forces.

Orthodox and Natural Styles of Gardening

Today, one of gardening's ever-recurring cycles has made it fashionable, once again, to invite Nature into the garden. The places where plants grow naturally—referred to by the cognoscenti as "habitats"—and ways of matching them with settings in the garden—sometimes referred to by the trendy as "garden habitats"—have become talking points; articles are written and books published on the subject, and bandwagons can be seen in motion, some rolling steadily, others lurching haphazardly. When some guru tells us to consider the conditions in which plants grow naturally in order to improve our gardening, it seems a blindingly obvious statement of an eternal truth. But when they go on to tell us that we should match the places we put plants in our gardens to the conditions in which they grow naturally, doubts arise. How was it possible, we may wonder, for generations of gardeners to spend their lives growing plants with scarcely a thought about such things? When I watch television programmes or read articles in which punctilious attention is paid to separating plants that prefer sun from those that like shade, or those that prefer moist soils from those that like dry, then observe them being dotted around according to these perceived preferences, I spy a lurching bandwagon driven by someone who has failed to grasp the essence of this new approach to gardening.

Matching plant to place can be significant, but only as part of an alternative, radically different approach to garden making. Such discrimination is pointless when following orthodox techniques specifically designed to provide conditions in which plants will grow almost irrespective of their natural origins. Matching plant with place allows us to adopt fundamentally different methods, and to forget most of what we have been taught to do by orthodoxy. Then possibilities open up and advantages are gained which are especially relevant in situations where lack of water, infertile soils, unrelenting sunlight or prolonged warmth and humidity create stressful conditions that orthodox methods fail to address satisfactorily.

All that digging and delving, mucking and manuring, watering and feeding carried on by the orthodox create conditions in which plants survive irrespective of their natural likes and dislikes. If some mad fancy ever persuaded me to make the deep bed of homogeneous, fertile soil needed for an herbaceous border, I would not hesitate to grow wetland plants like ligularias and wachendorfias beside drought-adapted salvias and euphorbias, or compose colour schemes with dianellas from the forests of Australia combined with osteospermums from the sunlit veld of South Africa. In such benign conditions all would grow happily together, partly because they are looked after to ensure that they do not compete with one another, partly because I would be using what might be termed "good garden plants"—that is plants capable of thriving in a broad range of conditions regardless of their natural preferences. Centuries of western gardening has selected a corps of tried and tested, tolerant, broadly adaptable plants that do well in gardens. One problem with introducing new plants to our gardens, such as those of the Southern Hemisphere, is lack of the experience that enables us to pick out the compliant from the recalcitrant. The result is successive disappointments as we learn by trial and error which are the good garden plants and which need special conditions in order to thrive—in other words depend on matching plant with place.

Just as there are plants with special needs, so are there gardens with special needs that are not amenable to orthodox approaches. Few of us choose our gardens, but instead have them thrust upon us by circumstance and happenstance. We may find ourselves with a plot that is impracticable to dig deeply; soils may not be fertile; water is often a limited resource. Organic

New Zealand is a country of abundant water and rich plant growth; here the two are combined in a water garden that embodies the character of the countryside. Ayrlies, Bev McConnell's garden, Howick, North Island, New Zealand.

matter may be so meagre, or so rapidly destroyed, that its role is insignificant. Even the most favoured gardens include places beneath well-established trees, on steep banks or above beds of sticky clay where it is impossible, uneconomic or ruinously time-consuming to practise orthodox techniques. We have all met the owners of such properties, and listened to their lamentations and complaints—repeated over and over again—that "nothing grows there," a notion difficult to reconcile with the sight of wild plants flourishing in the surrounding countryside, where exactly the same features exist.

We have a choice between orthodoxy and nature, and the time to abandon orthodoxy is when we encounter plants or gardens with special needs.

This relaxed planting of bulbs and grasses amongst bird-of-paradise flowers, proteas, milkworts and other shrubs is aptly described by its owner as a "back to nature garden." Nevertheless, the grouping and siting of the plants clearly establish that it is a garden, and its informality matches the mood of the suburb in which it is situated. O.G. Malan's garden, Uniepark, Stellenbosch, Western Cape Province, South Africa.

Then it can be rewarding to look beyond the garden to identify where and how plants grow, and to use what we observe as a guide to the plants we choose to grow and the ways we manage them. Natural models are everywhere—forest, bush, veld, scrub, pampas—the word we use depends on where we live. They may seem a world away from the contrivances and artificialities of gardens, but these structured, ordered and stable communities teach us that plants grow naturally in communities, not as individuals, and illustrate the importance of compatibility within such communities if plants are to grow amenably together—compatibilities based on matching vigour and complementary life cycles, and compatibilities derived from inborn qualities that enable plants to cope with the problems and benefit from the opportunities posed by different situations. When we start looking beyond the garden we discover that some of the plants we fancy seem so dependent on the circumstances in which they grow naturally that they thrive in cultivation only when reminded of those conditions. Proteas, celmisias, banksias, kangaroo paws, moraeas and many more, amongst the brightest and most exciting items in the Looking-Glass Garden, are more likely to succeed with us when we forget the teachings of orthodox gardening and aim instead to provide for their particular needs and preferences.

Gardening with Native Plants

Many people assume that we can only bring the bush into the garden by turning the garden into bush, and that the result will be some kind of "wildflower" gardening. Sometimes this assumption is reinforced by the belief that local or regional character can be expressed only by growing native plants, and there are those who insist that even design concepts from outside should be excluded. The development of new styles of gardening has never, hitherto, depended on such restrictive definitions, and I do not accept that gardening lore condones such restrictions on what we should grow. Those who prefer to grow native plants in their gardens do so because that is their fancy, and good luck to them. But the development of broadly appealing, innovative styles of gardening that respond sympathetically to the particular problems and opportunities of different places should be based on selecting plants and ideas from anywhere in the world which contribute in any appropriate way. When South African, Australian or New Zealand garden styles eventually emerge, I hope and believe, they will be broadly based, rather than restricted to the indigenous plants of each country or confined to ideas about design and function that renounce fertilisation from outside sources.

The idea of growing only native plants seems beguilingly simple, and can lead to the creation of gardens with an overall unity that is extremely effective, conferring a powerful sense of place and an overall serenity that is most appealing. But bestowing nationality on wildflowers creates huge problems of definition and logic. I find it disturbing that gardeners in Melbourne or Sydney in eastern Australia blithely include species from Western Australia in their so-called native plant gardens, but reject wholeheartedly the idea of using plants from New Zealand—a place closer to home and

Narrow, winding paths between small trees and ground-carpeting shrubs provide a formalised structure, composition and scale that fit the location of this small garden in the inner suburbs of Melbourne. Diana Snape's garden, East Hawthorn, Victoria, Australia.

only slightly more isolated by time and the Tasman Sea than Perth is by the deserts. What if the fortunes of European settlement had taken a different turn, and Western Australia had been colonised by the French and was now an independent country called Provencia? Then the inhabitants of New South Wales or Victoria would be no more inclined to consider its plants as natives than I am to count plants that grow in Spain as part of the British Flora. In South Africa similar incongruities arise when gardeners in the Mediterranean climate of Cape Town cannot resist the temptation to include plants from the summer rainfall areas of KwaZulu-Natal in their "native" gardens. The arbitrary national divisions established by centuries of human political history have little or no relevance to the natural distribution of plants.

Ernst van Jaarsveld pointedly exposed the dilemmas raised by conferring nationality on plants in a series of articles in *Veld and Flora*. He explored the idea of defining native gardens by the situations in which the plants grow naturally—thus the Karoo Garden would contain only plants that grow naturally in the Karoo Desert of South Africa; the Bushveld Garden, only plants of the bushveld. This approach seeks to establish affinities between the occupants of gardens based on the climatic conditions, soils and other features of their environment on which their survival in the wild depends. It is more rational than basing affinities on political divisions, but it represents a complication of a simple idea that puts it within the realm of the botanic garden and beyond the reach—and probably the inclination—of most gardeners.

The variety of plants to be seen in gardens devoted exclusively to native plants always astonishes me, particularly in South Africa and Australia. One garden after another reveals almost completely different sets of plants—in contrast to my experience in orthodox gardens where similar plants appear repeatedly, and the main interest lies in the imaginatively varied ways they are combined. These Southern Hemisphere countries are the homes of almost overwhelming numbers of plants which, but for the efforts of a comparatively few dedicated gardeners and designers, would continue to remain neglected, their garden potential largely unexplored. Even though I do not believe that gardening styles expressive of local or national character can, or will, only be achieved by restricting the plants used to those that grow naturally in the area, I recognise the valuable role that indigenous gardens play. These pioneering explorations of the possibilities of the southern flora furnish information about ways to propagate and grow its plants. They enable us to find out which are amenable and easy to grow in gardens, and which need special conditions in order to thrive. They make it possible to compare unfamiliar plants with those we are accustomed to seeing in traditional garden settings, which is an essential part of the process of developing ideas about how to use them. And, in addition to benefiting everyone with an interest in gardening, they give their owners enormous pleasure and satisfaction by focussing their attention and interest on worthwhile and thoroughly rewarding projects.

This traditional garden is so blissfully constructed that it provides an entirely satisfying response to the challenges of creating a garden, transcending the question of what constitutes a "New Zealand" garden. Greagh, Clark and Kathleen Abbot's garden, near Whangarei, North Island, New Zealand.

Exotic plants combined with natives can impart distinctive local character or atmosphere. The spiky forms of the native cabbage trees and the broad-spreading fronds of pongas (*Dicksonia fibrosa*) combine so very effectively with the broad foliage of ground-covering hostas. Gordon Collier's garden, Titoki Point, Taihape, North Island, New Zealand.

Accommodating Southern Hemisphere Plants

Winter's nights bring frosts rolling down the surrounding hills into my garden, and the first question I ask about any plant I hope to grow is, "How hardy is it?" Unless it can tolerate frosts down to at least −15°C (5°F), there would be no point in exposing it in the hurly-burly of the garden itself. That question would seem to exclude a high proportion of the plants of the Southern Hemisphere, so many of which are not notable for their tolerance of low temperatures. But plants are tolerant beings, and gardeners long ago learnt ways to grow them in places where they could not otherwise survive. Greenhouses or frames in which plants can be overwintered or protected during early, vulnerable stages are the most obvious of these devices. Sowing and planting seasons can be manipulated, as exemplified by the annuals and vegetables from around the Mediterranean Sea that have been grown since time immemorial. Their seeds germinate in autumn under natural conditions; the plants grow through the winter and flower and fruit in spring. They would be impossible to grow in cold northern gardens if gardeners had not discovered that when sown in the spring the plants grow successfully and flower and produce fruits during the summer and early autumn—a complete reversal of their natural responses, but one so easily accomplished that it is easy to overlook what a giant step forward it represents.   Trees, shrubs, long-lived perennials and many other plants are not so easy to manipulate, though some of us manage to grow a few in containers that can be moved into a conservatory or glasshouse in winter. It is rewarding to grow correas, leucadendrons, banksias and other winter-flowering shrubs in this way, but these are a tiny proportion of a vast range of temptations.

Fear of frost is the main concern that limits more adventurous and imaginative use of these plants in gardens, and frost is a killer, an overnight assassin. Nevertheless, the northern gardener's preoccupation with frost tolerance represents a narrow view that ignores contributory effects. Drought, infertility, short dimly lit days, waterlogged soils, exposure to wind and salt sprays all create stressful conditions. They operate more insidiously by reducing the performance of ill-adapted plants, making them vulnerable to competition from other plants, to the effects of cold, or to pests and diseases. Hardiness is a most elastic term that refers to a plant's ability to survive in a particular situation, and any combination of the stresses which make life

difficult can result in a plant's demise. That is a negative view. A more positive approach is to see what can be done to alleviate these effects. Shelter can
be provided in the form of walls, hedges or trees acting as screens or providing overhead cover from branches and foliage. I encountered a striking
example of the effects of shelter at the Royal Botanic Garden in Edinburgh.
Here a remarkable variety of semi-tender Southern Hemisphere plants grow
out of doors in walled, sometimes sunken spaces, partially surrounded and
sheltered by buildings and glasshouses. This arrangement provides conditions very similar to those in city and suburban gardens, where buildings,
high walls or fences offer similar protection. If these plants can grow in a city
like Edinburgh, which is less than favoured climatically, there must be many,
many other places where they would do equally well and better. I have often
been surprised to find so-called tender plants growing, even thriving, in

In this garden by the sea, native phormiums and astelias provide striking contrast to the
level, softly textured path, and are framed by a variety of low-growing perennials, shrubs
and small trees. Bellevue, Vivien Papich's garden, near Wipe, North Island, New Zealand.

small town and suburban gardens far beyond the limits suggested by the plants' recognised tolerance of frost or exposure. We might fare better if we looked further than ceanothus, a hebe or two and a Moroccan broom when inclined to garden adventurously, and tried out more of the less familiar plants of the Looking-Glass Garden. That would be bound to lead to losses and some disappointments, but it could also produce some memorably pleasant surprises.

Water-logged soils and frost are widely recognised as a lethal combination, even to reliably hardy plants that grow naturally in situations where soils remain more or less amply supplied with water throughout the year. Many shrubs and trees from South Africa and Australia grow where seasonal, prolonged droughts are normal, and perfect drainage around the roots can be a positively life-enhancing feature. Planting these in deep beds of gravel or road metal in place of or overlying normal soils can transform their tolerance of low temperatures.

Gardeners know plants by their names; to most of us a grevillea is a grevillea whether its ancestors grew in the benign coastal conditions of the Royal National Park just south of Sydney or the snowy, frost-inclined Bogong High Plains in the Alpine National Park. Foresters use the word provenance to describe the precise origins of the stocks of seed they use, and when establishing plantations recognise the importance of matching provenance with the conditions in which the trees will be growing. Gardeners have not paid much attention to this, preferring to create conditions in which plants will thrive regardless of where they came from. But attitudes are changing, and as more trouble is taken to collect high-altitude, cold-adapted forms of familiar grevilleas, prostantheras, callistemons and other trees and shrubs, we can hope that our experience of the frost hardiness of many attractive plants that we now fear to grow will change for the better.

Treasure-Trove or Pandora's Box

One of the delights, for me, in the otherwise desolate scenery of Central Otago's High Country in New Zealand is the colourful presence of lupins. These plants were deliberately introduced, first by Florence Cambridge during the 1940s, who found that they grew well in her garden on Dalrachney Station close to the Lindis Pass, and she scattered around the countryside quantities of Russell lupin seed obtained from England. A decade later roadworks around Burke's Pass provided another opportunity, and Connie Scott and her son David deliberately sowed several kilograms of seed on areas of bare exposed soil. The lupins now grow in groups along the roadsides in a range of colours that any gardener would be content to obtain from a packet of commercial seed—all the usual shades of pink and blue, but also creams, yellows, whites and brick reds, many as bicolors. They are practically the only bright element in a landscape that is otherwise unrelievedly sub-fusc in tones, with mile upon mile of tussock, often so evenly spaced that it forms repetitive patterns as though deliberately planted. The lupins are regarded as pests by conservationists because they harbour cats and ferrets, and their nitrogen-fixing abilities may change conditions for a natural flora which is notably deficient in species that fix nitrogen. Graziers regard the lupins rather differently because, contrary to experience else-

Descendants of introduced Russell lupins have colonised many areas of the Otago High Country, providing a conspicuous, beautiful and possibly beneficial addition to the scene. By contrast, the little yellow hawkweed *(Hieracium)* growing amongst them is a pernicious weed that is harmful to extensive areas of range-land near Lake Tekapo in South Island, New Zealand.

where, they have proved to be potentially valuable as a fodder crop and produce quantities of feed with limited fertiliser input.

Many other plants have made themselves so thoroughly at home in different parts of the Southern Hemisphere that they have become colonists, sometimes threatening the survival of native species. In one place or another, hakeas, melaleucas, acacias and leptospermums have developed into weedy infestations, deeply deplored by people who appreciate the native flora, and exceedingly costly and difficult to control. The issue of alien introductions is a serious one in both the Northern and Southern Hemispheres, but gardeners should not be unduly defensive nor submit meekly to suggestions that because some tea trees or wattles have proved to be nuisances—usually exploiting gaps in the environment's defences first breached by human disturbance of natural ecosystems—they should refrain from growing others. As a Pom visiting Australia I have several times been fixed with a penetrating look and asked, "Who introduced the rabbits?"—my part in this ploy is to confess that it was a deed personally undertaken by a direct ancestor. A reasonable answer would be to accept responsibility for rabbits, and add in mitigation a claim for wheat, Hereford cattle and Merino sheep, which have been essential elements in the country's agricultural prosperity. So too with garden plants. Most of the trees and other plants we grow provide enjoyment, contribute some degree of economic benefit, and create no problems of any kind. A very few become colonists, but we are unlikely to be able to forecast which these will be. Pohutukawas, *Metrosideros excelsus*, are causing concern in their native New Zealand because they are failing to regenerate successfully. Who would have predicted that seedlings produced from a few trees grown in a garden in Betty's Bay in South Africa would thrive in such an abandoned way that they are defying attempts to reduce their numbers along the neighbouring coastline? We should dutifully and scrupulously obey quarantine regulations and other measures designed for the protection of precious environments, but be wary of, and oppose, unreasonable restrictions on freedom to grow plants that contribute to the pleasures of the garden.

Regions of the Looking-Glass Garden

The plants of the Looking-Glass Garden grow in all sorts of different situations. Some grow in Mediterranean climates which gardeners long ago learnt to cope with and use to their advantage; others, like the plants of the rainforests, come from places that are less familiar and hitherto underrepresented in gardens. The climates, the soils and the terrain vitally affect the needs and preferences of plants, and can be guides to the conditions they need in cultivation. The remainder of this chapter looks briefly at the diverse conditions that provide for the world of plants in the Southern Hemisphere.

MEDITERRANEA
The Dutch established the first man-made Looking-Glass Garden in Cape Town three hundred years ago, in conditions much like those in which the first western gardens were conceived around the Mediterranean and the Near East by Neolithic gardeners three thousand years earlier. Compared to the long, dark, freezing, grey and leafless winters of the Netherlands, the warm sunlit days, mild nights and ample rain must have made the Cape Town winters seem like paradise, with colourful flowering shrubs covering the mountainsides followed by brilliant mixtures of annuals and bulbs carpeting the ground each spring. In summer, beneath a sun blazing from rainless skies and buffeted by hot north-easterly gales, paradise became a strictly seasonal phenomenon as the land dried out and plants ceased to grow. Mild, moist winters and hot, dry summers define the climate of Mediterranea, a scattered province that comprises the lands around the Mediterranean Basin and in California in the Northern Hemisphere, and central Chile, parts of Western and South Australia and the south-western Cape in the southern.

On a global scale, Mediterranea is a small province, and in the Southern Hemisphere its total area is tiny, but it has a significance for gardeners far greater than its geographical extent. Western gardening was founded on annuals that grew wild around the Mediterranean Basin. Southern annuals like the South African nemesias and osteospermums, helichrysums and brachyscomes from Australia or salpiglossis and schizanthus from Chile were easily fit into long-established practices, either by sowing them in protected conditions and planting them out, or sowing them straight into the ground after severe frosts were past. Petunias, lobelias and other tender perennials easily grown from seed responded to similar treatment, and only small modifications were needed to extend these methods to pelargoniums and heliotropes raised from cuttings. Similarly, gardeners already familiar with tulips, crocuses and daffodils quickly grasped the possibilities of bulbous plants discovered in South Africa. Most of these were too vulnerable to frost to be planted during autumn in cold situations to produce flowers in spring—even though that corresponds to the way they grow naturally—but unlike daffodils and tulips, gladioli, ixias and sparaxis amongst others can grow at high soil temperatures and in long day lengths, and it was soon discovered that when planted in spring they produced flowers during the summer. In New Zealand, Western Australia, California and other parts of the world where winters are less severe, South African bulbs, reverting to their natural growth patterns, form a major and brilliant part of spring displays, and many are so comfortably at home that they naturalise themselves in the countryside.

Mediterranea is not kind to herbaceous perennials, which make up only small proportions of the flora, but shrubs are another matter. The brilliant colours, exotic forms and prolonged flowering periods of ericas, proteas, banksias, grevilleas, bottlebrushes and mint bushes from Australia and South Africa caused a sensation when they were first discovered, and briefly but significantly became the backbone of collections in every fashionable conservatory or heated greenhouse. Once this phase ended, the plants slipped back into obscurity in western gardens, condemned for their lack of hardiness; in these chilly parts of the world Southern Hemisphere shrubs played little part in the garden styles developed during the nineteenth and early twentieth centuries. As a result these plants still play lesser roles in popular garden styles, even in gardens in the Southern Hemisphere where mild winters are no bar to their cultivation, and elsewhere in the world, such as California, coastal Oregon and southern Europe, where climates are equally suitable. Many of these plants flower during the winter, and their huge potential is now being recognised where frosts are absent or light, revealing the beginnings of what could develop into dramatic changes.

Trees from Mediterranean areas of the Southern Hemisphere are even less likely than shrubs to be included in gardens in places with severe winter frosts, but psoraleas, virgilias, melaleucas, jacarandas, maytenus and a few others have nevertheless become popular garden plants in milder parts of the world. Small, highly decorative and attractive trees are particularly well represented in these floras, and there are rich pickings to be had as the species become better known.

Horticulturally, the most significant single feature of Mediterranea is bare earth. For long periods each summer, high temperatures, drying winds and lack of rain create arid conditions in which much of the plant life of the previous growing season disappears, and large areas of bare earth are made available for colonisation by seeds when rains fall in the autumn. This condition provided the model for the earliest cultivators of cereal grasses and annual vegetables of many kinds. In Mediterranea the spade, the hoe and the rake remain essential tools for producing a tilth in which to plant or sow seeds that are the foundation of orthodox gardening. If, however, western gardening had been based on rainforest plants like those introduced in the following section, where bare earth is a rare phenomenon and annuals almost unknown, the methods of cultivation devised would have been very different to those we take for granted today.

TEMPERATE RAINFORESTS

From afar, impressions of the African veld, the Australian outback and the Patagonian pampas coloured my vision of the Southern Hemisphere. I imagined it as a place where the sun shone from blue skies, drought was a recurrent fact of life and plants survived by finding ways to cope with infertile soils. My ideas were rudely revised amongst the rolling fields of sugar cane that surround Eshowe in KwaZulu-Natal, when I first encountered dense, darkly luxuriant, dripping evergreen forests, both within the town itself and in the steep-sided valleys where cane could not be grown. Later I came across other places where ample, sometimes excessive rainfall and rich, fertile soils support forests of broad-leaved evergreen trees, podocarps, palms and tree ferns upon which shrubs and climbers grow above verdant carpets of ferns, mosses and liverworts, to create some of the most luxuriant temperate forests in the world. Rainforests dominate the landscape in New Zealand, western Tasmania, and southern Chile wherever coastlines face into the prevailing, westward-driving Roaring Forties. Elsewhere, forests occupy moist valleys and sheltered situations in cool temperate to subtropical regions in Southern Africa and eastern Australia, as scattered remnants where once they ranged much more widely. Epiphytic plants, including ferns, tree lilies and orchids, are a characteristic feature of the vegetation. Even trees, including the ratas in New Zealand and figs in Africa and Australia, may start life perched high above the forest floor, before eventually becoming earthbound members of the forest community after engulfing and strangling their hosts.

The plants in these forests are naturally sociable, highly competitive, and grow in well-watered, fertile situations, and many of them make excellent, amenable garden plants. Widely grown trees from these parts of the world include pittosporums and lacebarks *(Hoheria)* from New Zealand, eucryphias and embothriums from Chile, the Australian native frangipani *(Hymenosporum flavum)* and firewheel tree *(Stenocarpus sinuatus)* and the South African Cape chestnut *(Calodendrum capense)* and Outeniqua yellowwood *(Podocarpus falcatus)*. Few survive severe frosts but some tolerate temperatures down to at least −10°C (14°F), and although they may be chancy in gardens in cold climates, their potential in areas where severe frosts are unusual has scarcely been tapped. The temperate rainforests hold the major under-exploited flora left for gardeners to explore, a flora in which the plants for the most part are easily grown in gardens. Although abundant rainfall is the norm in their native habitats, these plants experience periodically recurrent droughts, and once established many grow surprisingly well even in gardens where summer droughts are severe.

The constantly competitive, continuously recycling conditions of the rainforest provide few spaces in which annuals can find a roothold. Plants survive by holding their ground and remaining evergreen and active. In gardens too, they lend themselves to techniques that are based on establishing more or less permanent matrices of roots, shoots and leaves within which the plants exist as communities, held in balance by mutual compatibilities and natural adaptations to the conditions.

SUMMER RAINFALL AREAS
Summer visitors from Europe or North America flying into Johannesburg during the Southern Hemisphere winter may be surprised to find the grass beside the runways sere and brown—the result of drought and frequent frosts. Here, as in the remainder of what used to be known as the Transvaal, and in KwaZulu-Natal, the Free State Province, Swaziland, Lesotho and into the Eastern Highlands of Zimbabwe, winter is a dry season and, at higher altitudes, a cold one too. Away from the narrow coastal plain bordering the Indian Ocean, plant growth is restricted during the winter as much by drought as by cold. Species of *Agapanthus, Rhodohypoxis, Eucomis* and *Berk-*

heya grow naturally at high altitudes in the Drakensberg, a mountain range in eastern South Africa, but are vulnerable to frosts in lowland gardens in Britain, the Atlantic States and the Pacific Northwest, frosts which they would survive unscathed in the dry winters of their homeland.

During winter droughts there is a build-up of highly inflammable, desiccated plant material, and frequent grass fires restrict the development of scrub and forest, except in places that fires seldom reach. Consequently, extensive grasslands are typical features of the landscape, providing homes for numerous perennials and bulbs that die down in winter, and flower when soils are moist during the summer, often most profusely in the wake of fires. Gladioli, crinums, nerines, galtonias, cyrtanthus and other bulbs from this area have been particularly successful in gardens, and are easily grown even in very cold locations by storing them through the winter and planting out in spring, or planting deeply in well-drained soils or in the rain shadow of buildings, walls or trees.

Fire also affects the growth patterns of the shrubs and trees that grow in the summer rainfall areas of eastern Southern Africa, and many, like sagewood, *Buddleja salviifolia,* and oldwood, *Leucosidea sericea*, produce burls below the ground from which buds emerge when the tops are killed; others, like *Protea caffra,* have epicormic buds buried within the recesses of ridged or corky bark that regenerate rapidly from the fire-scarred superstructure of the original plant. Most develop into vigorous, large, open bushes very amenable to garden culture. Trees are found mainly in small patches of forest deep within steep-sided gullies and along water courses where fringing screens of shrubs protect them from the effects of fire. However, three characterful and notable components of the landscape grow in more exposed situations, and no gardener could fail to notice them: the African cabbage tree, *Cussonia paniculata,* the mountain bottlebrush, *Greyia sutherlandii,* and the tree fern, *Cyathea dregei.* Another characteristic group of plants that grow here are the cycads with harsh, angular, spiky forms that confer unique landscape qualities both in their natural surroundings and in gardens.

HUMID SUBTROPICS
Few places expose the weaknesses of orthodox gardening styles and methods so mercilessly as the almost, or entirely, frost-free areas where summer-

long periods of warmth and humidity favour luxuriant growth (except during sporadic more or less severe droughts), and winters are sufficiently mild and moist for plants to grow throughout the year. In Northland in New Zealand, the Hibiscus Coast of KwaZulu-Natal and coastal New South Wales, plant-to-plant competition in the form of weeds, and assaults from flourishing pests and diseases—rather than climatic factors—are the major threats to successful gardening, and orthodox gardening is under continual siege. In such situations bare earth is rapidly occupied by weeds at any time of the year, and monocultures are a sacrifice to insects and fungi. Other ways to garden need to be followed which reflect the complex structures of the communities of plants that grow naturally in the humid subtropics.

Warmth, moisture and recycled fertility appear to be the plant equivalents of health, wealth and the pursuit of happiness, but for plants such conditions create difficult and competitive places in which to make a living. The presence of persistent, luxuriant vegetation makes the annual lifestyle hopelessly forlorn, and the absence of dry or cold seasons when vegetation dies back ensures that retreat into subterranean storage organs is unlikely to be a successful strategy, so few annuals or bulbs are found here. Possession of space is the key to survival, accompanied by the ability to move as necessary in response to changing patterns of light and shade. Therefore many of the perennial plants, including species of plectranthus and ferns, are stoloniferous or rhizomatous. Established colonies survive by spreading across the ground in search of sunlit or less shaded situations, without sacrificing the roothold from which they derive the vigour that gives them a competitive edge. Many plants have broad entire leaves that may persist for several years, enabling them to maintain a presence even in conditions so densely shaded that they are scarcely able to grow.

Shrubs are few and far between where the forest canopy is complete, but numerous species grow in company with seedling trees and climbers beside water courses, along the forest edges and wherever gaps allow sunlight to penetrate the canopy. Many respond well to garden situations and are notable for their attractive, often fragrant flowers and the quality of their lustrous foliage. The strikingly effective forms of tree ferns, bananas, bromeliads and palms make this a most distinctive flora of great interest to gardeners, but one that for lack of hardiness has played no part at all in the development of western gardens. Legend has it that during a visit to the tropical plant collection in the botanic gardens in Berlin, Roberto Burle Marx's eyes were first opened to the possibilities of the familiar but disregarded flora of his native Brazil, with results that changed the face of tropical gardening forever. The early stages of the trends to explore similar opportunities in New Zealand, Australia and South Africa—usually under the increasingly fashionable tag of "the tropical garden"—are leading to the creation of some of the most exciting and innovative Looking-Glass Gardens.

SEMI-ARID AREAS

The semi-arid areas correspond most closely to my preconception of the Southern Hemisphere as a place of blue skies, unrelenting sunshine, recurrent drought and infertile soils; though, as in the Little Karoo in South Africa, the apparent infertility of these places may sometimes be caused by drought rather than lack of nutrients. Such semi-arid regions include Namaqualand and the Karoo; Western Australia apart from its extreme southwestern corner; inland southern and eastern Australia; and parts of Madagascar and Patagonia. Summers are very hot and winter days frequently warm, but nights are often cold and temperatures that fall well below freezing are not unusual. Plants survive by adaptations to heat and drought, and by strategies through which they make the most of capricious favourable periods of heavy rain when vigorous growth enables them to flower and fruit prodigiously for short periods.

Faced with challenging conditions, plants respond in interesting ways. Some grow as annuals relying on seeds for survival; some as bulbs finding security underground. Some store water in their leaves or stems. Mesembryanthemums with succulent, jade-green leaves provide plant forms distinctively different from more conventional plants. Euphorbias, cotyledons, tylecodons and crassulas have succulent stems and sculptural forms that set them apart from all other shrubs. Leaves may be produced briefly only when water is available, or may be persistent and like those of eucalypts — sclerophyllous. This unattractive but rather apt word describes the dry-textured foliage produced by many trees and shrubs in hot, arid conditions. Sclerophyllous foliage is said to snap rather than bend when folded, and in a sense it is an onomatopoeic word since it conveys an impression of the rustlings such harshly constructed leaves make when disturbed by the wind. Plants with sclerophyllous leaves grow most often in sunlit situations that enable them to produce quantities of carbohydrates, on infertile soils where lack of nutrients, particularly phosphorous and nitrogen, restrict protein production. The plants respond by producing foliage that contains little protein but large amounts of woody fibres derived from carbohydrates, and high levels of tannins. These strongly constructed, broad, flat evergreen leaves with leathery textures and hardened cuticles to conserve water often remain on the plants for years. They are unpalatable to most insects and unrewarding because of their low protein levels. Few mammals, apart from koalas and other creatures with specially adapted digestions, enjoy the experience of eating them for poor returns—low protein and mineral contents, an excess of indigestible fibrous carbohydrates and distasteful, often toxic, tannins that upset digestions. Not surprisingly, many sclerophyllous plants turn out to be deer resistant in gardens.

Other trees and shrubs produce leaves that are narrow, even needle-like, presenting small surfaces to the sunlight and avoiding water loss by sheltering stomata within rolled-up margins. In windswept places like Patagonia, plants may grow as ground-hugging, densely compact cushions, relying on boundary layer effects created by their close-knit surface structures to conserve water.

The variations of climates and habitats in the Southern Hemisphere offer an array of forms and textures that provide gardeners with opportunities to make innovative gardens, and present impressions dramatically different from those of established styles. I have seen the plants used to create an alternative view of the tropical garden, one in which the luxuriance of the humid subtropics is replaced by the austerity of arid lands in the form of spiky aloes sparsely posed with succulent shrubs and trees, cycads and brightly floriferous annual daisies amongst rocks and pebbles. Gardeners throughout the world, and especially in South Africa, California and countries around the Mediterranean Sea, are being made aware that it is increasingly unacceptable to lavish water on lawns and other plants in the garden. Even in places like the United Kingdom where in the past such shortages have been transient and not critically important, water-wise gardening has become a fashionable topic, and one in which plants from these semi-arid areas play a vital role.

PART I

Gardens in Sunshine

W HEN I am faced with the chill reality of November in England, nothing restores my spirits more effectively than a migration to New Zealand. The antidote to winter blues for me is an early morning arrival at Auckland Airport and the drive to the city past farm shops selling strawberries and asparagus. Mounds of marguerites, pelargoniums, and osteospermums in gardens bright with watsonias, ixias and sparaxis raise spirits still further. Bird-of-paradise flowers are displayed amongst agapanthus, and scarlet bottlebrushes and the fragrant yellow flowers of the Australian native frangipani replace the forsythias and flowering cherries that brighten gardens in the spring in Britain.

The flowers that make gardens here as lovely as any in the world are different from those that are so welcome and so colourful in springtime in western Europe. Daffodils and tulips are few and far between, and although magnolias may be splendid, flowering cherries open raggedly and lack the full-blown sumptuousness of places where winters are colder. Some of the brightest flowers are produced by shrubs, perennials and bulbs from Australia and South Africa—many familiar enough to gardeners anywhere. But here pelargoniums, gazanias, osteospermums, and freesias appear in spring, not summer, as I am used to. Where winters are mild, these plants thrive outdoors, coming into flower early and growing with such rude vigour, with such profuse displays of brilliant, uninhibited colour that "sophisticated" gardeners disdain them. They banish these gems to remote corners, and put David Austin roses, cottage garden plants, and chocolate-leaved heucheras just arrived from the States in the places where gardening friends are most likely to notice them.

Previous pages: This desert garden in an outstandingly challenging situation is full of interest and attractions. The planting displays an excellent sense of form using kokerbooms, *Aloe dichotoma,* with occasional halfmans, *Pachypodium namaquanum,* to provide height and structure. The sparsely planted forms of aloes, tylecodons and euphorbias complement the austerity of the rocky landscape. The Hester Malan Garden at the Goegap Nature Reserve, near Springbok, Northern Cape Province, South Africa.

Those for whom life has no meaning without a rose should visit the Regional Botanic Garden at Manurewa, beside the motorway south of Auckland, to see one of the most impressive trials of these plants anywhere in the world, in full flower at the end of November. Jet-lagged northerners homesick for familiar plants can look in on the herbaceous borders, and for further comfort, try the herb garden too. But, once the nostalgia fix has been attended to, other parts of the garden provide a gentle and enlightening introduction to the pleasures of the Southern Hemisphere flora—and, for once, the plants are well labelled and the names of the unfamiliar can easily be discovered. There is a garden of South African plants, another of natives of New Zealand, including numerous garden forms and cultivars. Nearby are collections of the grasses and sedges so well represented in these islands. Elsewhere, representatives of Australia include a dazzling display of kangaroo paws (*Anigozanthos*), and bottlebrushes (*Callistemon*) in brilliant scarlet and dashingly lurid tones that are neither quite shocking pink nor vulgar magenta— guaranteed to frighten the neighbour's cats. The clear, bright colours of the flowers—yellows, scarlets, flames and oranges, bright pinks, blues and purples—are characteristic of these plants. Muted tones and pastel shades of cream and mauve, soft rose, violet, lilac and pale aubergine fade in the clear light of this part of the world, and seem lustreless and less appealing than in places where smog is more prevalent, sunshine more diluted and the air a quieter shade of grey.

Familiarity with the genteel, tasteful colour schemes of English gardens can make all this colour hard to take. Some find it too insistent and attention demanding—brash and vulgar may be words that spring to mind, or to be a little more charitable, cheap and cheerful. If your reaction to unaccustomed things, to new experiences or to unexplored situations is defensively unfriendly—eliciting the response that you know what you like, and this is something you do not know, so do not like—then perhaps you should read no further. The Looking-Glass Garden is often unfamiliar, often demands a new viewpoint or adjustments to established responses, and would be less interesting if it were not so. If we are to find innovative approaches to gardening and new ways to use plants, we must expect the unfamiliar where fashionable taste, artistic respectability and established conventions no longer provide familiarly comfortable routines that tell us how we should react.

A changing attitude to colours, expressed by describing as fresh and vibrant what we previously would dismiss as cheap and cheerful, is only the start of this process of discovery. The briefest tour of these gardens of the sun will reveal other suitable cases for amending our perceptions and our gardens. Plants will be encountered that have shapes and forms seldom or even never seen amongst the familiar occupants of borders in western gardens. Aloes similar enough to agaves to ring bells of recognition but with heads of scarlet or orange tubular flowers—some containing narcotic nectars to which, I am told, baboons and even children can become addicted—look nothing like the gigantic asparagus-like stalks of an agave. Other surprises include the flowers of proteas, in which petals and stamens cupped within colourful bracts are transformed into shapes unrecognisable from more familiar flowers; or the bottlebrushes, and many other Australian myrtles, in which masses of stamens form the colourful, attractive part of the flower, and petals decline to insignificance. This is a world quite different from that in which roses, snapdragons and michaelmas daisies play their parts; a world so original and so full of opportunities that it should not be diminished by making carping comparisons with plants of other kinds and quite different qualities.

The plants are not the only strange things introduced to us in this garden. The ground in which they grow often bears no resemblance to the fine

Strong textural contrasts and bright colours complement the clear light of gardens in many parts of New Zealand. Valley Homestead, Diana Anthony's garden, near Whangarei, North Island, New Zealand.

loams that we have been taught to strive to create. Proteas in the South African garden and many of the New Zealand native shrubs emerge from beds of stones. If we were to grub around a little we would find that these stones are not mere dressings sprinkled over the surface, but foot-thick beds of harshly textured, crushed volcanic scoria or finely broken basalt. Proteas, and the plants that grow with them in the fynbos (scrub) that covers much of the countryside in western and southern South Africa, grow on ground derived from rocks from which most of the minerals were long ago leached away. The flamboyantly beautiful shrubs of Western Australia often grow in almost pure sand and gravels, or infertile laterites more like hard baked beads than soil. These plants are so adapted to austerity that they may even decline and fail when asked to cope with plenty. In sunlit parts of the world where droughts, high temperatures, poor soils and, in places, windblown sea spray are the norm, these plants become the mainstays on which success in the garden depends.

Few places exemplify the problems of gardening in the sun more convincingly than the Hester Malan Garden in the Goegap Nature Reserve near Springbok in the Northern Cape Province. The splendid displays of spring flowers bring flocks of tourists to Namaqualand, but for most of the year this hot, dry place is forbiddingly inhospitable to rose beds and cottage gardens. I visited the Hester Malan Garden on my first trip to South Africa and recently returned. Full of interest and attractions in an outstandingly challenging situation, this desert garden depends entirely on natural, often very limited, rainfall. The planting displays an excellent sense of form using kokerbooms, *Aloe dichotoma*, with occasional halfmans, *Pachypodium namaquanum*, to provide height and structure. Around and beneath them, upright, rounded, spiky or columnar forms of aloes, tylecodons and euphorbias complement the harsh rocky landscape, and mesembs, geraniums and low-growing shrubby perennials form spreading mats across the ground, illuminated in spring by brilliant orange daisies and other annuals. The result is an eye-opening example of the benefits of relying on plants naturally adapted to local conditions as the foundation of a garden. The smoothly surfaced fingers of the mesembs, the rough textures of the pelargoniums, the silken surface of the kokerboom bark and the sculptural forms of the tylecodons all provide interesting detail that adds depth to the attractions of this garden, and are an inspiring introduction to the possibilities of gardening in sunlit situations.

CHAPTER 3
Oases with Trees

E VEN IN the cool temperate north, human comfort in the garden often depends on finding somewhere cool, shaded and tranquil to retreat to on hot summer days. In warmer climates, gardens without shade can be unbearable, and trees provide essential life-enhancing relief from the heat of the sun. Gardens should be places for people—part of our living space where children can play safely, where we can sit and unwind, enjoy a meal, chat with friends, relax around the pool, canoodle or sip a cup of tea— and our comfort demands that shade as well as sunshine be part of the mix.

The Looking-Glass Garden is a world where the heat and power of the sun can often be unremitting, but where warm air fanned by breezes— which in parts of South Africa and Australia are often more robust than gentle—makes shade and shelter comfortable, attractive features of a garden. Fortuitously the vegetation in semi-arid climates and in Mediterranea as well as the summer rainfall areas of South Africa in savanna or bushveld includes numerous small to medium-sized trees. Many grow in dispersed groups or as individuals in open conditions where they are exposed to heat, periodic drought, sometimes frost and frequently violent winds, which they have to contend with throughout their lives. Unlike the more sociable forest trees in areas where rainfall is ample and more evenly distributed, the trees of semi-arid regions have to be pioneers, designed by nature to make their way without the support and shelter of neighbouring trees. As a result these trees have little difficulty establishing and thriving in similarly exposed situations in gardens.

Perennials and shrubs can usually be quickly replaced following losses, but trees are more significant hostages to fortune. Few of us care to risk plants that are such important structural elements or provide hard-won screening or shelter in our gardens. Even occasional losses are too serious to be accepted blithely and casually replaced, and gardeners in

Previous pages: In this garden on the edge of the Little Karoo, karrees (*Rhus lancea*) and other small, drought-resistant trees provide a tranquilly cool and restful retreat from the heat of intense summer sun. The Nature Garden, Montagu, Western Cape Province, South Africa.

54

cold climates have chosen to be prudent rather than adventurous when selecting trees. Hardiness matters less in milder situations, yet on visits to garden centres in places like Launceston in Tasmania, Auckland in New Zealand and Krugersdorp in South Africa, I am struck by the overwhelming representation of trees from the Northern Hemisphere compared to those that grow naturally south of the equator. Such stubborn adherence to the plants and traditions of orthodox gardening denies gardeners opportunities to grow many more plants with great potential from the Southern Hemisphere.

A number of trees suitable for hot, dry situations are introduced in this chapter—a very small number indeed in relation to those that exist—and since some shrubs can be turned into trees with a little judicious pruning, a few more appear in the following chapter. Eucalypts and wattles alone could fill the available space twice over, and to make room for others these genera are deliberately underrepresented. Trees that remain small enough to be easily contained within a garden are favoured, as are those that have bark, flowers, foliage or form that make them particularly attractive to gardeners, and are either generally adaptable and broadly tolerant of conditions in cultivation, or grow well under particular conditions that create problems for gardeners. I have not, however, attempted to assess or indicate their potential as escapees. *Caveat conservator!*

Acacias, or wattles, include many valuable small garden trees, often notable for the beauty of their foliage. The foliage usually consists of imitation leaves formed from flattened shoots, known as phyllodes, rather than true leaves. Wattle flowers are almost always yellow, and many species bloom during winter or early spring. The genus includes numerous drought-tolerant, fast-growing and often short-lived pioneer species that quickly provide shelter and shade in gardens, and nitrogen-fixing bacteria in nodules attached to their roots enhance fertility. A few of the more useful garden kinds are described here.

The Cootamundra wattle, *Acacia baileyana,* is an upright tree from southeast Australia with feathery, silvery phyllodes, and masses of small, golden puff balls on thread-like stems along the length of slender trailing shoots. The selected variety *purpurea* has foliage that is suffused with a multi-hued sheen of violet and purple, as though some tinsmith had constructed a tree from burnished metal.

Acacia caven is the only wattle that grows in Chile. It can be seen growing unimpressively amongst low scrub on barren hillsides around Santiago, where it is cut for fuel and cropped by goats. Left to grow, as in Ruth Bancroft's garden at Walnut Creek in California, it becomes a fine round-headed specimen tree with deeply furrowed, russet-red bark beneath billowing clouds of yellow flowers in early spring.

The ferociously thorny sweet thorn, *Acacia karroo*, is widely distributed in Southern Africa, usually in dry places, and often in cold areas, where it is deciduous. When well grown, it develops into a fine specimen tree with fragrant flowers like deep golden bobbles along the branches in midsummer. The flowers are an excellent source of pollen and nectar for bees. The plant's formidable yet decorative ivory-white thorns make an impenetrable security screen, and serve a useful purpose as impalers of insects, small frogs and other tit bits caught by local shrikes.

The Sydney golden wattle, *Acacia longifolia*, is hardy and broadly tolerant of garden conditions, even on infertile sandy soils. More often a large shrub, this species can be trained into tree form, and produces cylindrical inflorescences of fragrant yellow flowers along its branches in spring. It is a serious weed species in South Africa, and attempts are being made to control it through the introduction of a gall wasp that parasitises the flowers, preventing seed development.

The pearl acacia, *Acacia podalyriifolia*, is remarkable for its intensely silver oval foliage ranked along the shoots, with clusters of bright yellow flowers. One of the most decorative species, it forms a small to medium-sized tree, and is widely grown in gardens in California, southern Europe and elsewhere.

The Ovens wattle, *Acacia pravissima*, grows on the forbiddingly dreary and chilly Bogong High Plains and Mount Buffalo in Victoria, vying with *A. dealbata* for the title of hardiest wattle. It should be tried where temperatures fall at least to −5°C. Starting as a dense, lax shrub, remarkable for its ranks of deep green, small, triangular leaves, it grows eventually into a small tree with sinuous stems and attractive, smooth, silvery grey bark. In spring the semi-weeping shoots are covered with masses of glistening bobbles like tiny bright yellow powder puffs. Garden forms include 'Golden Carpet', 'Kurunga Cascade' and 'Tricolor', their cultivar names each indicating their essential characteristics.

The ivory-white spikes are a formidable yet decorative element of the sweet thorn, *Acacia karroo*. Karoo National Botanic Garden, Worcester, Western Cape Province, South Africa.

Several out-of-the-ordinary wattles are also good candidates for gardens. These include *Acacia iteaphylla,* a drought- and frost-tolerant tree with long, narrow phyllodes suffused with pink when immature; the brigalow, *A. harpophylla,* a robust and strikingly individual tree with broadly sickle-shaped, pewter-coloured phyllodes; and the shoestring acacia, *A. stenophylla,* a slender tree that eventually grows tall, with trailing, elongated phyllodes up to half a metre long. *Acacia sieberiana* var. *woodii* is a sturdy, small and flat-topped species from Southern Africa, remarkable for the beauty of its flaking cream and tan bark, reminiscent of a river birch *(Betula nigra)*.

I first met the graceful willow peppermints amongst the tuart forests south of Bunbury in a typically Mediterranean part of Western Australia. The tuarts, *Eucalyptus gomphocephala,* were well spaced and formed a light canopy above a scattering of peppermints, *Agonis flexuosa.* The peppermint's long clear stems and narrow crowns with clustered shoots and leaves at their extremities cast little shade on the ground below. I next saw this tree in Ayrlies, Bev McConnell's garden near Auckland, in a very different form. Here, in a moister climate on more fertile soil, in an open situation on the edge of a lawn, it had grown into a broadly spreading, dome-shaped tree, casting a most welcome pool of shade on the lawn below. *Agonis flexuosa* makes an elegant shade tree with short, bright green leaves on pendant branches. Small, lightly fragrant white flowers almost smother the tree in spring. Variegated forms like 'Belbra Gold' and 'Peppermint Cream', with creamy yellow leaf margins, are beautiful but less vigorous, with a tendency to revert to green.

The Sydney apple or red gum *Angophora costata* is a close relative of the eucalypts, and it is a mystery how it could possibly have reminded anyone of an apple. But that aside, this medium-sized to large tree has the character and presence needed to serve as a specimen in gardens or larger landscapes. The bark flakes off like rosy tan cornflakes to reveal fresh cinnamon-coloured underbark often beautifully marbled with pink and cream. Masses of creamy flowers are followed by grey-brown, leathery capsules.

Even the biggest and most robust banksias grow more like shrubs than trees and need to be pruned by removing their lower branches to accentuate the tree form and to reveal the main stems, which are often covered with remarkably textured bark. Many species grow naturally in impoverished, well-drained conditions, and the fertility and water retention of typical garden soil is more likely to be excessive than inadequate. Levels of phosphates no more than moderate by general gardening standards can be toxic to banksias. In infertile situations they respond to modest quantities of slow-release fertilisers, provided these contain minimal amounts of phosphates. Mulches may be beneficial by reducing soil temperatures in hot, sunlit situations and, in impoverished conditions, by releasing nutrients as they decay. They encourage the proliferation of surface roots that are vulnerable to drought, however, and in gardens where nutrient levels and rainfall are adequate, the plants derive little benefit from mulches, and may even be adversely affected.

More often than not banksias grow where fires blaze sporadically, and many species produce large woody masses, known as lignotubers, just below ground level, from which new shoots sprout after the fires. Such species respond extremely well to occasional complete removal of stems just above the base to encourage the development of strong new shoots. Other species form no lignotubers, but produce new shoots from buds towards the top of each flush of new growth. Tip-pruning year by year encourages the new shoots needed to keep the plants compact and bushy, and once they become leggy and untidy, they are unlikely to grow away strongly if cut back hard. The seeds of banksias are produced in follicles on cylindrical inflorescences. They do not open when mature, but remain closed until the plant dies, usually as a result of bush fires, when they open to release the seeds.

In Western Australia I encountered banksias growing in a profusion that was quite bemusing. Eighty-five different species grow in the Stirling Range alone, from the large *Banksia grandis* with sturdy yellow "candles" that would

The seed follicles of *Banksia serrata* are an essential part of the shrub's fire-adapted survival strategy. Mount Tomah Botanic Garden, the Blue Mountains, New South Wales, Australia.

grace the altar of the grandest cathedral, to the prostrate *B. repens* with small cones of pinkish cream flowers almost hidden amongst the foliage at ground level. Soils in the area have become infected with the fungus *Phytophthora cinnamoma,* and many of the plants were dying when I visited. This condition is highly relevant to gardeners, especially those with well-established gardens, which frequently harbour the disease; the presence of the fungus combined with previous applications of fertilisers are responsible for many failures, not only of banksias but of other proteaceous plants as well. These plants are often at their best in gardens recently created from virgin bush, scrub or chaparral.

On a happier note, gardeners who live in or visit California can enjoy a magnificent collection of banksias at the Arboretum of the University of California at Santa Cruz. The presence of banksias, along with other Australian shrubs such as grevilleas and correas, have made this an excellent place to see hummingbirds as well. During my visit several were buzzing and darting around the shrubs as they fed from the flowers. The introduction of winter nectar sources from these plants, supplemented by the flowers of phormiums and Cape heaths, have made conditions here so congenial that birds which formerly migrated each autumn to Mexico now stay as year-round residents.

The bull banksia, *Banksia grandis,* must be the most macho of the species. It has substantial inflorescences of light, acid yellow flowers and attractive deep green, leathery, serrated leaves. It is a conspicuous presence in the jarrah forests of south-western Australia, and in exposed places close to the sea at Cape Leeuwin waist-high individuals still carry the great yellow candles.

The coast honeysuckle, *Banksia integrifolia,* is the most common banksia on Australia's east coast. It develops into a twisted, small to medium-sized tree that becomes progressively more gnarled and characterful with age. Tolerance of salt spray makes this species suitable for coastal gardens, and it is hardy enough to be grown in south-western England.

The silver banksia, *Banksia marginata,* named for the silvery reverses to its deep olive-green leaves, is a compact shrub in exposed coastal situations, but a small tree in sheltered gardens. It is one of the hardiest species, and its presence on Wilson's Promontory in southern Victoria on sandy soils overlying "coffee rock" (an iron pan that forms an impermeable crust just below the surface and limits root development) attests to its ability to thrive on infertile, dry, testing soils. The pale yellow flowers produced on small cylindrical inflorescences resemble corn cobs and, appropriately, smell like buttered popcorn.

An avenue of wisteria trees, *Bolusanthus speciosus,* lines the way to the offices of the Kirstenbosch National Botanical Garden, and these were in full flower when I visited one September. Very pretty they looked, too, resembling sturdy, round-topped standard wisterias. But the wisteria tree can be raised only from seed, grows slowly, and does not start to flower for some years. When they appear, the flower trusses are short-lived, so despite the plant's appeal, more patience is necessary during the wait from sowing to flowering than is perhaps justified by the reward.

The South African cabbage trees or kiepersols are also slow growers, but their bold, deeply lobed, blue-green leaves, gawky, roughly furrowed stems and strong structural forms make an impression in gardens even when small. The impact of these trees gathers strength as they mature and start to produce groups of cylindrical fruits on awkwardly angled short stems amongst the crowns of dense foliage. Their succulent fleshy roots were used as a source of water by the San or bushmen. *Cussonia spicata* is the species most often grown in gardens. It develops into an imposing tree with im-

The bull banksia, *Banksia grandis,* growing near Armadale in Western Australia.

pressive deeply fissured brown-grey bark and magnificent sturdy branches supporting a fine head of deeply lobed, blue-green leaves, but it is seen like this only in very mature gardens. The greenish yellow flowers, produced in close clusters on cylindrical inflorescences, are followed by small purple berries. In summer rainfall areas of eastern South Africa the mountain cabbage tree, *C. paniculata*, grows naturally amongst cliffs and rocks in exposed situations in the Drakensberg, where it is seldom more than 4 metres high. It makes an excellent small garden tree, and is hardier than the previous species, becoming deciduous in cold situations.

The most widely grown hop tree, or sand olive, is the purple-leaved form, *Dodonaea viscosa*, 'Purpurea', which can thrive in all but the coldest gardens, including lowland parts of the British Isles. As a group the hop trees are broadly tolerant of garden conditions, very drought resistant and moderately or very hardy to frost. Many of the sixty or so species have garden potential, but few are grown. Most produce decorative hop-like fruits often deeply flushed crimson, which are a major attraction, but hop trees are dioecious and produce fruits reliably only when male and female plants are both present. *Dodonaea rhombifolia*, from dry parts of Victoria and New South Wales, has elongated paddle-shaped foliage similar to that of *D. viscosa*, but the leaves are broader and the hops larger. *Dodonaea sinuolata* has delicately fern-like pinnate foliage, and its foliage and fruits are used in flower arrangements. Also worth a try are *D. microzyga*, notable for its bright crimson and gold hops from midwinter to spring, and *D. procumbens*, a ground-carpeting, broadly spreading shrub with small, pointed leaves and dark crimson hops in spring and summer.

The unique character of *Eucalyptus* makes this vast genus instantly recognisable—and sometimes as instantly rejected as alien—wherever they grow. Although almost anyone can identify almost any eucalypt, far fewer can say which one it is, and the complexities and infinite variations of the genus have dumped such an indigestible excess into the laps of gardeners that the plants are seldom used in ways that make the most of their potential in gardens. Species are combined in almost random associations, where harmonies are indistinguishable and contrasts imperceptible in a mishmash that lacks the visual logic and evidence of intention necessary for the composition of an attractive garden. The most successful effects are often seen where eucalypts are not planted but grow naturally, where the repetition of particular bark patterns, leaf shapes and growth forms of a few kinds create harmonious settings for other plants.

With literally hundreds of species to choose from, a tiny proportion of eucalypts are described here and elsewhere in this book. Rather than select a limited number in an arbitrary way, I prefer to make a short circular tour of the countryside south and east of Perth in Western Australia, introducing some of the gum trees that grow in this part of the world. I have chosen this small corner of Western Australia because many of the species that grow here have brightly coloured flowers that are particularly attractive in gardens.

We start from Perth on a carousel that takes us south to Augusta in the lea of Cape Leeuwin, where one of the first European settlers, a redoubtable lady called Georgiana Molloy, found the wildflowers of Western Australia so fascinating that she made collections of them in about 1835, under conditions that would have defeated all but the most resolute of characters. We then circle east through Albany to Esperance before turning north to Kalgoorlie and returning to Perth.

The first stage of the journey passes though the sand plains south of Perth, grass-covered and, in spring, bright with the yellow flowers of Capeweed *(Arctotheca calendula)*, and grazed by herds of Aberdeen Angus and Hereford beef cattle. The fields are dotted with large eucalypts—mainly jarrah, *Eucalyptus marginata*, and marri, *E. calophylla*—giving the countryside an expansive park-like appearance, with numerous small water-filled depressions patrolled by white-faced herons and often occupied by ducks. These two eucalypts are characteristic components of the bush in this part of the country, and jarrah, in particular, is an outstanding timber tree.

Farther south, groves of tuart, *Eucalyptus gomphocephala*, grow beyond Bunbury, forming extensive stands of beautiful open woodland on deeper, more fertile, water-retentive soils derived from limestone. These graceful, elegant trees branch fairly low down, and their ascending shoots with semi-trailing tips clustered with fragrant cream flowers are ideal as providers of light shade—though seldom grown in gardens.

At the extreme south-western tip of Australia, ample, more evenly distributed rainfall and fertile, reddish brown gravelly loams, very different to the Mediterranean areas a few miles to the north, sustain luxuriant forests of karri, *Eucalyptus diversicolor.* Here the third tallest tree in the world rises high above the forest floor with long clear stems that eventually branch to form compact heads—remarkably small in relation to the great bulk of the trees. The outer layers of bark are shed during late summer and autumn to reveal an underlying layer, skin-smooth with grey and mushroom marbling streaked with cream or pinkish grey.

The next stage on the carousel brings us to the land of the tingle trees: giant-sized, immensely venerable eucalypts that include the red *Eucalyptus jacksonii* and the yellow tingle *E. guilfoylei*. They grow in small patches of fertile ground only where rainfall is ample, along the southern coastline, clustered in exclusive groups or mixed with karris. Many are ancient, some in decline. The decaying remains of fallen trees lie amongst the massive columns of rugged, fissured bark of those that still stand, above tangled masses of shrubs, tassel flowers, clematis and climbing coral peas, in luxuriant contrast to the stark, often austere open woodland characteristic of so much of the Australian bush.

A short way farther east, and rainfall is already more erratic, less abundant and more seasonal, and by the time we reach the vineyards on the northern slopes of the ancient Porongurup Range, the luxuriant forests of the southwestern tip of the continent give way to more open woodland that reflects the drier conditions. But the plants—including the eucalypts—are even more diverse, amongst them several species widely grown in gardens. *Eucalyptus tetragona* is an outstanding small multistemmed mallee with bold silvery foliage, conspicuous amongst the overall tones of grey-green, especially after fire when vigorous upright shoots with extra-large leaves grow strongly from lignotubers below the ground. *Eucalyptus preissiana* is known as the bell-fruited mallee for its fine red-capped buds. It produces large, intensely chrome yellow flowers, but these barely compensate for a tendency to develop misshapen, spindly stems. The fuchsia mallee, *E. tetraptera,* grows naturally as a multistemmed small tree, again with a tendency to straggle, but it is notable for the bright pink flowers produced during the winter from angular crimson-scarlet buds, followed by attractive and persistent red box-like fruits.

Eucalyptus ficifolia is one of the most popular and widely distributed of all garden eucalypts, and the one that gardeners in cold climates are most likely to long for. It grows naturally in only a few places with well-drained sandy soils close to Albany. The striking scarlet or crimson flowers of this medium-

The towering karri, *Eucalyptus diversicolor,* has trunks like majestic marble columns. It grows in the luxuriance of south-western Australia amongst a variety of shrubs, climbers, perennials and terrestrial orchids. Boranup National Park, Western Australia.

sized tree make a lasting impression in frost-free gardens in Mediterranea, and as a street tree in similarly mild locations like Cannery Row in Monterey and elsewhere in California. More surprisingly, this tree with a tender reputation succeeds as a street tree in Launceston in Tasmania, where winter temperatures fall well below the two or three degrees of frost usually cited as its limit.

Beyond Albany the countryside is progressively more subject to drought and the trees more widely spaced. Yet another contingent of eucalypts appears: the yates. Amongst them are *Eucalyptus cornuta,* with pale yellow flowers, and *E. megacornuta,* the warted yate, with greenish yellow flowers and long, warty, finger-like buds. These medium-sized trees attract attention with their shaggy, fraying dark bark hanging from the tops of their short trunks and the lower parts of their main limbs. The Bald Island marlock or bushy yate, *E. lehmannii,* is an excellent drought-resistant, medium-sized, round-headed tree well known to gardeners. It is notable for its pale yellow flowers, and for the curious way in which the tops of the buds are drawn out into finger-like extensions. These are followed by clusters of decorative, brown, box-like fruits. This species grows close to Esperance in Cape le Grand National Park at the eastern limit of our circuit.

The pale yellow flowers and curious red buds of the Bald Island marlock, *Eucalyptus lehmannii.* Cape le Grand National Park, Esperance, Western Australia.

From Esperance the carousel circles north through an increasingly arid countryside, where salt pans turn into shallow lakes after rain. We are near the Fraser Range to the east, where the rare *Eucalyptus caesia* grows. Best known in gardens for the weeping form called 'Silver Princess', the species itself is a small multistemmed tree with silver bark, relatively broad blue-green leaves and rose-pink flowers. It is an attractive garden plant, but takes second place in gardens to the promise of its weeping offspring. The cultivar too often develops as a gangly drooping brat rather than a graceful weeping maiden, but its small size and weeping form—the Australian equivalent of the Kilmarnock willow (*Salix caprea* 'Kilmarnock')—give it instant sales appeal in garden centres, and it is widely grown in mild gardens around the world.

The land amongst the salt lakes near Norseman is the birthplace of one of the most striking of all eucalypts, *Eucalyptus woodwardii*. Thought to be a natural hybrid of *E. striata* and the coral gum *E. torquata*, this compact, well-formed small tree has smooth grey bark that sheds to reveal pink patches streaked as though with verdigris. It produces clusters of large, chrome yellow flowers. The coral gum itself is the special plant of the little town of

The broad, blue-green leaves on pendant shoots make *Eucalyptus woodwardii* attractive at any time, but when the large, bright chrome yellow, honey-scented flowers are in bloom, the appearance justifies this species's popularity in cultivation. Near Salmon Gums, Western Australia.

Coolgardie, where the streets, broad enough for teams of oxen to turn in former times, are lined with this small tree bearing its beautiful soft, coral-red flowers.

The carousel's circuit is completed by returning to Perth via the goldfields of Kalgoorlie, then back through bush, where despite the aridity of this part of Australia, surprisingly large and well-developed trees grow, including blackbutts with bark peeling from blackened bases as though scorched by fire, replaced abruptly by smooth grey-green bark; and the oddly named gimlets, *E. salubris*, with fine, sage green foliage and clean, pale, gleaming silver or copper toned stems springing from the red soil, often in small groups, or the dominant tree over extensive areas of bush. Finally, in the open countryside of the wheat belt, and on the last stages of the circuit, we encounter one of the most striking and characterful of all Australian trees, the salmon gum, *E. salmonophloia*. Often standing isolated and mercilessly exposed to the heat of the sun, this tall tree has smoothly gleaming rosy tan bark beneath a high canopy of glistening, burnished leaves dark against bright blue skies.

Far away from Australia and its eucalypts, the small town of Barrydale lies on the edge of the Little Karoo, where carpets of purple, crimson, magenta and pink flowers cover the veld for miles on end in wet seasons; when I encountered it, the carpet was threadbare and tatty, the result of the second drought year in succession. Ochres and sage greens, donkey browns and greys merged in the middle distance into a uniform dun-coloured mat, the monotony interrupted only by small trees dotted across the landscape. These interruptions were guarris, *Euclea undulata*, looking like giant mushrooms with closely knit, intertwining stems below domed crowns that seemed deliberately clipped into shape. In a sense they had been, by goats and buck who rest their feet on the trunks and nibble shoots and leaves as far as they can stretch—the grazing line establishes the uniform height, and what is out of reach spreads out to cap the mushroom. These little trees send roots down deep into the soil, and they not only survive but with their glossy deep green leaves manage to look as though life is thoroughly enjoyable under conditions that most plants merely endure. The closely related *E. racemosa* is a characteristic plant of coastal thickets, and an excellent plant for gardens where shelter from extreme exposure is needed, whether by the sea or in exposed situations inland.

A light green, open, graceful "conifer" provides a contrast to the grey-green flattened foliage of the sclerophyllous bush of eastern Australia. This tree is no relative of the conifers, however, but the cherry bullart, *Exocarpus cupressiformis,* a small to medium-sized tree semi-parasitic on the roots of eucalypts. This trait has given the plant the reputation of being difficult to cultivate, but it flourishes in gardens where it is able to practise its parasitic lifestyle. The flowers are minimal, tiny and green, and are followed by hard, globular, green nuts attached to a yellow or red succulent receptacle barely a centimetre long—only extreme nostalgia could have brought cherries to mind when confronted by such a paltry fruit.

My first visit to South Africa started with a sunlit breakfast in the open air at the old restaurant of the Kirstenbosch National Botanical Garden, where my first floral experience was the sight of a little flock of white-eyes sipping nectar from the scarlet flowers of a large mountain bottlebrush, *Greyia sutherlandii.* This plant grows naturally as a small, crooked tree, and is notable for the brilliant colour of its cup-shaped flowers on dense spikes from late winter into spring. The branches are bare at flowering but are soon clothed with broad, heart-shaped leaves, which are amongst the few in this part of the world that display colourful autumn tints before falling. It is a coloniser of crevices and rock falls along the cliffs below the crest of the Drakensberg, and its pioneering qualities make it an excellent garden plant. In spite of its origins in a summer rainfall area, the mountain bottlebrush is not addicted to winter drought but thrives even in places like Cape Town and Auckland where winters can be very wet.

The most striking of all trees to be seen at Kirstenbosch is the silver tree, *Leucadendron argenteum,* aptly named for its gleaming silver foliage. They grow wild close by in a small area on the eastern slopes of Table Mountain, the only place in the world where they can be seen growing naturally. Not very amenable as garden plants, silver trees do well only on perfectly drained soils where winters are mild and summers hot and dry.

Few trees grow amongst the large paddocks east of Albany towards Esperance in Western Australia, apart from ribbons of eucalypts around the margins and small, scattered, upright, rather tousled looking specimens dotted across the landscape. The Western Australian Christmas tree, *Nuytsia floribunda,* makes a break from the conventional association of Christmas with red flowers, enveloping itself in a bright yellow cloak that conceals the foliage. Although a tree, *N. floribunda* is in the same family as mistletoes

The aptly named silver tree, *Leucadendron argenteum,* creates a dramatic effect at the Kirstenbosch National Botanical Garden in South Africa.

(Loranthaceae), and it too has parasitic tendencies, tapping into the roots of grasses and other plants growing around it. Seeds germinate freely when sown soon after collection, and seedlings in containers amply supplied with nutrients and water grow with no need for a host plant; before they are planted in the garden, grass or some other not too vigorously competitive host should be planted beside them. The tree makes haste slowly. For the first few years it produces shoots from the base that build up a substantial rootstock. Eventually a shoot is produced that develops into an upright stem and, in time, forms the trunk of the tree. It will be ten or more years before the tree flowers, but with so much of interest going on meanwhile, and such a display to look forward to, what gardener could resist a try?

Most proteas, like banksias, are more shrubby than tree-like. However, a few species that do develop into trees give their name to the protea savanna amongst the grasslands of the Little Berg beneath the crests of the Drakensberg. *Protea caffra* is the more widespread species, an often multistemmed small tree with a spreading crown and flowers with pink or cream bracts and white centres. The bracts of the silver sugar bush, *P. roupelliae,* vary in colour from creamy yellow to deep pink with pale pink to deep purple centres.

Cottage gardens in northern Tasmania are based on flower power. Bold splashes of bright colour and rounded masses of white marguerites set off by pelargoniums, particularly the flamboyantly coloured and luxuriantly textured regals, grow amongst heaps of brilliant magenta, crimson or pink mesembs, competing for attention with mats of osteospermums, gazanias and arctotis. Psoraleas are the favoured ornamental trees, and their clouds of purple-blue flowers add an aerial dimension to the display, supplemented in places by pink clouds of virgilias. The brilliant eruptions of colour are eye-catchingly intrusive, in contrast to the grey-green tones of the eucalypts and other members of the native bush. But they are by no means out of place in this cultivated countryside, where the bright fresh colours of verdant fields of lush grasses, alongside pink opium poppies, potatoes and cereals, alternate with the rich chestnut-brown earth of uncropped fields, punctuated by the white walls of houses and farm buildings.

Psoralea pinnata is a small, fast-growing pioneer tree from Mediterranean and other parts of South Africa, wherever soils are moist in winter. It needs ample water through winter and spring to do well, but is naturally adapted to summer drought and grows rapidly even in the most exposed situations. The nitrogen-fixing roots enhance the fertility of soils in which it grows. The tree's obvious possibilities in gardens were recognised long ago. In Britain, where it was amongst the first South African trees to be tried, *P. pinnata* survives only in mild situations, but is widely grown wherever winters are not too cold, forming a small multistemmed tree with a billowing head of dark green, soft needle-like foliage. The sweetly fragrant, purple-blue and white flowers are massed at the tips of the shoots.

The South African species of karee or wild currant in the genus *Rhus* are shrubs or small trees easily overlooked beside their more dazzling compatriots. But these trees have understated attractions that grow on me as I get to know them better. One place where I particularly appreciated their presence was on the way north from Springbok to the Orange River and the border of South Africa with Namibia, where *Rhus lancea* provides shade for the roadside picnic tables. Its shade was equally appreciated along paths leading to a small stream in the beautiful little Nature Garden at Montagu, on the edge of the Little Karoo. This very widely distributed dioecious tree occurs naturally around water holes and along the courses of river beds, but can cope with more exposed hostile conditions, like those beside a road. Its tolerance of drought and frost make it suitable for gardens in a variety of testing situations, where it will grow into a low, rounded shade tree with an open, slightly lax habit, producing bunches of small yellowish flowers during late summer. Dark, fissured bark and, usually, several twisted stems support a spreading head composed of similarly contorted branches.

The quandong, *Santalum acuminatum*, is a large shrub or small tree that attracts attention in many parts of the Australian bush where rainfall is low or moderate. Its form and foliage would scarcely be noticed but for the globular fruits hanging from slightly pendulous shoots. The fruits, consisting of dry, slightly tart flesh enclosing round stones, are green and deeply flushed with scarlet as they ripen. They can be used to make preserves—perhaps I would find them more palatable than those I tasted raw. A cultivar, hopefully the first of many, bred to be grown in gardens or orchards has now been released, appropriately under the name 'Powell's Number One' after its selector. The quandong is another of the semi-parasitic trees of Australia, related to the cherry bullart, described earlier. Young plants grown in containers need no host, and they quickly establish connections with other plants when grown outside, so their parasitic lifestyle has caused few problems in cultivation. *Myoporum parvifolium* has proved to be a suitable host as well as useful ground cover, but other plants would probably be equally satisfactory.

Keurbooms have long been recognised as fast-growing, extremely floriferous, broadly tolerant garden trees that are widely grown in gardens where winter frosts are not too severe. The Knysna keurboom, *Virgilia divaricata*, produces masses of fragrant mauve-pink flowers from early spring into summer. The Cape keurboom, *V. oroboides*, is a short-lived, fast-growing pioneer tree that flowers more or less throughout the year in constantly moist soils. Like psoraleas, these leguminous trees enhance soil fertility by fixing nitrogen.

The dark green needle-like foliage and purple-blue and white flowers make *Psoralea pinnata* a popular garden plant in mild situations. The Regional Botanic Garden at Manurewa, near Auckland, North Island, New Zealand.

The fruit of quandong, *Santalum acuminatum*, are much appreciated by the Aborigines. They appear to be an acquired taste, but are rated high amongst the bush tucker of neo-Australians (that is, amongst the edibles obtainable from the bush by trendy white Australians pursuing the foraging practises of the Aborigines). Scaddan, south of Norseman, Western Australia.

CHAPTER 4
Shrubs for Sunlit Spaces

I GARDENED once on gravel terraces beside the river Thames. My lawns became toast dry at the first hint of summer drought; water-wise gardens had not been thought of, and I struggled to apply the well-tried prescriptions of deep digging, ample manuring and constant watering. Today the infertile, droughty nature of the site could be turned into opportunities by growing plants that are impossible or difficult in richer, more moisture-retentive conditions. I would look first amongst the shrubs of South Africa and Australia, born to hold their own on drought-afflicted, infertile soils where competition for limited resources forces each to reserve its space and discourage over-familiar neighbourliness. Failure to understand the needs of such plants, or to take account of their aversions, explains why so many of these beautiful shrubs have acquired a reputation for being "iffy." In fact, far from being hard to please, they can ensure success in situations that gardeners generally regard as problems—provided traditional forms of cultivation and husbandry are modified or abandoned in favour of innovative approaches more suited to their needs.

Some time ago a marketing genius coined the term "The Garden Route" to entice tourists to the southern coastline of South Africa. The bait was brilliantly laid, and tens of thousands follow its trail, as I did, because of the appeal of that name. Taking the N2 national highway west from Cape Town on the way to the Garden Route, you drive through the Overberg—a fertile region bounded by the sea on one side and mountains on the other—never realising it is there. I was drawn to this small corner of the country by an article in *Veld and Flora* that described attempts by local farmers, landowners and conservationists, aided by local tourist agencies, to make people more aware of the attractions of the area. It

Previous pages: Many South African and Australian shrubs grow in dry, infertile situations, quite different from those provided by gardens. Here colourful expanses of fynbos cover impoverished, rocky mountainsides. Thys de Villier's farm, Boskloof, in the Overberg, Western Cape Province, South Africa.

all sounded too interesting to miss, and I found myself there barely a month later. I went, as they say, only for the plants, but there is so much else in the Overberg, including whale watching at Hermanus and extensive wetlands packed with ducks, geese and the largest flocks of blue cranes left in the country, now the site of South Africa's most recent national park. This ambitious project, involving many different people and interests, is neither uncontroversial nor without its teething problems, but for me it was an opportunity to see how the Looking-Glass Garden in its natural as opposed to cultivated form contributes to conservation, recreation and economic development.

Elim, a village in the Overberg, is an attractive settlement that was founded early in the nineteenth century by German Moravian missionaries to provide a livelihood for the emancipated slaves of the Cape. Its historical associations attract numerous visitors, and the adjacent Geelkop Floral Reserve is a site of great interest to conservationists, but I was particularly interested to see an area of natural fynbos being managed for commercial flower production. The possibility of harvesting flowers, fruit or foliage from the veld or the bush, either in its natural state or managed to a greater or lesser extent, is attracting increasing interest in South Africa as well as Australia. Such efforts open the way to the economic exploitation of countryside that is too steep, too infertile or too remote to have been used previously for anything other than light grazing. The financial attractions of finding ways to make such land productive are obvious, but there are dangers too. The dangers are exemplified by what is seen here, where alternate strips of virgin veld are ploughed and then sown with mixtures of seeds of species that produce desirable cut flowers. The hope is that this will lead to the establishment of semi-natural vegetation derived from seeds lying in the soil, supplemented by those that were deliberately sown and contain a higher than "normal" proportion of economically desirable plants. The unploughed strips are intended to preserve the original constitution of the veld, act as erosion breaks and also provide a continuing source of seeds that over the years reinforces the tendency to revert to "natural" vegetation.

Words like "normal" and "natural" are enclosed within quotes because the fynbos is a dynamic community of plants, subject to the effects of fire in particular, which makes words like these ambiguous and open to interpretation. Ploughing and sowing natural systems as delicate as these constitute drastic and almost certainly irreversible interference. Even more significantly, devising means of making it financially beneficial to cultivate strips opens the door to cultivating more extensive areas. Similarly, discovering how to reinforce natural communities by sowing a proportion of desirable species makes it tempting, and perhaps provides the expertise necessary, to grow only those species that are most economically productive. The difference between partial ploughing accompanied by management that encourages a high proportion of the original species to persist, and overall ploughing accompanied by radical changes in the vegetation is no more than a small step. If the enterprise proves successful, will it be possible to overcome the temptation to take that step? If not, huge expanses of previously untouched veld or bush could be changed forever. Such a development is particularly significant in places like the fynbos, where entire populations of a species are often concentrated in a small area—making them extraordinarily vulnerable to disturbance.

In South Africa wildflowers are increasingly being harvested for sale to florists, which has led formerly undisturbed stretches of countryside to be brought into semi-cultivation or management. The decorative female cones of *Leucadendron muirii* are long-lasting and sought after by florists. They also provide an attractive garden feature. Meerkraal, near Bredasdorp, Western Cape Province, South Africa.

The South African Fynbos

The more fertile land in this part of South Africa was originally covered by scrub dominated by the grey-leaved rhenosterbos, *Elytropappus rhinoceritis*. This land is now almost all cultivated, but an entirely different kind of vegetation known as fynbos (pronounced *fainbos*) dominates the less fertile areas, particularly the mountainsides. Covering vast areas of the south-west corner of Africa and along the chains of mountains that fringe the southern seaboard, fynbos is remarkable for the great variety of plants it contains. Using the term "it" is misleading because it implies uniformity, when in fact fynbos occurs in many different forms in all sorts of situations from the seashore to the tops of mountains. The land on which these communities grow is invariably infertile, usually seasonally dry, frequently exposed, and subject to recurring fires. Gardens that reproduce such conditions are to say the least unusual, so it is not surprising that the fynbos flora, as a whole, does not settle down comfortably in conventionally managed beds and borders.

A defining feature of fynbos is the presence of proteas, Cape heaths and reeds known as restios. Find these growing together, in association with numerous small, fine-leaved shrubs, and you can be pretty sure that you are amongst fynbos. You may also be struck by the feeling of being in a garden—partly because of the remarkable abundance of colourful flowers from winter till early summer, but also due to the juxtaposition of broad-leaved proteas, narrow-leaved heaths and the reedy restios. These strongly contrasting forms create compositions that are nonetheless beautiful for being haphazard, and provide excellent models for attractive visual effects in gardens.

Deeply dug, moisture-retentive, fertile loams have nothing in common with the rocky, free-draining landscapes almost devoid of nutrients where these plants live naturally. Cape heaths subsist by developing intimate associations with fungi—technically arbuscular endomycorrhizal fungi—through which they derive nutrients from extremely dilute or insoluble sources. Proteas develop specially adapted roots consisting of clusters of innumerable tiny, delicate filaments that are designed to extract every nutrient molecule in the plant's vicinity, and are produced only when soils are moist. In fertile garden soils these devices become redundant, and the fynbos plants, like those that grow on similar soils in Western Australia, tend to languish and die, becoming prey to soil fungi after a few years—if they last so long.

Fire is also a natural part of the fynbos flora's lifestyle. It is essential to development and survival here, but plays no part in the management of most gardens—and would likely lead to problems with our neighbours if it did. Without fire these communities become senescent after a few decades; they collapse and are replaced by the trees and shrubs that lead eventually to more persistent forest. Fire rejuvenates the fynbos. Shoots emerge from underground burls, long-suppressed bulbs flower by the thousand, and seedling shrubs, perennial plants and annuals appear and flourish for a few years, gradually being suppressed as the larger shrubs develop and shade them out. This dynamic, constantly changing pattern may not suit gardeners accustomed to more settled forms of gardening. Orthodox shrubs like philadelphus, lilacs and viburnums are so long-lived that in most gardeners' experience they never die. But longevity is not a strategy for survival in the fynbos, and is not built into the genes of the shrubs that live there. Drought, wet, fungal pathogens, plant competition and other adversities, which lilacs and viburnums would shrug off, lead to premature deaths and a reliance on seeds shed in the soil to replace the parents when better conditions return.

Shrubs of the Fynbos

My first trip to the Overberg was in July, midwinter in the Southern Hemisphere—a season in my own garden when, apart from snowdrops and a few flowering shrubs, all is grey and brown. I had come to the area to see the winter-flowering shrubs, but from a distance the mountain slopes appeared almost equally grey and brown, and I wondered if I had made a fruitless journey. I was going to Thys de Villier's farm at Boskloof not far from Caledon, which is an exceptional location for Cape heaths, and Thys is a man with a passionate interest in these plants. He took me on a drive to the neighbouring mountain, the Akkedisberg, which forms the greater part of his farm, and my fears of a wasted journey were soon forgotten. As we climbed the hill we encountered an astonishingly varied and colourful display. An almost unbelievable 250 different kinds of Cape heaths grow around Caledon, in an area of about 4500 square kilometres—scarcely larger than Shropshire, the county in which I live, and less than half the size of the Olympic Peninsula in Washington State. Some fifty species grow in and around Boskloof itself, and on that day I saw twenty-five in flower, besides many other fynbos plants.

The discovery of the Cape heaths transformed our view of heathers. Nobody had imagined that these plants could have orange, scarlet or bright yellow flowers, some shaped like long trumpets, others broadly urn- or bell-shaped, many far larger than anything seen before. Their forms are startlingly original compared to the traditional occupants of our borders. The Cape heaths were popular plants in conservatories and glasshouses in the early nineteenth century, and the Prince of Wales heath, *Erica perspicua*, is widely grown as a pot plant. Like proteas and their relatives the leucadendrons and leucospermums, these plants have tempted many gardeners to grow them, but even today the numbers that survive and make an impression are a tiny fraction of those sold. Most have an aversion to gardens that makes them hard to please; they emphatically do not fit the category of good garden plants on which orthodox gardening depends for success, but these plants repay attention to the conditions in which they grow naturally.

Amongst the first Cape heaths I encountered on my tour with Thys de Villier was *Erica cerinthoides*, a widely distributed and variable species, and one of the few that frequently appears in gardens. It has large, scarlet, tubular flowers from midwinter to late spring and rejuvenates vigorously after fires. Garden forms are mostly upright and a metre or more high, but here it grows as a low, sprawling shrub. The bottle heath, *E. ampullacea*, looked nothing like any heather I had seen before, with clusters of long, pure white, tubular flowers with crimson centres at the tips of the shoots, resembling delicately formed bone china flasks. *Erica sessiliflora* is tall and bushy, with bunches of lime-green flowers clustered at the tips of the shoots. It is one of the few Cape heaths that grows naturally on limestone, and is unique among heaths for its serotinous seed capsules—that is to say the capsules do not open to release the seed when mature, but remain closed until the plant dies, usually from fire. Capsules filled with seeds produced in earlier years cluster at intervals around the stems like brownish cylinders. *Erica tenella*, more like a familiar European heather, is small and bushy with masses of little cerise, urn-shaped flowers. It grows in colonies, making a major contribution to the colourful fynbos. A species with flowers more like a lily-of-the-valley than a heather is *E. bodkinii*, with short spikes of large, white, pendant globe-shaped flowers. The flowers hang on for months, losing something of their freshness as they change from white to pink and finally brown, but still looking attractive. Despite its name, the form of *E. coccinea* growing here has clusters of bright yellow flowers (*coccinea* means deep red), and is known commercially as lemon plukenetii—a case of confusion with the closely similar *E. plukenetii*. The flowers of the widely distributed *E. plukenetii* may be red, pink, orange, tan, yellow or green depending on where it grows, and would be the envy and despair of anyone planning a heather garden in the United Kingdom.

Boskloof, like many places where fynbos grows, is remarkable for the diversity of its shrubs. Some are widespread in nature but still seldom seen in gardens, such as the berzelias. These understated shrubs are densely bushy and deep, monotone green with off-white flowers massed in bobbles at the tips of their shoots. Usually found on moist soils, they are amenable and useful garden plants with a characteristic form and structure. Species include *Berzelia squarrosa*, a stiffly erect, densely evergreen medium-sized shrub, and the larger, more robust *B. lanuginosa*, with long shoots densely clothed with small, fresh green leaves and masses of small, ivory-white bobbles. More unusual is the closely related *Nebelia paleacea*. Like the berzelias,

Shown here displaying a pinkish tint, the flowers of *Erica plukenetii* can also be red, orange, tan, yellow or green. Silvermine Reserve, near Cape Town, Western Cape Province, South Africa.

this distinctive plant grows as a densely compact shrub with broad, flat heads of creamy greenish flowers just topping congested dark green whip-cord stems. It too has considerable garden potential.

Some very unusual shrubs grow here, including *Penaea mucronata*, with triangular four-ranked, close-set leaves, and short, tubular yellow flowers clustered at the tips of the short, erect shoots. The exaggerated shape and texture of *Phaenocoma prolifera* is stranger still, and of outstanding interest in a garden. It grows as a small upright shrub with strange, congested foliage composed of tiny grey leaves covering the stems and side shoots, creating an almost sculptural effect. The pink everlasting flowers appear at the tips of the shoots in summer. Easily grown from seed, the plant thrives in gardens and is relatively hardy in dry, well-drained conditions. *Retzia capensis* is a one-off, one of those rare plants so unlike any others that it is the sole representative

Densely evergreen shrubs like *Berzelia squarrosa* and *Brunia lanata* are not particularly showy but have considerable garden value. The vegetation in the background is regenerating after fire, an essential element in the survival of the fynbos. Thys de Villier's farm, Boskloof, in the Overberg, Western Cape Province, South Africa.

of its family. It regenerates rapidly from underground burls after fires, and for the first years after a burn its characteristic stiffly upright shoots—densely covered with green and orange needle-like leaves—dot the landscape. The stubby, tubular, red flowers are almost concealed amongst the foliage at the ends of the shoots. Finally, *Brachysiphon acutus* is a broadly dome-shaped shrub with obvious and exciting garden potential, looking much like a floriferous, neatly constructed daphne with clusters of bright pink flowers. When in full bloom, these flowers almost cover the surface, obscuring the leaves.

Numerous plants of *Leucadendron tinctum* grow on the rocky exposed slopes of the mountain overlooking Thys's farm. Notable for the glistening, treacly looking gloss that covers the inner parts of the female cones, this species is known in some places, appropriately, as toffie appels, and is widely grown in gardens. The bright yellow bracts of this fairly hardy, broadly spreading shrub persist throughout the winter, developing eye-catching crimson tones as the flowers age.

Before returning to Thys's farm, we stopped amongst the fynbos over-looking the farmland below, and opened the picnic hamper prepared by Thys's wife: meatballs, chicken legs, a sandwich or two and coffee, all the bet-ter for being eaten in such a beautiful spot. Making our way back down the track, Thys pointed out a large green bush growing in a crevice in a sheer cliff on the other side of the kloof (ravine). He mentioned that a pair of black ea-gles had nested on a ledge just above the bush for years. As he was speaking one of the birds glided into view below us, before sweeping up to land on the ledge beside its nest.

Proteas, restios and the Cape heaths may be the great stars amongst the constellations of the fynbos, but numerous lesser stars and planets shine brightly enough to please any gardener. Many flower during winter, and would long ago have been snapped up by western gardeners if they were hardy enough to survive severe frosts. Some are still almost unknown in gardens, while others are beginning to be appreciated. The shrubs of the fynbos have enormous potential in gardens where winters are mild, espe-cially where summer droughts and thin, infertile soils are part of the gar-dener's lot.

Acmadenia heterophylla is one of a number of compact, densely twiggy shrubs with glossy, small, deep green, aromatic leaves and small clusters of bright pink, starry flowers. This species and the closely related *A. mundiana* are both lime tolerant.

The china flowers are small shrubs with clusters of pure white, pink-flushed, solidly textured flowers that seem to be made of porcelain. Most species of *Adenandra* are moderately frost hardy and grow best in relatively well watered, fertile soils; all have aromatic foliage. *Adenandra obtusata* has pure white flowers at the tips of long, upright shoots and grows naturally on soils derived from limestone. Ranks of small leaves closely set along the stems confer a semi-whipcord effect. When pruned after flowering to retain a compact form, this shrub is not only attractive but quite distinctive.

Aromatic foliage is a feature shared by many fynbos shrubs, and the buchus are notable for the innumerable fragrances of their leaves. *Agathosma* is a large genus of usually small, densely twiggy, fine-leaved shrubs with close-packed clusters of tiny flowers that are very attractive to bees. Their unemphatic shapes, diminutive leaves and washed-out tones of lilac, mauve, pink and off-white flowers are the attributes of plants destined to play supporting roles, appreciated for the interesting fragrances of their leaves, for their long flowering periods from winter often running through till summer, and as neutral, inconspicuous space fillers amongst the more pronounced forms and textures of the structural planting. *Agathosma crenulata* is an exception to this general view. Larger and more individually striking than other species, this vigorous shrub produces masses of brilliant white, starry flowers followed by fruits like little pepper pots, amongst leaves that smell of anise. *Agathosma collina*, with greenish yellow flowers clustered towards the tips of the shoots, is small, densely foliaged and compact. A natural colonist of sand dunes, it does well in seaside gardens and on lime-rich soils. *Agathosma serpyllacea* is another compact shrub that grows naturally on sandy soils and on limestone. It has masses of faded pink flowers in small clusters, and leaves that smell of licorice. The bobbles of tiny white flowers of *A. apiculata* emerge from shoots covered with leaves that have a musky, some would say skunky, smell that many people find unappealing. One of the best and most amenable species, provided it is regularly lightly pruned to prevent it from straggling and flopping open, is *A. ciliata*, with tiny, pale pinkish lilac flowers clustered at the tips of the shoots. The false buchu is a compact, densely foliaged shrub with small, bright green, oval leaves and starry, pale rose-pink flowers with many of the garden qualities of a heather. Folklore credits the plant with beneficial effects on wounds, rheumatism and digestive disorders. A number of local forms of *A. ovata* have been selected, differing in small details, amongst them the white-flowered 'Outeniqua' and the densely compact 'Igoda', which has masses of tiny, faded rose-pink flowers.

My first encounter with a euryops was a plant of *Euryops acraeus* exhibited at an Alpine Garden Society Show in a freshly scrubbed clay pan all set about with little stones. At the time it was a recently introduced novelty, but now its silver foliage and bright yellow daisy flowers are often seen in rock gardens. More recently, *E. pectinatus* has been adopted as a standby bedding plant, to be seen emerging amongst geraniums, begonias and busy Lizzies *(Impatiens)* in displays in public parks around the world. Anyone visiting Cape Town will see the shrub growing naturally beside the corniche road through Chapman's Peak. One of the brightest euryops is *E. tysonii*, a small, exceptionally floriferous shrub with heads of fragrant yellow flowers that grows in groups on rocky mountainsides, or along stream beds in the Drakensberg bordering on Lesotho. *Euryops virgineus* is large, open and rather rangy. Its small but brilliant yellow, honey-scented daisies appear in profu-

The inflorescence of *Leucospermum cordifolium* is a dense hemispherical mass of flowers that can be white, cream, yellow, peach, pink, orange or scarlet. Kirstenbosch National Botanical Garden, Western Cape Province, South Africa.

sion amongst bright green, feathery leaves sporadically throughout the year, peaking in late winter and spring. It needs to be pruned to convert its naturally open structure into a more compact form as it matures. Excellent for coastal gardens.

Pincushions, otherwise known as luisies—so named by the Afrikaners because of the louse-like appearance of their seeds—rank amongst the major stars of the fynbos. Several species have proved their worth in warm temperate gardens throughout the world and as cut flowers—especially *Leucospermum cordifolium*, a native of the Overberg, and the parent of numerous cultivars. Notable selections include *L. cordifolium* 'Aurora', with light orange flowers; 'Caroline', crimson-red; 'Fireball', orange-red; 'Gold Dust', salmon and yellow; 'Moonglow', pale yellow; 'Riverlea', bright orange; 'Shrimp', salmon-pink and apricot; and 'Yellow Bird', clear yellow. Some cultivars change colour as they mature, like 'Patricia' which opens yellow, changes to orange and dies red. Pincushions grow in the winter rainfall areas of the southwestern Cape, and are amongst the most amenable of the proteas on light, well-drained, humus-rich soils. Unlike the true proteas and leucadendrons, leucospermums maintain a good shape without pruning, but are more sus-

The rocket pincushion, *Leucospermum reflexum*, is a widely grown and amenable plant, and the variety *luteum*, shown here, offers the additional option of yellow flowers. Sierra Azul Nursery, Watsonville, California, United States.

ceptible to frost, especially when young. *Leucospermum reflexum* does well in gardens and is widely grown, but confined naturally to a small area in the Cedarberg mountains of the western Cape. The flowers, produced freely from late winter to midsummer, resemble flaming rockets more than pincushions, and they are produced at the tops of vigorous shoots, clothed in dove grey leaves. A pale yellow form found originally at Heuningvlei in the Cedarberg of Western Cape Province has been named var. *luteum* and is also widely cultivated. Soft yellow flowers, pinkish grey foliage, and an upright stance make this a characterful plant. A much less emphatic species, but an excellent, attractive garden plant, is the sprawling tufted pincushion, *L. oleifolium;* its dense hummocks carry clusters of multicoloured flowers that open yellow and progress through orange to flame red from early spring to midsummer.

The eight-day healing bush, *Lobostemon fruticosus,* is a small shrub studded with rather wishy-washy pale lilac-pink flowers amongst silvery leaves. Like most members of the genus, this is a demurely tasteful shrub, too anodyne to make more than a whispered statement in a garden, but appealing to gardeners fearful of offending. *Lobostemon sanguineus* is the star of the genus, introduced to me by June and Micky D'Alton at Kosiers Kraal, where it grows on Aunt Jewel's Kop, a hill named after the renowned and respected local amateur botanist Jewel Albertyn. Its scarlet flowers stand out in contrast to the pale tones of other members of the genus. The plants I saw had few flowers, so that for all its brilliance this may be a shy flowerer. Perhaps I met it on the wrong day.

Few would guess from their appearance that the pagodas, with their robust spikes of bright red and yellow bracts, are cousins of the proteas. The most widely distributed naturally and the most amenable to garden conditions is *Mimetes cucullatus,* an excellent and effective garden plant that is also popular with florists as a cut flower. This medium-sized shrub grows naturally in marshy, acidic conditions, and is in flower from midwinter to early summer. *Mimetes hirtus,* another small shrub, has attractive top-knots of rusty red bracts crowning its spikes of flowers. It grows in only a few places along the southern coast, where it is severely threatened by housing developments. *Mimetes saxatilis,* with yellow involucral bracts and stamens, is one of a group known as the silver pagodas, and the only lime-tolerant member of the genus. These are compact and floriferous shrubs when young, but age brings a progressive gawkiness and a tendency to stop producing flowers, which can be corrected by hard pruning. *Mimetes fimbrifolius,* to be seen amongst the leucadendrons and restios in the Cape of Good Hope Nature Reserve, is large enough to be trained to grow as a small tree.

Numerous lesser known shrubs are found in fynbos, amongst them more than a hundred species of *Muraltia.* These little shrubs, seldom more than a metre high, form straggly rather than compact bushes with deep lilac, violet or vibrant purple flowers strung along their shoots. Brightly floriferous during the winter, many species are ideal for small gardens. *Muraltia squarrosa* is a prickly little shrub with pink flowers in spring that grows in coastal fynbos and is recommended as a post-pioneer species for dune stabilisation. *Muraltia heisteria,* common around Cape Town, has small but brightly coloured flowers, and although not brilliantly showy, is eye-catching enough to attract attention—it would have at least as much impact in gardens as, say, the European heathers. *Muraltia macropetala* is another promising species with rather larger flowers than most of the others.

Nylandtia spinosa is one of the most noticeable of the smaller shrubs in flower around Cape Town during the winter. Every shoot of this densely twiggy, medium-sized bush is smothered with purple flowers, followed by glistening red edible berries. The similar *N. scoparia,* with slightly larger flowers, grows in Namaqualand; it is more drought tolerant, more vigorous and graduates in maturity into a small tree.

Some plants have a distinctive appearance that impresses on first acquaintance but is inclined to pall if exposed to a longer relationship. I find *Phylica plumosa* to be one of these.

The flowers of *Mimetes cucullatus* are popular with florists, and the plant is effective in gardens. Kirstenbosch National Botanical Garden, Western Cape Province, South Africa.

It is a stylish, rather lanky small shrub with feathery heads of very pale straw-coloured flowers adorning the tip of every shoot. The flowers, which are a collection of bracts, last a long time when cut for arrangements, and this provides a satisfactory pruning regime—otherwise cutting back hard after flowering keeps the plant trim. It grows naturally amongst mountain fynbos on the Cape Peninsula, is notably drought tolerant, and has a tendency to self-seed in gardens when it finds conditions congenial.

The pea family (Leguminosae) includes numerous, mostly easily grown, showy shrubs that do particularly well on light well-drained soils and enhance fertility by fixing nitrogen; amongst them *Podalyria sericea.* The silver leaves have a satin sheen that complements the pale lavender-lilac fragrant flowers, produced from autumn into midwinter, followed by silvery seed pods that are equally or even more decorative. The sweet pea bush, *P. calyptrata,* is a large evergreen shrub easily trained into tree form that produces masses of pinky mauve "sweet pea" flowers in early spring, followed by furry pea pods.

Who could imagine that milkworts—known to me only as minute creeping plants on the chalk slopes of the Downs, with tiny spikes of bright blue flowers—would reappear in the Southern Hemisphere transformed into large shrubs, even small trees, with correspondingly more splendid flowers? Too good to ignore, several milkworts are widely grown in gardens in their native South Africa and elsewhere, including *Polygala myrtifolia* 'Grandiflora'. This large, erect and splendidly floriferous shrub develops with age into a small tree, and flowers more or less throughout the year, with a peak during spring and early summer. It grows naturally in coastal scrub and lowland fynbos. *Polygala virgata* is a large, graceful shrub with sprays of deep rosy purple flowers at the tips of the branches. It is another species well worth its place in a garden, especially in its semi-prostrate form, which makes excellent ground cover.

Elephants food, *Portulacaria afra,* is a distinctive, succulent-leaved shrub or small tree that is particularly useful in hot, dry situations, and exceptionally tolerant of exposure and salt sprays in coastal gardens. Although slow growing, it eventually makes a large, dense screen that responds well to clipping, and could be as valuable for formal hedges in coastal situations as yew is in cooler, moister situations. Traditionally a remedy for sunburn, blisters and exhaustion, this species sounds indispensable for those contemplating any kind of trekking. Two cultivars have been selected: 'Tricolor', with leaves coloured green, cream and pink, and 'Variegata', with cream-margined foliage.

The blushing bride, *Serruria florida*, has an appropriately romantic history. It was found originally in the eighteenth century by Carl Thunberg, one of the fathers of South African botany, growing on the granite slopes of the Assegaisboskloof near Franschhoek in the western Cape. It was then lost, apparently forever, before being found once again, almost in the same place a hundred years later. Most members of the genus are compact, low-growing, rounded shrubs with relatively inconspicuous, charming rather than beautiful flowers in clustered heads amongst or just above the level of the foliage. *Serruria florida* is up to 2 metres tall and produces its white, delicately flushed pink flowers through the winter and into the spring. Seedlings reach flowering size in less than two years. Although a popular cut flower, it is an awkwardly shaped shrub for a garden, and others like *S. elongata* are more promising garden material. This species forms a rounded, compact shrub with feathery foliage and small clusters of fragrant pink flowers at the ends of long bare stems. *Serruria decipiens* is another low, densely foliaged shrub, with fine pinnate leaves, amongst which fragrant pink flowers cluster at the tips of the shoots from midwinter till spring.

Though seldom seen in gardens, struthiolas are easily grown, graceful, floriferous winter- and spring-flowering shrubs that deserve to be better known. *Struthiola myrsinites* is a medium-sized, laxly rounded or upright shrub with slender, twiggy shoots clothed in narrow, pointed, rather heath-like leaves. The slender, elongated, tubular white flowers open from pink buds and cluster in the axils of leaves all along the shoots, and are fragrant at night. *Struthiola leptantha* is smal-

Despite a fragile appearance and rarity in the wild, the blushing bride, *Serruria florida*, grows well in cultivation. Fernkloof Nature Reserve, Hermanus, Western Cape Province, South Africa.

ler but equally graceful, with an open, upright habit and masses of yellow, narrowly tubular flowers in the axils of tiny leaves.

Sutherlandia frutescens, sometimes known as kankerbos, is believed to relieve the effects of cancer. The species is widely, and deservedly, grown in gardens, unmistakable wherever it is seen. The clusters of large, deep crimson flowers are followed by inflated pods, amongst silvery pinnate foliage. The plant ranges from a compact to medium-sized shrub, and a natural variant known as var. *incana*, notable for its silky, brightly silver foliage, grows on sandy soils around Hout Bay near Cape Town.

Wolfdoring, *Wiborgia monoptera*, has many of the qualities that gardeners appreciate in a shrub. It lacks the sophisticated beauty of a protea, but quieter attractions, and exceptional heat and drought tolerance, make it worth a place in many gardens, especially in the most testing situations. It is a twiggy, medium-sized, rounded shrub with numerous small, pale yellow, pea-form flowers inscribed with crimson pencillings, in flower from midwinter into spring.

The Succulent Karoo

Inland from the Mediterranean climate of the south-western Cape and north into Namaqualand is an area known as the Succulent Karoo. The name owes nothing to the presence of plants with juicy, tender shoots or river valleys filled with lush pastures, but to the semi-arid nature of a countryside where drought is the norm and even the seasonal rains can be scanty and fickle. The plants that grow here store precious water in swollen leaves and stems against the rainless days. Although almost absent from similar places in Australia, apart from a few creeping pig faces (*Carpobrotus*), succulent shrubs are amongst the most characteristic of all plant forms in many parts of South Africa, particularly the drier parts of the western Cape.

Winter sunshine during a visit to the desolate landscape between Vanrhynsdorp and Nuwerus tempted me to stop at a roadside picnic spot for a snack. Out in the open, a cold wind blowing meanly across the plain quickly persuaded me that this was not the place for an al fresco meal and drove me back to the warmth of the car. I turned off the main road more or less at random onto an unsealed road signposted Douse the Glim—a name that seemed appropriately expressive of hopeless resignation with its situation in this desolate place. Douse the Glim is reached by a road that winds through a landscape that is not flat, but a monotony of barely undulating ridges. A sandy track cuts through orange soil strewn with small, white, jagged pebbles. In places these fragments of quartzite cover the surface in dazzling sheets that reflect the sunlight, and in summer emphasise the hostile aridity of the withering heat. As I walked, the pebbles ground together under my feet, as they would have done, even more protestingly, beneath the wheels of the bullock carts of the trek Boers who came here long ago, naming the place Knersvlakte, the grinding plain.

The distantly indistinct grey wall of the more fertile, comparatively rain-blessed Bokkeveldberg rises far away on the horizon, and the eye travels for miles unimpeded by bush or tree across a landscape occupied by low, mounded shrubs widely spaced on the sandy stretches, even more widely spaced amongst the quartzite pebbles; sometimes, where drought and in-fertility combine to create intolerable conditions, disappearing altogether. A plant 20 centimetres high is normal, 40 centimetres is luxuriant, and 60 a phenomenon. Only those shrubs with thick succulent leaves survive, and their succulence takes many forms. In places pale green, silken-skinned fin-gers emerge in clusters from bare ground; elsewhere chains of small jade ovals straggle across the ground, or tiny crumpled beads are strung on slen-der twiggy shoots. The leaves of the low, mounded shrubs sometimes re-semble rugby balls, bananas, or tiny boats with prows pointed towards the sky to reduce the area exposed directly to the heat of the sun's rays. Others imitate the stones so closely that they are practically invisible, or bury them-selves in the ground, depending on transparent layers of cells at their tips for the light they need. Plants shun their neighbours; each is dependent on its own space for the life-giving water and nutrients it needs to survive. Small brown birds flit from here to there, somehow making a living where none seems to exist; occasionally a grey and white kite glides across the veld, or a pied crow flies up to its nest amongst the wires at the top of the telegraph poles. A young ostrich picked its way towards me, suggesting that I hand over something to eat, bowing deferentially with its head, while simulta-neously curtsying gracefully with its wings. The gesture was unmistakable but I left it disappointed.

At the appropriate season in the right year these grey-green shrubs, now littered with the debris of spent twigs, would be arrayed in brightly coloured glistening daisies—magenta, pink and crimson lake, every shade of orange, flame, primrose, yellow and white—splashed like bright paint across the landscape, vying for the attention of the birds and insects on which pollination and seed production depend. In midwinter in one of the driest years for decades the display existed only in my imagination apart from a few sad-looking flowers in drab tones of washed-out pink or white. Most of the plants are mesembs, a comfortable all-embracing term long used by gardeners to describe these succulent shrubs. The word is short for mesembryanthemum, once a great alliance of plants, and a convenient hold-all that served us well until examinations of minute structures in the flowers and on the surfaces of the fruits by botanists provided reasons to complicate this simple situation. They created a host of obscure new genera—well over a hundred in all—defined by characteristics that elude the eyesight and tolerance of most amateurs.

Mesembs include some of the world's great colonisers. Hottentot figs, or *Carpobrotus* spp., have emigrated from South Africa and established themselves along the Pacific Coast in California, on the Rivieras of Mediterranean France and Italy, in cooler Cornwall, and in many coastal areas around New Zealand. Species of other genera contribute colour to the wildflowers on California's Sonoma coast and the bare earth of cuttings beside roads out of Hobart in Tasmania. Most mesembs are a propagator's dream: pieces of stem detached from the parent plants rapidly produce roots and establish a new plant. Left to their own devices they do the same with equal ease, establishing themselves from seed or broken-off fragments in the roughest, stoniest, driest, most exposed situations where few other plants survive.

Such qualities are the key to growing mesembs successfully in gardens. They are not sociable plants and quickly succumb to competition for light and air when crowded by neighbours. That does not mean that they are weaklings, however. Once established they are amongst the most long-lived, indestructible and reliable plants in the garden. Wherever the sun shines hot and unrelenting on unshaded banks, where soils are thinned out by sand or composed of little more than stones and gravel, even on the sides and tops of dry stone walls, mesembs can be planted and will produce dazzling displays each spring of outrageously, vivaciously coloured flowers; flowers that resemble daisies, but belong to an entirely different family. The central eye of each flower is enclosed by glistening petals like slivers of satin, crowded so closely together that they drape the bushes in a mantle of colour.

Hundreds of different mesembs grow in South Africa, where these plants are known as vygies—pronounced as far as my ears could tell more or less as "faichies," meaning figgies or little figs, because that is what the seed capsules look like. Visits to wildflower reserves, or to the Karoo National Botanic Garden at Worcester, or the Mathew's Rockery or the Botanical Society Conservatory at Kirstenbosch in the spring provide eye-catching experiences of the variety and colourfulness of these plants, accompanied, probably, by a sense of bewilderment at the complexity of their names and the difficulties, very often, of distinguishing between one and another. Some, like the pigsroot, *Conicosia pugioniformis,* with broad, glistening sulphur yellow flowers, are so striking and individual that they are easily identified. The numerous magenta-flowered species of *Lampranthus* or *Ruschia,* on the other hand, require a persistence and attention to detail with which only experts can be bothered. Fortunately, gardeners need not be too concerned with botanical minutiae—any one or two of numerous magenta lampranthuses would be sufficient, and most ruschias are better left to grow wild than in the garden. A short list chosen to provide a wide range of different colours, and some variation in flowering season and plant form, is quite enough for most people.

The ground-hugging stems of cephalophyllums produce clusters of stubby succulent leaves above which moderate-sized white, yellow, salmon, pink or red flowers appear each spring on short stems. They occur in many of the drier parts of the Cape, including the coastal sands. They are best for gardens in Mediterranean situations because flowers are freely produced only following long periods of drought. *Cephalophyllum alstonii,* a species with striking red flowers and smooth bluish green leaves, is particularly dependent on summer drought for flower initiation. *Cephalophyllum spongiosum* produces beautiful, moderately large, deep magenta-rose flowers with yellow centres above elongated bluish green leaves.

Cheiridopsis is a genus of dwarf, succulent subshrubs that are seldom tolerant of more than light frosts. They produce large white, yellow or orange flowers above long, bluish green, boat-shaped leaves. *Cheiridopsis cigarettifera,* a remarkable name for a most garden-worthy plant, produces masses of brilliant yellow flowers above compact mounds of succulent, cylindrical, grey leaves.

Dorotheanthus is a small genus of low, spreading annuals that compensate for their brief existence by the unusual brilliance and varied colours of their flowers. *Dorotheanthus bellidiformis* is familiar to gardeners everywhere as the Livingston daisy. Various colour forms occur naturally, and selective breeding has extended the range to include cerise, red, salmon, rose, tan, orange or white. This annual is easy to grow and tolerates light summer rain, but is inclined to grow excessive foliage at the expense of flowers on rich, well-watered, fertile soils. The plant is also fragile and easily damaged, as I discovered when a litter of puppies chose a particularly thriving display as a romping ground. *Dorotheanthus oculatus* is similar but the petals are a uniform canary yellow, surrounding jewel-like crimson centres.

Known as dew flowers because of the tiny, dew-like raised dots that cover the small cylindrical leaves, *Drosanthemum* species are amongst the most drought tolerant of the mesembs. *Drosanthemum speciosum* grows into a low, hummocky bush densely covered with orange, crimson or tan flowers with white centres. Its life tends to be brilliant but brief, and attractive colour forms should be replaced from cuttings every few years.

The bright orange-crimson, white-centered flowers of *Drosanthemum speciosum* are densely produced on a low bush. The Regional Botanic Garden at Manurewa, near Auckland, North Island, New Zealand.

A fascinating feature of many mesembs is the varied shapes of their succulent leaves, and *Gibbaeum* is a genus that seems to specialise in extra-compact, extra-succulent, congested growth forms. It spreads as low domed mats just above ground level—sometimes closely resembling colonies of lithops. The leaves are characteristically produced in unevenly sized pairs fused for part of their length, each pair producing a single, usually rather small flower, more often than not that dangerous but brilliant colour magenta. Most, like *Gibbaeum pubescens*, are easily grown garden plants that are content to grow in the hottest, driest, least fertile situation.

The genus *Lampranthus* includes

many of the best known, most showy garden mesembs. They grow as ground-covering mats, broadly spreading shrubs or upright bushes. Most are exceptionally floriferous and characterised by fiery orange, red or yellow colours. Their tolerance of summer rainfall makes them rewarding and easy plants to grow in gardens in many places, but even lampranthuses have their limitations, and like most mesembs, they can be disappointing in any but the most brightly lit settings in gardens. *Lampranthus aureus* is a widely grown species with bright orange flowers in spring on small, mounded bushes. Another good, widely grown garden plant is *L. blandus,* with pale pink flowers on spreading, rounded hummocks during late spring and sometimes midwinter. *Lampranthus coralliflorus* has dazzlingly bright magenta flowers—not for the faint-hearted or the genteelly tasteful. The species is valued for its broad tolerance in gardens of summer rainfall and even moderate frosts in winter. *Lampranthus glaucus* is notable for its beautiful ochre-yellow or lemon flowers. *Lampranthus spectabilis* has rich cyclamen

cerise flowers with yellow centres that appear in late spring and are useful for extending the flowering season. It is a flexible friend that will follow the contours of rocks and slopes, and tumble over the tops and down walls.

A genus of only two species, *Oscularia* is similar to *Lampranthus,* but its flowers are fragrant. *Oscularia caulescens* is compact and bushy with washed-out rose-pink flowers over a longer period than most mesembs. It is unusual for its tolerance of partial or even fairly dense shade, enabling it to grow on light sandy soils beneath trees, provided the canopy is not too heavy.

Ruschia is a huge genus of more than three hundred species, ranging from creeping ground-covering forms to upright shrubs, that often makes

Gibbaeum pubescens has succulent, pebbly, sage green leaves and magenta-purple flowers. Karoo National Botanic Garden, Worcester, Western Cape Province, South Africa.

up a major component of the low, succulent scrub that covers arid sandy and rocky places in the western Cape. The flowers are usually quite small, and the colour range limited to magenta, pink or white, but they are numerous enough to produce a pleasant, if not very notable, display. The main drawback of these plants is the tendency of the older leaves to hang on after death, looking tatty. They thrive in very hot, dry situations, but most tolerate summer rain and light frosts in gardens. *Ruschia parviflora* forms tight, ground-hugging mats with tiny leaves that may be flushed with crimson in cold situations. Flowers are small and mauve. *Ruschia macowanii* is an upright bush that regularly and profusely produces moderate-sized, pinky-mauve flowers towards the tips of the stems.

Sun-loving Shrubs from Australia

Leaving South Africa and travelling east a third of the way around the world brings us to Western Australia. Seasonally hot, dry climates and infertile soils echo those of the western Cape, and the drought-adapted vegetation known as kwongan shares some of the qualities of the fynbos, although the plants are entirely different.

Gardeners have regarded plants from Western Australian with even more suspicion than those from other parts of the Southern Hemisphere, regarding them as fickle, pernickety beauties, all too inclined to give up and die. Attempts to grow spectacularly desirable species like the flamboyant orange-scarlet *Banksia coccinea,* from the extreme south of Western Australia, are almost inevitably frustrated by phytophthora fungal disease in any situation where soils remain moist throughout the summer.

Australian plants are often as challenging to grow and exasperating there as elsewhere, and repeated attempts have been made to introduce them to gardens. Even in the earliest days of European colonisation, when nostalgia for "home" was acute, and the bush was regarded solely as an obstacle to the improvement of land for farming, there were some settlers who were fascinated by the wildflowers. Amongst them was the unfortunate Thomas Shepherd, the first professional gardener to work in the colony of New South Wales. He recognised some of the qualities of the bush at a time when it was being ruthlessly cleared, and in an imaginative transference of ideas derived from Humphry Repton, Shepherd advocated styles of gardening sympathetic to the bush's existence. Sadly he died soon after delivering the first of an intended course of lectures, and the rest were published posthumously. His ideas failed to work in practise, a problem also encountered more recently by followers of Edna Walling in the twentieth century. Edna Walling's books created widespread popular interest in Australian plants, leading almost to a cult for planting them in gardens. Often they were planted in ways that took little account of their needs, and either killed them by kindness or left them to fend for themselves in the belief that being wild they would be able to do so. The result was widespread exasperation at their contrariness and condemnation of their garden qualities.

Today's renaissance of interest in Australian plants coincides with greater awareness of their ecological requirements, and a willingness to modify orthodox approaches to match them. I had read about John Hunt's method of creating mounds and channels to provide the combination of free drainage and available water needed by many of these plants. While I was staying in northern Tasmania with Colin and Jill Roberts, and after being shown her beautiful native garden in the shelter of a grove of *Eucalyptus viminalis*, within sound and smell of the sea, Jill took me to meet Marianne and. Bradley Stagg, who have applied John Hunt's ideas in their garden near Devonport. Trenches are dug through the beds before planting, and the spoil heaped up to form ridges or mounds, like an extreme version of the ridge and furrow of a ploughed field. The trenches are then partially backfilled with stones and other free-draining material before the plants are set out on the sloping, mounded parts of the bed—in time the plants may well grow over and bridge the channels. Rainwater runs off the mounds into the channels, so the soil around the plants never becomes waterlogged, and subsequently returns to the mounds via capillary action, alleviating water shortages in times of drought.

The Stagg's garden demonstrates the success of the system, but the work entailed in mounding and channelling is evidently not essential for the cultivation of Australian plants in all situations. On an earlier visit to Melbourne I had found my way to Karwarra, a garden devoted to native plants, originally designed and planted by Kath Deery, at Kalorama in the Dandenong Hills. Later I met Rodger Elliot there, who introduced me to the curator Marilyn Gray and gave me a guided tour of the garden. We then went on to see Rodger's old garden of exclusively native plants, in nearby Montrose, now in the care of Elspeth and Garry Jacobs. On the same day, a mile or two away at Wandin, I visited Katandra, the garden of Bob and Dot O'Neill. Impressive collections of Australian plants grow in these three gardens under systems of management that take account of shaded or sunlit settings, and of variations in water-holding capacity of the soil from one place to another, but make no attempt to modify the soil profile drastically, or introduce other fundamental changes (apart from the generous use of wood chip mulches in Bob's garden). Like many who garden with native trees and shrubs, Bob recognises sudden death syndrome as part of the gardener's lot, and regards it positively as opening the way for changes that allow new ideas to be tried out. He attributes some of these deaths to seasonal variations in rainfall, finding the casualties most numerous in excessively wet years—though other gardeners in other gardens have suggested drought as a major cause of losses. Although naturally adapted to grow in drought-prone parts of the world, many of these shrubs appear to be surprisingly vulnerable to drought in gardens. In common with the plants of the fynbos, they grow in fire-adapted associations, in which successful survival strategies may depend on giving way gracefully in the face of adversity—to take advantage of opportunities to rise from the ashes when better times return.

A small but exciting selection of shrubs from this part of the world which may find their place in gardens in the north is presented here.

The swamp daisy, *Actinodium cunninghamii,* is a coolly elegant, small, shrubby plant, but it is no composite. This unusual member of the myrtle family (Myrtaceae) has daisy-mimicking inflorescences consisting of a central zone of small, red fertile flowers surrounded by white, sterile ray flowers.

A most splendid and, as it happens, easily grown Western Australian shrub is the native hibiscus, *Alyogyne huegelii.* Cultivars bred at the University of California at Santa Cruz include the purple 'Santa Cruz' and 'White Swan', with palest lilac flowers fading to pure white. The native hibiscus is an amenable garden plant in any frost-free area, and selected forms flower every day of the year in some gardens. Left unpruned it develops into a lanky, awkward-looking specimen, and should be cut back hard from time to time to discourage this tendency. *Alyogyne hakeifolia* also has large, fragile-looking flowers that are usually pale purple-mauve with crimson centres amongst narrow, flattened, needle-like foliage.

Numerous banksias from Western Australia have garden potential. *Banksia ashbyi* has attractive deeply serrated foliage and orange flowers that drip with nectar—the nectar is said to give Europeans headaches, but is enjoyed by Australian aborigines with impunity. I first saw the possum banksia, *B. baueri*, a few years after it was planted at Lotusland in California, where it looked as though some child had populated its stems and leaves with a little group of cuddly toys. Its inflorescences are plump little woolly cylinders that cluster together, at first more or less at ground level but, as the shrub develops, ascend to higher levels. This banksia has an easy, amenable nature and grows well in many gardens in Mediterranea. The medium-sized *B. media* produces golden yellow, cylindrical inflorescences. The Australian banksias require little or no pruning, in contrast to the South African proteas, which need regular hard pruning to maintain shape and flower production.

Boronias are mostly small to medium-sized evergreen shrubs, with aromatic foliage, that tend to have a bright but brief existence in gardens. Slightly acidic, free-draining soils suit them best, and mulches are usually beneficial. Boronias, like croweas and correas, are related to citrus fruits, and since half the population of the United States goes to work on California orange juice, the importation of all these plants is strictly controlled

Alyogyne hakeifolia may be less well known than *A. huegelii*, but it is a similarly large, easily grown shrub that produces a long succession of satin-textured, mallow-like, purple flowers. Ruth Bancroft's garden, Walnut Creek, California, United States.

to guard against the introduction of disease. The brown boronia, *Boronia megastigma*, has the biggest reputation, but is by no means the most amenable garden plant. It grows amongst the moist karri forests of southern Western Australia, and resents dry, infertile soils. Leggy and short-lived, it should be cut back hard after flowering. The chocolate and yellow flowers are intensely fragrant, and a commercial source of essential oils. The numerous cultivars include the brown and yellow striped 'Harlequin'; 'Heaven Scent', a popular cultivar with brown flowers; the deep cerise-crimson 'Jack Maguire's Red'; 'Lutea', notable for its yellow-green flowers; and less leggy than the others, 'Royale', with brown flowers. The red boronia, *B. heterophylla*, grows rapidly into a substantial medium-sized shrub that should be repeatedly tip-pruned to encourage dense growth. Its masses of deep pink to cerise flowers combine sparky colour with aromatic foliage. Provided it has excellent drainage combined with moist soil at all times, it is a reliable garden plant. *Boronia heterophylla* 'Just Margaret' is a cultivar with coral-pink flowers, and 'Morandy Candy' is early flowering with sprays of flowers on upright stems. *Boronia citriodora* is a compact, broadly spreading shrub of considerable quality and appeal reminiscent of a daphne, with deep green,

In this ground-hugging form of the possum banksia, *Banksia baueri*, the large, furry, cuddly looking inflorescences sit on the surface like, well, squat little possums. John Taft Garden, near Ojai, California.

sharply and pleasantly aromatic foliage, and masses of white or pale lilac, starry flowers.

Surely, the best known Australian shrubs must be callistemons, the scarlet bottlebrushes, closely related to the almost equally familiar honey myrtles and paperbarks, species of *Melaleuca*. Both genera have a preference for damp, even waterlogged, situations, and soil moisture is not the critical factor for these shrubs like so many of the others from drier places, and as a whole they respond amenably to cultivation. The weeping bottlebrush, *Callistemon viminalis,* is a small tree with pendant tips to the shoots. It is widely grown in gardens, and frequently planted as a street tree in California. The foliage smells of myrtles. 'Dawson River' is tall with silky grey foliage and a pronounced weeping form. Other selections of *C. viminalis* include 'Wilderness White', a dense, medium-sized shrub with white bottlebrushes; and two popular, relatively dwarf cultivars, 'Captain Cook' and 'Little John', which offer softer, broader leaves than the type and striking clusters of deep red bottlebrushes. *Callistemon citrinus* is one of the hardier species, with broad leaves and large, open-textured scarlet bottlebrushes. The soft texture of the immature shoots and foliage, silky grey and shot with crimson, are particularly attractive. 'Anzac' grows low, spreads broadly and has white bottlebrushes. Only two species grow in Western Australia: the more striking is the Albany bottlebrush, *C. speciosus,* with the most substantial, brilliant scarlet bottlebrushes of any. It develops into a large shrub with sparse, stiff, greyish green leaves on rangy branches. The other Western Australian species is *C. phoeniceus,* an upright shrub with long twiggy shoots clothed with narrow leaves. It produces very bright vermillion-scarlet bottlebrushes over a long period and retains an attractive, presentable appearance with little attention. Two species that buck the prevailing trend for scarlet flowers are *C. pallidus,* notable for its lemon-yellow bottlebrushes, and *C. viridiflorus,* with even more unusual green flowers and the one to choose if your garden happens to be cold and wet. *Callistemon pallidus* is naturally a vigorous shrub or small tree with lemon-yellow bottlebrushes and bronze-tinted immature growth. It grows on rocky sites near watercourses in the mountains of eastern Australia, and does well in cool, even cold, gardens on damp, infertile soils. The cultivar 'Candle Glow' is broadly spreading and low-growing, and 'Mount Oberon' has fine, silvery immature foliage. Finally, *C. salignus* makes a fine specimen tree that innocent gardeners might mistake for a melaleuca.

It has stems swathed in shreds of peeling bark, and immature foliage as scarlet as a pieris's, studded with little bottlebrushes of creamy white flowers.

Roadside planting around Perth in Western Australia includes numerous bushes with washed-out pink flowers and narrow aromatic foliage—shrubs that might be mistaken for tea trees except that they are broader and more open than any leptospermum. Geraldton wax, *Chamelaucium uncinatum*, is a medium-sized shrub that is very sensitive to fertilisers and intolerant of moist soils in summer; the species and its many cultivars must be planted on relatively infertile, very free draining soils in sunny, frost-free situations. Rapidly becoming a florist's favourite, cultivars include 'Purple Pride', with clusters of large, bright magenta-pink flowers; 'Album', more demurely white with staring yellow centres; and 'University', with purple flowers deepening in intensity with maturity. Hybrids with the smaller and very ornamental white-flowered Esperance wax, *C. axillare*, have produced 'Esperance Pearl' and 'Esperance Velvet'.

Shrubs with blue flowers are invariably sought after, and the intensity of colour of the blue or purple flowers of dampieras makes them particularly desirable. Two good garden plants are *Dampiera linearis*, which forms

Callistemon pallidus is one of the few Australian bottlebrushes with yellow rather than red flowers. The Arboretum of the University of California at Santa Cruz.

ground-covering mats of slender shoots with narrow grass-like foliage, or-
namented with masses of deep blue flowers from spring to autumn; and *D.
diversifolia*, with horizontal, lightly suckering shoots clothed with tiny fresh
green foliage and dotted with deep blue, yellow-centred flowers.

Shrubs of the pea family are so numerous in Australia that they seem to
be the result of attempts to combine the smallest possible differences in the
greatest possible number of variations. They range from ground-covering
shrubs to large erect bushes. Flowers are usually quite small, and frequently
yellow, golden brown or orange, often with crimson centres, and clustered
towards the tips of the shoots. All form symbiotic associations with nitrogen-fixing bacteria in their roots and are useful pioneer shrubs to enhance
soil fertility—a godsend on well-drained, sandy, gravelly or infertile garden
soils. Bitter peas include the hop bitter pea, *Daviesia horrida*. A bit of a cu-
riosity, this species is remarkable for and easily recognised by its seed pods
shaped like legs of mutton. Gorse bitter pea, *D. ulicifolia*, is small and prickly,
with orange and crimson pea flowers in small clusters of two or three in the
axils of the leaves. The bush peas in the genus *Pultenaea* are another large
group that includes *Pultenaea pedunculata*, which normally has red and yellow flowers, although 'Pyalong Pink' is a totally prostrate, ground-covering
shrub with distinctively different salmon flowers. Golden rosemary, *Oxylobium ellipticum*, has nothing whatever to do with rosemarys, but is another
member of the pea family. Some Western Australian species in this genus are
highly toxic and cause numerous stock deaths. Possums, kangaroos and
other native animals tolerate fifty to a hundred times the amounts that kill
introduced species, and oxylobium, the poison responsible, has been for-
mulated as a chemical known as 1080, which is widely used in Australia to
control introduced mammals that compete with or prey on native species.

Few shrubs have greater drought tolerance or cope better with infertile
soils than the Western Australian emu bushes, *Eremophila*, more evocatively
known as poverty bushes because of their ability to grow on soils too barren to provide a living. Their brightly coloured tubular flowers are showy
and effective, but the susceptibility of their roots to soil fungi in damp soils
during summer, and their aversion to fertilisers make the plants difficult to
grow in gardens. In eastern Australia the problem is largely solved by graft-
ing them onto the closely related and more amenable boobiallas, particularly *Myoporum insulare;* in California and around the Mediterranean where

summer droughts are the norm, they can be grown on their own roots. The most successful species in gardens are *Eremophila maculata*, a small, upright, rounded shrub with crimson tubular flowers; *E. divaricata*, with mauve flowers and fine grey foliage; and *E. bowmanii*, an attractive plant with lavender-blue flowers and silvery foliage.

Grevilleas play a leading part in any garden containing Australian plants. Numerous species are grown in cultivation, from the dense ground-covering mats of *Grevillea laurifolia* to tall trees like *G. hilliana* and the silky oak *G. robusta*. *Grevillea alpina* and *G. juniperina* vary considerably from one part of their range to another, and numerous natural forms have been selected—fourteen different variations of *G. alpina* are said to grow on Kangaroo Island off South Australia alone. Vast numbers of hybrids have been produced—taking advantage of widespread interfertility between species—amongst them those bred by Leo Hodge of Poorinda Nursery in East Gippsland, Victoria, who has included a bewildering miscegenation of species in his crosses. Many other hybrids have been produced elsewhere in Australia as well as in New Zealand and California. The very few examples mentioned here scarcely scratch the surface. Many grevilleas are easily grown, respond to frequent light tip-pruning, are tolerant of drought and are unattractive to deer. Several variants of *G. rosmarinifolia* and *G. juniperina*, including the yellow-flowered forma *sulphurea*, are hardy enough to be grown in the United Kingdom. The popular *Grevillea* 'Canberra Gem' (*G. juniperina* × *G. rosmarinifolia*), with cerise-red flowers in small trusses amongst needle-like foliage, is also hardy in northern gardens. The natural hybrid *G. ×gaudichaudii* (*G. acanthifolia* × *G. laurifolia*) is another popular, if slightly less hardy garden plant that forms an impenetrably dense ground cover of olive-green, deeply lobed leaves and reddish crimson new growth, dotted with inflorescences like burgundy toothbrushes. Bees and birds, including small honey-eaters, patronise it enthusiastically. *Grevillea banksii* is a large shrub, outshone in many gardeners' experience by its offspring, the ubiquitous *Grevillea* 'Robyn Gordon' (*G. banksii* × *G. pinnatifida*). This densely bushy, broadly compact hybrid produces an almost vulgar abundance of orange-scarlet flowers in large, slightly pendant trusses, and responds well to regular tip-pruning. It is tolerant of summer drought and coastal exposures, and is particularly amenable to Mediterranea, provided it is grown on very well drained soils. The royal spider flower, *G. victoriae*, from the mountains of south-eastern Australia, is large and one of the hardiest of the genus. Its clusters of orange-red flowers hang amongst broad, grey-green leaves with silvery reverses. Until *G. thelemanniana* produces its clusters of red flowers, it might be mistaken for an artemisia. It is known as the cob-web or spider-web grevillea. A valuable garden form grows as dense ground cover, making impenetrable mats that follow contours of the ground, spilling freely over low walls.

Hakeas and grevilleas are closely related, but the follicles of the latter open spontaneously to release the seeds, whereas hakea follicles are serotinous and remain closed until the death of the shoot that bears them—very often after fire, or when they have been picked in cultivation. The invasive tendencies of a few species, including *Hakea lissosperma* and *H. gibbosa* as well as *H. suaveolens* and *H. tenuifolia*, brought to South Africa to be used as hedges and screens, have given the genus a bad name amongst conservationists. But many are amenable garden plants that add to the attractions of gardens, without threatening to escape and become a nuisance. The willow-leaved hakea, *H. saligna*, is a tall shrub or small tree with clusters of creamy white flowers. It is hardy and broadly tolerant of garden conditions,

Grevillea 'Robyn Gordon' is possibly the best known, most popular hybrid grevillea. Its large clusters of brightly coloured flowers are produced almost continuously throughout the year. The Taft Garden, near Ojai, California, United States.

including wet soils, and is an excellent screen or shade tree for testing conditions. The royal hakea, *H. victoriae*, sounds good: broad, scallop-shaped leaves develop yellow and orange tints on a grey-green background that are most intense on the flowering shoots. The colours intensify throughout the life of each leaf—up to three years. The species is grown commercially for florists, but in gardens is generally a coarse shrub with poor structure and form. The flowers of the pin-cushion hakea, *H. laurina*, also popular with florists as a cut flower, have a fascinating resemblance to small, pale pink sea-urchins. This large, open shrub or small tree is broadly tolerant in cultivation and flowers during autumn and early winter. *Hakea salicifolia* is a small and attractive tree with very narrow sickle-shaped leaves, a gracefully weeping form and strongly textured, deeply furrowed brown bark. The fragrant flowers have an aroma reminiscent of a combination of licorice and wintergreen.

The almost invariably bright yellow, bowl-shaped flowers of guinea flowers resemble the hypericums or St John's worts of the Northern Hemisphere. The snake vine, *Hibbertia scandens*, so-called for the tangle of writhing stems that support the upper part of this scrambling shrub, is the most widely grown of the genus, and deservedly so. A first-class, trouble-free plant, it is equally effective as broadly spreading ground cover or as a climber, and flowers almost continuously. In contrast *H. stellaris*, a small shrub from Western Australian, is inclined to be choosy and difficult to please even in the sunlit situations and well-drained but not excessively dry soils in which it is reputed to be most at home, displaying a disconcerting tendency to die overnight. This and *H. miniata* are the only members of the genus without yellow flowers. Instead the flowers are a vivid shade of bright orange and cover the plant in a spectacular display, above a mound of twiggy stems and narrow foliage rather like a rock rose. The thyme guinea flower, *H. serpyllifolia*, is a creeping shrub with small yellow flowers from alpine situations in the Victorian Alps. It makes good small-scale ground cover, and is moderately hardy and broadly tolerant in gardens.

The Swan River myrtle, *Hypocalymma robustum*, is a small shrub with aromatic foliage and masses of bright pink flowers with prominent stamens, rather like a colourful, small tea tree. It flowers only during the winter in hot, dry situations but continues well into spring in cooler, moister settings. In nature it flowers most profusely a year or two after a fire, from new shoots springing from the base; hard pruning as the flowers fade improves its performance in gardens. *Hypocalymma cordifolium* 'Golden Veil' is a delicately attractive shrub with small white flowers and aromatic, variegated foliage with green centres and broad cream edges.

Kunzeas are sometimes rather dowdy little shrubs with flowers arranged like bottlebrushes. One of the best is *Kunzea ambigua,* a worthy garden plant that eventually grows into a well-formed small tree with masses of fragrant, creamy white flowers in early summer. *Kunzea ambigua* 'Wilson's Promontory' is shrubby with arching shoots, and a prostrate form is also available. The outstanding exception to any suggestion of mediocrity is *K. baxteri,*

good in all its parts. By far the most showy of the genus and a winner in gardens, this species produces substantial scarlet and gold bottlebrushes over a long period, followed by sculptured, dark chestnut brown, clustered seed capsules. It may take a few years to settle down, but once it does so develops into an attractive semi-weeping shrub or small tree with soft grey-green leaves. Another species with similarly bright, but smaller, scarlet flowers is *K. pulchella*. Gardeners looking for serviceable and attractive ground cover for well-drained sandy soils might go for *K. pomifera,* with its broadly spreading shoots producing clusters of white flowers during the summer.

At its best *Leschenaultia biloba* from the kwongan of Western Australia is dazzling: spattered with clear sky blue flowers through autumn and winter, culminating in a grand display each spring. Regular tip-pruning as the main display fades helps to keep the plants compact. 'White Flush' is one

Kunzea baxteri is the showiest in the genus and a winner in gardens, producing long-lasting scarlet and gold bottlebrushes. Garry and Elspeth Jacob's garden, Montrose, Victoria, Australia.

of several selected garden forms with white-centred flowers. Well-drained soils are essential, and mulches of washed gravel or pebbles right up to the stems of the plants are recommended. *Leschenaultia formosa* is an almost prostrate shrub with vivid, deep red flowers, and is the most widespread of several red-flowered species in this genus.

Melaleuca is a large, almost exclusively Australian genus of trees and shrubs, many of which are notable for their beautiful flaking bark. All honey myrtles and paperbarks produce inflorescences that resemble bottlebrushes, and many grow naturally on perennially or seasonally moist soils. Most species adapt readily to garden conditions, and several, like the weeping paperbark, *Melaleuca leucadendra,* are planted as street trees in many more or less frost-free parts of the world. Although excellent as a small tree, it eventually grows large, developing increasingly beautiful, deeply layered peeling bark, and long trailing tips to its shoots. Its small, creamy white, fragrant flowers appear from midsummer until autumn. Others that grow as trees include the swamp paperbark, *M. ericifolia,* with creamy white and grey exfoliating bark and small, ivory-white, fragrant flowers in spring; and *M. quinquenervia,* which flowers during the autumn and winter. The latter species is often seen as a large shrub but develops into a medium-sized tree, with peeling bark that makes a notable contribution to its beauty. *Melaleuca quinquenervia* 'Revolution Gold' is a widely distributed garden selection with bright yellow foliage. One of the most remarkable species, from limestone formations south of Perth, is the chenille honey myrtle, *M. heugelii.* This characterful small tree with whipcord foliage, rugged bark and a stiffly upright form might be mistaken for a cypress, until it flowers, when the best forms produce spectacular creamy white bottlebrushes. A showy species that flowers during the summer is the scarlet honey myrtle, *M. fulgens.* Notable for its colour and comparatively broad bottlebrushes, this medium-sized shrub should be pruned hard after flowering to maintain shape and density. Selected colour forms range from salmon to crimson-red—all embellished by the golden tips of the anthers. 'Stevemannii' grows more rigidly and stiffly upright than the type and has outstanding scarlet flowers. The green honey myrtle, *M. erubescens,* is remarkable for its lime-green bottlebrushes, and in addition is a large shrub with a distinctive structure and angular shape combined with stiff, densely ranked foliage that make it a conspicuous feature plant in any garden.

Many rice bushes have showy flowers that are attractive to bees. They tend to be short-lived, but most grow rapidly and flower when still young. Bushman's boot laces, *Pimelea nivea*, is a Tasmanian endemic. This high-quality medium-sized shrub has an angular, characterful appearance; it produces excellent, leathery, glossy deep green foliage and terminal inflorescences of pure white, well-formed, fragrant flowers. *Pimelea rosea* from the southern coast of Western Australia is a densely twiggy, round-profiled little bush with clustered heads of flowers that may be almost white, pale pink or a deep rose colour. *Pimelea ferruginea* is medium-sized and broadly domed, developing a middle-aged spread as it matures. It has bright, fresh green foliage in four close-set ranks along the shoots carrying hemispherical clusters of flowers at their tips. *Pimelea ferruginea* 'Bonne Petite' and 'Magenta Mist' are selections with deep pink flowers, the latter with more than a hint of the dreaded magenta. *Pimelea filiformis* grows either as a carpeting shrub or a low, hummocky ground cover. The fresh light green foliage is dotted with small, irregularly formed bobbles of white starry flowers.

The mint bushes, as their name suggests, are another group addicted to aromatic foliage—sometimes sharp and refreshing, at others cloyingly sweet. The leaves of the Victorian Christmas bush, *Prostanthera lasianthos*, smell of eucalyptus and are produced by an open, spindly shrub with multiple stems that become bare towards their lower halves. On deep fertile soils, it eventually grows into a tree with an open canopy above a short trunk. Quite large white flowers with orange and crimson markings, sometimes tinged with lilac, are produced in masses from spring to early summer; an attractive form with deep crimson stems and blushing blooms is also available. *Prostanthera lasianthos* grows from lowland forests to subalpine heaths in eastern Australia, and provenances from the latter provide plants sufficiently frost hardy to be widely grown in chilly gardens in the Northern Hemisphere. The alpine mint bush, *P. cuneata*, is another hardy shrub from high altitudes. It has small, semi-succulent, round leaves on upright shoots, and the flowers, like little slightly misshapen bells, may be pure white or pale mauve, with crimson and yellow markings. In the selection 'Alpine Gold', occasional leaves or twigs are suffused with golden tints. One of the most floriferous species is *P. rotundifolia*, a substantial round-profiled shrub that grows on rich loamy soils. It is broadly tolerant, growing equally well in sunlit or partially shaded settings, and does well in exposed coastal situations. The highly aromatic foliage is almost obscured by the purple flowers each spring. Selected cultivars include the pink-flowered 'Rosea' and the even more floriferous 'Ghost Cave'. *Prostanthera ovalifolia,* which also has a form with variegated foliage, produces masses of purple-mauve flowers on a lax, tumbling shrub with refreshingly aromatic foliage. It is widespread in gardens in Australia and elsewhere.

From semi-arid parts of Western Australia, the unforgettably named cockies tongues, *Templetonia retusa,* are tolerant of base-rich soils and are recommended for free-draining gardens subject to summer drought—Mediterranea would suit. This leguminous shrub with bright red flowers amongst long, grey, wedge-shaped leaves has none of the anonymity, and much greater impact, than the small-flowered yellow or orange shrubs of the pea family referred to earlier. Selections with white or yellow flowers are available if you find red a little too hot.

Springtime in the eucalypt forests of eastern Australia is enlivened by a number of low-growing shrubs, including the pink bells, which remind me of the daboecias that grow amongst the plantations of imported gum trees in north-west Spain. Black-eyed Susan, *Tetratheca pilosa,* is small and bushy with narrow leaves and masses of bell-shaped lilac flowers that can also be mauve or magenta in garden forms. Pink bells, *T. ciliare,* is more upright, often with slightly arching stems carrying mauvy pink flowers. It prefers moist but well-drained situations.

Thomasia solanacea is strikingly different from most Australian shrubs. Its distinctive foliage seems out of place in this flora, with soft, broad, lobed leaves that look as though they should be deciduous. This large, densely foliaged shrub produces sprays of white or pale pink, downward-facing, bowl-shaped flowers with dark centres. *Thomasia montana* is prostrate but capable of becoming a scrambler when it runs up into neighbouring shrubs. For months on end it produces a prolific succession of broadly bell-shaped flowers, in subdued shades of violet or light purple, along the lengths of the shoots. Although seldom seen in gardens, this species makes excellent spreading ground cover with a quiet attraction that would be welcome in many situations.

From quiet attractions to some of the brightest of the bright, we return to Western Australia and the feather flowers—feathers that surely come from some bright bird of paradise. Gardening lore condemns the feather flowers as difficult to please, but the plants are killed by kindness in rich, fertile, well-watered conditions; their aversion to moist soils in the summer leads to root infections. On infertile, well-drained soils where summer droughts are the norm, this genus is well worth trying. *Verticordia chrysantha* has yellow flowers that may be small individually, but massed together overlay the little flat-topped bush with a cloth of gold that seems to be a reflection of the sun itself. The scarlet feather flower, *V. grandis,* is equally flamboyantly beautiful, and would be more widely grown in gardens but for the difficulty of growing it from seed, due to low viability, and its extensive and deep root system, which makes transplanting difficult.

Looking-Glass Shrubs in the North

Travelling east by another third of the world's spin, and an excursion into the Northern Hemisphere, brings us to California, where chaparral is the name given to the drought-adapted plant communities growing in conditions markedly similar to those in the western parts of South Africa and Australia. Exceptional collections of Southern Hemisphere plants have been assembled at the Arboretum of the University of California at Santa Cruz, where correas, Cape heaths and Australian native hibiscus, amongst others, have been bred by Ray Collett, the founder and first director, and introduced into Californian gardens. A tour of the gardens with Melinda Johnson provided an inspirational introduction to the wealth and diversity of these shrubs, and the opportunities they offer gardeners in places like California and the Mediterranean—opportunities that have barely begun to be explored. Hitherto, garden makers in California reflecting on the fashions of the eastern United States and Europe saw little point in creating gardens that aped the dry hillsides around them, covered with golden grasses and drought-adapted trees and shrubs. They preferred visual reminders of the gardens they had left behind, based on flower beds and lawns, and these dreams of past glories in an alien land were nourished by abundantly available water. Nowadays, water can no longer be used as though it came from an inexhaustible source, and developing interest in gardens based as much on ecological principles as on nostalgic visions have created new perceptions of what we want from plants and how we can use them in gardens.

Another garden in California where Southern Hemisphere plants are grown in conditions similar to those they experience naturally in Australia or South Africa is John Taft's garden near Ojai, not far from Santa Barbara. I visited the Taft Garden one wet day in November—a matter for rejoicing since this was the first rain since February and, as it turned out, a prelude to the wettest winter for many years—and few plants were in flower on the day I was there. I was shown round by Vance Martin, director of the International Center for Earth Concerns, and now responsible for the management of the garden. We were joined by Jo O'Connell, an Australian who not only carries a torch for the native plants of her country, but does so with such conviction that she has established the Australian Native Plants Nursery in the heart of California. Amongst her many activities, she was responsible for planting and now for keeping an eye on the Australian plants in the Taft Garden. The plants were remarkable for their strong and vigorous growth, possibly because they respond to the deep, scree-filled soil that drains superbly in its upper layers but allows roots access to water at deeper levels. Their success also was aided possibly by the fact that this is not old garden ground that has been fertilised and managed in the past, with the risk of infection with phytophthora and other soil-borne fungal diseases, but a garden cut from the virgin chaparral that still covers the neighbouring hillsides.

My tours of the Santa Cruz arboretum and the Taft Garden reinforced more optimistic impressions of the potential of these gorgeous shrubs from the other side of the world. I saw many more Australian shrubs in a garden near San Diego, far to the south, situated on virtually frost-free, slightly sloping, free-draining ground. The owner, Andrew Wilson, first became interested in Southern Hemisphere plants while living in Dublin, before, very wisely, moving to California, where he was able to indulge his fancy to the full. The garden is a revelation of how broadly tolerant some plants can be, when given skilful care and attention. Cool temperate shrubs like camellias and azaleas grow alongside eucalypts, banksias and other sclerophyllous trees and shrubs, beside rainforest species like the firewheel tree, *Stenocarpus sinuatus*, and even the tree fern *Cyathea cooperi*, amongst numerous succulents and other plants adapted to arid conditions, accompanied by drifts of daffodils, in this case the paper white narcissus, the only one that can endure the heat and drought. Although Andrew is mainly interested in shrubs and trees from Australia, his garden also contains numerous plants from Southern Africa.

Those of us brought up on Rudyard Kipling's *Just So Stories* have a vivid image of the "great, grey-green, greasy Limpopo River—all set about with fever trees" where the crocodile did a nose-job on the elephant child. Fever trees, *Acacia xanthophloea,* grow naturally in summer rainfall areas of eastern South Africa, usually in moist situations, as Kipling implies. The last time I had seen one was at Amanzimnyama, a garden in the steaming, humid conditions of the Hibiscus Coast north of Durban. There, as here, the softly gleaming lustre of its pale gold bark provided ample justification for its ever-increasing popularity with gardeners.

Not far away, Andrew showed me a flourishing specimen of the Natal flame bush, *Alberta magna.* This plant has a resounding ring to its name, but the appellation "magna" can raise frustrated expectations, since in gardens it usually grows as an upright shrub, seldom as a tree. Rather than admire its size, gardeners are more likely to regret its slow growth and delayed production of its superb displays of clustered tubular, scarlet flowers in spring, prolonged throughout the summer by the persistent scarlet sepals. It grows naturally in the humid forests of coastal KwaZulu-Natal, and books invariably advise that its well being in gardens depends on rich, fertile soils well supplied with water.

Pride of de Kaap, *Bauhinia galpinii,* comes from much drier parts of the bushveld and open woodlands in summer rainfall areas of eastern Southern Africa. Its name has nothing to do with Kaap Stad (Cape Town) but refers to the de Kaap valley, near Barberton, in the province of Mpumalanga. The large flowers are irregularly shaped, a little like beautiful, soft apricot-orange nasturtiums clustered at the ends of the branches from summer into autumn. Its natural inclination is to sprawl over neighbouring shrubs almost as a climber, and in gardens it can be used to drape large boulders or tumble down walls. If preferred, it can be persuaded to grow in a more shrub-like fashion by cutting it back hard in late winter.

Numerous money plants, *Crassula ovata,* had sowed themselves freely amongst the other shrubs. This species, from the south-western Cape, grows in dry, often drought-afflicted situations. It is a strikingly individual looking shrub with thick, fleshy stems and rounded, succulent leaves overlaid with a bloom that gives them the texture and something of the appearance of grapes. Maturity and old age bring characterful sculptural qualities as the congested stems become progressively more gnarled and knotted.

Dombeyas are a group of shrubs from Madagascar and summer rainfall areas in Southern Africa. They have fragrant flowers that sometimes resemble mallows, sometimes more like apple blossoms. Their reputation as amenable garden plants was borne out here by a flourishing *Dombeya* 'Rosemound', a compact, spreading, flat-topped shrub with broad, lobed leaves and beautiful large, rounded clusters of pale pink flowers. Full of promise for gardeners, few species are widely grown in cultivation, and fewer still are seen often.

The coral trees are a group of leguminous shrubs and trees; almost all are easy to grow in gardens and have intensely showy, large, crimson-scarlet flowers. By far the most widely cultivated is the Brazilian *Erythrina crista-gallii*, seen in gardens all over Mediterranea and beyond. It is naturally a large tree, but is so undemanding that, when cut back annually—like a buddleja—it flowers prodigiously at the ends of the new shoots. The plant grown here was the coast coral tree, *E. caffra*, which is particularly admirable when its nectar-filled flowers appear on bare branches during winter and spring; I had previously seen it, like the fever tree, in the perennial humid warmth of Amanzimnyama. Nectar usually brings in hummingbirds, but in this garden it is the ravens that help themselves appreciatively. A cultivar known as 'Flavescens' has creamy yellow flowers.

One of many plants known colloquially as the crown of thorns is *Euphorbia milii*, more familiar to conservatory owners perhaps as *E. splendens*. This native of dry places in Madagascar was another plant growing freely and seeding itself happily in this California garden. Its green succulent stems, overlaid by a grey bloom and armed with formidably long spiny thorns, contrast distinctively with the forms and textures of neighbouring plants, but the brilliant scarlet bracts that surround the clusters of tiny, bright yellow flowers—like miniature poinsettias sprouting from some kind of cactus—are its chief glory for most gardeners.

Gasteria acinacifolia was another succulent shrub, adapted to drought-stricken areas, to be found growing amongst trees and shrubs from moist forests in Natal, and very often tucked in beneath them, since like many xerophytes, it has a natural—and rather unexpected—tendency to seek shade. It grows here exceptionally luxuriantly, with dropsical, spiky fans of leaden green leaves, not unlike those of an aloe.

The sausage tree, *Kigelia africana*, invariably attracts attention when seen growing in the Kruger National Park and other areas of the Low Veld in northern South Africa and southern Zimbabwe. The loose sprays of showy, open bell-shaped, glowing scarlet flowers are pollinated by bats and are attractive and interesting in themselves—but the tree is even more notable for its extraordinary cylindrical fruits hanging amongst the foliage like salamis from the ceilings of Italian grocers' shops. Gardeners often display a misplaced fascination with this tree, ignoring its natural preference for hot, moist summers and mild, dry winters, and planting it in unsuitable places, where it usually grows in a morose and unconvincing fashion—attributes left at the gate when planted in Andrew Wilson's garden.

The sticky flower, *Orphium frutescens*—a little more woody than a perennial, but barely a shrub—has clusters of large, purplish pink flowers at the tips of its branches. It has some of the qualities of its relatives, the gentians, and in gardens is usually an amenable and rewarding plant to grow. Although a native of Mediterranea from the south-western Cape, its natural preference is for places close to the sea, and it usually does best in gardens where adequate moisture is available year round.

Finally, *Pachypodium lamerei* comes from the dry, deciduous forests of central, western and southern Madagascar. In gardens it is the most frequently grown member of a sometimes dramatic, sometimes bizarre, always exciting group of plants. Its single stout stem is encased in a silver skin of bark, as though forged from aluminium adorned with sharp spines, beneath a stubby branching head, making a compelling focal point in any garden. At the height of the dry season, small clusters of fragrant white, yellow-centred flowers with voluptuous satin petals emerge amongst the austerity of its spiny stems.

This garden, set in an extreme manifestation of Mediterranea, cuts short too headlong a pursuit of the idea that shrubs and trees from Australia and South Africa can be grown successfully in gardens only by taking care to match plant with place. The places that many of these plants come from share few affinities with the climate of San Diego—some, like the Hibiscus Coast of Natal, might reasonably be described as diametrically opposite. We need to remind ourselves that Australia is a continent, and South Africa a landmass not quite as vast as Alaska, but twice the size of Texas—there is room here for all sorts and conditions of plants, from all sorts and conditions of situations. The plants of the South African fynbos and the Australian kwongan cope naturally with conditions so austere that it is scarcely surprising that they find the rich diet of gardens indigestible. Plants that grow naturally in the meadows of the Drakensberg, nourished by summer rains, or the fertile soils of the open woodlands of Gippsland in south-eastern Victoria, and in other places equally well endowed, come to our gardens better equipped to make the most of the feather bedding we can provide for them, and as in Andrew Wilson's garden, good husbandry enables us to grow many of them even though the conditions are nothing like those they would experience naturally.

In Chapter Two, mention was made of plants that are able to thrive in a broad range of conditions irrespective of their natural preferences—described as good garden plants, and identified amongst the pillars of orthodox gardening. A glance through the lists of plants offered by any broadly stocked nursery or garden centre will reveal many long-established garden plants from the Looking-Glass Garden that we grow with scarcely a doubt about their ability to thrive in our gardens without going to the trouble of changing the ways we garden to suit their fads. As interest develops in the native plants of these places, more and more are being brought to the attention of gardeners, and made available for all who would like to try them in their gardens. Some of these bring with them a fondness for specialised conditions that makes them recalcitrant in orthodox gardens and demands that we find ways to grow them that take account of their preferences. The great majority—and we come across increasing numbers of these in the chapters that follow—have or will show themselves to be amenable plants that we can grow alongside the familiar occupants of our gardens. Their presence will provide scope for new effects, for more dazzling colour combinations and for even more imaginative and exciting presentations in our gardens.

CHAPTER 5

Flowers of Veld and Bush

T HE CREATOR once spent a fragment of infinity composing variations on a theme of orange daisies, and having done so, sought a home for the results. A well-travelled angel—Gabriel perhaps—suggested that Namaqualand seemed more in need of brightening up than most places, and the whole lot were scattered over Springbok, or thereabouts. For twelve months of the year Springbok is a copper mining town; for a month, when the wildflowers bloom, it is a tourist resort. At the Springbok Cafe, now more trendily known as the Springbok Lodge, Jopie Kotze provides marching orders for the flower people after breakfast every morning. Each is issued with a map on which Jopie highlights the route to take and scrawls cryptic references to people and places while dealing with a stream of enquiries about where to go. "You will go to Steinkopf. After seven kilometres some eucalyptus trees beside the road. Go behind them—it's magic." "You go to Skilpad. It is two rands to enter, the best two rands you ever spent in your life—it's magic. Now go! You will miss the flowers."

Springbok is the heart of the Klipkoppe—an appropriate name meaning rocky hills—in Namaqualand. This 50-kilometre-wide escarpment is a winter rainfall area sandwiched between the Sandveld beside the Atlantic Ocean, where sea mists provide much of the scanty precipitation, and the high, dry Bushmanland Plateau, where rain, such as there is, falls mainly during the summer. In good years in favoured areas, the Klipkoppe may receive more than 500 millimetres of rain. Then the veld is carpeted with annuals, bulbs and succulents that create earthbound rainbows of orange, blue, yellow and purple stretching from horizon to horizon, making this one of the most astonishing spectacles any gardener could ever wish to see. In years when the rains

Previous page: The South African Sandveld is home to many annuals, bulbs and succulent plants widely grown in gardens around the world. This colourful display of flowers is growing in a semi-natural state in a garden on the Cape Peninsula. Silver Seas, Felicity Flint's garden, Fish Hoek, Western Cape Province, South Africa.

fail, as in 1998, the flowers scarcely appear and tourists go home disappointed.

Jopie's instructions first brought me to a farm called Skilpad close to Kamieskroon, which has been a wildflower reserve since 1988. Its position along the spine of a low ridge attracts any rain that is going, and the abandoned wheat fields and spaces between the shrubs are filled each spring with a myriad of colourful flowers. Yellow duck's eyes, dusky crimson horned diascias, blue felicias and orange gazanias carpet the ground between little outcrops of shattered rock; Namaqualand daisies and ursinias flourish amongst scattered shrubs; and an extraordinary variety of plants emerge from the crevices and cracks between the stones of rocky pavements. It is not a place where just a handful of species paint the landscape, but one of those rare wonderlands where every step seems to lead to something new. Many of the residents here are bulbs, a lifestyle that provides security where severe summer droughts are normal, and where in occasional years rains fail almost completely. Others are annuals that depend on the rain for renewal each year, growing through the winter, flowering in spring and shedding

Colourful wildflowers carpet the veld in Namaqualand. Near Steinkopf, Northern Cape Province, South Africa.

their seed as the land dries. Some are succulent shrubs that go virtually dormant during the heat and aridity of summer but grow rapidly from an established base in response to the first autumn rains.

Annuals and Some Perennials

Many species of *Arctotis* are amenable, widely grown garden plants with large, bold, daisy flowers. Botanists separate *Arctotis* from *Venidium* by the patterns of the scales on the backs of the flowers, but hybrids between the two genera provide gardeners with flowers in a wide range of colours. *Arctotis hirsuta* grows naturally in the Sandveld along the west coast of South Africa. It has large white, yellow or orange daisies on sprawling, branching stems. The gousbloom, *A. fastuosa*, also known as the double Namaqualand daisy, is a brilliantly colourful orange annual widely grown in gardens. The perennial, mat-forming *A. stoechadifolia* produces large cream flowers on short stalks just above the soft, grey, lobed leaves. This species is grown

This "garden" of annuals and succulents includes nemesias, ursinias, diascias and felicias growing with the broad yellow daisy flowers of pigsroot *(Conicosia pugioniformis)*. Skilpad Wildflower Reserve, near Kamieskroon, Northern Cape Province, South Africa.

in gardens in California, and does well elsewhere in Mediterranea, particularly on free-draining soils and in coastal gardens.

The little, yellow, button-headed flowers of duck's eyes are everywhere on the Klipkoppe. The most widely distributed species are *Cotula barbata*, also known as smelly weed due to its odoriferous foliage, and *C. leptalea*, which produces flowers on long stems above neat cushions of greyish green, feathery foliage. Neither quite makes it as a garden plant, but several perennial species are excellent as bright ground cover, especially in dry situations on free-draining soils, including: *C. turbinata*, with dense mats of finely divided pinnate foliage, dotted with bright yellow bobbles; and *C. lineariloba*, which forms a deep carpet of feathery, ferny, light green foliage beneath the yellow flowers.

Many good plants from this part of the world are hardly seen in gardens, including *Didelta carnosa*, a low-growing and semi-succulent shrub rather than a perennial. It has large, bright yellow daisies. Its extreme drought tolerance during summer, and ability to do well in freely drained situations in places with wet winters make it an ideal candidate for gardens in Mediterranea.

The large flowers of Namaqualand daisies, *Dimorphotheca sinuata* and the equally striking *Osteospermum hyoseroides*, are mainly responsible for the displays that paint any patch of waste ground around Springbok brilliant orange in the spring. *Dimorphotheca sinuata* is a popular garden annual notable for the satin sheen of flowers that range in colour from cream through yellow to vibrant salmon. White petals with crimson reverses are produced by the low-growing *D. pluvialis*, an annual that covers huge areas of the western Cape. Like many South African daisies, this species is reluctant to open its flowers fully except in bright sunshine, which can make it frustrating as a garden plant in places where sunshine tends to be variable or more elusive than in Namaqualand.

Kingfisher daisies include annuals, perennials and small shrubs, and characteristically have flowers with bright blue ray petals and yellow centres. Annuals from Namaqualand include *Felicia bergeriana*, with large blue flowers opening late in the morning, and *F. namaquana*. Several perennial or shrubby species are amenable garden plants already widely grown or potentially useful. *Felicia nordenstamia*, for one, is tolerant of wind and salt spray in seaside conditions. Equally useful for coastal gardens is *F. amel-*

loides, a shrubby perennial with sky blue daisies held well above the foliage, flowering on and off throughout the year, with the main display in spring. *Felicia echinata,* the dune daisy, is a rather tender, low-growing, freely branching subshrub also appropriate for coastal conditions. Its distinctive small triangular leaves have prickly pointed tips, and bluish mauve flowers are produced at the ends of the shoots in early spring. These and other perennial felicias should be trimmed back fairly hard once the first flush of flowers fades, to keep them bushy and encourage longevity.

One of the most attractive and conspicuous annuals in Namaqualand is *Grielum humifusum.* Its large, satin-textured, primrose-yellow flowers form pools of sunshine across the surface of the ground amongst finely divided leaves. *Grielum grandiflorum* is closely related and similar, but it is a perennial from the Sandveld with deeply dissected, lobed leaves. Although a lovely plant, it seldom flowers so profusely, and never achieves the vernal freshness of the annual version.

My visit to the Flower Reserve at Nieuwoudtville on a winter's day, before the spring flower display really got going, was brightened by the presence of a little, milky white annual, like a diminutive cuckoo flower *(Cardamine pratensis),* dotted by the thousands amongst grasses and a few iris-like moraeas. *Heliophila collina* is one species in a large genus of annuals with white or bright blue flowers. The blue-flowered types are particularly tempting, and when seen growing massed together their slender stems and numerous small but brilliantly colourful flowers make a lasting impression. The most widespread species is *H. coronopifolia,* often with flowers with pale or whitish centres. It grows well in gardens in Mediterranea when sown in situ during the autumn to flower the following spring, but is not hardy enough to be grown this way in colder gardens, and is insufficiently tolerant of summer rainfall to thrive when sown in the spring.

An intriguing feature of many South African wildflowers, amongst them nemesias, is a chameleon-like tendency to appear in a variety of colours. *Nemesia versicolor* is widespread especially on sandy soils; the flowers are usually bicoloured white and yellow, or blue and yellow, but may be plain pink or blue. The perennial *N. caerulea* is an exceptionally floriferous plant, almost perpetually in flower in mild climates, but becomes straggly unless cut back hard from time to time. 'Alba' is a robust form that produces dense terminal spikes of large white flowers with yellow markings that serve as honey guides for bees. *Nemesia caerulea* 'Rosea' is taller and has more open spikes of slightly smaller, pinky mauve flowers. *Nemesia strumosa*, the progenitor of the cultivated strains of annuals, grows wild on sandy soils to the north of Cape Town, usually as taller, more open plants than the forms seen in gardens. It branches freely from the base to produce numerous flowering stems.

Several pelargoniums from Namaqualand are notable garden plants. The best known is *Pelargonium fulgidum,* with heads of small glowing scarlet flowers above rich green, deeply lobed leaves produced on semi-succulent stems. The plants are comfortably bushy and have an attractively soft appearance that comes as a relief in this world of often uncompromisingly strange xeric forms. Since its arrival in western gardens early in the eighteenth century, *P. fulgidum* has given rise to the hybrids 'Ardens' and 'Scarlet Unique'. The clusters of brilliant cerise-purple flowers of *P. incrassatum* stand out even amongst the bright flowers that grow at Skilpad, and are all the more striking in contrast to the orange daisies amongst which they grow in nature. When flowering is over, the plants retreat underground into small, beetroot-like tubers. *Pelargonium sericifolium* is a branched dwarf shrub with silvery hairs on the leaves, and large, brightly coloured cerise or pink flow-

Although *Grielum humifusum* crops up everywhere in Namaqualand, I never tire of its beauty, and wonder why gardeners did not adopt it long ago. Near Bullertrap, Springbok, Northern Cape Province, South Africa.

ers with pronounced crimson veins. *Pelargonium klinghardtense* is far removed from the stereotypical garden geranium. Not only does it have yellow flowers, but it looks like a clump of sea kale with semi-succulent, wavy-margined, glaucous leaves carried on stout, fleshy stems.

Groundsels in this part of the world are not dowdy little plants with small, yellowish flowers, but eye-catching, vibrantly colourful annuals. Even so, the name hongerblom for *Senecio arenarius* suggests the dry, infertile nature of the places where it grows naturally, producing its large heads of bright mauve or pinkish purple flowers. *Senecio elegans,* with glowing purple flowers and slightly fleshy succulent leaves, is an excellent seaside plant, and an early colonist of disturbed ground that is equally at home in gardens.

Ursinias are graceful annuals distinguished by their light green, feathery foliage. Many are fully paid up members of the orange-daisy clan, and amongst the great contributors to the floral fireworks of spring in Namaqualand, but several *Ursinia* species have flowers that vary in colour from place to place. The flowers of *Ursinia cakilefolia* may be glowing orange or yellow or cream—all with dark centres. *Ursinia speciosa* carpets the ground with quantities of large, upward-facing daisies that are most often yellow, but a very pretty salmon-coloured form grows in some places, and elsewhere the flowers are ivory-white, contrasting particularly effectively with deep crimson, almost black, centres.

Grazing and Wildflowers

Venturing backstage at Kirstenbosch in search of John Winter the curator, I encountered first Mrs Thomas taking cuttings in the potting shed, and later Graham Duncan, who is in charge of the bulb collection there. Both asked me why I was in South Africa and on hearing that I was there to see the wildflowers responded with almost exactly the same words: "While you're here you must make sure you see Neil MacGregor at Nieuwoudtville." So a week or two later, I made a point of finding my way to Glenlyon at Nieuwoudtville in the north-western Cape, where Neil MacGregor farms several thousand merino sheep.

Impressive though his flock is, Glenlyon has more to offer than sheep. It is an inspiring example of management that brings sheep and wildflowers together for the benefit of both, and challenges methods that have led to the impoverishment of the natural flora over vast areas of veld. Driving along roads in Namaqualand it was impossible not to notice how frequently the bright ribbons of colourful flowers on either side stopped at the stock fences. Beyond them every vestige of edible leaf and flower had been eaten, to be replaced by tufts of unpalatable grasses amongst humped shrubs separated by bare rocky, sandy or stony spaces. Some years ago Neil became convinced that wildlife and farming—in the shape of a breeding flock of fifteen hundred ewes in an area too dry to grow wheat, and close to marginal for intensive sheep grazing—need not be incompatible. The results are a vindication of his belief.

The Bokkeveld Plateau where Glenlyon lies is remarkable for the high proportion of plants that produce bulbs or corms. Ploughing, as a means of

Uncontrolled grazing by sheep and other animals has stripped areas of the veld in Namaqualand bare of all but unpalatable shrubs and grasses, as seen on the far side of the wire stock fence here. Meanwhile, wildflowers flourish in the ungrazed area between the road and the fence. Near Steinkopf, Northern Cape Province, South Africa.

improving grazing, has devastating effects on the numbers of bulbous plants, and other ways had to be found to restrict the spread of unpalatable grasses. These included scarifying the surface, top-dressing with phosphates and sowing with nitrogen-fixing legumes. The vegetation here is not fynbos, so these improvements in fertility were no threat to its existence. Instead they led to an explosion in the numbers of bulbs, combined with improved grazing and increased stocking rates. A few hundred plants of *Bulbinella latifolia* var. *doleritica,* a rare local form that produces spikes of orange flowers, in contrast to the yellow ones of the type species, formerly hung on close to extinction. Now hundreds of thousands create a swathe of colour across these patches of clay derived from dolerite rocks, in the plant's only home. Sparaxis, ixias, geissorhizas, hesperanthas, cyanellas and others have also increased enormously, as have the dramatically beautiful, stately autumn-flowering amaryllids.

Neil has a magic bus on which he took me and a group of his friends on a tour of the farm, first to a paddock running with water where pools collected in every hollow—so remotely different from the conditions in which I had imagined South African bulbs might grow that I had to be persuaded that this was not an unusual event, but the normal spring condition in years of average or better rainfall. Even more remarkable was the sight of great drifts of annuals growing here: bands of yellow cotulas and purple senecios colour a landscape adorned with bright pink homerias, pale blue ixias and regal purple and crimson geisorrhizas. The grazing regime is timed to allow the annuals to grow undisturbed until their seeds have matured, at which point sheep are put in to spend a month or so clearing up the dried remnants, which are surprisingly nutritious. The controlled grazing, aided by the trampling effects of the sheep's feet, keeps the vegetation open and helps to implant seeds. This key element of the management of the land has resulted in the displays of flowers at Glenlyon, which are amongst the most remarkable to be seen anywhere.

These changes in management have had extraordinary effects on the wildflowers of the veld, while at the same time increasing their value as fodder for the sheep. The brilliantly colourful displays of flowers in the paddocks at Glenlyon each spring, compared to the desolate appearance of much of the surrounding countryside, are glowing testimony to the success of Neil MacGregor's methods. If only landowners could be persuaded to adopt such methods on a wider scale there would be little need for wild-flower reserves in this part of the world.

Bulbs of the Winter Rainfall Area

Gardeners long ago learnt to appreciate the possibilities of bulbs. Many South African bulbous plants are particularly amenable and even more flex-ible in gardens than the traditional spring-flowering daffodils, crocuses and tulips. Where winters are mild, the bulbs can be treated au naturel, planted in the autumn to flower the following spring. In colder areas, where winter frosts would be the death of them, many bulbs are equally happy to be lifted each autumn and stored in dry, frost-free conditions, before being replanted in spring to flower during the summer.

Few bulbs are as distinctive or delicately pretty as the cups-and-saucers, or paper boats. My first encounter was with a colony of *Androcymbium cili-olatum* scattered on the ground amongst shrubs close to Skilpad. The minute flowers are cupped within a pair of fragile white bracts, seemingly floating on a pair of deep green, ground-hugging leaves. The plants have the same sort of appeal that has made snowdrops and cyclamen such gardener's pets.

Most babianas are remarkable for the rich, glowing colours of their cup-shaped flowers, above pleated, sword-shaped leaves. They are easily grown and tolerant of moist soils in summer if drainage is good. Plants with bril-liantly colourful clusters of flowers, mostly in vibrant combinations of crim-son, purple, violet and similar shades, on short stems are represented by *Babiana geniculata,* one of the most eye-catching with rich crimson-magenta flowers; *B. dregei,* with one-sided, dense spikes of deep purple or mauve flowers; and *B. rubrocyanea,* with purple chalices stained crimson, as though with wine, towards the base. *Babiana villosula,* which delighted me on the Sil-vermine Reserve near Cape Town, is an exception with delicate flowers that resemble pale blue crocuses.

Chasmanthe floribunda is another plant of the South African winter rain-fall area that is easily grown and tolerant of moist soils in summer in well-drained situations. In Mediterranea the bright orange flowers appear on tall, branching inflorescences above fans of pleated leaves from midwinter. They are vulnerable to frost, however, and in colder situations should be stored in winter and planted in spring. The yellow-flowered var. *duckittii* is a natural variant. The species is widely naturalised in western and southern Australia. The related *C. aethiopica* naturalises freely around Santa Barbara in California, where its nectar attracts migrating rufous and Allen's hummingbirds.

Gladioli must be the most familiar of all South African bulbs, but the plants so often seen in gardens are hybrids of species from summer rainfall areas. The corms of species that grow in winter rainfall areas tend to rot in soils that remain moist in summer, and should be lifted and stored dry till autumn. *Gladiolus scullyi* is a small gladiolus, usually with only about three flowers on its short stems, but with a strong, spicy scent. *Gladiolus arcuatus* grows on sandy soils in Namaqualand and has smoky mauve-pink flowers, which are very fragrant in the evening. *Gladiolus tristis* is more broadly tolerant of garden conditions, and its pale yellow flowers, fragrant during the night, deserve more attention from gardeners. It grows naturally in depressions that become flooded during the wet season, known as vleis, often emerging and flowering in shallow expanses of water.

Tulbagh is an historic small South African town set in beautiful countryside amongst vineyards and orchards, where ostriches mingle in grassy paddocks with Angora goats up to their bellies in a sea of pink and apricot flowers. These are homerias, a group of robust plants, unpalatable to stock, with star-shaped flowers on branching inflorescences. Many species of *Homeria* grow naturally in seasonally wet situations on soils that dry out completely when the bulbs are dormant in summer, but most are broadly adaptable garden plants; attempts are being made to popularise them under the name "stars of the veld."

Ixias have long been established in gardens and are not only amongst the brightest of all bulbs, but amongst the most amenable. They naturalise freely in parts of Australia and New Zealand, where some species succeed when planted amongst grasses as meadow flowers. The strangely beautiful and elusive *Ixia viridiflora* has flowers that are a pale shade of electric blue with crimson-black centres. At the opposite end of the spectrum, *I. maculata* is notable for its brilliant orange flowers with purple or black honey guides. It grows amongst bushes on well-drained, coarsely sandy soils with gravel and small stones. Less dramatic than either of the previous two, *I. paniculata* has pale, parchment yellow flowers flushed with red in the throats on gracefully bunched spikes, fading as they mature.

The spikes of scarlet and yellow tubular flowers of the Cape cowslip, *Lachenalia aloides,* make it one of the most colourful species in a genus that runs from the large and showy to the dwarf and downright dowdy. It was introduced long ago to western gardens as an excellent conservatory plant. Like most of its kind, this species is vulnerable to moist soils in summer and, except in dry, well-drained situations, should be dried out after flowering. Variants with different coloured flowers and varying degrees of mottling on the leaves include the deep chrome yellow *L. aloides* var. *aurea.* Other species that qualify as bright and beautiful include *L. bulbifera,* with cerise-red flowers; the yellow-flowered *L. reflexa;* and *L. mutabilis,* with flowers that are cup-shaped rather than tubular. *Lachenalia matthewsii* has conspicuous inflorescences made up of numerous small, purple and pink flowers.

The ugly duckling, *Massonia depressa,* is seldom grown in gardens, and though not showy or obviously beautiful, it is an original with character that cannot pass unnoticed. Little coronets of white, nectar-producing flowers with yellow stamens sit in the centre of pairs of broad leaves, as large as dinner plates, that lie perfectly flat on the ground. Raindrops or dew on their surfaces reflect the sunlight like glass beads. *Massonia angustifolia* is brighter and more stylish, with clusters of orange flowers and glossy green leaves incised with deeply scored lines.

No irises grow naturally in the Looking-Glass Garden, but moraeas take their place, ranging from the delicately pretty to the sumptuously beautiful. Some species have slender stems each usually carrying a single or a few broad-petalled flowers, gracefully reminiscent of butterflies. One such species is *Moraea serpentina,* with moderately large yellow and white flowers on short stems, often in small colonies. This diminutively elegant bulb from Namaqualand looks particularly effective when grown in a pan. Cool, moist winters and hot, rather dry summers are its natural preferences. The delicate pale blue flowers, with yellow nectar guides, of *M. ciliata* have the fragrance of a vanilla pod. *Moraea fugax* grows from corms, deeply buried in unpromising aridly sandy soils, that produce a single attenuated leaf. Its strongly fragrant white, blue or yellow flowers open one or two at a time, each for a few hours and only after noon. The aptly named peacock moraeas include *M. aristata*, with pure white petals and shimmering blue honey guides. A tiny colony in a Cape Town suburb is all that remains of its natural population, but this species thrives in gardens and is widely established in Australia, where like many South African bulbs it has found a more congenial home away from home, away from porcupines, mole rats and baboons, which between them make the lives of bulbs in South Africa so tenuous. *Moraea neopavonia* is another plant restricted naturally to small and precarious populations, but is easy to cultivate and when grown from seed produces interesting variations. Flowers range in color from brilliant orange to rusty yellow with shimmering petals.

Papery white flowers that remain fresh (more or less) for six weeks or longer, and can even be dyed in tune with prevailing fashionable colours, sound like an interior decorator's dream plant, or the answer to a florist's prayers. *Ornithogalum thyrsoides* grows, often in large colonies, amongst

The large flowers of *Moraea serpentina* on slender stems appear to hover just above the ground. Near Kamieskroon, Northern Cape Province, South Africa.

grasses in the western Cape, and does equally well in gardens or in containers. Numerous other species occur, mostly with white flowers, but the bright orange flowers of *O. dubium* are colourful enough to justify the care needed to cultivate the plant successfully. Unlike most bulbs from this part of the world, *O. dubium* should not be planted deeply, but barely covered.

Carob orchards in north Cypress were once the home of orchids and other wildflowers; then, like many other places in milder temperate regions, the orchards were invaded by the so-called Bermuda buttercup, *Oxalis pescaprae*. Repeated sprays with herbicides have failed to eliminate the weed while largely destroying the native flora. *Oxalis pes-caprae* is native to South Africa, and with impartial poetic justice it is as inclined to invade the apple orchards in the Hottentots-Holland Mountains around Grabouw as carob orchards around the Mediterranean. *Oxalis obtusa* is a less invasive member of the genus, and another example of a chameleon plant with large flowers that may be creamy white, pale yellow, pink or brick red, their veins often delineated with crimson. *Oxalis purpurea* grows in lawns like daisies do in Britain, and despite the moans of greenkeepers, its shimmering patches of crimson-rose flowers look even prettier. This too varies in colour, favouring pale salmon in Namaqualand and variously pink, rose-purple, mauve or white elsewhere.

Small, bright bulbs resembling crocuses grow in seasonally wet vleis, even emerging in pools of shallow water during winter rains or along the edges of streams—these are most likely to be romuleas. Flowers vary in colour from yellow *(Romulea hirta)* to pink *(R. rosea)* to a glorious coral-red with black blotches at the base of the petals *(R. sabulosa)*. In cultivation the plants can be grown in containers, and even immersed in water during the growing season—though this tolerance of wet conditions does not extend into their summer resting period, and once flowering is over they must be allowed to dry out.

Soon after midwinter, when the spring display of most bulbs and annuals is still a promise, the star-shaped, bright yellow flowers of *Spiloxene serrata* and other members of the genus appear like sparks of sunlight spangling the ground beneath the shrubs amongst which they grow.

Grasses and Grass-like Plants

Two very different Southern Hemisphere plants colonise the crumbling cliffs facing the Pacific Ocean around San Francisco. Hottentot figs, *Carpobrotus*, are widely planted on roadside banks and elsewhere, spreading across the slopes and steep banks, stabilising them beneath colourful carpets of magenta or soft yellow and pink flowers each spring. The tufted clumps of pampas grass in untidy array amongst the gullies are less welcome. These clumps are more likely to be the Andean species *Cortaderia jubata* than the more familiar garden pampas, *C. selloana,* from Argentina. *Cortaderia jubata* has an apomictic lifecycle, based on automatic self-fertilisation, that guarantees the production of quantities of fertile seed, and makes it a formidable coloniser along the southern and central California coastline. That is a misfortune, not just for those who deplore such alien invasions, but for gardeners too—because dislike based on distrust of one species has led to the dismissal of other grasses in this genus that are of real garden value.

The garden pampas grass from Argentina has a magnificent presence, only too often demeaned by its use as a self-conscious, solitary clump in a corner of the lawn in small gardens. Unfortunately, such resolution and physical strength is needed to oust a well-established plant that removal is seldom attempted, and the tired, dowdy impression created by these plants has become so hackneyed and timeworn that suggestions to use them more imaginatively or in more expansive settings are seldom considered. The usual form of *Cortaderia selloana* has plain, rather uncharismatic inflorescences, like pale fox's brushes stuck on stiff poles, but cultivars like 'Sunningdale Silver', with elegant, open inflorescences on tall pliant stems, make unforgettably graceful impressions in groups against a background of trees,

This combination of grasses, ferns and phormiums around a small garden pool exemplifies the striking effect of compositions based on leaf shapes and forms—even when there is not a flower to be seen. Anne and Tom Stacey's garden, Te Puke, North Island, New Zealand.

or alongside a large pool or lake. A grouping of New Zealand toe-toes, *C. richardii*, can be equally impressive with tall plumes of off-white or cream flowers like banners at the tops of their stems. But at half the size *Cortaderia fulvida* has inflorescences like the flowing manes of Palomino horses and is a more amenable species in most gardens. Grasses are seldom thought of when wind breaks are planted, but vigorous, clump-forming species like *C. fulvida* provide excellent local shelter for plants close to them in a manner that is distinctively different to the trees and shrubs typically used for this purpose.

Another imposing plant, the giant cutty grass, *Gahnia xanthocarpa*, grows naturally on the edges of bogs and, more interestingly for gardeners, in light shade within and along the edges of forests. It is seldom seen in gardens, and its towering inflorescences are too tall for all but the grandest settings.

Despite its colonizing tendencies, *Cortaderia selloana* is one of the few grasses with the size and presence to make an impact on large-scale plantings. Powys Castle, Welshpool, Wales.

Thatch saw sedge or cutting grass, *G. radula,* from eastern Australia and Tasmania is more dramatic and more easily accommodated. Its inflorescences of black flowers erupt from large clumps of long leaves. In northern Tasmania its black spikes contrast starkly with the white flowers of *Diplarrhena moraea* beneath the eucalypts, a combination that would be equally dramatic in a garden.

The large and conspicuous inflorescences are what make these grasses and sedges interesting to gardeners. Generally speaking, large inflorescences come attached to large plants, but several grasses of no more than moderate size, like the New Zealand snow grasses, have outstandingly bold heads of flowers. *Chionochloa conspicua* is the largest, with relatively broad leaves and substantial plumes of flowers above flowing tussocks. The snow grass *Chionochloa flavicans,* from the higher rainfall areas of New Zealand, is half the size and forms dense tussocks beneath equally large plumes of straw-coloured flowers. Both species grow readily on average garden soils in full

Cortaderia fulvida produces flowing manes of inflorescences, as shown here on the Mahia Peninsula in New Zealand.

sun or dappled shade. *Chionochloa bromoides* forms smaller clumps of arching leaves with inflorescences that are neither as large nor as full as those of the previous species, and tend to be more laxly held, often drooping. Lastly, *C. rubra* is a knee-high tussock grass with rusty red inflorescences that are no more than modest, but its tawny clumps look particularly effective when planted in groups in landscaped settings. It also is broadly tolerant of a wide range of conditions, including drought. In parts of Central Otago in New Zealand's South Island, red tussock blankets the rounded hilltops and fills the valleys between them. The plants are so evenly spaced and so uniform in growth that they look as though each has been individually planted on a gigantic grid over the countryside.

The distinctive rustiness of *Chionochloa rubra* introduces another feature that characterises some New Zealand grasses and particularly sedges: foliage

The texture and shape of red tussock, *Chionochloa rubra,* contrasts with the rounded forms of hebes, corokias and pittosporums. The Regional Botanic Garden at Manurewa, near Auckland, North Island, New Zealand.

that is more or less permanently suffused with tan, bronze or crimson tones. As a nurseryman, I found this a doubtful asset because customers would assume that the plants were dead, and even if persuaded otherwise would decline to buy it, saying "Well! Anyway, it *looks* dead." A more serious concern, perhaps, than looking dead when alive is the fact that dead ones look little different to live ones, and customers are wary of those who happen to sell them dead plants. Such rusty foliaged grasses and sedges have to be used confidently and boldly as an assertion of their vitality and an assurance that they are meant to be where they are, when their warm tones and distinctive appearance create effects not achievable with more familiar green and blue-green grasses. One of the best known of these sedges is *Carex buchananii.* Its upright clusters of leaves have drooping tips and are usually coloured grey-brown or dull bronze in nature, rather than the copper-red of most of those grown in gardens. Several particularly intensely coloured forms of *C. testacea* with bright tawny orange, coppery bronze or red foliage have also been selected, and the attractive sheen on the leaves minimises the appearance of dead foliage. A less colourful but still interestingly different species—though one that can look more than a little in need of resuscitation—is *C. flagellifera,* with clumps of fine, grass-like bronze foliage with twisted, trailing, bleached tips.

Machaerina sinclarii is the sole representative of its genus in New Zealand. This striking sedge has slightly arching olive-green leaves that set off the warm russet- or tan-coloured panicles on more upright stems. The species is naturally inclined to more or less permanently moist soils and appreciates ample water in gardens, but is sufficiently drought tolerant to be a broadly amenable garden plant.

The giant *Poa flabellata* is one of the most imposing tussocks of them all. It is now found only on offshore islands after being systematically destroyed in pursuit of improved grazing on the main Falkland Islands. In maturity, the tussocks develop fibrous "trunks" a couple of metres high under great mops of leaves, below which penguins nest, and where even animals as large as sea elephants find shelter. Plant them if you want sea elephants at the bottom of the garden. The medium-sized *P. labillardieri* is more in scale with the needs of most gardeners. This Australasian tussock grass has dense blue-green foliage, and purplish green spikes of flowers that fade to a greyish tan. Other species of *Poa* in Australia include bog snow grass, *P. costini-ana*, which forms broad, dense tufts of rigidly spiny, shiny blue-green foliage; the small velvet tussock grass, *P. morrisii*, with compact mounds of grey-green foliage; and the more vigorous coastal tussock grass, *P. poiformis*, with dense hummocks of blue-green leaves below tall inflorescences. The most graceful of all is the New Zealand silver tussock, *P. cita*. Its silvery brown leaves radiate from the centres of the tussocks in such perfectly symmetrical hemispheres that one almost expects each one to be terminated by a bright point of light, like fibre-optic fountains.

For one who is intolerant of the unceasing demands that lawns can make, the attitude towards lawns is an admirable feature of the Looking-Glass Garden. Most people, sensibly, avoid the fine fescues, the carefully tuned strains of rye grass and other sirens that tempt gardeners in cooler, moister climates with promises of perfect velvet swards—provided that, forsaking all else in the garden, they offer themselves in perpetual bondage to the never-ending demands such lawns make. Instead gardeners of the Southern Hemisphere prefer to use work-a-day grasses. The vigorous, drought-resistant kikuyu grass, *Pennisetum clandestinum*, has both deep-running and surface rhizomes that form a dense, hard-wearing turf. Though inclined to be invasive, this species is popular and widely used in South Africa and Australia. Buffalo grass, *Stenotaphrum secundatum*, is a most serviceable perennial with surface rhizomes that root at the nodes and spread vigorously across the ground. It makes a resilient surface capable of enduring the exposure and saline conditions of coastal situations, is useful for a water-wise lawn, and grows only moderately high even when left uncut. Buffalo grass turns brown in severe drought, and goes yellow in response to frost, but recovers rapidly afterwards. The advantage of these species and the broad-leaved, shade-tolerant kersny, *Cynodon transvaalensis*, is that however much time and effort is put into mowing, top-dressing, scarifying and generally titivating, none will ever form a perfect sward. So the temptation never arises, and gardeners can enjoy the pleasure of deeply resilient, rug-like green mats to walk on, without being slaves to their lawns.

Finally, there is *Zoysia tenuifolia*, which I saw in Ted Smythe's garden in New Zealand making a soft carpet beneath bromeliads and palms, and later in Andrew Wilson's garden near San Diego. Although both men assured me that it was a living plant, it looked to me just like the green grass-like matting that butchers and florists use in their shops, forming a close-set, fine-leaved covering that faithfully followed the contours of the ground. Naturally low growing, it needs little mowing, and although it turns brown in very dry or cold weather, it recovers rapidly afterwards. This is a plant for cosmetic lawns, not those that are heavily used, since its network of fine, surface-rooting rhizomes do not appreciate being walked on—still less played on—and it should be mown much less frequently and more gently than regular lawn grasses.

Restios

Retios belong to a family of reeds, the Restionaceae, that grows only in the Southern Hemisphere and, of all the grass-like plants, are the least familiar to gardeners. Most grow naturally in South Africa, some in Australia and a very few in New Zealand and Chile. Although many restios have qualities of great potential interest to gardeners, scarcely any have a significant presence in gardens because, until recently they could not be easily propagated. All but a few resent division and recover slowly afterwards or die, and although many produce seed in abundance, seedlings were seldom produced in gardens. The discovery at Kirstenbosch that many species germinate rapidly and in quantity after exposure to smoke, or even when watered with infusions of the constituents of smoke, has made it possible to produce the plants in large enough numbers to support their widespread use in gardens. As a result, their sculptural qualities, their affinity with rocks and buildings, and the intriguing qualities of the flowers on the female plants—often enhanced by conspicuous and long-lasting tan, rust or golden brown bracts—are now more widely recognised. A garden devoted to these plants recently established at Kirstenbosch has played a leading part in their increasing recognition.

The restio garden at Kirstenbosch provides an opportunity to get to know these plants better, and as the first major public display of this group of plants it serves the double purpose of introducing species that are unfamiliar to most people, and demonstrating their possibilities in gardens. As a means of introduction, I was sad to find the garden's value reduced by inadequate labelling, which left many species unidentified, and felt that the manner of planting numerous species in large groups did not display these plants to advantage. Restios tend to be sombre. Deep greens and olive drabs are overlaid with khaki tones and even deeper coppers and bronzes almost bordering on black. Sometimes this is relieved by variegation on the stems, usually in the form of banding, but the contrasts created are more often subtle than obvious. Highlights tend to be absent, and en masse restios appear lifeless and lacking in movement, quite unlike the characteristic qualities of the grasses, with which these plants are often rather misleadingly compared. Inflorescences may be stiffly, spikily upright, or feathery in densely congested, billowing heads, but with such weight and substance that the buoyancy and lightness of feathers is lost.

Many restios have valuable horticultural qualities that contrast with broad-leaved plants and even with grasses, and perhaps even more significantly with large rocks and boulders, with which they display particular affinities. Comparisons with grasses which imply that restios could be used as grass substitutes or supplements are superficial and misleading. These plants possess qualities that are fundamentally different to those of grasses, but when well-used could play effective roles in gardens nonetheless. *Elegia capensis* is an elegantly stylish plant that would be an adornment to any garden. The great stiffly, spiky clumps of thatching reed, *Chondropetalum tectorum*, now also widespread in gardens, create a fundamentally different impact that is highly effective, especially in contrast to softer foliaged plants like *Rhodocoma capensis*. This plant creates impressions of an entirely different kind, with billowing, feathery masses of foliage quite unlike the reed-like forms of the previous two species. As they die, the

The conspicuous inflorescences of many restios are not the least of their attractions. Flowers of male and female plants can be so different that it is hard to believe they are produced by the same species. Kirstenbosch National Botanical Garden, Western Cape Province, South Africa.

plumes shrivel and go brown but remain conspicuously present—spoling the fresh appearance of the green foliage. The obvious response is to cut them off, but some gardeners contend that the plant resents this and is inclined to die as a result. Others do it with impunity.

These three relatively familiar restios are the vanguard of many more, and the display at Kirstenbosch provides a valuable introduction to the diversity of form possessed by these plant. Their day will come, as we learn better how to handle them and bring to bear the flair and imagination that will display their true appeal in gardens. Already there are signs of where that may lie only a few yards away in the fynbos garden at Kirstenbosch, where restios are grown amongst the proteas, heaths and other shrubs that are their natural companions. I have already suggested that areas of fynbos

Chondropetalum tectorum, with its lance-like shoots and dark bronze inflorescences, has a strong form that creates effective contrasts with other plants. Sierra Azul Garden, Watsonville, California, United States.

often have the appearance of gardens because of the contrasts and visual impact created by the juxtaposition of these plants, and when this effect is applied to gardens, reinforced by grouping and placing the plants to create visual logic and a sense of design, it immediately leads to attractive and striking combinations.

Another example of the value of restios can be seen near Cape Town, at Tierboskloof on land overlooking the sea at Hout Bay. I was shown round this development of some fifty or so houses by Elaine Campher, the landscape architect who provides help and advice on the planting of the gardens. The development extends into the veld, and styles of architecture and landscaping are rigorously controlled and managed to avoid intrusive effects as much as possible. The plants used in the gardens reflect the wildflowers of the veld, and create effects that are sympathetic to their surroundings. In practise the planting consists exclusively of native species—and here that means plants native to the Cape Peninsula—except in spaces

The dense "ostrich feather" foliage of *Rhodocoma capensis* can be very effective in a garden setting. Kirstenbosch National Botanical Garden, Western Cape Province, South Africa.

immediately adjacent to houses. When houses are sited and constructed, the landform is changed no more than is absolutely necessary, topsoil is conserved and replaced, and—critically important—rocks, which are so characteristic of this part of the world, are not cleared away or buried but retained as essential features of the landscaping.

These restrictions confer a unity on the planting that I found extremely restful and agreeable, achieving an impressive overall quality of character and sympathy with the location. The site is not an easy one to garden in conventional ways. The terrain is steep and extremely rocky, and in many places there is little soil. The climate has a pronounced Mediterranean character. It can be very wet during the winter, with frequent heavy storms capable of causing flash floods, and extremely hot and droughty through the summer; strong winds are experienced in winter and summer. The local plants are adapted to these conditions and grow well in the gardens with-

Native restios and rounded rocks combine to create an effect clearly appropriate to a garden yet retaining essential elements of the local character and individuality of the Cape Peninsula. Garden at Tierboskloof, Hout Bay, Western Cape Province, South Africa.

out depending on orthodox methods of cultivation, soil improvement, supplementary nutrition or watering; and because of the richness and variety
of the flora, there is no shortage of plants to choose from. Nevertheless, the
restios, which are expertly used here, play crucial roles that could not be du-
plicated by any other group of plants. Their strong shapes and the unusual
textures and forms of their foliage provide essential contrasts and patterns
amongst the shrubs, annuals and other plants, lifting the planting and con-
tributing structure and form. And, possibly even more significant, they are
plants with an extraordinary affinity with rocks, and the two together create
a uniquely appropriate atmosphere that is responsible for much of the character and ambience of the estate.

The great rounded boulders and other natural features in this garden are an essential part
of the landscape. Planting around the natural elements, rather than removing them, helps
to maintain the sense of place, which is so often lost when housing estates are developed.
Garden at Tierboskloof, Hout Bay, Western Cape Province, South Africa.

The Looking-Glass Garden abounds with plants bearing outlandish, exaggerated or accentuated shapes, providing a rich source of material for dynamic and provocative effects in gardens. The Abbey Gardens, Tresco, the Isles of Scilly.

CHAPTER 6

Plants with Attitude

A GARDEN where strange and wonderful experiences abound is to be found almost out of sight of land in the Atlantic Ocean beyond Land's End. The Isles of Scilly seldom experience killing frosts or extreme heat, and the Abbey Gardens on Tresco shelter a great variety of plants that are too tender to be grown elsewhere in Britain—it is famous for its collections from the Southern Hemisphere. Close to the entrance, two New Zealand cabbage trees, *Cordyline australis* 'Lentiginosa', with leaves the colour of coffee cream, and gaunt, wind-torn, gnarled stems, demonstrate how full of character ancient specimens of this plant become. Swathes of the silvery rosettes of saw-edged, narrow puya leaves cover rocky banks beneath barrel-sized inflorescences of theatrically coloured, tart lime-yellow or electric blue flowers. The broad fronds of tree ferns unfold above columnar trunks, and the lance-like inflorescences of phormiums thrust into the air from striped yellow, green or pink leaves. The distinctive shapes of aloes, grass trees, cycads, phormiums and cordylines introduce exotic atmosphere and novelty into gardens and invite bold planting and audacious grouping, rather than the timid balancing of forms. These possibilities have been fully grasped at Tresco. Sunlit rocky terraces sweep across the centre of the garden, dominated by the spiky forms of aloes, dasylirions, yuccas, puyas, agaves and cordylines playing point and counterpoint with shaded forests where ferns, palms and myrtles grow amongst lancewoods, pittosporums, pohutakawas and other southern evergreen trees. The gleaming columns of eucalypt stems with marbled bark and silvery foliage create another change in atmosphere.

As in many major gardens, there are also tensions here between ambitions to gain respect as a botanical collection and aspirations to create theatre appropriate to a pleasure garden. The former poses the temptation to specialise, making collections of particular plants and segregating them according to taxonomic divisions into families or genera, or into geographical or other sets based on scientific notions. The latter seeks to create artistic effects by juxtaposing one form with another and combining them to create visual logic and dramatic impact. It should be possible to reconcile the two by combining scientific insight with good design, but it is too often regarded as a choice between academic respectability or artistic license; the serious study of plants or their trivialisation; the advancement of knowledge or the pleasuring of our senses. The restraining hand of botany is presented as the virtuous path; artistry as self-gratifying indulgence. The plants described in this chapter bring academics and artists into head-to-head conflicts wherever they are grown, just because their exotic appearance attracts attention and stimulates interest.

There was a time when Tresco was nearly plunged into academic respectability, serious study and the advancement of knowledge by becoming a satellite of the Royal Botanic Gardens, Kew. Thankfully, those plans came to nothing, and this garden, which offers opportunities, unique in the United Kingdom, to explore and demonstrate what imagination, flair and artistic ingenuity can do with plants, is still free to explore those opportunities. The outcome remains finely balanced, and each time I take the helicopter across to the island I find myself hoping that the contest between science and art is still an open one.

Aloes

Aloes bring colour and activity to the garden in winter: colour from their glowing scarlet, flame or orange flowers; activity because they attract sunbirds, honey-eaters, tuis, starlings, white-eyes, hummingbirds and other nectar-feeding birds, depending on the location. Aloes are succulent plants that store water in their thick, fleshy leaves. Their drought tolerance is an asset in dry gardens, but it is best not to push them to extremes; many aloes react to severe drought by sacrificing the tips of their leaves, and the withered reminders of their ordeal spoil the appearance of the plants long into the future. A hundred or more species occur in South Africa, mostly in summer rainfall areas, but a few in winter rainfall areas, and success in cultivation depends on recognising their need for alternating regimes of drought and plenty. All succumb to root rots and decay unless planted in exceptionally free-draining conditions.

Aloe arborescens forms a large, rounded bush with branching spikes of brick red flowers above the leaves during early to midwinter. Hybrids with the tree-like *A. ferox* occur naturally and are widely grown in gardens, where they do best in warm, sheltered sites—although they are not easily damaged by frost. Two fine hybrids selected at Kirstenbosch are *Aloe* 'Jack Marais' and 'Ryecroft', with broad branching infrastructures supporting well-formed spikes of brilliant orange-scarlet flowers.

Several aloes grow as trees. The most widely planted used to be known as *Aloe bainesii,* now rechristened *A. barberae.* It usually appears in gardens as a small, sturdy tree beneath a rounded head of stubby branches and long, narrow succulent leaves. It gains strength and character with maturity, eventually developing into a striking specimen tree, tall and imposing with a characterful sinewy trunk. The quiver tree or kokerboom, *A. dichotoma,*

The spikes of scarlet flowers of hybrids of *Aloe arborescens* and *A. ferox* illuminate the garden in winter, and provide nectar for white-eyes and other birds. Kirstenbosch National Botanical Garden, Western Cape Province, South Africa.

grows in the Northern Cape Province and Namibia occasionally forming "forests" of well-separated individuals. In youth and maturity these are wonderfully evocative, statuesque plants with strong but elegant trunks on which splits in the thin bark reveal silken smooth surfaces marbled with striations of various colours. Blunt spikes of vibrant orange-yellow flowers emerge amongst rounded heads of succulent leaves. The bastard kokerboom, *A. pillansii*, might be described as the masculine equivalent of the kokerboom and is a closely related species with stouter stems and broader, less elegant fans of leaves.

The rounded rosettes of olive-green leaves studded with blackish crimson spines of *Aloe melanacantha* are produced in clusters at or close to ground level. They look as though a fairly ordinary aloe has been rolled into a ball and trundled through a pile of soot, but the results are better than the description suggests. This exceptionally drought tolerant species from the northern Cape produces fine spikes of orange-scarlet flowers on long stems, well above the foliage.

The short, strap-like, blue-green leaves of *Aloe plicatilis* are arranged in bunches like fans at the ends of a framework of blunt, bare stems. This large shrub branches repeatedly as it grows, developing with maturity into a striking accent plant, with strong sculptural qualities that depend on careful placing to be effective. Naturally distributed on mountainsides in the western Cape, it is one of the few aloes that appreciates winter wet.

The widely grown soap aloe, *Aloe saponaria*, is a notably drought tolerant species that can survive long periods without water, but the shrivelled tissues of dead leaf tips can be disfiguring. This broadly amenable garden plant has rosettes of mottled succulent leaves with spiny margins at ground level, beneath branching inflorescences of flame and orange flowers in winter.

The coral aloe, *Aloe striata*, is another drought tolerant species. It grows naturally in dry situations in the Eastern Cape Province, but copes well with varied patterns of rainfall in gardens, provided the soil drains freely. The stemless rosettes of this medium-sized aloe bear pale green, smooth, spineless foliage that becomes heavily tinted with red and crimson during droughts or in cold situations. Orange- to coral-coloured flowers are carried at the tops of short, branching stems in broadly round-topped tumbled clusters that (so it is said) resemble some kinds of coral.

Aloe variegata forms small, ground-level rosettes of overlapping fleshy leaves dotted and edged with white, beneath spikes of orange-red flowers in spring. Growing naturally in the Karoo, this species is extremely drought tolerant but liable to basal rot in damper conditions unless planted in exceptionally well-drained sites.

Cycads

Long before Gondwanaland began to drift apart, cycads dominated the world. Today these most primitive of seed plants still hang on, superseded but not entirely replaced by more recent versions of plant life. Cycads have not held their own for so long by being meek and mild—few plants are more assertive, and they are impressive wherever they are encountered, nowhere more so than in the Modjaji Nature Reserve in South Africa's Northern Province, where a forest of *Encephalartos transvenosus* covers the hillsides. I found these strange plants one hot day in late spring, with the sun blazing from a bright blue sky, and the nearby mountain crests of the Strydpoortberge, a shadowy presence to the south, veiled by heat haze.

I was met at the entrance to the reserve by the custodian of the cycad forest, a small woman who was surprised to learn that I came from England. "Overseas!" she exclaimed, and threw the gates wide open to let me in. The forest was unforgettable; the great, dark, harsh, spiky, primitive plants stood gaunt and crowded in the heat. Broken fronds, hanging loose, clattered and scraped together in the warm breeze. Like aloes or palms, but somehow nothing like either, these cycads were altogether more primitive leftovers from a time unimaginably long past: their scaly, fibrous trunks blackened by old dead fires, their fronds cut jaggedly from thick, insensitive material daubed a dark, uniform and burnished green. Their shapes were compositions of discords: some upright, others writhing; some with long scaly stems like the bodies of giant reptiles, others with bulbous, lumpen, improbable-looking excrescences erupting from twisted limbs. Great yellow cones sat gracelessly, awkwardly posed and angular amongst the fronds. These were the survivors of an earlier age of plant creation, before grace, balance and beauty became the hallmarks of the plant kingdom.

Gardeners covet cycads for their distinctive weirdities, and because these slow growers become increasingly erratic and bizarre with age, mature plants dug from the wild are extremely valuable. Digging up wild plants is illegal, however, and cycad owners in South Africa must be licensed, and be

Millions of years before humankind inherited the earth, forests of cycads were characteristic features of its vegetation. Today, the gaunt shapes of *Encephalartos transvenosus* in the Modjadji Nature Reserve in South Africa are amongst the last reminders of an earlier age of plant creation.

able to prove that theirs were obtained from legal sources, either raised painstakingly in nurseries or rescued from the paths of roads or other developments. Nevertheless, a lucrative black-market trade offers cycads "rescued" by poachers, who try to sell them off the backs of trucks. Gardeners covet these plants for the wrong reasons, and usually use them in the wrong ways. Cycads individually, or in moderation, even in excess under some circumstances, are exciting garden plants, but the harshness and angularity of their primitive forms, the ungainliness of their cones and the metallic gloss of their bronze, steel blue or coppery olive fronds are not easy to accommodate in gardens. When used as dot plants to introduce contrast for the sake of contrast, they merely look out of place; when assembled in collections they can be overpowering.

But cycads can do things to gardens that other plants cannot match. Their angular stems and foliage have aesthetic affinities with certain man-made materials, as I found when Pieter de Jager took me to Viktor and Gretchen Hesse's garden at Waterkloof near Pretoria. A low-slung, burly, grey and white bull terrier met us at the iron gates, a natural choice to play Bill Syke's dog, Bullseye, in *Oliver Twist*. The dog remained profoundly suspicious of me, and deeply doubtful of its mistress's judgement in allowing me past the gates. As we went round the garden the dog followed, breathing heavily at my heels, turning a cold eye on every movement, balefully supervising every step and alert to the slightest indication from its mistress of compliance with its urge to express its disapproval.

People attuned to the soft forms of cottage gardens might find the planting here as prickly and as threatening as the dog. The garden is small, scarcely more than the borders around the driveway and entrance to the house—but intensely effective in the way it was planted. Constructed of poured concrete, the house is modern and uncompromisingly austere in appearance. It lacks romantic qualities like coziness and soft comforts conveyed by country cottages. Instead hard surfaces, clean lines and sculptural effects predominate inside and out. The style is matched by the planting, based on cycads, some succulents, boophones and other equally assertive plants—plants with attitude, with shapes that make statements, very often with forms that are themselves uncompromisingly unsentimental. The design of the house, the drive and the planting achieves a logical underlying unity that is most impressive and aesthetically satisfying.

Drought and infertility do not kill cycads, but the plants stand still and wait for better times. In gardens, freed from such restrictions, they grow steadily, but hoeing, forking and similar routine cultivations can damage the networks of roots close to the surface and seriously reduce their growth rates. At the Witwatersrand National Botanic Garden near Krugersdorp these plants are grown amongst the grasses, bulbs, succulents and broad-leaved perennials with which they would associate in the veld where they grow naturally, avoiding the need for surface cultivation between the plants. It is hoped that this will improve their performance, and that cycads like *Encephalartos humilis,* which fail to produce cones under more orthodox garden conditions, will grow better as a result.

Encephalartos altensteinii is the epitome of all that is primitive in plants: heavy masses of deep green, spiny fronds carried by massive, scaly trunks curving upwards, like the limbs of great antediluvian reptiles, from a central point of origin. A single plant of *E. friderici-guilielmi* growing by the old Botanical Society offices at Kirstenbosch demonstrates how outlandish these plants can look. Its upright, stubby trunk has an open, densely woolly crown from the centre of which ten or more cones stick up into the air, surrounded by a broad head of blue-green, stiffly feathery fronds. This fairly frost tolerant species grows well in gardens in sunny situations with good drainage. *Encephalartos horridus* is one of the more architecturally striking species, with ferociously jagged, intensely silvery blue fronds curved back at the ends — the foliage seems to have been crudely cut from thin sheets of metal. *Encephalartos lehmannii* from the eastern Cape develops no more than a short trunk, but has rather distinguished regularly placed, upright, narrow, glaucous fronds tipped with decidedly assertive spines.

Australia also has its share of cycads, and amongst those that populate the dry forests in coastal regions of eastern Australia is the burrawang, *Macrozamia communis.* This species has long, graceful pinnate leaves that arch from the tops of short, barrel-shaped trunks; on deep soils, contractile roots pull these below ground level.

Stangeria eriopus is a diminutive relative of the cycads. Not only is it the only species in the genus, but the only genus in its family, the Stangeriaceae. It grows in eastern South Africa, never very far from the sea in evergreen forests or in short grassland. The forest plants have large leathery fronds; those from grasslands are lighter and more feathery.

Cycads have an almost outlandishly bizarre strength of character wherever they are planted—as demonstrated by this *Encephalartos friderici-guilielmi* specimen at Kirstenbosch.

Grass Trees

While South Africa reaches back to cycads, born in the distant past, for exotic and unusual plant forms, Australia, which has its share of these strange plants, also finds these qualities in the relatively recent guise of the grass trees, at the other end of the evolutionary time scale. These plants belong to an obscure family, the Xanthorrhoeaceae, an outlandish scrambling together of consonants and vowels that, believe it or not, contains plants that are cousins of the lilies. Ancient or modern, from the gardener's point of view cycads and grass trees have much in common. Both grow naturally in drought-prone, infertile situations; both develop into intensely individual and distinctive specimens capable of creating powerful impressions in gardens; both can be propagated from seed, but seedlings grow slowly and take years to reach maturity, ensuring that the architectural affinities and sculptural qualities that make these plants so desirable remain elusive.

Although grass trees are often seen in dry, infertile situations, they do not have a preference for such conditions—like fynbos plants do—and grow faster, in gardens as in nature, on fertile, moist soils. They are not difficult to grow from seed, but since ten years and more will pass before seedlings develop the first vestiges of trunks, and many more years before maturity brings the character and pose that makes them so sought after, gardeners contemplating growing these plants should lay in stocks of patience first. Some species never develop the trunks that turn them into trees, or those they do possess remain hidden below ground, such as in *Xanthorrhoea resinosa*, with bluish green leaves and dense spikes of flowers, and *X. minor*, with rhizomes that form small colonies of tussocks topped by dense spikes of tiny, aromatic flowers. The saw-edged grass tree, *X. macronema*, recognised by its prominent inflorescences that look like drumsticks or robust butterfly antennae, is another with no visible trunk.

As its Latin name suggests, *Xanthorrhoea arborea*, the broad-leaved grass tree, eventually develops tree-like trunks in mature plants. The grey-green, broadly flattened leaves emerge below tall flower spikes. *Xanthorrhoea australis* is similar but has mop heads of long, narrow, silvery green leaves and lance-like spikes of fragrant cream flowers. Dense clusters of long, needle-like, glaucous blue leaves make *X. quadrangulata* an impressive garden plant, with or without a trunk, and *X. preissii* is another that is sufficiently attractive and distinctive even when immature to be well worth a place in gardens.

The drumhead blackboy, *Kingia australis*, is one of the most striking of the grass trees. It slowly produces a long, slender stem crowned by narrow silky leaves. Ellis Hill, near Perth, Western Australia.

Eventually these species grow into great bulky mop heads, sometimes with several dark stems, beneath slender columns of cream flowers.

The most elegant and impressive of the grass trees is the drumhead black-boy, *Kingia australis*, which eventually—but on a time scale that would try most gardeners' patience—develops a flexuous trunk topped by a graceful head of long, narrow silky leaves. It grows in the higher rainfall areas of south-western Western Australia, punctuating the heath-like scrub on the Stirling Range with columnar trunks crowned by globular heads of creamy white flowers amongst the leaves, creating an unforgettable impression. Like the cycads, it is protected by laws that criminalise those who dig up wild plants. Gardeners owe it to their heirs to sow today so others can enjoy these remarkable plants tomorrow.

Cabbage Trees

Grass trees, aloes and cycads are exotic creatures, to be regarded from afar by gardeners in cold temperate parts of the world where they are restricted to exceptionally favoured places, or must be grown under cover, protected from excessive rain and frost. Plants that share some of their qualities but develop character and maturity much more quickly, and are more tolerant of damp soils and chilly conditions, are the New Zealand cabbage trees or cordylines. I have driven for miles through farmland in many parts of New Zealand where scarcely any native plants can be seen, apart from phormiums, maybe a few totaras, kahiakateas or rimus left as specimens in paddocks—and, almost ubiquitously, cabbage trees. The cabbage trees acquire great character with age and size, and the gnarled, contorted and weather-beaten appearance of groves of these old trees remind me of the forest where Tweedle Dum and Tweedle Dee boasted of their encounter with the Jabberwocky.

Over the last few years *Cordyline australis* has become a regular garden feature in many parts of Britain, not merely as juvenile plants scattered amongst beds of annuals, or planted in containers by gardeners in search of instant contrast, but as well-established specimens. This plant is one of the sights at Logan in south-west Scotland, a satellite garden of the Royal Botanic Garden in Edinburgh. Here the Gulf Stream reduces the severity of frosts, and the conditions closely resemble parts of the plant's homeland in New Zealand. The tree becomes progressively more frost tolerant as it develops, and old trees in gardens in inland Britain survive temperatures of −10°C (14°F) regularly and −15°C (5°F) occasionally. Other species, and even forms of this species, are less tolerant of intense cold—but who can say what we may be growing after a few more years of global warming?

Cordyline australis, or ti kouka, is the hardiest, fastest growing species. In New Zealand many trees are dying from an unidentified affliction known as sudden decline syndrome (SDS). Some people say this is caused by infection with a mycoplasma, a mysterious, elusive and almost untraceable kind of pathogen; others associate it with the effects of excessive ultra-violet radiation due to the notorious hole in the ozone layer centred on Antarctica. Among the numerous selections of *C. australis* are 'Coffee Cream', with regular yellowish veining in the centre of light brown leaves; 'Pink Stripe', deep purple with a central pink stripe down each leaf; 'Purple Tower', with bold, broadly arching, deep reddish purple foliage, that often grows into a

The mountain cabbage tree, *Cordyline indivisa,* develops imposing sword-shaped leaves. Noeline Garden's garden, Avennel Station, South Island, New Zealand.

multi-headed tree; and 'Green Goddess', a compact form that branches close to the base with a rounded head that needs sheltered conditions and freedom from frost, especially when immature.

Cordyline kaspar is one of a number of plants from offshore islands around New Zealand that differ from mainland forms, and often possess qualities of special interest to gardeners. This species grows on the Three Kings Islands, isolated from the northernmost part of New Zealand by 60 kilometres of ocean. It is a cabbage tree on steroids. A short, robust trunk is capped by a broad, widely branching head packed with densely clustered leaves—unfortunately also appreciated by a caterpillar that can leave them in unsightly tatters. The large, exceptionally fragrant panicles of flowers are followed by blue and white berries. The discerning reader will already have noted the link between Three Kings and Kaspar and perhaps be wondering when Melchior and Balthazar will make an appearance. Melchior appears, later; Balthazar does not.

The dwarf or pygmy cabbage tree, Ti koraha, *Cordyline pumilio*, is an oddity amongst cabbage trees: it grows as a stemless tussock, a clump of grass rather than a tree. The clusters of white flowers are strongly fragrant. The mountain cabbage tree, *C. indivisa*, eventually develops a massive trunk with a great tuft of sword-shaped leaves at its apex. This imposing plant requires cooler conditions than *C. australis*, and is less amenable to cultivation, most likely to grow well in constantly moist, well-drained soils in cool, temperate situations.

Euphorbias

The New World has cacti; the hot, dry areas of South Africa have euphorbias—another group of succulents remarkable for shape and spines. The candelabra tree, *Euphorbia ingens*, is the giant of the genus, with a specific name meaning, appropriately enough, massive. And massive it is with a short, stout stem and a great outstretched, upward-pointing head of solid, angular, spiny edged succulent branches. This species and the closely similar *E. cooperi* are amongst the most conspicuous and characterful plants of the summer rainfall areas of South Africa, growing naturally in dry grassland, often in company with *Aloe ferox*. Candelabra trees are equally effective in gardens, with qualities of form and structure that associate positively with buildings. An extraordinary weeping form of *E. ingens* exists, a plant with no pretensions to be a tree but ambitions to be mistaken for a nest of giant, writhing serpents.

Some euphorbias resemble the smaller species of *Cereus* or the Chilean *Eulychnia* species, with clusters of slender, spiny organ pipes ascending vertically from ground level. The taller ones provide sculptural effects in gardens, and all are enduringly drought tolerant. *Euphorbia caerulescens* has clusters of angular, very spiny organ pipes crowned by coronets of small yellow flowers in spring. *Euphorbia virosa* is an upright, urn-shaped succulent shrub with numerous deeply ridged, spiny cylindrical stems branching on short trunks, just above ground level. The decorative and characterful *E. tuberculata* is a small plant that spreads broadly from the base to form an upward-facing mass of warty cylindrical stems, each topped with numerous greenish inflorescences amongst a frieze of short-lived, stiff leathery leaflets. The columns of euphorbias may be both warty and spiny, like those of the little *E. mammilaris* from the Karoo. Few plants are more bizarrely extraordinary than *E. esculenta*. It forms a spherical bole about the size of a football from which numerous long fingers emerge with upwardly curving, pale green tips that appear to be exploring the space around the plant—like the tentacles of some gross sea anemone. It is, as the name suggests, edible, and stock appreciate it as a succulent treat amongst the drier, spinier and more bitter offerings of its arid home in the Karoo.

Pachypodiums

The road to Sun City from Pretoria passes through the mixture of shrubs and low trees typical of the bushveld—the product of dry, rather harsh conditions that inhibit any hint of luxuriance in the vegetation. Once within this land of fantasy, austerity is replaced by luxuriance in the shape of broad-leaved evergreen trees, palms and plants of all kinds. Within the gardens of the Palace of the Lost City, the opportunities that unfold when unlimited water is made available are displayed in the bold use of exotic shapes and forms, imaginatively combined with extravagant architectural features, to create a fantasy world totally removed from the natural character of the veld beyond the fence. During my visit, fantasy was sustained at breakfast on the Palm Terrace, where peacocks competed to outsplendour each other amongst the ferns beneath the palm trees, and vervet monkeys chased each other through the fronds, and were chased in turn by staff vainly attempt-

More like surreally sculptured aluminium or shining, spiky steel than a plant, *Pachypodium lamerei* has a rugged individuality that creates an unforgettable impression. The Royal Botanic Gardens, Sydney, New South Wales, Australia.

ing to prevent them grabbing delicacies from the plates of half-awake guests. Additional sound effects and atmosphere were provided by weaver birds looking for crumbs around the tables, so bold that one bright yellow cock, like a burly, beetle-browed canary, used my milk jug as a perch while making a closer survey of the opportunities for plunder.

The plants matched the exotic spirit of the fauna, none more pointedly than the spiny trunks of *Pachypodium lamerei* emerging from beds of sansevierias below the palms. Pachypodiums, like lemurs, are at their happiest and most variable in Madagascar, where they inhabit the spiny forests and other dry situations—but, unlike the lemurs, they also occur across the sea in Southern Africa. All pachypodiums have an austerity that belies the voluptuous beauty and bright colours of their flowers, for they are members of the periwinkle family (Apocynaceae), something that is revealed only when the buds unfold to display luxuriantly large periwinkle-like flowers with satiny petals in clear, bright shades of pink, yellow, cream or apricot. *Pachypodium lamerei* offers unexpectedly delicate-looking, fragrant white flowers with yellow centres amongst the broad leaves of its sparsely branching head. One of the most interesting species is *P. namaquanum*, the halfmans tree from Namaqualand and the Richtersveld in the extreme northwest corner of South Africa. I encountered it in isolated places beyond Steinkopf, where these strange succulent plants inhabit the dry, rocky slopes of small kopjes, and in the Hester Malan garden near Springbok. They grow tall with tubular spiny stems bearing a tuft of leaves at the top, always slightly inclined towards the sun, like nodding shock-haired heads. Successive rings of long spines cover the stems—if, as some people suggest, every ring represents a year's growth, some plants must be centuries old.

Phormiums

One thing that I wanted to discover during my first visit to New Zealand was the kind of places where phormiums grow naturally. Having followed advice to plant them in sheltered, sunlit situations in my own garden, I had been surprised to see how well they grew on Tresco in moderate to deep shade beneath trees, and to find them flourishing in seaside gardens, untroubled by wind or salt spray. Once I was in New Zealand it quickly became obvious that they grow almost anywhere. They were growing amongst short grass on the most exposed slopes overlooking the sea near Cape Reinga.

Plants thought at first to be reeds fringing the shallow waters at the edge of the Mirror Lakes near Te Anau turned out to be phormiums. They grew in forests deeply shaded by tree ferns high on Mount Taranaki, and as hedges amongst the bare, sunlit, windswept paddocks close to the sea at the base of the mountain. They greeted me from well-drained sandy soils, from water-logged clay and from peat-filled meres below the volcanoes in the centre of North Island.

This ubiquity owes something to the fact that there are two phormiums: the mountain flax, *Phormium cookianum*, a yellow-flowered plant of exposed, well-drained situations on mountainsides and seaside cliffs; and *P. tenax*, known simply as flax (with or without "New Zealand"), which has reddish flowers and a preference for wet, shaded or sheltered situations, but with naturally catholic tastes that enable it to thrive in a variety of habitats. Hybrids between the two produce fertile seed, and are the source of numerous

The varied colours of phormium foliage is only part of their attractions. Stance also varies, from upright spiky forms to those with laxly arching leaves, conveying distinctively different impressions in gardens. The Regional Botanic Garden at Manurewa, near Auckland, North Island, New Zealand.

garden plants. The genes of mountain flax tend to produce plants with lax, arching foliage that is less likely to shred and tear in exposed positions than the more stiffly upright leaves of flax itself. These two forms, upright or lax, mark plants with distinctively different appearances that create quite different impressions in gardens. The intractable qualities of the leaf are due to the fibres within them, perhaps most significant today for the ease with which they become inextricably involved in the moving parts of lawn-mowers—garden planners should ensure their absence from any situation where contact between the two is likely. Previously the leaves were valued because, like the stems of true flax, the fibres within them could be spun, and long before the white settlers, or Pakeha, reached New Zealand, the Maoris had selected numerous forms which they grew for different purposes; 'Taiore' and 'Kohunga' were two kinds that were grown for their long, white, silky fibres woven into material for cloaks.

A great many garden forms now exist, from the diminutive *Phormium* 'Chocolate Fingers', barely 20 centimetres high, to the 3-metre-tall 'Goliath', some with green leaves, some with variegated and others suffused to varying degrees with crimson. The crimson-suffused forms date only from the 1930s and '40s, when several plants with pink- or red-flushed longitudinal stripes on their leaves appeared amongst a batch of seedlings raised by Walter Brockie at Christchurch Botanic Gardens. Upright, spiky forms include 'Sundowner', with bold tussocks of long leaves banded with green, cream and pink lateral stripes. 'Green Dwarf' develops compact, broad-leaved tussocks that combine the stiff, upright green leaves of *P. tenax* with the yellow flowers of *P. cookianum*. 'Radiance' has very broad, sword-shaped leaves with cream stripes. 'Bronze Elf' is a compact plant with olive-green or bronze, narrow, spiky, twisted foliage. The medium-sized 'Sunset' has green and cream striped leaves flushed with crimson, and deep, dark bronze flower stems and flower buds that contrast strikingly with the foliage. Cultivars with lax arching foliage include 'Maori Maiden', with short green and cream striped leaves overlaid with crimson, and particularly brightly coloured immature foliage. 'Dark Delight' is an outstanding medium-sized selection with very broad, blackish bronze leaves with a high gloss. Another excellent cultivar is Felix Jury's popular hybrid 'Yellow Wave', which has broad, arching, pale yellow and green foliage. Unfortunately, in some gardens brown blotches on the leaves, caused by a rust fungus, spoil their normally fresh appearance.

Astelias

The main entrance to the "Glasshouse Experience" at the Royal Botanic Garden in Edinburgh is flanked by two large beds in which phormiums, cortaderias, astelias and other plants with strong lines and pronounced textures grow amongst large, rounded granite boulders. The planting exemplifies the powerful impressions that can be created with these Southern Hemisphere plants, and their curious affinity with rocks. The presence here of cortaderias and phormiums is not surprising, but astelias are less well known, and their appearance outdoors and unprotected in this cold and windy city is an encouraging indication of their hardiness.

Astelias are plants with great garden potential, similar in many ways to phormiums, and on the threshold of much wider use in gardens, as phormiums were thirty or forty years ago. They are widely distributed across the Southern Hemisphere, often in exposed, testing situations. Some species are epiphytes—such as *Astelia solandri* growing in the crotches of trees high above the forest floor in Chile and New Zealand—but also able to colonise the raw, jagged scoria of lava flows on the inhospitable volcanic island of

A large clump of *Astelia nervosa* planted amongst the figureheads of wrecked ships at Valhalla. The burnished bronze or filigreed silver colours of some of the cultivars might look even more effective in this setting. The Abbey Gardens, Tresco, the Isles of Scilly.

Rangitoto in Auckland Harbour. The most widely grown species is *A. cha-thamica*, sometimes listed as *Astelia* 'Silver Spear' in a bid to encourage market appeal. It grows naturally on wet, peaty soils in exposed positions in the Chatham Islands. The promise of its brilliantly silver foliage is hard to resist, and it can have dramatic impact when well placed, although the effect is too often diminished by the ragged, battered appearance of the ends of the leaves. The mountain astelia, *A. nervosa*, grows amongst tussock grasses with celmisias in montane situations. This bold and beautiful species has already given rise to a number of selected forms and hybrids, many remarkable for the silver, bronze, crimson and copper tones of their foliage, as though their leaves have been cunningly inlaid with gleaming metal. *Astelia nervosa* may not have the knock-em-dead impact of *A. chathamica*, but it possesses other subtler qualities that could make it a better long-term bet for gardeners. The pale tan, fragrant flowers are curious rather than beautiful, but the orange-red berries are a decided asset.

Using "Attitude" in Gardens

Aloes, cycads, cabbage trees and phormiums all have the potential to create dramatic effects in gardens, but also the potential to overwhelm their fellow garden residents. Often used as accent plants—where their bold, contrasting forms and textures can be clearly displayed—many of these Southern Hemisphere plants make the statement that they are different so blatantly that we can feel as uncomfortable in their presence as they appear to be. Not only are we more used to handling harmonies than contrasts in gardens, but even when handled incompetently, harmonies seldom lead to faux pas. They are so anodyne that they fail to arouse our senses enough to do so. On the other hand, a contrast is not a contrast unless it arouses our senses and excites reactions, forcing us to choose between condemnation or approval—a much more dangerous field of operations, and one with which the incisive shapes of the plants discussed in this chapter confront us every time we are tempted to use them.

Visual logic dictates that mixtures of plants form compositions only when they share qualities that make it evident, however subtly, that each is intended to be there, and the simplest way to suggest this is through shared affinities. Contrasts are often the zest or spice that makes the planting exciting, but successful contrasts need the support of harmonies of colour, texture, form or whatever to establish visual links with other members of the group. A cabbage tree, an aloe or a cycad in the midst of a group of more conventional trees or shrubs inevitably creates a contrast. That is the easy bit; the harder part is to establish the links that also create a composition. A cycad with harsh, jagged, sharply toothed leaves might be used to contrast with broader leaved plants—choosing a steel blue form will provide the complement to other plants in the group with glaucous foliage. The long leaves and emphatic shape of cabbage trees erupting amongst more amorphous small-leaved shrubs or trees looks simply out of place, but grasses, phormiums or other long-leaved plants amongst the shrubs establish affinities that reveal the logic behind their presence.

A garden that has effectively brought such striking forms into a garden setting can be found on the northern side of the looking-glass, in California. Lotusland, near Santa Barbara, is a garden inspired by a search for theatri-

Plants with emphatic shapes, like these aloes, have greatest impact when planted in groups. Their presence instantly creates distinctive spaces within a garden, varying the atmosphere and ambience. Huntington Botanical Gardens, San Marino, California.

cality and artistic effect. Here Ganna Walska, a Polish-born opera singer, devoted a fertile imagination to the creation of a garden where plants were used with rare freedom and inventive flair. Visitors today may notice signs of an inclination amongst her successors to favour academic respectability at the expense of artistic integrity. Flair seems in danger of being replaced by virtue, but some of Ganna's fantasies still flaunt themselves—in particular in a garden filled with aloes.

Planted late in the 1950s, the garden evidently failed to please, and was altered twenty years later by Charles Glass, a grower of cacti and succulents, under Ganna's direction. The plants were dug out, and sand, gravel, topsoil and compost were dug in and embellished with tons of black volcanic rocks from southern California. The result is a dramatic intensity that is lacking in other gardens devoted to a single group of plants—all the more interesting since this one is limited to the plants of a single genus, albeit a large and ex-

Aloes and palms around a clam-shell-rimmed pool create a theatrical and striking impression at Lotusland. Lotusland, Montecito, California, United States.

tremely characterful one. Variations in height introduce diversity through changes in level, stance and viewpoint within the mass of the planting, where the repetition of succulent, spiky forms provides a strong sense of unity. The effect is a tortuous, enchanted forest of writhing foliage on snaking columnar limbs, unexpectedly and brilliantly reinforced by a strange, lucent pool of pale blue water surrounded by the sun-bleached shells of abalones, and giant clams whose gaping mouths display rows of jagged, menacing teeth. The pool is fed from a fountain also made of clam shells mounted on a column decorated with lumps of coral, down which water runs in a ceaseless, puny flow, dropping from one great shell into the next.

Elsewhere at Lotusland, the cycad garden contains a superb collection of plants from Australia, Africa, Mexico and Asia, of great value to people interested in comparing one species, or exhibit, with another. All display the harsh forms and metallic textures that comprise cycadness, but the impression made by each is too emphatic, within even a limited diversity of shapes and textures, to provide unity. Landscaping, done when the garden was planted, created a varied topography of mounds and broad valleys, within which most of the paths run at a slightly lower level than the plants themselves, enhancing an overwhelming feeling of exposure to these strange and characterful plants. After a short time my only feeling was an urgent desire to leave the scene and move on somewhere else.

Softer and less assertive than cycads, New Zealand cabbage trees are widely available plants that develop rapidly to maturity, and are unlikely to burn holes in our pockets. They provide an economical way to create new and unusual effects. When I travel to the south-west of England I encounter cabbage trees promoted beyond their station. Vegetable connotations in the name are forgotten in favour of up-market names like Torbay Palms. They are set out along promenades, outside railway stations, in shopping malls and other places where people might be impressed, as though they were palms. But they are not; they have other qualities. Cabbage trees lack the presence of palms, and when widely spaced in exposed situations they become weatherbeaten, harum-scarum little trees, an impression that does little justice to their potential. Planted in groups where they benefit from each others' shelter, a grove of cabbage trees—even, if there is room in a small garden for only three or four together—not only makes a confident assertion that they are meant to be there, but transforms the setting in which they stand, immediately conferring an atmosphere that is uniquely different from other parts.

At the south-western tip of England in Cornwall, Trebah is a garden in a long valley sloping steeply down to the estuary of the Helford River. It once held great collections of rare and exotic plants from Chile, New Zealand and elsewhere; today it looks back to a great past, and hopefully forward to a glorious future—but that is still in the future, and for now it is a most pleasant and atmospheric place to walk or sit and ponder amongst tree ferns, rhododendrons and great conifers. The horticultural treasures of yesterday are mostly a memory, but new ideas are beginning to make their mark on a high sunlit bank close to the house which has been planted with a broad array of spiky Mediterranean plants, including palms, grevilleas, echiums and pelargoniums amongst yuccas, cabbage trees, aloes, puyas and phormiums. Diverse forms and textures are used in a dynamic planting scheme quite distinct from the motifs present in the rest of the garden, and one which accords well with the lines of the long, white-painted house beneath a grey slate roof. These spiky leaved plants create contrasts with broad-leaved plants, and with palms in warm situations, but significant variations in stance and other qualities possessed by different narrow-leaved plants that can also be used to create diversity and interest are frequently disregarded.

I have already noted the striking effect of stiffly upthrusting foliage of some phormiums contrasted with those species in which leaves arch gracefully. Grouping phormiums that share a similar form—whatever the other differences in size and leaf colour—immediately introduces structure and visual logic into a planting, an effect that is lost completely when the two forms are mixed haphazardly together. Similarly the relatively soft, lax foliage of the cabbage tree is quite different to that of most yuccas and can be used to create subtler variations within an overall theme. Aloes and agaves, although structurally so similar, differ not only in the monocarpic character of the latter, but in the more defined, emphatic forms of their rosettes. Handling this material effectively depends on inspired orchestration of macro and micro effects: taking a broad-brush approach to the overall impact of grouping, repetition and emphatic contrasts, and adding subtlety and interest through the detailed treatment of variations available within the range of forms, textures and other qualities used to compose the planting.

CHAPTER 7

Gardens by the Seaside

A TRIP TO the seaside is a childhood treat. Hours can be spent making cities, fortifications, canals and harbours out of sand. For half a day, mess and disturbance do not lead to trouble—all is smoothed out when the tide comes in. The sea has similar effects on some gardeners, encouraging flights of fancy that level-headed citizens with feet firmly set on terra firma would never dream of indulging. How else could gardens in the north of Scotland be blithely described as "subtropical" merely because the absence of frost allows cabbage trees, tree ferns and pittosporums to be grown in them? Harold Peto designed a famous "Italian" garden on Ilnacullin Island in Bantry Bay off the south-west coast of Ireland, in a place that has no affinities whatever with Mediterranea—as the luxuriant growth of myrtles, fuchsias, crinodendrons and other plants from the cool, humid forests of Chile and New Zealand demonstrates. On fine days the views from its terraces and colonnades create magical moments. At other times rain, cool winds and lowering grey clouds challenge anyone to enjoy Harold's Italian experience.

The sea is a great leveller, in the literal sense that gardens in its vicinity do not differ due to the effects of altitude, but also because its presence greatly reduces temperature extremes, often eliminating frost as a significant concern. Frost is one of the two great forces that restrict our freedom to grow whatever plants we wish. Drought is the other, and in seaside gardens, even in places where rainfall is low, the impact of drought is reduced by equable temperatures and humid atmospheres often reinforced by sea mists. Far-ranging consequences stem from demoting frost and drought to minor importance—amongst them delusions that gardens two-thirds of the way to the North Pole are in the subtropics.

Previous pages: This garden, designed in Italian style by Harold Peto, is located on an island in Ireland's Bantry Bay, an area that has no affinities whatever with the Mediterranean. Ilnacullin Island, Bantry Bay, Kerry, Ireland.

174

That is the good news. The disadvantages of seaside gardens include exposure to wind and periodic drenchings with salt spray, and the combination can be devastating. Shelter is easier to provide than protection from frost, however, and gardens like Glanleam on Valentia Island off the extreme south-western tip of Ireland, Inverewe in north-west Scotland and Tresco on the Isles of Scilly provide remarkable examples of the benefits of shelter. They exist in landscapes dominated by wind, in situations so exposed that surrounding vegetation is reduced to closely knit dense scrub or heath within which only a restricted range of plants can survive. But within the sheltering belts of pines and cypresses, these gardens are filled with exotic plants, many of which are beyond the dreams of even the most optimistic gardeners in places farther inland that seem much more benign.

Shelter is essential in most seaside gardens to protect plants from winds and salt spray. In this New Zealand coastal garden, the first line of defence is a sombre screen of pines, but cabbage trees, pittosporums and other plants tolerant of sea exposure provide a belt of inner shelter that effectively combines utility with beauty. Coehaven, Cynthia Coe's garden, Otaki, North Island, New Zealand.

While few of us garden in conditions so persistently hostile as the Atlantic fringes of western Europe, the wind, rain and stormy conditions of the Cook Strait between the North and South Islands of New Zealand challenge those who garden on its exposed shores. Christine and Gerald Curran's L'Amour Garden looks directly across the strait at the tip of the promontory that forms the eastern shore of Wellington Harbour. The countryside on the way to the garden becomes so bleak and windswept that I thought I must have misread directions for finding it, and almost turned back before a road sign confirmed that all was well. The Currans seem to have become gardeners almost by accident, and Christine told me that "hard work, perseverance and madness rather than horticultural genius" produced the happy results seen today—but the results display no shortage of the last quality, both in the construction of the garden and the way it is planted.

Views are one of the great pleasures of seaside gardens. Here at Christine and Gerald Curran's L'Amour Garden, a gazebo placed in the enclosing shelter of trees and shrubs provides both shelter and views—and a place to sit and look across the sea to the distant mountains of South Island. Near Wellington, North Island, New Zealand.

As in many seaside gardens, a dense windbreak of trees is an essential part of the Currans' success. Now nearly twenty years old, these sheltering trees include pines and manukas *(Leptospermum scoparium)*, supplemented by pohutukawas *(Metrosideros excelsus)* and sand olives *(Dodonaea viscosa)*, placed not, as might be expected, between the garden and the sea, but on the landward side. This arrangement causes winds from the sea to lift before reaching the trees, so that they flow over the top of the garden, and has the great advantage that views across the straits are not blocked by the trees. Shrubs are used generously within the garden, amongst them numerous banksias, proteas, grevilleas, leucospermums, leucadendrons and phormiums, all solidly reliable seaside plants that might be expected to do well here, but numerous herbaceous perennials testify to the effectiveness of the screen of trees. The sheltering effect is reinforced by hedges and screens, quite a low one across the front of the garden and others within, that divide the garden into sheltered areas. Some of these areas are small and intimate, with seats on which to relax out of the wind; others are more open and spacious. Once within the garden, one is aware of the presence of the sea, but isolated from its effects. Two elegant little gazebos break the line of the hedge along the front of the garden, where I sat and looked across the sea to the distant snow-capped Kaikoura Mountains.

Trees and Shrubs for Seaside Shelter

The Monterey cypress, *Cupressus macrocarpa*, and the Monterey pine, *Pinus radiata*, are ace shelter plants for those who garden by the sea. Both can be impressive and beautiful trees, but their widespread use imposes an unimaginative and predictable uniformity on seaside gardens, and in the Looking-Glass Garden they can be intrusively alien. The Norfolk Island pine, *Araucaria heterophylla*, at least comes from the Southern Hemisphere, but its exaggeratedly characterful profile looks no less alien, and its use ad nauseam in seaside situations has made it just as hackneyed. But the Southern Hemisphere is rich in plants that thrive in coastal situations, and unimaginative planting when seaside shelter is needed in this part of the world is inexcusable.

The coast wattle, *Acacia longifolia* var. *sophorae*, occurs naturally on seaside sand dunes, where branches root into the sand, stabilising the dunes. It has shorter, broader leaves than the type. Many other wattles are equally effective, including *A. leprosa*, with fluffy, lemon, powder-puff flowers that smell of cinnamon, and *A. cultiformis*, with large, erect heads of fragrant flowers. Several wattle species have become intractable weeds in coastal situations and on sand dunes in South Africa, so all should be used with caution.

The Australian she-oaks were all classified in the genus *Casuarina* until botanists segregated them for differences that are unimportant to gardeners. The coast she-oak, *Allocasuarina verticillata*, is a medium-sized tree with deeply furrowed bark and fine drawn, pendant shoots that makes an excellent screen in exposed situations. The smaller black she-oak, *A. littoralis*, is another easily grown species with deeply fissured, characterful dark bark and slender shoots like the finest whipcord. The rose she-oak, *A. torulosa*, is upright and multistemmed with attractive, granulated bark almost as ruggedly textured as that of cork-oak *(Quercus suber)*. It is widely planted for shade and fast-growing coastal shelter. The remarkable dark bronze tones of its slender, trailing shoots remind me of a tree in widow's weeds.

Several banksias revel by the seaside, particularly the silver *Banksia marginata* and the coast banksia, *B. integrifolia*. Both are capable of providing dense, windproof screens, and are unusually tolerant of salt, winds and frost. Like others of their kind, these species also attract birds. *Banksia ericifolia* ranges from a small tree to a large shrub, with tiny heath-like leaves and long, columnar, ginger to deep red heads of flowers. Another banksia that is tolerant of a broad range of soils and conditions is *B. collina* from the coastal hills of Queensland and New South Wales. It grows into a dense, upright shrub with smallish, golden, cylinders of flowers in late spring. Other banksias that do well in the impoverished sandy soils often found at seaside gardens include *B. ornata*, a dense, rounded shrub suitable for internal screening, with short cylindrical inflorescences of yellow- or bronze-tinted flowers. It grows on sandy soils in coastal and inland areas of south-eastern South Australia and the south-western Victoria desert and is very drought tolerant. *Banksia attenuata* is another so-called coast banksia. This large bushy tree has long, narrow leaves with serrated margins and bright yellow perfumed flowers arranged in slender cylinders. A characteristic plant of the coastal scrub around Esperance in Western Australia is *B. speciosa*, which has a tall straggling tree form that flowers during late winter. Unfortunately this species is very susceptible to phytophthora, but its tolerance of sandy soils and hot, dry conditions makes it a useful plant in gardens where the fungus is not a problem.

The South African num-num, *Carissa macrocarpa,* rapidly develops into a densely thorny hedge impenetrable by wind or person. The pure white, star-shaped flowers are followed by crimson-scarlet, edible fruits. Garden forms, useless for shelter but useful as soil binders, include 'Horizontalis', a close-set trailing cultivar on which the fruits are particularly effectively displayed, and 'Emerald Carpet', which grows into robustly mounded ground cover.

Another shrub from South Africa that is pre-eminent for almost frost-free gardens is bitou, *Chrysanthemoides monilifera.* Its flowers may be common little yellow daisies, but they have a shining intensity and depth of colour that marks them out as something special. No other shrub—not even the sunshine conebushes—brings the sensation of summer sun into a garden in winter more effectively. The flowers are followed by fleshy, juicy fruits that are attractive to birds. This pioneer shrub can be used to stabilise shifting sand dunes, or as primary shelter in the most exposed situations where eventually it will grow into a characterful, bulky, not-quite-small tree, or as clipped hedges for secondary shelter within the garden. In Australia, where it is known as tick-bush, its ebullience and questing nature have earned it a less than welcome reputation. Plants that have escaped from gardens and from erosion-control schemes have made themselves at home in every state, apart from the Northern Territory. Attempts to control it involving manual removal, herbicides and predatory insect species have been minimally successful.

Several coprosmas grow naturally

Banksia attenuata grows naturally in coastal regions, and requires infertile, well-drained situations to thrive in gardens. Near Jurien, Western Australia.

Bitou or tickbush, *Chrysanthemoides monilifera,* may be damned in Australia for its invasive tendencies, but its dense evergreen foliage and brilliant yellow flowers make it an excellent seaside shrub. Table Mountain, Western Cape Province, South Africa.

by the seaside and make robust supplementary shelter in combination with trees. Despite its name, *Coprosma repens* develops into a large shrub, highly tolerant of the shade of primary shelter trees, and with glossy deep green leaves. Variegated cultivars like 'Picturata' or 'Pink Splendour'—with shiny, leathery green leaves brilliantly suffused with pink, particularly in cold weather—are less vigorous but decorative and useful for back-up shelter within a garden.

One of the most amenable of all plants for seaside gardens is *Corokia* ×*virgata*. It is invaluable for gardeners in search of a dense and reliable hedge or screen within or on the boundary of a garden. The plant is tolerant of a broad range of conditions, including moderate frosts and drought.

Many eucalypts tolerate exposure and salt sprays well and are useful shelter trees within and around coastal gardens. These include *Eucalyptus viminalis*, a substantial, broad-headed tree; *E. macrandra*, a multistemmed mallee with attractive smooth bark and clusters of greenish yellow flowers in late summer and autumn; *E. ficifolia*, one of the most widely planted ornamental eucalypts, with stunningly beautiful crimson-red flowers; and *E. sideroxylon*, notable for its deeply furrowed, dark brown to black bark and white, pink or red flowers.

Those in search of a garden talking point might settle for *Ficus sur*. This species is most remarkable for the clusters of figs that emerge straight out of the trunk and major limbs. These are edible and make good jam. The plant has none of the austerity so often found in seaside shrubs, but despite its large leaves and more luxuriant appearance is surprisingly tolerant of wind and salt sprays. It needs fertile, moist soils and frost-free conditions, where it will grow into a large, densely foliaged shade tree; it is evergreen or deciduous depending on conditions.

The New Zealand broadleafs, *Griselinia lucida* and *G. littoralis*, are tolerant of wind and salt spray and grow into impenetrably dense thickets of glossy, apple green shoots and leaves. They are hardy and are often seen providing invaluable shelter in gardens in cool, moist situations, where they self-sow liberally.

Tea trees as a group are almost all worth considering for primary shelter around and within gardens. *Leptospermum laevigatum*, the Australian tea tree, is a large shrub or small tree, tolerant of lime-rich soils, shade and salt sprays. It makes an excellent screen or hedge in even the most exposed coastal settings. *Leptospermum rotundifolium* and cultivars like 'Jervis Bay' develop into vigorous shrubs with large, broadly open, single, pink, waxy textured flowers in spring, and are useful on sandy soils and in exposed, but frost-free, coastal settings. The well-known manuka, *L. scoparium*, grows naturally in some of the most exposed coastal situations in New Zealand, such as the approaches to Cape Reinga in the extreme north, where many of the plants have pale pink flowers. It is a thoroughly reliable, moderately hardy plant for coastal gardens, and is the progenitor of a wide range of garden forms with single or double flowers ranging in colour from pure white to deep crimson. Some are vigorously upright and develop into small trees, whereas others are broadly shrubby or even completely prostrate.

Kawakawa, *Macropiper excelsum*, will grow in deep shade and can be planted amongst taller trees and shrubs to intensify their shelter. Large leaves are a feature of the plant, but they are liable to be disfigured by holes made by a leaf-eating insect. A form from the Three Kings Islands known as 'Melchior' is less hardy but has bigger, glossier foliage free from holes that makes it a more attractive plant for gardens in mild situations.

Puka, *Meryta sinclairii*, is another useful product of New Zealand's offshore islands. This compact, dense-headed, sturdy-trunked tree has huge, leathery, deep green leaves that, despite their size, are remarkably unaffected by winds, salt spray and summer drought, but are susceptible to frost. Congested clusters of pale green flowers are followed by shiny black berries. The variegated foliage of 'Moonlight' is equally bold with yellow margins.

A tree that almost invariably grows naturally within sight and sound of the sea is the New Zealand pohutukawa, *Metrosideros excelsus*, eventually growing enormous with great strength and character. Several colour forms have been selected with flowers in varying shades of deep, vibrant crimson, others tend to orange, and one is a rather faded yellow.

Ngaio is a smaller tree that also grows in coastal situations in New Zealand and makes excellent front-line shelter. *Myoporum laetum* has long, glossy evergreen foliage and small, white, speckled flowers. The Australian boobialla, *M. insulare*, is also useful for coastal shelter, but it usually forms a densely leafy shrub, rather than a tree. Its white flowers during winter and spring are followed by fleshy berries that are attractive to birds.

Some of the New Zealand and Australian daisy bushes are excellent for primary shelter, developing from dense, broadly rounded, often grey-leaved shrubs into equally dense, multistemmed small trees. *Olearia traversii* from the Chatham Islands, where it grows as a small, upright tree, is one of the best. It thrives in exposed situations, even on pure sand. *Olearia macrodonta* is large, leggy and multistemmed, more attractive than it sounds, and the bare sinewy stems with peeling bark beneath dense heads of grey-green holly-like leaves have considerable structural value. *Olearia ilicifolia* is similar and may be a parent of *O. macrodonta*, distinguished by the white tomentum on young twigs and the leaf undersides. It is a small multistemmed tree with bark hanging in long tatters, and innumerable clusters of fragrant white flowers emerge in early summer. *Olearia paniculata* has lightly glossy, bright green leaves with undulating margins, rather like a pittosporum, until its clusters of creamy white, lightly fragrant flowers appear in the autumn. Another multistemmed small tree, *O. virgata* has sinuous stems and narrow, leathery, sage green leaves on a twiggy superstructure, with clusters of white flowers in the axil of every leaf.

Pohutukawa, *Metrosideros excelsus,* provides most effective and attractive seaside shelter with its dense head of silvery grey leaves. Muriwai Beach, near Auckland, North Island, New Zealand.

For many years the bulb fields in the Isles of Scilly were sheltered by karo, *Pittosporum crassifolium,* until exceptional frosts struck the species down one winter. This large evergreen shrub grows into a sturdy small tree with leathery, silvery grey, oval leaves, and clusters of crimson-black tubular flowers that are most fragrant in the evening and during darkness—an exception to the general rule that night-flowering species produce pale-coloured or white flowers. The flowers are followed by apple green capsules filled with shiny, slimy black seeds. *Pittosporum crassifolium* 'Variegatum' has soft, sage green leaves with cream edgings, reminiscent of the variegated pohutukawa, but smaller and neater.

Yet another plant from the islands off New Zealand is rautini, *Brachyglottis huntii,* a small, round-headed ornamental tree from the Chatham Islands. This species has bright silver foliage—though some forms are more green than silver—and yellow flowers massed in heads that almost obscure the foliage from midsummer till autumn. It is tolerant of winds and salt spray and withstands prolonged periods of drought.

Some Do Like to Garden by the Seaside

Somewhere I read, but goodness knows where, that "all Mediterranean plants thrive in coastal gardens," and the writer meant plants from Mediterranea in general. Broad, confident assertions like that challenge us to find exceptions and smugly point them out—and they are there to be found. Nevertheless, it is true enough to serve as a guide for most purposes. Mild, frost-free or almost frost-free winters are similar to the cool, moist conditions of Mediterranean winters. Soils in coastal gardens frequently consist of well-drained sands and gravels that favour the survival of these plants, and though they may dry out in summer, they cause minimal problems for plants adapted to cope with drought. Sands derived from sea shells rich in calcium are base-rich, like many Mediterranean soils derived from limestones. Winds, hot or cold, are characteristic of many places where Mediterranean plants grow. Their leaves are constructed to withstand boisterous conditions, and salt has less effect on leathery, narrowly rolled or otherwise protected leaves than on the broad, soft surfaces of deciduous plants from gentler climates.

The Atlantic seaboard of north-western Europe is an exception to this rule, as are gardens facing the Pacific in western Canada and the north-western United States, and those on the west coast of South Island in New Zealand. In these places eucryphias, tree ferns, fuchsias, olearias, myrtles and pittosporums from the equally cool, wet forests of southern Tasmania, Fjordland in New Zealand and southern Chile are likely to be a better bet.

Driving past seaside gardens as far apart as the Coromandel Peninsula in New Zealand, the deep inlets south of Hobart in Tasmania, the Sonoma Coast in California and at Hermanus in South Africa on the coast of the Atlantic Ocean, I have been struck by the similarity of the flowers in the gardens. Pelargoniums, arctotis, gazanias, crocosmias, kangaroo paws, osteospermums, helichrysums, verbenas, watsonias, mesembs, ixias and sparaxis appear repeatedly in small front gardens, often directly facing the sea with little or no shelter. The plants in these gardens are the accumulation of years of exchanges, self-seeding, gifts and casual purchases, a selection process that owes little to expert opinion on what should or should not grow, to carefully sited shelter belts, or to attention to the conditions in which the plants grow naturally. What better way could there be to arrive at a list of reliable, easily grown, colourful and satisfying plants for seaside gardens than to look around and see what the neighbours are growing?

Gardening by the seaside is more commonplace in the Southern Hemisphere because higher proportions of the population live close to the sea, and it is more rewarding than in northern Europe. Sunnier skies and warmer conditions encourage people to garden with fewer inhibitions and a greater appreciation of the sea's attractions. Vivien Papich's garden on the west coast of New Zealand's "winterless north" is one where this positive approach has paid off brilliantly. The garden has a spectacular coastal setting with views across the water to the Hen and Chickens Islands, and is crammed with shrubs, trees, grasses, palms and other plants in imaginative medleys of colours and textures. Plants as diverse as cymbidiums, bromeliads, echeverias, camellias, aloes, phormiums, cabbage trees, cacti and roses combine to create exceptional opportunities for exciting effects. Vivien groups plants in different parts of the garden in bold, often unashamedly exaggerated ways, making full use of the shapes and textures to produce sometimes bewildering compositions of contrasting forms. Dense masses of plants establish more or less permanent communities that shelter one another from gales and salt spray, while providing few spaces for weeds—and time saved in maintenance on that account is productively and more imaginatively spent on great attention to detail. As though in response to the restless, ever-changing nature of the nearby sea, the garden itself frequently undergoes radical changes, including the creation of elaborate set pieces based on seats, driftwood and other artifacts. These are arranged, painted, planted, enjoyed and then taken down and replaced with an uninhibited verve and exuberance that sometimes comes perilously close to over-the-top, and would certainly incur the disapproval of straight-laced members of the British horticultural establishment.

The garden displays a revolutionary approach, always looking for ways to use plants to create new effects, providing the plants with unexpected settings and revelling in the use of contrasts between bright colours, exaggerated shapes and the full gambit of textures, from the soft fronds of ferns and the mossy textures of confetti bushes to angular, spiky phormiums,

Astelias, coleonemas, phormiums and other Southern Hemisphere plants combine with conifers and mulleins in a rich composition of shapes and textures in Vivien Papich's garden overlooking the Pacific Ocean, with the Hen and Chickens Islands in the distance. Bellevue, Vivien Papich's garden, near Wipe, North Island, New Zealand.

cabbage trees and puyas. It is not a restful garden, but it reflects the sudden mood changes of the sea in a way that is entirely appropriate to its setting. Even the element of shifting instability introduced by Vivien's willingness to dismantle and start again can be seen as recognition of the possibility that the patient years of work might be destroyed, at any time, by exceptionally stormy weather. The willingness to change, to discard what is there in order to try out new ideas reflects her positive acceptance of the sea—rather than a defensive posture against it.

Plants for Seaside Gardens

The Southern Hemisphere is exceptionally rich in plants able to hold their own in seaside gardens—some with a little help, some without. Many of these would greatly enhance seaside gardens elsewhere, particularly around the coasts of Britain, where frosts are seldom severe, but where gardeners too seldom explore the imaginative opportunities this profusion offers.

The dauntingly spiny spear grasses or Spaniards from New Zealand and Australia are outstandingly characterful plants, but only for the foolhardy, the armour-plated or the brave. *Aciphylla dieffenbachia* is the exception; its soft, blue-grey foliage is so unlike the others that the species was previously classified in a separate genus, *Coxella*. This rare and endangered plant from coastal cliffs in the Chatham Islands is broadly tolerant of garden conditions.

Most of the Australian kangaroo paws are short-lived, rhizomatous, herbaceous perennials that colonise bare spaces after bush fires, before they are replaced by shrubs and more persistent vegetation. The garden hybrids derived from *Anigozanthos flavi-*

The scarlet and green kangaroo paw *Anigozanthos manglesii* is a striking perennial for gardens in Mediterranea. Gingin Cemetery, near Perth, Western Australia.

dus—a robust species from seasonally, even perennially wet places—are introduced in the following chapter. Those discussed here are likely to be unreliable and short-lived in cultivation, but rewarding for gardeners adventurous enough to give them a try. The stunningly brilliant scarlet and emerald *A. manglesii* is the state flower of Western Australia, but not an easy plant in a garden, requiring well-drained soils that retain moisture at lower levels; in semi-natural situations like Gingin Cemetery north of Perth, however, it grows profusely and hybridises with *A. humilis*, a smaller species with yellow flowers. *Anigozanthos viridis*, with brilliant emerald-green flowers, is another challenging species, and the red kangaroo paw, *A. rufus*, has bright orange flowers deeply suffused with crimson. Like the others it does best on sandy soils that retain some moisture deep down, even in drought.

Arctotheca calendula is known as Soetgousbloom in its native South Africa, but as Capeweed in Australia, where it invades and beautifies lawns and pastures, providing seeds for parrots, fodder for stock, and dissent between those who appreciate it and those who claim it is harmful. This small plant is not golden, it is not orange, it is not cream. It is none of the euphemisms used to avoid confessing that a flower is the brightest of all the primary colours. It is just a wonderful, deep, full yellow, like the reflection of sunshine and the very essence of summer. Wherever it is found—for this plant is a great traveller and coloniser—*A. calendula* brings the sun to earth in great expanses of bright gleaming yellow that refreshes the soul and enlivens the landscape for mile after mile. The sea pumpkin, *A. populifolia*, is a pioneer species on the loose, shifting sands of dunes. This vigorously spreading, colonising plant has densely felted silvery leaves and large, bright yellow daisy flowers throughout spring and summer.

The confetti bush, *Coleonema pulchellum*, is a small evergreen shrub with heath-like aromatic leaves spangled with rose-pink flowers during the winter. It is broadly tolerant of garden conditions, moderately frost hardy and widely grown wherever winters are mild enough for it to survive, which includes sheltered gardens in London. Cultivars include 'Dwarf Pink', a compact green-leaved form, and 'Sunset Gold', with bright golden yellow foliage, very similar to a large, golden-leaved heath. The taller *C. album* is another seaside shrub. Its crushed foliage is used by fishermen as a deodorant to mask fishy smells.

Few groups of shrubs contain something for everyone in quite the same way as the coprosmas. Some species have broad leaves, in others they are little more than scales; some are upright, some completely prostrate and capable of following every contour of the ground. Some are gently rounded, others assertively divaricating. Coprosmas may grow in dense shade, in exposed sunlit situations, on the tops of mountains or beside the sea. Leaves may be drably olive or lustrous, shining apple green and suffused with yellow, bronze or crimson. Their translucent berries are similarly unstandardised in a colourful assortment of yellow, orange, brown, blue, purple, scarlet or white. These plants are related to coffee plants, and their seeds have been used as substitutes for coffee beans, though sadly the colours of the berries are not reproduced in the brew. Several coprosmas are of particular value for coastal gardens. *Coprosma* ×*kirkii* 'Variegata' is an excellent dense, low-growing ground cover with narrow leaves variegated green and cream. Tangled masses of ground-hugging stems form the rounded hummocks of *C. acerosa*, spangled with beautiful light blue berries. *Coprosma crassifolia* is a shrub or small tree with stubby interlacing branches and very small, thick, rounded leaves dotted with translucent whitish berries. *Coprosma repens*, sometimes known as the mirror plant, offers numerous selections remarkable for the brilliant gloss on the surfaces of their leaves. In addition to those with potential as shelter plants discussed earlier, notable cultivars include 'Beatson's Gold', with small gold and green variegated leaves; 'Coppershine', upright and twiggy with clusters of thick-textured, brilliantly glossy leaves with bronze margins; 'Gold Splash', an upright shrub, each leaf of which has a broad cream margin and central deep green flash; 'Karo Red', a recent selection with leaves that are glossy crimson, especially during colder weather; 'Kiwi Gold', with leaves broadly splashed with gold; and 'Painter's Palette', with glossy crimson, green and cream variegated foliage on an upright bush that opens out as it matures.

The Australian fuchsias are of great value in gardens because their pendant, nectar-bearing, bell-shaped or tubular flowers, which are pollinated by birds, appear during the winter. Many correas are short-lived but amenable, whether beside the sea or in inland gardens. Several are remarkable for the great variety of forms in which they occur naturally. One of the most variable is *Correa reflexa*, a low, twiggy shrub common on coastal heaths that usually has red tubular flowers with green-yellow flared ends to the petals. Two recognised botanical varieties are var. *coriaceae*, with lime-green flowers and grey leaves, and var. *nummularifolia*, a low, broadly spreading shrub with greenish white tubular flowers. *Correa reflexa* 'Fat Fred', a cultivar with a name not easily forgotten, has unusually large, inflated, cardinal red bells; 'Point Hicks' is taller, with shorter leaves and broadly tubular red flowers outlined with yellow. 'Ringwood' is tall and upright with long, green, tubular flowers. 'Tricolor' has multicoloured bells banded with pink, yellow and green. The prostrate and ground-hugging *C. reflexa* 'Yanackie' has broadly triangular leaves and pink tubular flowers with yellow tips. 'Mt Lofty', a selected form of *C. aemula*, is low growing with slightly scrambling, sometimes twining stems; its startling sea green, slender, tubular flowers are flushed with purple. *Correa alba* has star-shaped white flowers from spring to autumn on broadly compact shrubs with grey-green leaves. *Correa pulchella* grows naturally in a variety of habitats, including calcareous soils in very exposed situations. It is usually a small shrub, but coastal forms often grow as ground-hugging mats. The tubular, bell-like flowers may be white or salmon-pink, and a low-growing form has bright orange flowers.

The Australian cushion bush, *Leucophyta brownii*, is a pioneer shrub capable of growing in the most exposed situations, but it usually lives only a few years. During its brief life the shimmering mounds of silver stems and narrow leaves below clustered balls of creamy yellow daisies make for an inspiring presence in a garden. A form from Cape le Grand National Park in Western Australia has extra-bright silver-white, intertwining stems.

The legendary plant of the Chatham Islands—and one already loaded with gardening lore about its likes and dislikes—the Chatham Island forget-me-not, *Myosotidium hortensia*, is now widely grown in gardens, and is beginning to be recognised as an amenable garden plant. Have successive generations grown in gardens led to selection of strains that are more amenable to cultivation, or have gardeners become more understanding of its needs? In apparent contradiction to its natural situation almost on the shoreline, just above high-water mark, the plant prefers shaded conditions in gardens on humus-rich, moisture-retentive soil. This is perhaps explained by the fact that the sand in which the plant grows naturally overlies peaty soil, and the Chatham Islands enjoy an exceptionally temperate climate with a high proportion of days when cloudy, misty conditions maintain humid atmospheres. The broad, pleated leaves and great trusses of forget-me-not blue flowers are irresistible garden treasures. Gardeners who like their puddings with extra cream might try 'Alba', a form with pure white flowers.

One of the sights of Jill and Roelf Attwell's garden facing the Atlantic Ocean at Betty's Bay is *Osmitopsis asteriscoides*. This bushy, evergreen shrub with pure white daisies at the tops of long stems grows naturally in peaty marshes beside the sea in South Africa. It grows lax and gawky with age, and the stems should be cut to the ground in rotation every few years to encourage regeneration from new basal shoots. This treatment not only keeps the shrub compact but also greatly increases its flower power.

Plectranthus are usually thought of as plants for shaded situations, but several of these autumn-flowering, ground-covering perennials do well in coastal situations, amongst them *Plectranthus madagascariensis* and *P. verticillatus*. Both are tolerant of strong salt-laden winds and can be planted very close to the sea. *Plectranthus ecklonii* and *P. fruticosus,* regarded as shade lovers in inland gardens, grow in sunlit situations by the seaside.

The South African crane flower *Strelitzia reginae,* known elsewhere as bird-of-paradise, grows readily in situations where summer droughts and frosts are not too severe. It is wind tolerant and good in exposed seaside gardens.

The white form of the Chatham Island forget-me-not, *Myosotidium hortensia* 'Alba', is increasingly being grown in gardens. Margaret Barker's garden at Larnach Castle, near Dunedin, South Island, New Zealand.

'Mandela's Gold' is a selected form with sepals that are pale gold partially suffused with orange—more subtle perhaps than the bright orange of the typical bird-of-paradise, but less dramatically effective. *Strelitzia juncea* has flowers just like those of *S. reginae*, but instead of being paddle-shaped the leaves are long, narrow and lance-like, with considerable landscape quality.

The Australian rosemarys are easily grown shrubs that are becoming increasingly popular in gardens. They produce flowers over long periods, but seldom with the profusion of true rosemarys. *Westringia fruticosa* has a reputation for being able to grow anywhere. It is a densely foliaged, aromatic shrub with whorls of linear or narrow leathery leaves and white or pale mauve flowers that responds well to tip-pruning after flowering. Two variegated, comparatively low-growing cultivars are 'Morning Light', with green and pale yellow leaves, and 'Smokie', with green and creamy white foliage. *Westringia angustifolia* is a broadly spreading coastal and montane shrub that looks much like a rosemary, with flowers ranging from white to a moderately strong lilac. *Westringia glabra* has high-quality dark green foliage, and bright lilac-pink flowers that appear in succession for several months.

Strelitzia reginae is a strikingly effective and accommodating plant in gardens that experience only light frosts during the winter. Ayrlies, Bev McConnell's garden, Howick, North Island, New Zealand.

CHAPTER 8
Particularly Perennials

TWO MAIDS, a Maltese terrier, Fred the gardener and a husband named Douglas lived or worked in a house called Beamish, in a small town in the English Midlands during the 1920s. How do we know? Because their memory lives on in the names of one of the smallest of all perennial plants. Dry soil and desiccated bits of grass in a parcel delivered to Mrs Garnett-Botfield's house in Albrighton were handed over to the head gardener, Mr Fred Broome, to see what he could make of them. He crumbled the mixture between his hands, mixed it with a little potting compost in a container, watered it and waited to see what might happen. In time, clusters of narrow leaves emerged amongst which appeared first a little starry rose-pink flower, and then a white one. They were rhodohypoxis collected on the Drakensberg in South Africa. Plants raised from their seeds produced flowers ranging in colour from white through various shades of rose-pink to deep crimson, and Mrs Garnett-Botfield named them after members of the household. A deep crimson one was called 'Douglas' after her husband; two maids were united in memory as 'Margaret Rose', a vigorous cultivar with bright rose-pink flowers; 'Perle' commemorates her white Maltese terrier; and 'Fred Broome', a deep pink, recognises the contribution of the gardener who grew them. These plants are still with us, and numerous other cultivars have since been named, including one with pale pink double flowers like tiny rose buds, called 'Bright Eyes', raised in New Zealand in the early 1990s.

I came across rhodohypoxis growing on the grassy slopes beneath the Sentinel Peak that dominates the Amphitheatre, a broad arc of precipitous cliffs, bitten out of the side of the escarpment overlooking Royal Natal National

Previous page: This novel version of the herbaceous border is almost entirely filled with Southern Hemisphere plants, including galtonias, agapanthus and red hot pokers. The stance of the flowers, well clear of foliage, makes exceptional use of the clear, bright colours of these perennials. The Savill Garden, Windsor Great Park, England.

194

Park. Several forms of *Rhodohypoxis baurii* grow in the Drakensberg, including var. *baurii*, usually with deep pink flowers in moist, partially shaded situations; var. *platypetala*, more likely to have white flowers, and growing amongst grasses on dry stony slopes; and the form sent to Mrs Garnett-Botfield, var. *confecta*, which grows amongst rocks at high altitudes often on shallow soils that dry out in winter but run with water through the summer. I first visited this area in early spring during a year of severe drought, and the pink or white stars of *Rhodohypoxis* and the pale lilac blooms of *Moraea alpina*, like tiny irises, were amongst the few flowers to be seen. Nobody else was on the mountain, and as I poked around looking for plants, a lammergeier descended, gliding by a few yards away with his ginger beard clearly displayed. Perhaps he interpreted my bumbling, uncertain movements as a sign of imminent collapse and the possibility of lunch. I returned in summer during a much wetter year, to a very different place. The grass-covered slopes of the mountain were bright with familiar garden flowers. Agapanthus, kniphofias and osteospermums, lobelias and geraniums, helichrysums, diascias and pineapple flowers grew amongst the grasses in a floral profusion more like the hay meadows of the Picos de Europa in northern Spain, or the Tuolumne Meadows above the Yosemite Valley in California, than the desolate scene of my first visit.

Little rain falls on these mountains during the winter, but frosts are frequent and light snowfalls not uncommon. The plants that grow here experience severe frosts, but this can give a misleading impression of their hardiness when grown in gardens, especially in areas with wet winters where they may fail to survive temperatures that would not threaten them in nature. One species to be seen here is *Agapanthus campanulatus*, a herbaceous perennial and the parent of numerous relatively hardy garden plants, including the widely grown seed strain *Agapanthus* 'Headbourne Hybrids' and the cultivars 'Castle of Mey', 'Isis' and 'Profusion'. The evergreen plants found in gardens in milder parts of the world are more likely to be derived from two species that are more tolerant of winter wet, but more vulnerable to frost. *Agapanthus praecox* comes from the eastern Cape, where rain may fall at any time of the year; it is usually represented in gardens by the particularly robust subsp. *orientalis*. The other, *A. africanus* from the winter rainfall area of the western Cape, is similar but smaller, with deeper blue or even violet-purple flowers. My experience of agapanthus in Britain had fixed them firmly in the category of sun lovers, until I saw them growing profusely in the gardens of Mon Repos on Corfu in deep shade, demonstrating the versatility of these plants under more congenial conditions. Escapees from gardens have established themselves in North Island of New Zealand, in Tasmania and even in south-west England, developing colonies that are almost ineradicable; spraying with glyphosate (Round-up) merely destroys their competition, and the agapanthus come back stronger than ever. Numerous cultivars are available: *Agapanthus* 'Baby Blue' and 'Lilliput' are miniature; 'Purple Cloud' and others have been selected for the intense colour of their flowers, 'Snowball' and 'White Ice' for the purity of their white ones. A variegated form with boldly striped, deep green striated leaves with creamy white margins is a recent novelty.

A plant from a different mould is *Agapanthus inapertus* subsp. *pendulus,* which grows naturally around Graskop in the northern Drakensberg in

The meadows below the Sentinel Peak in the Drakensberg are filled in summer with many flowers familiar to gardeners. Photographed from Tendele Camp, Royal Natal National Park, KwaZulu-Natal, South Africa.

company with St Joseph's lily, *Lilium formosanum,* an immigrant from Taiwan. Clusters of tubular flowers hang from the tops of upright stems and provide nectar for the sunbirds, and in gardens elsewhere for humming-birds, honey-eaters, tuis and other nectar feeders. The species comes from a summer rainfall area and, like *A. campanulatus,* loses its leaves in winter. At Kirstenbosch National Botanical Garden *A. inapertus* subsp. *pendulus* is interplanted with the winter-flowering *Chasmanthe floribunda,* which goes dormant in summer, forming a neat couplet of plants that play "box and cox" through the seasons—one losing its leaves and ceasing to flower as the other produces leaves and starts to flower.

Another plant of the Sentinel meadows is a little red hot poker, *Kniphofia porphyrantha.* Even though its lemon-yellow flowers open from orange flame buds, they appear much cooler than red hot, and its specific name, meaning purple-flowered, is mystifyingly wide of the mark. Only a few miles away, but on the other side of the Continental Divide in neighbouring Lesotho, drifts of *K. caulescens* grow in boggy places around Oxbow, on stream banks and in the shallow streams that mark the source of the Orange River. Gardeners who appreciate this plant's broad, glaucous foliage and substantial, low-growing stems—not unlike a super-decorative leek—topped with blunt spikes of orange and cream flowers, soon discover that it does well only in extremely well drained soils, a preference that has even enabled it to colonise sand dunes on the shores of the Firth of Forth in Scotland. The paradox of a plant that can be found in flower in extremely wet situations but depends on good drainage for survival when grown in gardens applies to many plants from South Africa, whether from summer or winter rainfall areas. In this case the wetlands in which *K. caulescens* luxuriates are short-lived and seasonal; once summer is over, winter droughts ensure that the ground dries out and remains dry throughout the winter, when dormant plants become vulnerable to wet.

The grand, old-fashioned red hot pokers of herbaceous borders are descendants of *Kniphofia uvaria,* a plant of damp slopes and marshy meadows in the western Cape. An impressive example is *Kniphofia* 'Lord Roberts', with bold spikes of vermilion-scarlet tubular flowers from vigorous clumps of deep green leaves; unfortunately, like many of its kind, this plant is all too inclined to degenerate into a bedraggled, tangled bundle. Hybrids of *K. galpinii* and other smaller species are less inclined to be messy, and their more slender spikes of flowers range from almost white through cream to yellow to flame to orange to vermilion.

South Africa is the home of many other herbaceous plants familiar to gardeners in the north, and few visitors to Cape Town in late winter or spring could miss seeing the arums that grow so abundantly around the city. They are most at home in seasonally wet vleis and are widely distributed in damp spots over vast areas of the less arid parts of South Africa. Arums, *Zantedeschia aethiopica*, were one of the crops grown on my father's nursery, in a large heated greenhouse. At that time we only knew the typical pure white wild form, and since sales were almost confined to Easter, any flowers that appeared for weeks beforehand were cut and stored in a cool cellar, to be sent to the shops just before the great day. These memories were revived years later in KwaZulu-Natal, when Henry Rasmussen and his wife showed me round the nursery where they grow arums of many kinds. Several were variants on the 'Green Goddess' theme, amongst them *Zantedeschia* 'Green Tip' and 'Emperor', varying in the proportion of the spathe that was suffused with green pigment, and 'Emerald Green', with broad flowers on vig-

The arum lily, *Zantedeschia aethiopica*, is hardy enough to be grown in many parts of the Northern Hemisphere, and repays those adventurous enough to try it. Its large leaves and elegant, pure white flowers make an impression that has no substitute. Sissinghurst Castle, Kent, England.

orous, rather coarse stems, that are so heavily infused with pigment that they are hardly distinguishable from the leaves. The so-called pink arum is also grown here, neatly formed and white apart from a delicate pink flush at the base of the flower. This selection was discovered by Henry growing in the shade of a fig tree nearly thirty years ago, and a tangled web of events has led to it now being marketed under the name 'Kiwi Blush'.

Zantedeschia 'Crowborough' is a cultivar with a reputation for hardiness, but it is impossible to be sure that the original strain on which this reputation was based is still maintained. Nevertheless, arum lilies can now be seen in many parts of Britain in gardens where winter frosts are at least moderately severe; the plants are sometimes, but not always, grown in shallow water where they are protected from winter's worst effects. There can be no doubt that this plant could be used much more widely than it is. Its pure white spathes above broad, deep green leaves contribute an air of subtropical luxuriance to any setting that few other hardyish plants can match.

Several dwarf forms of the true arum lily have been selected—including *Zantedeschia aethiopica* 'Little Darling', specially bred as a pot plant, and 'Childsiana', with small, neat foliage and flowers—but the most truly dwarf, and the most colourful, members of the genus are the calla lilies, with flower colour ranging through cream, yellow, orange, pink and plum purple. Unlike the arum lily, which grows mostly in winter rainfall areas and remains evergreen in mild situations, calla lilies grow naturally in the Drakensberg and the Eastern Highlands of Zimbabwe, where they lose their leaves and go deeply dormant before the onset of winter. They can be grown in gardens where winters are very cold, provided soils remain dry or drainage is exceptionally good; the plants are generally unreliable in western Europe and parts of the United States where wet soils combined with frosts create intolerable conditions. *Zantedeschia albomaculata* grows naturally in seasonal marshes amongst grasses and in rocky situations, and is drought tolerant. It has green, arrow-shaped leaves spotted with white, and the flowers, though usually yellow, may be white or pinkish white with deep crimson blotches at the base of the spathe. *Zantedeschia rehmannii* has greenish white, deep maroon, pink or red spathes, varying in intensity of colour depending on the conditions in which it is grown. These and other species have been hybridised, particularly in the Netherlands and New Zealand, to produce numerous commercial cultivars that are now widely grown as cut flowers, and to a lesser extent as container plants. Though rather neglected by gardeners, they are a group with attractive leaves, elegantly beautiful flowers, and a generally amenable temperament that would repay a more adventurous interest.

Almost the first plant I grew was montbretia, rescued from a rubbish heap and painstakingly separated corm from corm with childish diligence before planting. This plant, derived from *Crocosmia aurea*, is a traveller and coloniser of cool, moist maritime situations, as at home in the Orkney Islands as in southern Chile. The corms piled one upon another are a defence against the baboons and porcupines that grub it up for food in its native South Africa. Probing fingers or grubbing snouts may account for most of them, but a few corms will be missed and live to grow another day.

Crocosmias grow naturally in summer rainfall areas of South Africa and are represented in gardens by numerous mostly hardy, broadly tolerant, vigorous hybrids lumped together under the rather awkward name *Crocosmia* ×*crocosmiiflora*. Apart from *C. aurea*, which often grows in deep shade, two other species are involved in their parentage: *C. masoniorum*, with large, widely flaring, rich orange or orange-vermilion flowers in one-sided spikes just above the leaves, naturally partial to moist, humus-rich soils; and *C. pottsii*, with narrow, tubular red flowers, from lighter, well-drained soils. Crocosmias are reliable, pest- and disease-free, floriferous plants that excel in late summer and autumn. The flowers may be star-shaped or more or less tubular, usually flaring at the mouth. The inflorescences may be neat and orderly, with flowers in precisely aligned ranks, or follow more carelessly abandoned styles. Some flowers are held well clear of the foliage; some are level with the tips of the leaves—any lower and they become partially concealed and much of their impact is lost. Colours range from soft yellow flushed with peachy apricot shades to intense burnt orange-red, even crimson. Size is similarly variable, but cultivars with the largest flowers are not necessarily the most attractive or garden worthy, particularly when large size is associated with fragile petals that are vulnerable to the effects of wind and rain. The upright, sword-shaped leaves provide excellent contrast to broad-leaved perennials, but the crowded masses in which they grow makes this more of a contrast in texture than in form.

Large flowers, inherited from *Crocosmia masoniorum*, can be vulnerable to wind and rain, but 'Lady Hamilton', a cultivar with large, shapely and finely coloured flowers, shrugs off wind and rain, and remains beautiful even under trying conditions. The bronze-flushed leaves and soft apricot-yellow flowers of 'Solfatare' make a change from the others, but this cultivar is not one of the hardiest and needs warmth and shelter to do well. Some of the best recent crocosmia hybrids have been produced by Alan Bloom of Bressingham Nurseries in East Anglia. Most of his hybrids have markedly tubular, firmly constructed flowers that are notably weatherproof and reliable in gardens. Two of the best are 'Lucifer' with flame red flowers, which flowers earlier than most crocosmias, and 'Firebird' with bright vermilion-orange flowers that are rather larger than other Bressingham hybrids.

Another familiar plant of the meadows below the Sentinel Peak was associated in my mind with an unpleasant whiff of rotting meat in a greenhouse on my nursery, and a fruitless few minutes searching for the dead rabbit which I suspected one of the cats had left behind. Eventually the penny dropped, and I traced the smell to a plant of the pineapple flower, *Eucomis bicolor*, in full bloom. All the more surprising, then, when Gaye Simmons took me round her Shosholoza Nursery near Mooi River in KwaZulu-Natal and showed me some of her beautiful eucomis hybrids, with the comment that she hoped they would catch on as house plants. When I suggested that dead-rabbit smell might not be a selling point to those looking for a plant for their sitting room, she enlightened my ignorance by pointing out that the flowers of most species are sweetly fragrant. These fascinating plants have a character all their own, with bold, broad leaves and pineapple heads of green or cream flowers flushed, veined or outlined with crimson. Several species from summer rainfall areas of Southern

The large, open flowers of 'Lady Hamilton' show the influence of *Crocosmia masoniorum*. It is one of the best of the large-flowered hybrids. Powys Castle, Welshpool, Wales.

Africa are notably hardy, broadly tolerant garden plants, and their distinctive appearance and long flowering season are beginning to be more appreciated by gardeners. Few herbaceous plants are more impressive than *E. pole-evansii*, with its pineapple-like heads of green flowers, raised shoulder high on stout stems in midsummer, above clusters of broad, glossy leaves. The flowers of *E. comosa*, produced on shorter stems, range in colour from white flushed with pink or crimson to an overall deep wine-red. Hybrids that have inherited these deeper, more colourful tones may soon radically transform our present view of the attractions of pineapple flowers. *Eucomis autumnalis* is usually said to have smaller flowers than other species, a reputation which for me was entirely refuted by the impressive appearance of plants growing around World's View near Nyanga in the Eastern Highlands of Zimbabwe. The flowers are a delicate shade of pale apple green, and lack the crimson pencilling and shading that distinguishes some other species, but the robust inflorescences beneath the top-knots of green leaves would add distinction to any garden. Attractive features of eucomis include the foliage, whether plain green or deeply suffused with crimson, and the long-lasting qualities of the flowers, which remain open and appealing, some even until the seeds are released several months after the first buds open. Some species contain toxic compounds in their leaves that have lethal effects on snails—perhaps they should be grown as companion plants among hostas or rengarengas.

Eucomis autumnalis illustrates the characteristic pineapple inflorescence of the genus, growing beneath a top-knot of green leaves. World's View, Eastern Highlands, Zimbabwe.

The summer hyacinth, *Galtonia candicans*, has been grown in gardens in Britain since the middle of the nineteenth century—without ever quite becoming established. It is a plant of the summer rainfall area of the Drakensberg and is perfectly happy in Britain's wet summers, but not able to cope with winter wet and cold. Sometimes it will get by, especially on well-drained soils, sometimes not. Close relatives include G. *princeps*, a gawky, rather ungainly look-alike, but with 2-metre stems that seem to outgrow its foliage and relatively small, sparse flowers that dance around the top. *Galtonia viridis* is a much more attractive proposition, with flowers like the palest jade-green ivory and a more sturdy form, but it is even less tolerant of cold, wet winters than the white summer hyacinth. When lifted in the autumn and stored over winter like gladioli, both can easily be kept alive from one year to the next.

The southernmost parts of the Overberg are remarkable for the presence of limestone, and on a visit to one such area at Meerkraal Farm with June and Micky D'Alton, I came across a most splendid display of the perennial lion's ear or wild dagga, *Leonotis leonurus*. Masses of plants grew all the way along the sunny side of the woodland edge amongst the grasses where a paddock met the fynbos. Each one bearing several stems and multiple whorls of glowing orange flowers, the lion's ears were a brave and striking sight that illuminated a dull day. In summer rainfall areas, and that includes gardens in Western Europe, this plant flowers during autumn and early winter. Here in a winter rainfall area, its flowering period is late winter and early spring, as it is in gardens in Mediterranea generally. The tropical orange-flowered species is a most beautiful plant that one might well think could not be surpassed, but the white form, 'Harrismith White', by no means just a pale variation, is an equally arresting and beautiful plant in its own right. A close relative, L. *dysophylla*, is rather smaller with shorter leaves and similar flowers, but with one significant difference, pointed out to me by Lynn Page during a tour

The white-flowered summer hyacinth, *Galtonia candicans*, from the Drakensberg has long been used in British gardens. Near Mont-aux-Sources, Royal Natal National Park, KwaZulu-Natal, South Africa.

of her garden at Gillitts, outside Durban in KwaZulu-Natal. Lynn described the nectar of this species as being like the best liqueur chocolates for the sunbirds, as opposed to that produced by *L. leonurus*, which was quite evidently not the connoisseurs' choice.

Most bulbs flower in spring or, like pineapple flowers, galtonias and gladiolus hybrids, during the summer, but a group of South African amaryllids flower in the autumn. Gardeners in western Europe, parts of the United States with cold winters, or the summer rainfall areas of South Africa see nerines, amaryllis and brunsvigias as the last fling of colour before the onset of winter cold or drought. In Mediterranea their appearance is the first sign of rejuvenation at the end of long hot summers. *Nerine bowdenii*, from the Sentinel meadows, has heads of rather shocking bright rose-pink flowers, at the tops of bare stems, that appear shortly after the leaves have disappeared. It is the hardiest of several species from summer rainfall areas of KwaZulu-Natal and the Drakensberg. Others species include *N. filifolia*, which is easy to grow, flowers freely and makes a good garden plant where winters are not too cold; it is notable for the grass-like foliage which develops almost into a thick sward. *Nerine masonorum* is another, with slender, almost evergreen leaves and paler pink flowers, small enough to be useful as an edging plant. The rainbow diversity of *N. sarniensis* is a striking contrast to the narrow colour range of other species, and is also the only one from winter rainfall areas. It exists naturally in several colour forms, but the most widespread has clusters of scarlet flowers with gracefully reflexed petals sprinkled with gold dust at the tops of the bare stems. Cultivation has released a bewildering variety of pink, scarlet, crimson, orange and intermediate

The glowing orange flowers of the wild dagga, *Leonotis leonurus*, are attractive to gardeners as well as nectar-feeding birds. Meerkraal, near Bredasdorp, Western Cape Province, South Africa.

hues, including violets and purples, some clear, true hues, others with clouded, almost smoky tones that are unusual and attractive. Although moderately winter hardy, the Jersey lily, as some call *N. sarniensis*, takes its summer resting period seriously and decays in soils that remain moist during dormancy. Outside Mediterranea it is best grown in a container and sheltered from rain in summer.

The colour range displayed by *Nerine sarniensis* is remarkably similar to that of the zonal pelargoniums, as though they share the same paint box. As with nerines, this brilliant diversity is not typical of the genus as a whole. The impressions conveyed by the brilliant colours of geraniums in our gardens, or the opulence of regal pelargoniums in conservatories, are very different to those of most of the pelargonium species to be seen growing naturally. Often they are little more than a pallid presence amongst grasses, tucked in amongst shrubs and other vegetation, revealed by a glimpse of washed-out lilac, barely enhanced by the crimson figurings in the centres of their flowers. But some species are bold, vigorous plants with strongly marked leaves and luxurious heads of colourful flowers. The elegant, open clusters of bright salmon-pink flowers of *Pelargonium frutetorum* from the eastern Cape

Nerine sarniensis, from the winter rainfall area of the western Cape, is the species with the brightest and most variously coloured flowers. The Carmichael garden, Welland, Worcestershire, England.

are an example, and this species is one of the progenitors of the zonal pelargoniums. 'The Boar' is a selected form of *P. frutetorum*, very similar to the species, with a dark brown central blotch in place of the zonal marking. Other brightly coloured species include *P. inquinans*, also from the eastern Cape, and the source of the brilliant colours of the bedding geraniums; its straggly and pale-leaved appearance, with awkward gawky shoots, has been greatly improved by hybridisation with the pink-flowered *P. zonale* and other more compact species. On the other hand *P. peltatum*, ancestor of the ivy-leaved geraniums and another species from the eastern Cape, is naturally a vigorous scrambling plant capable of climbing into and over shrubs and small trees. Unfortunately it has been utterly spoilt by the fashion for miniaturisation; instead of a valuable, long-flowering, brightly coloured climber that clambers into dull shrubs and over ugly trellis fences in gardens in Australia and New Zealand, modern hybrids are so small and unambitious that they are fit only for window boxes and hanging baskets. The common origin of these easily grown, amenable species in the eastern Cape is significant. This is a place where rain may fall at any time of the year, but where periodic, prolonged droughts are not unusual—a combination of plenty and austerity that enables plants in cultivation to respond to the good times, and equips them with the stoic endurance needed to survive periods of neglect. Most gardeners' first experiences of pelargoniums away from the popular zonal, regal or ivy-leaved hybrids are with the scented-leaved hybrids and species. One widely grown in gardens in mild situations is the peppermint-scented *P. tomentosum*. Its spreading inclination and broad, soft leaves make a most attractive ground cover in lightly shaded situations, or on dryish banks beneath trees.

Beyond these, the genus *Pelargonium* includes huge numbers of plants that challenge the imagination to find ways to use their diversity in gardens. A few, like *Pelargonium* 'California Brilliant', are rhizomatous, and Jim Gerdiman showed me plants in his garden, near Yachats on the Oregon Coast, that had been cut to the ground by frost and recovered successfully by producing shoots from their underground stems, raising hopes of pelargoniums that can be grown outdoors in cold climates. Another tempting change from the usual is suggested by *P. tricolor*, a small species with distinctive flowers of deep crimson upper petals contrasting with white lower ones. It grows naturally in the shade of shrubs in drought-afflicted situations in the western Cape. It seldom does well in gardens, but hybrids with *P. ovale*, a more amenable garden plant, have produced 'Splendide'. Bigger than either parent, this cultivar combines the striking flowers of *P. tricolor* with the tractable nature of *P. ovale*.

Another most attractive and unusual little pelargonium is 'Pretty Lady', close to *Pelargonium ovale* itself. This is a compact plant that produces clusters of finely textured silvery green leaves at ground level, with numerous bi-coloured white and bright pink flowers densely distributed just above the foliage. It bears little resemblance to the pelargoniums we are accustomed to seeing in gardens, and has qualities that are eminently garden-worthy. When shown the plant growing in their beautiful informal woodland garden in the Blue Mountains west of Sydney by Cec and Rita Sullivan, my immediate reaction was the hope that further hybridisation and selection would lead to a new race of garden hybrids with similarly attractive foliage and compact form in a wider range of colours.

This pelargonium has seeded itself in the crevices of a wind-carved rock, illustrating just how resilient these plants can be. Whangarei, North Island, New Zealand.

Pelargoniums were amongst the first Southern Hemisphere plants to be discovered by western gardeners, and their hybrids have long played a part in gardens and conservatories. The kangaroo paws and their relatives, just as tempting, have by comparison played very little part at all. The tallest and most vigorous species is the yellow kangaroo paw, *Anigozanthos flavidus*, from swampy situations in south-western Western Australia. Plants from such habitats often make amenable garden plants. They are at home in comparatively fertile soils that seldom dry out completely, and they are members of competitive communities where longevity and the ability to hold ground are at a premium—just the sort of qualities we like to find in our garden plants. Numerous cultivars derived from this species are now making their presence felt in gardens, but even more notably as cut flowers for florists, for whom they are being grown on an ever-increasing scale by nurseries in Australia, Zimbabwe and elsewhere. A series known as the Bush Hybrids are

These brilliantly coloured Bush Hybrids at the Regional Botanic Garden at Manurewa in New Zealand are hybrids derived from the amenable *Anigozanthos flavidus*.

claimed to be resistant to ink spot, a crippling disease that disfigures foliage and kills the plants. These hybrids made an impression on me during a visit to the Regional Botanic Garden at Manurewa near Auckland, where in beds close to a display of *Hemerocallis,* they glowed with such intense colours that they entirely outshone the daylilies.

Strong golds, velvety (if slightly musty) crimsons, burnt oranges, yellows and pinks—the colours represented a broad spectrum, and provided an eye-opening demonstration of the possibilities that recent cultivars of kangaroo paws offer gardeners. Some cultivars are around knee-high, with the flowers too often crowded into congested, shapeless masses close to the ground, almost obscuring the leaves and becoming progressively more faded and tacky at the edges as they age. Flowers on the taller cultivars are gracefully presented on open, branching inflorescences that reveal the form of the individual flowers, and enable the foliage beneath to contribute to the overall composition and structure of the plants. Several of the Bush Hybrids are small, including 'Illusion', with glowing flame orange flowers with bright yellow tips; 'Heritage', tawny red with yellow reflexed tips; 'Pearl', with rosy mauve self-coloured flowers, a little too reminiscent of faded velvet curtains; and 'Twilight', with very heavy heads of tawny orange and crimson flowers with yellow tips, inclined to collapse and flop around in disarray—sunset would have been a more accurate description. Amongst the taller cultivars are 'Radiance', which has upright, slender, self-supporting stems and deep rose-pink flowers well spaced on short, lateral branchlets; and 'Dawn', with clusters of bright yellow flowers at the tips of the branchlets of open inflorescences. Good points of these kangaroo paws are their glowing rich colours, velvety textures, mass flower power and, for the taller forms, their elegant stance. Limitations include an inclination to fade as the flowers age, tumbled/jumbled form of the dwarf cultivars, blotched foliage and unemphatic, weak forms.

The black kangaroo paw, *Macropidia fuliginosa,* is a short-lived, rather choosy perennial but with an appealing style and dramatic intensity possessed by none of the *Anigozanthos* hybrids. Its well-spaced black and straw yellow flowers at the ends of branching inflorescences have all the qualities that make gardeners open their eyes wide, and it is proving amenable enough in gardens to support hopes that it will become a much appreciated occupant of our borders.

Beyond the topographically challenged continent of Australia, in the Southern Alps of New Zealand, we find the slopes amongst the glaciers of Mount Cook covered with grasses, low shrubs and numerous perennial plants—reminiscent of the high heathlands of Lesotho beyond South Africa's Sentinel Peak, but with a very different cast of plants. The most remarkable has to be *Ranunculus lyallii*, a buttercup, but so beautiful that those who found it could not bring themselves to call it one, naming it instead the Mount Cook lily. Its flowers, more like pure white single roses than buttercups, cluster on branching stems above luxuriant deep green, rounded leaves. They stand out amongst the ochre, olive-green and other drab tones around them, making no concessions to the wind and harsh conditions.

Like the plants of the Sentinel, the plants here live in a world where winters are cold, but here they are also wet, and combinations of frost and moist soils are not so lethal. The herbaceous Mount Cook lily avoids the worst of the winter weather by dying down after the first frosts to branching rhizomes with long, brittle roots. These roots are easily damaged, making transplanting difficult, and frustrating anyone wicked enough to attempt to lift

The black kangaroo paw, *Macropidia fuliginosa*, has a style and intensity that gardeners find irresistibly tempting. The Regional Botanic Garden at Manurewa, near Auckland, North Island, New Zealand.

this species from the wild. Gardeners who covet *Ranunculus lyallii* can propagate it from seed, or with care by dividing the rhizomes, but must grow it
in ground that remains constantly cool, drains freely and never dries out.

Mount Cook lilies are visible from afar, and my first sight of a group of
them sent me plunging through the grasses to reach them, giving way immediately to a much more cautious approach as I ran into plants of a very
different nature—the giant Spaniard, *Aciphylla scott-thomsonii*. This aggressive relative of Queen Anne's lace and carrots infested every approach with
spiny, spiky leaves that jabbed at my calves and ankles. Aciphyllas of many
kinds grow amongst the mountains of Australasia. *Aciphylla scott-thomsonii*
is the largest, with chest-high clusters of spiky leaves beneath imposing inflorescences of yellow flowers behind protective screens of sharp spines—
defences made redundant by the extinction of the moas. Few gardeners can
pass by plants with so much character and individuality without thoughts
of how they might use them, and by degrees aciphyllas are being found
places in gardens; the impressions they create more than repay the courage
of those who plant them. Gardeners at Logan, in Scotland, are falling under
the spell of this genus, and species to be seen there include *A. montana*, with
neat but cruel-looking hemispheres of lance-shaped, and lance-sharp,
leaves, as friendly as the backside of a porcupine. Also, the handsome and
substantially built *A. glaucescens*, with distinctive blue-green foliage and tall,
pale yellow inflorescences. Although the leaves are lax in comparison with
those of most other species, giving the plant an agreeably "soft" appearance, the leaflets are sharply pointed. This species grows best in fertile, moist,
well-drained situations and will tolerate semi-shaded settings. Another fine
structural plant, rejoicing under the name the horrid Spaniard, is *Aciphylla
horrida*, with metre-high clumps of spiny leaves and rather magnificent—
but equally spiny—compound spikes of yellow-green flowers. The closely
related *A. aurea*, with russet rather than golden leaves, colours most brightly
and grows better on well-drained soils, and is a good choice for gardens in
drier situations.

Gardeners learn early on that plants with grey or silver leaves most often
grow naturally in drought-prone places—all the more surprising, then, in
a place where drought is unusual, to find the bold, brilliant silver rosettes
of *Celmisia semicordata*, and to observe the silken, silver undersides of the
leaves of *C. petiolata* growing amongst aciphyllas, hebes, sedges and other

moisture-loving plants. But the plant that finally proved the exception to this rule for me, seen on a visit to Doubtful Sound in Fjordland National Park on a wet day, was *C. holosericea* growing in the midst of torrents of water cascading down the cliff faces.

Celmisias have a reputation for challenging the gardener's skills. Their preferences are for exposed situations with humid atmospheres, free from extremes of heat, cold or drought, on soils that drain freely but remain consistently moist. Gardeners in western Scotland, Puget Sound and similarly moist, temperate parts of the world find them easier to grow than those who live in eastern England or northern California. The cotton plant, *Celmisia semicordata,* from New Zealand herbfields is the species most often seen in gardens. Its broad rosettes of gleaming pewter, sword-shaped leaves highlighted with silver, and the large pure white daisies on strong stems are as stunning in nature as in cultivation. But this and the golden-leaved subsp. *aurigens,* like other species of celmisia with large rosettes of leaves and substantial rootstocks, are susceptible to phytophthora and other soil-borne pathogens. *Celmisia holosericea,* despite its apparent affinity with water in

Celmisia semicordata is a magnificent plant and the one most frequently seen in gardens. Jack's Pass, Hanmer Springs, South Island, New Zealand.

Fjordland's Doubtful Sound, often grows well in gardens even in places like Christchurch, where summer droughts make conditions more like Mediterranea than the west coast of New Zealand. Another good garden plant, both drought and lime tolerant, is *C. gracilenta*. This species has clustered crowns of pointed, narrow, deep green leaves heavily spangled with silvery white, like attenuated, multilimbed starfish. The spangling varies, and the most attractive cultivated forms are those in which it is most marked. The herbfields and grasslands of the relatively dry mountains in the north of South Island from Nelson to the Lewis Pass are the home of *C. allanii*, a plant with spreading clusters of leaves densely covered with soft, white hairs that does best in cultivation in drier climates. The Australian silver daisy, *C. asteliifolia*, has robust tufts of stiff, usually erect, silver-backed, lance-shaped leaves, and large white daisies carried individually on stout stems. The silky daisy, *C. sericophylla*, from the Bogong High Plains of south-eastern Australia, has large flowers with broad, pure white ray petals above tufts of limp, flat, silky grey annual leaves from a perennial rootstock. Celmisias are self-sterile and produce seed only when cross-pollinated from another plant. However, collective promiscuity replaces individual celibacy when species meet, and many hybridise freely. Gardeners who want to collect seed that is true to type should plant several of each species in a group, widely separated from other species.

Continuing our journey east around the globe from South Africa through Australia and New Zealand brings us across the Pacific to South America, where we are introduced to a plant that dwarfs even the grandest inflorescences of New Zealand's giant Spaniard, *Aciphylla scott-thomsonii*. The giant rhubarb, *Gunnera manicata*, not quite a plant of the Looking-Glass Garden, grows in swamps and bogs in wet valleys in the mountains between Brazil and Colombia, just north of the equator. Its size fascinates gardeners, and planted at one end of a large pool it has an imposing presence, although it has become a bit of a cliché plant in such situations. In nature its rhizomatous roots colonise swampy ground, and while the garden at Trebah in Cornwall lay neglected, the giant rhubarb reverted to nature, monopolising a large area of the valley below. The plants make a remarkable sight in spring, as the multitudes of crowns burst into growth, and the great leaves unfold above thrusting inflorescences—a convincing example of the rewards of planting boldly. We should all be so lucky to have such opportunities!

A smaller version, and a true Southern Hemisphere plant, that more gardens could accommodate is *Gunnera tinctoria*. This vigorous pioneer of cleared forest in its native Chile is beginning to make itself at home on Mount Taranaki in New Zealand. On banks beside ditches on Chiloe Island, the phallic inflorescences and broad leaves of the gunnera create compositions of contrasting textures and forms with the foxgloves, fuchsias and ferns amongst which it grows, an effect that would transfer most effectively to a garden. As though to compensate for *G. magellanica*'s excess, most gunneras are modest plants, more suitable as discreet ground cover along stream banks and beside pools than for the dramatic impact of gross leaves. In situations like these where the leading shoots will dip into water, *G. magellanica* from Tierra del Fuego and the Falkland Islands grows as a thick carpet, its round leaves with green and bronze tints full of texture and interest. *Gunnera hamiltonii* is the rarest of the New Zealand species, and the largest, but size is relative, and the plant's massed rosettes of mid-green leaves with toothed margins can also be used to produce deep-piled, ground-covering carpets.

The trees that fill this small garden form a cool overhead canopy even on the hottest days. Lower branches have been pruned out to provide views through the garden. The stems of the trees provide structure, and the constantly changing interplay of light and shade offers dynamic interest. Steve Shapiro's garden, Hout Bay, Western Cape Province, South Africa.

PART II

Gardens in Shadow

T
HE ROAD beside the Tasman Sea along South Island's west coast in New Zealand passes through countryside that becomes progressively wetter, greener, wilder and more luxuriantly forested as it goes south into the domain of the Roaring Forties. Greymouth sees the last of the Norfolk Island pines, Canary palms, pohutukawas, agapanthus and South African daisies that characterise the coastal gardens of these temperate islands, and the start of a world of evergreen forests, through which glaciers rise high in the mountains and flow almost to the sea, and deep fjord-like inlets penetrate miles inland. Shade is the norm for the plants that grow here. They thrive in it, providing new insights into ways to convert places where trees overshadow the ground below into some of the most rewarding parts of our gardens. This forest taught me lessons that I had overlooked during trips round hundreds of gardens. And I was not even here to look for plants, but crested penguins.

Tree ferns and penguins seem a biological paradox, but here these birds nest in burrows amongst the ferns' roots. Monroe's Walk is a short and easy path beside the Moeraki River through the forest to a beach where the penguins come ashore. I planned to sit quietly amongst the trees and watch them ride through the surf and waddle over the sand to their nests, a plan that took no account of the appetites of sand flies. Penguins are shy and, if they spy a movement, stay at sea until reassured that danger has passed— but I defy anyone to sit immobile enough to deceive a penguin when sand flies are biting. After a short while, smarting but wiser, I gave up and walked back through the forest, looking at it more closely than I had on my way out. This forest is multi-layered, complex and varied. The broad trunks of enormous kahiakateas, rimus and southern beeches are widely spaced, their tops

217

scarcely visible through the foliage of the lower growing kamahis, tree ferns and fuchsias, reinforced by broadleafs, wineberries, scheffleras and pigeon woods. This is a very wet place. Mosses, liverworts and filmy ferns cover the trunks and main limbs of many trees, and they carpet the ground. Water drips from leaf tips, and drops hang on the fern fronds glistening in shafts of sunlight. For this evergreen forest is not dense but fairly open; looking through it you can see the trees from the wood, and enough light reaches the ground to support a rich growth of astelias and ferns.

With so many trees, so many plants, one might expect a confused medley of impressions, but as I walked through this forest I became aware of differences that gave each space a distinctive character. Some parts seem predominantly grassy, though there is no grass to be seen at all. The impression is due to the presence of plants with long, narrow, grass-like foliage. The trees are wrapped around by kiekies; and clumps of astelias and perching lilies grow in their forks amongst wispy tresses of epiphytic orchids. Cutty grasses, more astelias, and dianellas with blue berries grow on the forest floor. Fern fronds provide the major themes a little further on. Numerous tree ferns rise through shrubs and small trees beneath the canopy. On the ground the sea green fronds of shield ferns, so charged with water that they appear oily, grow like loosely formed shuttlecocks; the pale tips of groups of crown ferns reflect light from the forest floor; and in places the Prince of Wales feathers, like supremely stylish miniature tree ferns, produce fans of deep green lace-like foliage. Filmy ferns, trailing club mosses and foliose lichens cover the lower limbs of the trees, reinforcing an overall impression of a more ancient world constructed before the advent of broad-leaved plants. Then I stepped into a leafy forest where the glossy deep green foliage of scheffleras, pseudopanax, broadleafs, and mahoes filled the spaces between the giant columns of the kahiakateas. Few ferns or long-leaved lilies were to be seen, but the ground and lower parts of the trees were carpeted with mosses and broad rugs of liverworts.

A walk through this wood is like progressing through a French *chartreuse* in which each enclosure provides a different experience. Small variations in exposure, soil moisture, past history and present circumstances generate different communities within which plants with similar textures or forms come together to create the dominant themes and provide atmosphere. This is a familiar design device in gardens too—we need only think of the

endless copies, variations and likenesses inspired by the red borders at Hidcote, the white garden at Sissinghurst or the blue garden at Lotusland to
understand that. But how often do we develop this idea beyond colour to
embrace texture or form, which is what we see on this path along the Moeraki River?

The complex four-dimensional matrices formed by trees challenge garden designers to create impressions that are not overpowering in their detail and diversity. Simplification through the use of repetition, as described
here, is particularly useful in woodland settings in which the urge to pile in
as many different plants as possible fragments the unity that confers tranquillity. But this preference for diversity and exaggerated concern for detail
applies also to the design of borders. Taught to seek balance between harmonies and contrasts, we offset a rounded plant with a spiky one, soft foliage with rough, an upright stance with something spreading. Rather than
using repetition to introduce rhythm and character, we dismiss it as monotonous, and inspiration is measured by diversity per square metre. I have
seen the results so often in the garden make-overs that television producers
like to present as gardening. In the final act there is a frolicsome raid on the
local garden centre, and the gathering together of a band of plants that
caught the eye and promised to combine in tasteful ways. This is followed
by an exhilarating spell setting the plants out in the freshly prepared borders—the round bun of a hebe posed beside an upright spiky phormium;
three mat-forming euonymuses overhung by a cut-leaved crimson maple;
the broad, bright foliage of a variegated hosta contrasted with a ferny, crim-
son-leaved astilbe. The first law of this kind of garden making is that every
effect must be balanced by another; the second is that, apart from groups of
three, even five if boldness prevails, to form a clump, no plant should appear more than once. The programmes conclude with a self-congratulatory
gathering of the cast to admire their handiwork, and when seen through the
camera's lens, the admiration is invariably justified by the appeal of the result—but that is because plants are very appealing creatures. Dismiss the
camera, stand back and take an overall view of the composition of the garden, and we see a mishmash of unrelated impressions jostling for attention. We search in vain for the integrity and individuality that would distinguish one border from another and turn a stroll through the garden into
a passage through a series of experiences.

The evergreen forest described earlier owes nothing to artifice and little to human intervention, yet its combination of overall unity with individuality would be the envy of many aspiring garden designers. Overall unity results from the presence of dominant trees throughout the forest. Wherever we look we are conscious of their presence, providing a setting for the smaller scale happenings, which we perceive in greater detail close to where we stand. We have to deliberately look up and around to become aware of the repetitive vertical lines of the columnar stems, the tracery of the overhead canopy against the sky, the subdued light and the tranquil, sheltered atmosphere that makes the forest environment. Within that environment different impressions are formed by a combination of diversity and repetition. Diversity from the presence of plants that differ from one place to another; repetition of particular plants or particular forms within a setting to confer a strong, easily recognised sense of local character.

There is nothing monotonous about this constructive repetition. It establishes overall unity, it creates structure, it reinforces individuality and it instils rhythm as the eye travels around the set, picking out patterns and inventing motifs. And all this happens in the wild wood, where nothing has been deliberately arranged and everything we see appears to be the result of chaotic, unplanned and seemingly arbitrary events. The gardener's view of the haphazard nature of wild plants and the ways they grow together in communities is misplaced and, amongst other misunderstandings, has led to the lack of appreciation of the virtues of repetition that so inhibits our use of it in gardens.

CHAPTER 9
Trees for Cool Gardens

*C*HILE starts in the tropics in the rainless Atacama Desert, becomes part of Mediterranea around Santiago, passes through the cool, cloud-ridden forests of Chiloe Island and Aisen, and eventually runs out on the windswept, stormy Wollaston Islands, where Cape Horn faces Antarctica across the Southern Ocean. The Canary palms, eucalypts, oleanders and crape myrtles that greeted me in the Jardin Alexander von Humboldt in the Parque Quinta confirmed the Mediterranean character of Santiago, as did the flowers in the gardens on the little hill of Cerro Santa Lucia in the city centre. This bizarre combination of narrow stony steps winding steeply through mini-ravines and elaborate, grandiose set-piece compositions of formal pools and gilded fountains is topped by the castellated battlements and turrets of what appears to be a toy fort, but which once preserved the lives of early Spanish colonists during a prolonged siege by the Mapuches. While cautiously making my way down the steepest and narrowest flight of steps, I thought war had broken out again, when an explosion, seemingly directed straight into my left earhole, announced the firing of the midday gun.

A long night's train journey to the south brought me to Puerto Montt in time for lunch. The countryside north of the city is farmed, prosperous and densely populated amidst beautiful lakes and impressive volcanoes. South of the city a single road, interrupted by inlets of the sea crossed by ferries, passes through a scantily inhabited landscape between the inland sea of the Golfo de Ancud and the cliffs and glaciers of the Andes Mountains towering above screes of shattered rocks. Puyuhuapi, a tiny settlement of carpet weavers, aimless dogs and invisible cats, where meagre gardens produce cabbages, peas or carrots for the pot, is a slow journey 300 kilo-

Previous page: This garden is planted like a forest ride, with a clear sunlit "meadow" flanked by a woodland edge, beneath which perennials, tree ferns and shrubs flourish in light shade. Titoki Point, Gordon Collier's garden, Taihape, North Island, New Zealand.

metres south of Puerto Montt. The nearby Parque Nacional Queulat, is a wet and chilly place, though severe frosts are unusual, and many trees and shrubs familiar to western gardeners grow in a relatively undisturbed tract of forest.

None is more familiar than *Fuchsia magellanica*, a plant that appears in many forms, depending on its situation. In the shade of forest trees at Queulat this species is an open, rangy shrub with sparse flowers amongst soft, pale green leaves and upright branching stems covered with pale, ragged peeling bark. In meadows beyond the forest, where cows graze, it forms dense, congested ground-hugging mats of small, hard, dark green leaves, more like a cotoneaster than a fuchsia, with flowers that are few, small and far between. Close to the sea at Ancud on Chiloe Island, it is a densely twiggy, medium-sized shrub resplendent with masses of long, tubular, crimson and purple flowers that we would be proud to grow in our gardens. This plant is the parent of numerous hardy fuchsias, particularly valuable because they continue to flower well into the autumn. Then, they display the resilience to wind and rain inherited from ancestors that grew wild on the exposed coasts of southern Chile, which makes them excellent plants for hedges and screens in seaside situations elsewhere.

These hardy forms are evergreen in very mild situations, deciduous in cooler, and herbaceous when faced with severe frosts, dying back to ground level each winter. Amongst the best cultivars are *Fuchsia* 'Mrs Popple', with extra large purple and crimson flowers, and 'Variegata', with white flowers from palest pink buds and leaves with green centres and yellow margins. Another selection with white flowers from pink buds is 'Sharpitor', a relatively vigorous shrub with green leaves that have narrow, precisely delineated white margins. The *Fuchsia magellanica* cultivars 'Aurea' and 'Tricolor' have bright golden and variegated leaves, respectively, and small purple and crimson flowers. 'Whiteknight's Blush' is a vigorous, upright shrub with arching branchlets and relatively large, pale rose-pink flowers. *Fuchsia magellanica* var. *pumila* is a minute form with correspondingly tiny foliage and flowers —petite, but no weakling.

Another shrub in Queulat has foliage so similar to a holly's, but flowers equally obviously not those of a holly, that it thoroughly confused a group of women whom I met discussing its identity in a garden in Cumbria. Their confusion was understandable, because *Desfontainea spinosa* is an odd plant in an obscure, mainly tropical family, the Loganiaceae. In Chile its orange and scarlet tubular flowers are pollinated, like the fuchsias', by green-backed, firecrowned hummingbirds, and are followed by many-seeded berries.

Two other familiar garden plants grow in Chile's Queulat national park: one a shrub, the other a tree, both with white berries. The spready and prickly *Gaultheria mucronata* (formerly *Pernettya*) is a thicket-forming plant in cultivation, with attention-grabbing, rather vulgarly gawdy clusters of outsized crimson lake or white berries. *Azara lanceolata*, like other species in its genus, is not hardy in cold gardens in western Europe, and suspicions of their reliability have led to the attractions of this group of plants being overlooked in gardens in milder situations. One of the best and hardiest species, meriting a trial in all but the coldest places, is *A. microphylla*, a small tree with finely wrought, slender stems with scaly bark. Minute yellow flowers are produced amongst fans of tiny, deep green leaves as winter turns to spring, filling the air with the fragrance of vanilla.

Roadworks around Queulat had cut swathes though the forest, exposing tracts of cleared ground that was being colonised by two pioneer trees, canelo, *Drimys winteri*, and notro, *Embothrium coccineum*. Canelo is sacred to the Mapuches and widespread in southern Chile. In maturity it is a large tree with smooth, elephant grey, aromatic bark and clustered racemes of pure white flowers amongst broad evergreen leaves. This close relative of the magnolias is always found in association with water or high humidity, sometimes growing vigorously in shallow water overlying waterlogged ground, and does best in gardens in mild, humid climates on soils amply supplied with water.

Notro is another tree that seldom excels in dry gardens or in places with dry atmospheres. Although it lacks the presence of canelo, it compensates by its brilliantly fiery display of scarlet flowers in spring. Trees that play the role of pioneers in nature usually do well in gardens, and this is no exception. Seedlings grow rapidly into gawky, upright trees, and in nature the few that survive eventually develop into large, isolated individuals in mature forest. 'Norquinco Valley', said to be a more frost tolerant plant, is named after its place of origin, and two New Zealand selections, reputed to be rather less hardy than the type, but even more floriferous, are 'Inca Flame' and 'Inca King'.

Evergreen southern beeches dominate the forests of southern Chile. The largest and grandest of these is coigue, *Nothofagus dombeyi*, a tall, impressively robust tree with columnar trunks supporting clusters of branches from which the canopy fans out to produce a comparatively small, dense, slightly convex head. In gardens it tends to grow slowly, seldom creating an impression comparable with the trees seen in the wild. It often grows with another large evergreen southern beech, *N. nitida*, and sometimes with coigue de Magellanes, *N. betuloides*. The latter is a tree of the coolest, wettest, most exposed situations, a castaway on islands exposed to the unrelenting wind and rain of the Roaring Forties, and it copes with equally rigorous conditions in gardens. Its timber is as enduring as the tree, and is used to make the wooden shingles used as cladding for houses in this part of the world.

At higher altitudes north of Puerto Montt, *Nothofagus obliqua* grows in the Central Valley and forests high in the Andes. This vigorous tree develops rapidly into an imposing specimen even in cold gardens. Nire, *N. antarctica*, and lenga, *N. pumilio*, are hardier still, but smaller. Both grow in Tierra del

Notro, *Embothrium coccineum*, from the forests of Chile offers brilliant scarlet flowers in spring, even when still quite young. Mount Usher Garden, Ashford, near Dublin, Ireland.

Fuego. The former, sometimes little more than a shrub, grows in the highest forests and the coldest, wettest places in the mountains. Lenga is a small to medium-sized tree, depending on its situation, that grows to the timberline and is another source of shingles.

Southern beeches are amongst the great trees of the Looking-Glass Garden, strongly represented in cool, wet forests in South America, New Zealand and Australia as well as the high montane forests of New Guinea and New Caledonia. None are drought tolerant or likely to do well in hot, exposed situations. New Zealand representatives dominate forests in cooler or higher situations: red beech, *Nothofagus fusca,* on lowland forests and warm slopes; *N. solandri* and var. *cliffortioides,* the smaller mountain beech, in subalpine forests; and silver beech, *N. menziesii,* in the most rain drenched situations. All are evergreen, and *N. fusca* in particular, with beautiful copper-flushed immature foliage, can develop into a fine specimen tree in a garden, though it is not quite as hardy as the others. Several, including the Australian myrtle, *N. cunninghamii,* and New Zealand mountain beech, *N. solandri* var. *cliffortioides,* make excellent tall hedges, forming dense green walls of small, dark, lustrous leaves when clipped. Beech is a notoriously slow coloniser, and seedlings are said to grow well only in the vicinity of their parents—possibly because healthy growth depends on forming symbiotic associations with mycorrhizal fungi, which occur only in the root zone of established trees. Several fail to grow as rapidly in gardens as they would in the wild, but develop slowly and remain small—perhaps they are missing the support of their little fungal friends.

The Australian National Botanic Gardens at Canberra contains an ambitious and interesting garden feature known as the Rainforest Gully. Ambitious because this place has little in common with situations where natural rainforests occur in eastern Australia, and interesting because, although it is not particularly difficult to provide the water needed to keep the soil moist and the air humid in imitation of the conditions in which these plants grow naturally, it is impossible to exclude the frequent, often moderately severe frosts that Canberra experiences every winter. Plants here and elsewhere in the gardens survive conditions scarcely less severe than those experienced by lowland gardens in many parts of the British Isles, plants that would be regarded as too tender to grow in even the mildest gardens on mainland Britain. Midwinter days in Canberra are longer and have higher light intensities than those in Britain, and this must reduce stress and improve chances of survival. Nevertheless, the frost tolerance of the plants here suggests that if we ventured a little we might discover more that are amenable to cold conditions than we recognise at present.

The Rainforest Gully contains tree ferns, amongst them the fast-growing *Cyathea cooperi*, and several figs, such as the Port Jackson fig, *Ficus rubiginosa*, and more surprisingly the Moreton Bay fig, *F. macrophylla*. There are also two Australian species of southern beech. *Nothofagus moorei* is remarkable for bearing leaves more like the large, leathery foliage of a Portugal laurel *(Prunus lusitanica)* than that of a beech tree. This species grows amongst palm trees and other exotics close to the coast on the border of New South Wales and Queensland, but in colder situations at higher altitudes it is often the dominant forest tree. The other species in the Rainforest Gully is myr-

Nothofagus solandri var. *cliffortioides* makes an excellent tree for gardens in cool, wet conditions, similar to the subalpine forests of its native New Zealand. Near the Homer Tunnel, Fjordland, South Island, New Zealand.

tle, *N. cunninghamii*, which no visitor to the west coast of Tasmania could miss, with its small, deep green, leathery triangular leaves that look almost black in overcast conditions and from a distance. This is another tree that often fails to grow well in gardens. Under natural conditions, assertively erect leading shoots and a conical immature form are replaced in maturity by a substantial single trunk and a rounded crown. The battered remnants of weather-worn trunks, a few ragged major limbs and irregular tufts of surviving shoots and foliage are characteristic features of the forests on the west of the island, and an indication of the exposed conditions in which they live. The immature trees do bear a strong superficial resemblance to South American myrtles—hence the vernacular name—which brings us back to the forests of Chile, a stronghold of the southern myrtles.

Myrtles and Pittosporums

There was a time when the myrtles of the world were united in the genus *Myrtus*, then botanists ordained the division of the southern myrtles into several genera. *Luma* and *Amomyrtus* account for the Chilean species. No problem there, except for the unfortunate twist that the tree with marbled cinnamon and ivory bark and four-petalled flowers that was once *Myrtus apiculata* reappears as *Luma apiculata*, but the closely similar tree, known vernacularly as luma, is *Amomyrtus luma*. The flowers of the latter have five petals and appear rather earlier than those of *L. apiculata*. Meanwhile, New Zealand's myrtles—previously *M. bullata* and *M. obcordata* and natural hybrids between the two, formerly known as *M. ×ralphii*—are now all *Lophomyrtus*. *Lophomyrtus bullata* is a small to medium-sized tree with neat leaves, dark green in shaded situations, often suffused with crimson in sunlight. The hybrid *L. ×ralphii* produces variegated forms almost as prolifically as *Pittosporum tenuifolium*, including 'Gloriosa', with green and gold leaves; 'Kathryn', a good plant for a hedge, with deep bronze-red puckered, or bullate, foliage and an upright stance; two dwarfs known as 'Lilliput' and 'Pixie', the first with green leaves suffused with crimson, the second with tiny bronze foliage suitable for the rock garden; 'Sundae', with creamy yellow leaves splashed with pink; and 'Kaikoura Dawn', purplish bronze and cream with a rose-pink tinge on the immature foliage.

The New Zealand myrtles sound like a bright and cheerful lot, but like many trees and shrubs with small leaves, the variegated foliage is effective only at close range; stand back a bit and the hoped-for display of diversely coloured leaves merges into a nondescript, rather muddy hued melange. This problem of definition afflicts the use of evergreen shrubs generally, and was responsible for that maligned style of planting known as the Victorian Shrubbery, in which groups of evergreen shrubs, once past the flush of youth, became a byword for dull, unimaginative planting. The label "Victorian" implies that it is a thing of the past, but one need not travel far to find it reincarnated. The entrance to the gardens at Glendurgan in Cornwall are flanked by deep borders recently planted with camellias and evergreen trees, amongst them myrtles, pittosporums and other Southern Hemisphere species. They are colourful when the camellias are in flower, and not unattractive, but seemed to me unlikely to mature well.

This pitfall can be avoided by recognising the significance of differences in textures, tones and forms and finding ways to contrast and complement these to introduce structure and emphasise diversity. The interplay of light and dark is a major contributory factor to the interest and beauty of any garden, but is never more critical than when planting evergreens. Contrasting areas too easily become fragmented and the effects lost in a complex mosaic. The small bronze-green leaves of *Luma apiculata* create dark, heavily shaded masses that are relieved by slender cinnamon-coloured stems, especially when the bark peels and becomes marbled with cream. Grouping plants together emphasises their mass, and pruning to reveal their stems accentuates their form and contrasting tones. The larger, lighter green foliage of pittosporums, especially *Pittosporum eugenioides* and to a lesser extent *P. tenuifolium,* reflect light strongly, in contrast to the myrtles, and those with pale variegated foliage accentuate the differences in tone. Other opportunities for changes of mood and contrasts of effect are provided by trees with pinnate leaves like acacias, gevuinas and weinmannias or species with unusually broad leaves like pseudopanaxes and schleffleras. When dotted around in a border or landscape, these differences create pleasant impressions for a few years; in maturity they grow one into another and their impact is progressively lost until they merge into a dull wall of evergreenery. Exciting, stimulating planting depends on bold grouping to create masses in which the shapes, textures and tones of each have space to develop and reveal themselves, and to preserve spaces between them occupied by lower growing plants, so that variations in height, stance and texture retain the individuality of each group.

Pittosporums were my first introduction to southern evergreens. In a sheltered corner of my father's nursery a group of strange, black-stemmed shrubs with wavy margins to their silvery green leaves attracted my attention. They were being grown to provide foliage for florists in Bath. This was at a time when most of our customers thought Mexican orange *(Choisya ternata)* and Spanish broom *(Spartium junceum)* exotic, and there was no question of persuading them to plant anything as outlandish as these pittosporums; added to which, doubts about their hardiness would have condemned them as a foolishly bad investment for those whose cautious natures spent five minutes debating whether a pound of sprouts would be a wild extravagance when half a pound might do. Like many shrubs—and other plants—from the Looking-Glass Garden, pittosporums will be killed from time to time when frosts are exceptionally severe. But like ceanothus, bay trees and the Moroccan pineapple broom, they are quite likely to reward those who grow them for many years before a killer frost puts paid to them.

For much of the year the bark of *Luma apiculata* is a warm, bright cinnamon colour with an appealing textural quality, like soft leather. Patches flake away in spring to reveal the cream underbark. Abbotsbury Gardens, Dorset, England.

Pittosporums are so firmly associated with New Zealand that, unless you live in Mediterranea, where the Asian *Pittosporum tobira* excels as a hedge or densely foliaged small tree with fragrant flowers, it is easy to overlook species in this genus from elsewhere. South Africa is the home of *P. viridiflorum*. As solid in its own way as *P. tobira,* this broadly spreading tree is sturdily robust rather than elegant, with its speckled elephant grey bark, darkest green glossy foliage and heavy limbs. It is a pioneer species with small orange berries that attract birds, and the seeds carried in their droppings play a crucial role in the replacement of grasslands by scrub and eventually forest. This species is equally effective when called on to play a pioneering role in gardens.

New Zealand's wildlife not only remained isolated for tens of millions of years, but experienced extraordinarily turbulent conditions involving extreme tectonic activity, during which mountains rose and fell, and much of the land subsided beneath and rose again from the ocean. Plants and animals reacted in ways that make the flora and fauna of the islands uniquely interesting. Woody plants devised a form of growth, almost confined to this part of the world, in which the stems divide repeatedly to form an angular network of slender twiggy shoots. Species distributed amongst no less than twenty different families developed this divaricating growth form, as it is called. It is most often present only when the plant is immature, changing abruptly to a normal pattern with maturity. It has been suggested that the complex tracery of often sharply pointed twigs served as a defence against the moas that were formerly New Zealand's main herbivores, in much the same way that ostrich farmers around Oudtschoorn in South Africa carry branches of karoo thorn that can be used as threats to the eyes of cock birds to discourage aggressive approaches. Two divaricating plants that excite interest and comment in the garden are *Pittosporum anomalum,* an attractive low-growing shrub with small aromatic leaves and tiny yellowish flowers, and *P. obcordatum* var. *kaitaiaense,* now rare in the wild but better known in gardens. Once past its divaricating stage, the latter develops into a small, practically fastigiate tree with ivory, cream or pale purple flowers emerging directly from its branches, like a Judas tree *(Cercis siliquastrum).*

Another unusual, though not unique, peculiarity of New Zealand trees and shrubs is the significant number of species that start life as seedlings high above the ground in the forks of trees, where they may perch for years before sending roots down to ground level. In gardens these natural epiphytes can be grown in the ground like any other tree or shrub. The perching kohuhu, *Pittosporum cornifolium*, a lesser known member of the genus, is one such epiphyte, found in deep shade or sunlit situations in kauri forests. In gardens it is a strikingly effective medium-sized shrub with broad, deep green leaves.

Another pittosporum that deserves to be more widely grown is *Pittosporum umbellatum*, which has clusters of hanging bell-like, fragrant, pink to reddish flowers. It usually grows as an upright shrub or small multistemmed tree with deep crimson stems and prominent midribs, reminiscent of a *Skimmia* in the quality and texture of its foliage. Lemonwood, *P. eugenioides*, with dark brown bark and a broad head of glossy, moderately large, wavy edged leaves, is a vigorous, densely foliaged shade tree widely grown in cool temperate gardens. The clusters of pale yellow flowers are more decorative than the green or dark crimson equivalents produced by other pittosporums. 'Variegatum', a form with silver-white margins to the leaves, is also an exceptionally attractive small tree for gardens; 'Platinum' is a more recent introduction with white margins to its silvery, light green foliage. The plants that I first met on my father's nursery were forms of *P. tenuifolium*, by far the

The deep green, lustrous foliage and clusters of pale yellow flowers make lemonwood, *Pittosporum eugenioides*, an excellent evergreen tree. Marcelle Garden's garden, Avennel Station, Miller's Flat, South Island, New Zealand.

best known species, and the source of numerous cultivars. When given the space and light it needs to display its qualities, the species makes an excellent garden tree, but the numerous forms with variegated foliage are more popular. These include 'Pixie', a waist-high bush with correspondingly tiny, bright green leaves; 'Irene Paterson', with green and white foliage in a pallid shade of jade; and the compactly rounded 'Green Pillar', with fresh green foliage, which can be shaped by light pruning with a pair of shears. 'James Stirling' has small grey-green leaves and wiry black stems. 'Silver Sheen' is an open bush with black stems and pale green leaves, remarkable for the absence of veining, shading or other variations in tone. W.R. Stuart, a nurseryman in South Otago, has produced hybrids with black mapou, *P. colensoi*, that are said to be more frost tolerant. The results include 'Elizabeth', with large cream and green leaves with pink rims, most prominent in cold weather; 'Moonlight', slow growing with small yellow leaves with deep green margins; and 'Victoria', with small, pale silvery green leaves with creamy white undulating margins, flushed with pink in cold weather.

Trees from the Forests of Tasmania and Eastern Australia

Southern Chile, New Zealand's Fjordland and south-western Tasmania share wet, stormy, oceanic climates akin to those of the Atlantic coasts of Europe and the Pacific Northwest of North America. Strahan in western Tasmania, surrounded by mountains covered with temperate rainforests and by lakes amongst expanses of orange button grass, is a pleasant little town and the end of the road. Further exploration is done by boat, by taking a flight across the wilderness to the south-west, or by trekking on foot. Myrtle and sassafras dominate the forests here. Neither is what it sounds to British or American readers, but aliases for *Nothofagus cunninghamii* and *Atherosperma moschatum,* respectively. The edges of the forest and clearings within it contain other trees, none more unexpected or extraordinary than pandani, *Richea pandanifolia.* Botanically it is related to the New Zealand grass trees or dracophyllums, but is sufficiently like a pandanus palm to bring an exotic air of the South Pacific to these cool, rain-drenched forests. This strange plant has a long, slender trunk topped by a crown of lax, strap-shaped leaves and bears pink or cerise flowers in spring into midsummer. It would have tremendous potential value in gardens, if only it did not take quite so long to grow tall.

Leatherwood, *Eucryphia lucida,* is more conventionally beautiful, and the source of a honey that is one of Tasmania's gifts to the world. In nature it is a substantial evergreen tree with delicately fragile, bowl-shaped white flowers, but like so many plants from these oceanic forests, it often fails to reach its natural size in gardens. 'Pink Cloud' is named for its pink flowers, and variegated selections include 'Leatherwood Cream', with creamy white margins to the leaves, and 'Gilt Edge', with pale yellow. *Eucryphia milliganii* is compact with tiny leaves, often recommended as the ideal eucryphia for smaller gardens; but, although it starts to flower when still very young, for me it lacks the cool distinction of the other. Eucryphias also grow in Chile, one of many links with the time when the Southern Hemisphere continents were united in Gondwanaland. Anyone familiar with the well-regulated appearance of *E.* ×*nymansensis* will scarcely recognise the infant in the shape of one of its parents. When seen in maturity in the forests on the flanks of the volcanoes in the Chilean Lake District north of Puerto Montt, *E. cordifolia* is the true patriarch of the genus. Venerable, stag-headed specimens emerge from the regenerating forest of myrtles, drimys, laurels and embothriums, their massive limbs smothered with lichens and Spanish mosses amongst congested clumps of astelias and other epiphytes. A full-grown specimen covered from top to bottom with clusters of single, bowl-shaped white flowers is one of the inspirational sights of the world of trees.

The cool montane forests of Tasmania are illuminated by the scarlet flowers of another small tree that many gardeners would, as the saying goes, be ready to die for. The Tasmanian waratah, *Telopea truncata,* usually found on fertile soils derived from dolerite, has trim blue-green foliage and disc-shaped heads of conspicuous scarlet-crimson flowers surrounded by equally colourful bracts. Forms with beautiful clear yellow flowers have been found several times, the first and best known on the slopes of Cathedral Rock above Hobart. It is a relatively hardy and, after an often slow start, amenable garden plant with an attractive branching form. The same can scarcely be said for the more famous New South Wales waratah, *T. speciosissima.* A clump of these at the Olinda Rhododendron Gardens in the Dandenong Hills east of Melbourne exemplified all the attractions and all the drawbacks of this plant. The flowers are a glorious dusky, velvety crimson-scarlet grouped in opulent hemispherical heads a handbreadth across, with an ooh-aah quality that was not in the least diminished by comparison with the most gorgeous rhododendrons. The effect is spoilt by the stance of the shoots, with the flowers awkwardly and gracelessly stuck on the top of long, straight stems. Hard pruning as the flowers fade is recommended to correct this defect, but seldom results in a truly well formed plant. In gardens it can be a finicky, difficult plant, but for years gardeners were too besotted by its beauty to recognise the attractions of other, more amenable relatives.

Waratahs grow in south-eastern Australia on deep, humus-rich, fertile soils. Heavy loams suit most of them in gardens, provided they drain freely, except for *Telopea speciosissima*, which grows naturally on sands and responds better to lighter soils. All benefit from surface mulches. Waratahs have a reputation for establishing slowly, and there is a belief that a spadeful of soil from around an older plant encourages transplants to grow better. This points, once again, to symbiotic associations with mycorrhizal fungi—which is curious because, in general, the Proteaceae are one of the few families that, it is believed, do not form such associations. The Gippsland waratah, *T. oreades*, is a relatively hardy and easily grown species with disc-shaped heads of flowers. It has been hybridised with *T. speciosissima* to produce the Shady Lady series, in which the bold globular flower heads of the latter are combined with the more amenable nature of the former. Other

In late summer *Eucryphia cordifolia,* an impressively large and rugged evergreen tree, becomes covered with bowl-shaped white flowers. Logan Botanic Garden, Stranraer, Scotland.

cultivars include 'Cardinal', with bright crimson-scarlet flowers, and 'Fire & Brimstone', with large leaves and large heads of bright red flowers. Hybrids with the Braidwood waratah, *T. monganensis,* are floriferous and compact, amongst them 'Braidwood Brilliant', with brick red flowers in spring, 'Burgundy', with velvety crimson flowers, and 'Canberry Coronet', in which the inflorescences lack the normally prominent scarlet bracts. Flowers without bracts are more popular with florists than gardeners because, although beautiful, the bracts are fragile and easily damaged in transit. 'Wirrimbirra White' is a cultivar with heads of greenish white flowers, and the crimson flowers of 'Fire 'n Ice', as its name suggests, are marked with white.

The Tasmanian waratahs grow on deep, fertile soils in places where rainfall can exceed 1000 millimetres a year. Their companions include *Eucalyptus delegatensis, E. regnans, E. obliqua* and *E. sieberi,* all valuable hardwood-timber species whose high canopies and open growth allow numerous shrubs and other plants to grow beneath them. This extraordinarily flexible and prolific genus is a peculiarly Australian institution, occupying a bewildering variety of habitats and situations. Until recently, few eucalypts were considered reliably hardy, a belief that could scarcely survive even the shortest visit to the ski resorts in the snow fields of New South Wales or Victoria. On my way there from Melbourne, the first climb up from the meadows and vineyards of the Yarra Valley brought me into forests of messmate, *E. obliqua,* and mountain ash, *E. regnans,* around Black Spur. The latter is a monumental species, rivalling the karris and tingles of Western Australia in size and impact. The lower parts of its trunks are covered with rough bark, transformed as they ascend into smooth, marbled grey columns beneath a compact canopy of silvery leaves 50 metres and more above the ground. These species, and other relatively hardy ones such as *E. delegatensis, E. cypellocarpa* and *E. dalrympleana,* extend far up the mountains, often towering above the smooth tree fern, *Dicksonia antarctica,* sheltered in damp gullies, till, nearly 1500 metres above sea level just below the ski resort of Falls Creek, they are replaced by snow gums, *E. pauciflora.* When first encountered, the snow gums are tall with sinuous ivory, grey and greenish brown stems, but they steadily become smaller, more weatherbeaten and contorted as one ascends to Falls Creek and onto the exposed landscape of the Bogong High Plains. This windswept plateau, with its frequent frosts in winter and snow cover for months on end, tests the hardiness of any plant, but forests of snow gums cover some of its highest and most exposed slopes.

The Bogong High Plains and other Australian highlands, including nearby Mount Buffalo, Mount Kosciusko and mountains in western Tasmania like Cradle Mountain, are a storehouse of hardy shrubs that gardeners worldwide are only beginning to tap. Foresters use the word *provenance* to specify where stocks of seed were collected, and they recognise the importance of matching origin (provenance) with the conditions in which the trees will be growing in plantations. Hitherto, gardeners have paid little attention to provenance, preferring to create conditions in which plants will thrive irrespective of their origin. But attitudes are changing, and the prospects of finding hardy forms amongst plants that grow naturally in the high, cold places of the world are exciting more interest, nowhere more so than with eucalypts. This genus is of major importance to foresters, whose experience has finally persuaded gardeners that if they want hardy eucalypts they should look for them amongst the Tasmanian mountains, the Bogong High Plains and similar places.

Putting good advice into practise, and following extensive trials by the Forestry Commission in Britain, Celyn Vale Nurseries in Wales have targeted eucalypts that grow naturally in places with unusually cold winters, frequent out-of-season frosts and exceptional exposure to the effects of wind-chill. As a result of this attention to the plants' provenance, Celyn Vale have put together a remarkable collection of hardy eucalypts, several of which survive temperatures as low as $-14°C$ ($7°F$). The snow gum, *Eucalyptus pauciflora,* long recognised for its hardiness, makes an outstanding garden tree with conspicuous, subtly painted python skin bark. In nature the trees seldom grow straight or single-stemmed, and in gardens too should not be staked or planted individually. Planting the inclined or twisted stems of several snow gums close together in one or more clusters is the most effective way to present them. An equally hardy, graceful weeping form known as 'Pendula', with upright main stems and trailing shoots, was found growing on the cold Kiandra Plain in the Kosciusko National Park of New South Wales. The jounama snow gum, *E. debeuzevillei,* from the mountains above Canberra, is reputed to be one of the hardiest of all eucalypts, and is also tolerant of exposure to high winds and salt spray. The spinning gum, *E. per-*

riniana, is another decorative species from the mountains of Victoria and New South Wales with glaucous foliage and boldly formed circular leaves, long grown by gardeners with mixed success until the importance of provenance became recognised.

Several species from high, wet sclerophyll forests across the Bass Strait in Tasmania grow well in gardens that are wet or cold or both. These include the alpine cider gum, *Eucalyptus archeri,* and the common cider gum, *E. gunnii,* with grey-green or silver foliage. The mountain gum, *E. dalrympleana,* is hardy and naturally adapted to base-rich soils, and the Tasmanian snow gum, *E. coccifera,* is a small to medium-sized tree found on rocky, doleritic outcrops, often in exposed, cold situations where snow is not unusual. Like many Australian trees and shrubs, these eucalypts develop a more compact, denser, bushy form with light tip-pruning, which consists of removing the tips of the shoots with no more than one or two leaves—simulating the kind of light grazing that kangaroos might perform naturally—and should be repeated frequently during the plants' formative years. The work sounds simple, and is not physically demanding, but you will quickly discover the enormously large numbers of tips even a moderately small eucalypt offers the pruner to prune.

I first visited the Garden of St Erth in Victoria when its creator, Tommy Garnett, was close to being forced by infirmity to find someone to take it on. A year or two later I returned to find the garden undergoing a new lease of life under the care of Clive Blazey, founder of the Digger's Club. I had previously admired Clive's successful synthesis of European styles and Australian opportunities in Heronswood, his garden on the Mornington Peninsula south of Melbourne, and will be interested to see what he makes of the rather different problems and possibilities of St Erth. Winters there can be cold and windy, and in the early days of the garden an Omeo gum, *Eucalyptus neglecta,* was decapitated by a gust of wind but regenerated so successfully that most of the eucalypts in the garden are now regularly pollarded. Eucalypts retain epicormic buds, buried in the bark where leaves once emerged, from which they regenerate rapidly and vigorously when cut back—a practise that has been standard treatment for cider gums and spinning gums in chilly British gardens for many years. The new shoots revert to an immature form, producing leaves that are often more colourful and more attractively diverse than the mature foliage of untreated trees. Some species respond particularly satisfactorily, including *E. archeri,* with silvery pink immature foliage; *E. coccifera,* with neat apple green immature leaves often flushed with crimson; *E. glaucescens,* with brilliantly silvery blue foliage; *E. nicholii,* with characteristically long narrow leaves, like those of a willow; and *E. subcrenulata,* with distinctive, lightly glossy, apple green foliage often more or less suffused with bronze.

Between the forests of snow gums on the windswept Bogong High Plains, expanses of heath contain alpine representatives of many genera introduced in earlier chapters. Grevilleas growing here include the royal grevillea, *Grevillea victoriae,* with striking terminal inflorescences of red flowers, and the alpine spider flower, *G. australis,* a prostrate shrub with night-scented, pinky white flowers. The endemic Bogong daisy bush *Olearia frostii* displays its pink, lilac or white flowers above grey, lightly felted, velvety leaves. The gardener's favourite *O. phlogopappa* also grows here, with flowers that reproduce the colours and appearance of michaelmas daisies. One or two species of hardy mint bushes tempt gardeners in cold places to give them a try, amongst them the showy Victorian Christmas bush, *Prostanthera lasianthos.* This upright shrub has aromatic leaves and large, irregularly petalled white flowers with orange and purple markings. The beautiful little alpine mint bush, *P. cuneata,* forms a dome of small, almost stemless, aromatic leaves densely covered with ragged, bell-shaped, pale mauve flowers. A small and spiky relative of pandani, the candle heath, *Richea continentis,* is another plant of these high plains, and the only member of its genus found outside Tasmania. Its upright stems with narrow, closely overlapping leaves are topped by "candles" of white flowers. Groups of lemon bottlebrushes, *Callistemon pallidus,* a shrub or, sometimes, small tree with pale yellow heads of flowers on stiff stems, grow in the wetter parts of the heaths and along streamsides.

CHAPTER 10

Flowers of the Forest

T HE JOYS of my visits to the Looking-Glass Garden went far beyond discovering strange plants and new ways to use them. They included travels through magnificent countryside, encounters with native birds and animals, visits to out-of-the-way corners I would never otherwise have gone to, and, above all, the pleasure of meeting other gardeners, amongst them Jeanne Villani. Jeanne responded to my request to visit her garden near Manly, Australia, with a warm welcome and an offer to take me to other gardens in and around Sydney that I would like to see—a gift indeed for a visitor to a city in which the road network had been reduced to a baffling maze by preparations for the 2000 Olympic Games. Jeanne's streamside garden, Waterfall Cottage, lies on steeply sloping ground amongst rainforest. Stone walls and flights of steps uncovered during clearing operations confirmed rumours of a previous garden; and camellias, abelias, hibiscus and hydrangeas emerged as testimony to a garden made there earlier by someone with nostalgic memories of England.

Frost and exposure have minimal impact here, soils are fertile, and rainfall is adequate or ample, except during periodic droughts, and the plants virtually never stop growing. It sounds like the Garden of Eden, and perhaps it is, but before The Fall that garden must have been maintained by angels—at least Adam and Eve had plenty of time to get up to mischief; afterwards they had to learn to wrestle with weeds. And in situations like these where there is no off-season for plant growth, weeds, pests and diseases display a relentless quality unknown to those whose gardening year is punctuated by periods of drought or cold, which slow down the pace of

Previous pages: In places like this garden in the rainforests near Sydney—where frost and exposure have minimal impact, soils are fertile and rainfall generally adequate or ample—conditions are so favourable for plants that they virtually never stop growing. It sounds idyllic, but poses problems for gardeners of the orthodox persuasion, and alternative means of holding the garden in check must be devised. Waterfall Cottage, Jeanne Villani's garden, Bayview, New South Wales, Australia.

242

events. For easy to grow does not mean easy to garden. Competition is intense and the plants that survive are those adapted to make most effective use of light, water, nutrients and other resources, by growing vigorously and overshadowing their neighbours, or are able to function when overshadowed and in perpetual shade—for here there is no season of the year when the leaves fall from the trees and allow light to reach plants at lower levels.

The overgrown orthodox English garden before Jeanne's would have survived only as long as weeds were kept at bay, and would have been overwhelmed within a season when left to itself. Jeanne's new garden takes its inspiration from the natural structure of the rainforest in which it is made, and the plants themselves control much of what goes on. It is a form of gardening which I would call "Matrix Planting" and which Phoebe Noble, who gardens near Victoria on Vancouver Island in Canada, refers to more picturesquely as "Layer-cake Gardening." The planting is relaxed and informal, with layers of tree ferns, shrubs and perennials beneath a canopy of coachwoods, *Ceratopetalum apetalum*. The tree canopy, taller shrubs and immature trees filter out much of the sunlight, and maintain shaded, sheltered, humid conditions for the plants below; the lower layers of smaller shrubs, perennials, ferns and bulbs reduce light reaching the soil surface, to levels that make life impossible for most weed seedlings.

The wildlife, too, revealed differences between this rainforest setting and the familiar gardens of my home in Shropshire. A kookaburra sat on a branch, on the lookout for lizards; flocks of little fire-tailed finches descended on the bird table; brightly coloured rosellas flew between the trees; and the distinctive calls of whip birds replaced the trills of blackbirds and wrens. Familiar complaints about rabbits, deer, moles, the neighbour's cats and the minor delinquencies of jays, sparrows and badgers were replaced by descriptions of the varied tastes and capacities for inflicting damage of wallabies, possums, spiny anteaters, lyre birds and bandicoots.

In this kind of gardening the management of trees, especially the ways their shade and presence are used to create atmosphere and provide a setting for the plants beneath them, is the key to success. The woodland floras of the evergreen, warm temperate rainforests of Australia, South Africa, New Zealand and South America, in particular, offer a huge choice of trees, shrubs, perennials and other plants that thrive in shade, some in situations that are periodically sunlit or lightly shaded on the woodland edge, others in the deepest recesses of the forest.

Forming a Forest

Few gardeners enjoy favoured patches of rainforest around Sydney or live in places like the Waitakere Forests in New Zealand or the Karkloof in the Natal Midlands, and for those who do not, this talk about trees might seem irrelevant. Later in this chapter, I make fleeting reference to the "jungle" at Lotusland, which might reassure those without trees who would like to have them. The blessings of Santa Barbara's climate do not include abundant year-round rainfall, and forests of this kind do not occur in the surrounding countryside. It had to be made from scratch, by someone who refused to acknowledge that climates, soils and other natural features should be allowed to limit her imagination. Imagination, you might say, but also time. Trees take years to grow, and in nature the combinations of trees, shrubs, vines, ground-covering perennials and ferns that compose a forest come together after aeons of growth, and decline as one set of plants succeeds another in a series of transformations that can last thousands of years. The kauris, *Agathis australis,* that overawe us in the Northland forests of New Zealand are only one stage in a series of changes, each lasting a millennium and more, that ultimately prepare the way for forests of tawa, *Beilschmiedia tawa,* and other broad-leaved evergreen trees. With time scales like that, thoughts of creating forests in our gardens tend to be relegated to the back-burner.

But Nature can be fast-forwarded. Events and transformations that would take hundreds or thousands of years—if they happen at all—can be compressed into a decade or two, and on a scale that matches the space that gardens provide. Jill and Roelf Attwell's garden in Betty's Bay overlooks the Atlantic Ocean on the southern coast of Africa. In origin and appearance, most of the garden might be described as managed coastal fynbos, in essence a heathland of small shrubs, perennials and bulbs in which each plant provides its neighbours with shelter from wind and protection from salt spray. It lacks most of the qualities that forest trees depend on for survival, yet within it there is a forest—one that measures only a few square metres. This forest was made from scratch by planting carefully chosen trees. Cape holly, *Ilex mitis*—ultimately a substantial tree with whitish bark and shiny dark

green, entire leaves that produces shiny red berries eaten and spread by
birds—grows beside the pioneer species *Pittosporum viridiflorum*, and wild
peach, *Kiggelaria africana*, with the tree fuchsia, *Halleria lucida*, and camphor
wood, *Tarchonanthus camphoratus*, a pioneer tree recognised for its value as
a dune stabiliser. Growing with them is *Protea mundi*, a tree protea that appreciates the areas of permanently moist soil created by seepage from the
springs here. The space occupied is tiny, the trees crowded together, but the
resemblance to forest is so real that the forest birds come to it to feed on the
fruits and nectar.

The birds in Jill and Roelf's garden reminded me of another, more ambitious attempt to create a forest. Tiritiri Matangi, an island in New Zealand's Hauraki Gulf National Park, is a short boat trip across the 4 kilometres of sea that have kept it free from cats, ferrets and most other predators.
Those that were there have been eliminated, and the island has been made
into a refuge for New Zealand native birds. Many of these birds are flight-
less, or poor fliers, and such easy prey to predators that they more or less disappeared from the mainland after the arrival of the Pakeha. The island was
farmed for many years, when most of the woody plants were destroyed.
Now the grassy paddocks are being planted with trees to provide food and
shelter for the birds, which at present depend largely on the patches of natural forest that survived in a few gullies. Speed is of the essence; the birds
cannot wait, and its value as a reserve depends on their well-being.

Tree planting follows the natural successions that would lead to the re-
establishment of native bush, but vastly speeded up. First the pioneer species go in, planted amongst the grasses, which are neither killed by herbicides nor mown. These first species are a mixture of trees and shrubs naturally adapted to grow in exposed windswept situations, and capable of the
vigorous growth necessary to shade out grasses and weeds. They include
ngaio, *Myoporum laetum*, a tree that grows naturally along coastal or lowland
forest margins; koromiko, *Hebe stricta*; several kinds of New Zealand brooms,
Carmichaelia spp.; pohutukawa, *Metrosideros excelsus*, that great standby for
seaside situations; tauhinu, *Cassiope leptophylla*; and *Coprosma robusta*, to in-
crease the density of the undergrowth and help suppress the grasses.

Only a couple of years later, these trees and shrubs are interplanted with
vigorous species that can tolerate wind and high light levels, but need a little shelter, including several that provide food for birds. The cabbage tree

Cordyline australis has proved its worth, also kowhai, *Sophora tetraptera*, a small tree with clusters of yellow nectar-bearing flowers; taupata, *Coprosma repens*, a large shrub with glossy leaves, naturally confined to coastal situations; kanuka, *Kunzea ericoides*; five-finger, *Pseudopanax arboreus*, a small, much-branched, round-headed tree; and houpara, *P. lessonii*, from coastal forests and scrub. Wharangi, *Melicope ternata*, is a large shrub or small tree that grows along the margins of coastal and lowland forests. Flax, *Phormium tenax*, and akeake, *Olearia traversii*, also grow vigorously in these conditions and provide excellent shelter. Somewhat surprisingly, puriri, *Vitex lucens*, an exceptionally beautiful true forest tree, also succeeds at this stage.

Only five years later, this fledgling forest is ready to receive the true forest species that will eventually suppress the lesser trees and shrubs that gave them shelter, to become the dominant species of the forest canopy. They include rewarewa, *Knightia excelsa*, a tall slender tree with considerable character and attractive and interesting spiky, crimson and yellow flowers; this species is tolerant of relatively dry situations and makes a good garden plant. Also planted are kohekohe, *Dysoxylum spectabile*, suitable only for mild, relatively sheltered districts where frosts are not severe; karaka, *Corynocarpus laevigatus*, a densely leafy canopy tree that is moderately tolerant of exposure and can be used as a hedge in seaside situations; and pigeonwood, *Hedycarya arborea*, a small, erect tree, with aromatic foliage and bright reddish orange drupes, that needs sheltered sites and protection from frosts during the first few years. The trees on Tiritiri Matangi are not a forest yet, and will not be for many years, but already they provide cover for the birds, as well as the berries, nectar and insects that the birds need for food. They also provide food for thought for gardeners in exposed situations or in places bereft of trees, and a living demonstration of their resilience and capacity for growth—given an understanding of their needs and a little tender loving care.

Rainforest Trees Suitable for Gardens

Although unusual in the rainforest, deciduous trees have special value for gardeners in places where evergreens prevail. Aesthetically, they introduce diversity; ecologically, they provide spaces in which plants can be grown that need more light in certain seasons. One of the most attractive deciduous trees for the shady garden is red cedar, *Toona ciliata*. Formerly widespread around Sydney, this species has excellent, easily worked timber that was too tempting for loggers to resist, and it was almost logged out in early colonial days. It is an imposing, fast-growing tree with pink flowers and glossy pinnate foliage, but in gardens the buds of the leading shoots are liable to be destroyed by infestations of tip moths, resulting in a branching, multilimbed tree rather than one with a strong central leader. *Brachychiton bidwillii* has flowers like velvety red balls followed by clusters of "glove-fingered" fruits, and the broad-leaved bottletree, *B. australis,* has fairly small, bell-shaped flowers and broad, deeply lobed leaves that fall during the summer. The South African Cape chestnut, *Calodendrum capense,* is semi-deciduous, tending to be more or less completely so in cooler situations. Its clouds of pink flowers and deep green glossy foliage are a memorable sight in the forests around Knysna on the border of the Western and Eastern Cape Provinces during spring and summer. Another deciduous tree, seldom grown in gardens, is the marula, *Sclerocarya birrea* subsp. *caffra,* from KwaZulu-Natal. It forms an attractive bole and broadly spreading crown. Its yellow berries smell cloyingly sweet, and the white slimy pulp looks less than appetising, but try them—they make a pleasant drink, and the seeds taste of walnuts.

Although usually shrubby and addicted to sunlight, grevilleas include a few rainforest trees. *Grevillea hilliana,* a tall, upright tree with numerous long, lacy racemes of white flowers, is one; another is the better known silky oak, *G. robusta,* which has large orange inflorescences and deeply lobed foliage that contrasts most effectively with the entire, rather solid leaves of many evergreens. The firewheel tree, *Stenocarpus sinuatus,* has even more striking inflorescences, consisting of a ring of bright scarlet flowers like spokes of a wheel around a central disc—not unlike those of the Tasmanian waratah, *Telopea truncata,* but all the more valuable for being produced in autumn.

Numerous rainforest species attract birds and other wildlife in search of nectar-bearing flowers or fruits. Figs like the Moreton Bay, *Ficus macrophylla,* are pre-eminent fruit producers over long periods. This magnificent tree, with buttressed roots, elephant grey bark, massive limbs and broad glossy foliage, is almost a rainforest in itself. Too big for many gardens, and inclined to produce continuous carpets of fallen fruit that tidy gardeners find intolerable, the Moreton Bay fig needs careful placing. It is a menace overhanging a lawn and should never, ever, as I once saw in California, be planted by a swimming pool. The Port Jackson fig, *F. rubiginosa*, is another substantial, but less overpowering, tree that tolerates dry situations better than most of the trees referred to here. Its yellow fruits turn red and are dotted with warts. The medium-sized tree fuchsia, *Halleria lucida*, from South Africa has clusters of rusty red tubular flowers growing straight from the trunk and stems. The flowers attract sun birds, honey-eaters and other nectar-feeding birds, from autumn to spring in winter rainfall areas, and during spring and early summer where winters are cold. Numerous fruit-eating birds are also attracted by the black berries that follow the flowers. The wild plum, *Harpephyllum caffrum*, from the same part of the world, is a broadly spreading, medium-sized, round-topped tree with pinnate foliage like that of an ash. The small, oval, rather sour, rusty red fruits produced by the female trees are poor apologies for plums, but birds and fruit-eating bats enjoy them—with unfortunate results when fences, paths, cars and whatever else lies beneath their roosts become stained with crimson droppings.

Several rainforest trees are notable for the beauty of their foliage, including the Australian lilly pillys like the white apple, *Syzygium cormiflorum*, with creamy white flowers directly from its trunks and main limbs, and the rose apple, *Syzygium moorei*, with masses of bright pink, fluffy flowers during the summer. The immature foliage of both species is pink and crimson, turning pale lime-green before maturing to a deep, glossy green, on gracefully pendant young shoots. As with the wild plum, the name "apple" owes more to imagination than to reality, but lorikeets and other parrots accept them enthusiastically. Two Australian rainforest trees that are now widely grown in gardens are the umbrella tree, *Schefflera actinophylla*, and the native frangipani, *Hymenosporum flavum*. The former has leathery, glossy dark green leaves that hang in clusters of up to sixteen from the tips of the branches; its tiny bright red flowers, curious rather than beautiful, emerge on stout brown stalks radiating from the tips of the shoots like octopus tentacles. The Australian native frangipani is a fast-growing small to medium-sized pioneer tree grown for its fragrant, scrambled-egg flowers—opening creamy white and turning yellow as they mature, in spring. A form that grows no larger than a shrub has limited appeal and an even more limited inclination to produce flowers.

On first acquaintance, the colourful flowers, fruits and even foliage of the forest trees of Australia and South Africa outshine those from New Zealand. But the tui appeals to me as an apt metaphor for the New Zealand flora. Seen perched, or skulking, half hidden in a tree, the tui is a bird of limited appeal: clothed overall in black, relieved only by a few tufts of white feathers around the neck, a clerical dress more suited to the presbytery than the garden. Then it calls — a fluting, melodious and distinctive call as beautiful as any blackbird's or gold finch's and yet entirely different to these Northern Hemisphere introductions. Or as it moves amongst the branches of a kowhai, *Sophora tetraptera,* probing the golden flowers for nectar, its sombre dress turns into an iridescent mantle in the sunlight, cloaking its back and shoulders with filigreed silver and gold that shimmers and glistens with the bird's movements. The trees and shrubs of the New Zealand bush present a sombre guise of heavy, verdant foliage and flowers that play endless themes on shades of green and white. But on other occasions or in different situations, they display unexpected subtleties of colour, texture and form.

Kohekohe, *Dysoxylum spectabile,* mentioned earlier, has spectacularly glossy, large leaves. Even when young it produces long, drooping panicles of creamy white flowers, sprouting directly from the trunk and main

Kowhai, *Sophora tetraptera,* grows into a small, spreading tree notable for its racemes of nectar-bearing, bright golden yellow flowers. Larnach Castle, near Dunedin, South Island, New Zealand.

branches, followed a year later by capsules that split to display black seeds enclosed by fleshy, scarlet fruits known as arils. It flowers every other year, so that flowers and fruit, although produced at similar seasons, alternate year by year. Few forest evergreens have a more notable display of flowers than the ratas. *Metrosideros umbellatus* and *M. robustus*, the southern and northern ratas, respectively, both frequently start life as epiphytes, high above the ground, but in gardens can be planted and treated like any other tree. They flower so profusely in good years that the entire tree becomes crimson-scarlet, and hybrids with the pohutukawa, *M. excelsus*, have produced a variety of different-coloured flowers. Their display varies from year to year, and in places disappoints more often than not, especially where possums, which enjoy the flowers as a delicacy, are numerous. The New Zealand tree fuchsia, *Fuchsia excorticata*, lacks the brightly coloured flowers and obvious garden charms of hybrids from South America, but it more than pays its way in gardens. It grows naturally in quite extraordinarily varied situations. I have met it on dry exposed ridges in the Port Hills above Christchurch, and in the wettest parts of the moss-enshrouded Goblin Forests on Mount Taranaki, where the gnarled, twisted, rusty brown trunks with bark peeling in long strips cluster in small groups. Elsewhere they grow immersed in the chilly, swift-flowing waters of Pupu Springs near Nelson, and along the cold divide of the Southern Alps pass that leads to Milford Sound, where it is regularly exposed to frosts and heavy snowfalls. The nectar in their inconspicuous green and purple flowers is a valuable resource to bellbirds and tuis during the winter and spring, and the berries that follow attract a variety of fruit-eating birds. The New Zealand tree fuchsia is an excellent small tree in gardens where, pruned to thin out the lower branches to display the multiple sinuous stems and peeling bark, a group becomes a little grove full of atmosphere and interest.

Climbers in the Forest

Gardeners tend to be wary of climbers, but many are most useful garden plants that add an extra dimension to woodland gardens, not necessarily by climbing over the trees but by decorating structures like pergolas and arbours in more controllable situations close to the ground. The pure white puawhanganga, *Clematis paniculata*, is a moderately vigorous climber from New Zealand, as is its Australian look-alike, *C. aristata*. If these are too vigorous for you, the natural hybrid between *C. aristata* and the clump-form-ing *C. gentianoides,* known as 'Garden Surprise', is a plant of most modest vigour that produces propeller-shaped white flowers in spring. *Clematis hookeriana* is another New Zealand clematis, seldom seen in gardens, but most desirable nonetheless, with fragrant pale ochre or green flowers. The South African *Jasminum multipartitum,* notable for the intense fragrance of its large, pure white flowers offset by deep green glossy foliage, is naturally a vigorous climber that can be curbed by hard pruning after flowering.

The Australian wonga vine, *Pandorea pandorana,* is a vigorous climber that develops over time into an impressive multistemmed liane with robust, sin-uous stems dividing into a mass of twining, twiggy branchlets, as you dis-cover when you sit beneath its shade on the terrace at the Mount Tomah Botanic Garden in the Blue Mountains. The flowers are usually soft straw yel-low, but forms exist with white, gold, pink, red-brown, purple or maroon flowers. The related bower plant, *P. jasminoides,* is another vigorous climb-ing shrub with clusters of much larger white to pink flowers with maroon centres. 'Pink Magic' is a recent introduction with deep rose-pink flowers.

The Australian coral peas include several useful climbing or scrambling

Puawhanganga, *Clematis paniculata,* is a floriferous climber with clusters of white flowers that illuminate New Zealand's evergreen forests. Cobb Lake, near Takaka, South Island, New Zealand.

shrubs. *Kennedia rubicunda*, the red bean or dusky coral pea, is a rampant, irrepressible plant with ground-covering capacity that puts it in the "mega" league, but which also makes a fast-growing, effective and decorative screen. The dusky red flowers are produced in small clusters amongst handsome, heavy, dark green foliage with well-defined texture and a light sheen; the flowers are followed by decorative seed capsules. *Kennedia nigricans* is another vigorous climber, also attractive to birds, and remarkable for its extraordinary black and yellow flowers. Happy wanderer, *Hardenbergia violacea*, an evergreen climber with masses of violet-purple flowers in spring, also has considerable covering capacity. The equally vigorous 'Free 'n Easy' has white flowers blotched with crimson. For gardeners who need them, there are cultivars with more restrained ambitions, including 'Mini-haha', a low-spreading plant with deep violet flowers.

Eccremocarpus scaber from Chile and *Thunbergia alata* from the Knysna forests in South Africa have glowing orange flowers, the first tubular, the second broadly open—and there are garden forms of both with flowers in various shades of cream, yellow, orange, flame or red. These short-lived climbers are easily grown from seed, flower in their first year, and provide excellent stop-gap coverage for pergolas, arbours and other structures. Another climber from the Chilean forests is the highly desirable but rather elusive *Lapageria rosea*, with deep green leaves and pendant, crimson-rose, tubular flowers. This cool beauty from the shadowed depths of the forests needs humid atmospheres, shaded root runs and equable conditions to grow well.

The spectacular flowering display of the Natal flame bush, *Alberta magna*, is extended by the scarlet bracts that remain colourful after the flowers fall. Andrew Wilson's garden, San Diego, California, United States.

Shrubs for Shady Places

Shrubs occupy the lower layers in matrix gardening, a hopelessly shaded situation for those that live naturally in the fynbos or open bush, but the natural home of many forest species. The Natal flame bush, *Alberta magna*, eventually becomes a small tree, but is generally seen in gardens as a large shrub. It has splendid tubular scarlet flowers, all the better for their equally scarlet bracts that remain colourful until the end of summer. The plant is reputed to grow well only on rich, fertile soils well supplied with water, but I have seen it thriving in the hot, dry conditions of southern California. *Mackaya bella* is pretty and amenable and will grow almost as a climber, scrambling into plants around it, but hard pruning after flowering limits its exploratory tendencies. The delicate-looking tubular, pale lilac flowers have broadly flared open ends and finely drawn crimson veins. Frosts cut this shrub back, and can kill it, but it grows well in shade, sheltered beneath overhanging evergreen trees. If you enjoy a little drama in the garden, you might like to try a shrub I first met in Lynn Page's imaginatively planted indigenous garden in the Natal Midlands. The pistol bush, *Duvernoia adhatodoides*, is worth growing for its dense clusters of slightly fragrant white flowers veined with lightly traced crimson pencilling and its large, deep green, slightly glossy foliage. But this plant truly announces its presence when the seed pods crack open with loud snaps, like mini-explosions of the percussion caps of toy pistols.

The Vireyan Rhododendrons

First impressions of the Looking-Glass Garden might disappoint gardeners looking for new treasures to grow. They would look vainly for roses, as none grows naturally in the Southern Hemisphere; would find no new species of cherries, silver birches or magnolias. There are no delphiniums, hostas, daylilies, true lilies or lupins—and, would you believe it, no rhododendrons? Or so I, like many others, thought, until I came across *Rhododendron lochiae* in the Temperate House at the Royal Botanic Gardens, Kew, and was astonished to discover that it came from Queensland. Like many gardeners familiar with the rhododendrons to be seen in England or the Pacific Northwest of the United States, I had encountered innumerable kinds of these sumptuous plants without suspecting the existence of a vast group, numbering one in three of the species in existence. Vireyan rhododendrons, as they are called, grow in forests along the mountains that stretch through Malaysia and extend beyond the equator, through the chain of Indonesian islands to New Guinea, and eventually to the Cape York Peninsula in Australia. They are one of gardening's better kept secrets.

Most vireyan rhododendrons are epiphytes, perching on trees or bedding down on leaf and bark litter on the forest floor. They grow in the tropics, and the temperate seasons of spring, summer and winter mean nothing to them; instead they grow, flower or become dormant in cycles that respond to rainfall and drought. Flowers, leaf shapes and general appearances vary, depending on where the plants live and the ways their flowers are pollinated. Some hold nectar in tubular or trumpet-shaped, cerise-pink, red or purple flowers that attract birds. Others produce their nectar for bats, and their fragrant flowers are large and pale to attract attention at night, with short, broad tubes for the bats' short, broad tongues. Those with equally sweetly scented pale flowers with long, narrow tubes are designed to be pollinated by moths, and butterflies are attracted by brilliantly coloured yellow, orange, or flame flowers with broad petals for them to land on.

Vireyan rhododendrons live in the mountains, but none survives more than a degree or two of frost. A few—including *Rhododendron macgregoriae*, forms of *R. javanicum*, *R. commonae* from high forests in Papua New Guinea, and *R. saxifragoides* from alpine parts of the same country—are sometimes referred to as hardy, but this highly relative term should not be interpreted too optimistically. On the other hand, their inclination to flower when periods of drought are followed by rain makes it possible, by alternately withholding and then providing water, to bring the plants into flower more than

Vireyan rhododendrons such as *Rhododendron phaeochitum* provide gardeners with a new view of a well-known genus. The Royal Botanic Garden, Edinburgh, Scotland.

once a year. In the treetops, where they live on layers of moss and litter, waterlogging is practically unknown, and nutrients, phosphates in particular, are normally in short supply. In gardens they do best in very free draining, well-aerated composts or soils containing mixtures of coarse organic and mineral particles and low levels of nutrients; they do not always have to be grown as epiphytes. At Eden Gardens in Auckland plants thrive in the hollow sections of tree ferns set in the ground with their upper third above the surrounding soil level.

The intensity and clarity of colour of the vireyan's flowers provide relief from the puce, mauve and purplish magenta tones so often seen in rhododendrons, and their varied shapes will surprise aficionados familiar with the legions of hardy cultivars. The fragile-looking, white, bell-shaped flowers of *Rhododendron taxifolium* are produced amongst yew-like foliage. *Rhododendron nervulosum* has long, willow-like leaves and clear, bright orange, bell-shaped flowers with flared mouths. *Rhododendron stenophyllum,* also with glowing orange, short, bell-shaped flowers, is an upright shrub from Sarawak in Malaysia, and is remarkable for its podocarp-like foliage. *Rhododendron phaeochitum* is an unusual and arrestingly beautiful species from New Guinea with clusters of long, tubular, curved, pink flowers; a dense, tan-coloured indumentum covers the young shoots and undersides of the leaves. Perhaps the largest flowers of any vireyan are the deep carmine, tubular flowers of *R. leucogigas,* which shade to white at the tips of their flared ends. *Rhododendron christii* has pointed, textured leaves surrounding the stems in whorls of three, and lime-green, tubular flowers with brick red flared ends.

Plants for the Ground Layer

When the overhead matrix of trees and shrubs has been well constructed, the ground beneath will be in shadow most or all the time. When the forest floor is filled with plants that thrive in shade, no room is left for intruders to make themselves at home. An example of the effects created by this kind of planting surprised me on my way to the Cycad Garden at Lotusland along a path through an area of "jungle" where shell ginger *Alpinia zerumbet, Clivia miniata,* and *Philodendron* grew beneath *Eucalyptus* and the broadleaved, wild banana, *Strelitzia nicolai.* Few plants are more tenacious or tolerant of shade than clivias from the dark recesses of evergreen forests in summer rainfall areas of South Africa. Their leaves maintain a fine balance that stops just short of coarseness, and their flowers combine the most dangerous tones of orange in a glowing intensity that nevertheless displays subtlety and refinement. Now hybridisers are busy producing flowers with greater substance that too often descends to voluptuous coarseness, in colours that range from ivory-white through pale yellow to orange and on to flame tones. Most that I have seen demonstrate how easy it is to be gulled into paying more and faring worse for the sake of novelty. A close relative of *C. miniata*, *C. nobilis* has a distinctively different inflorescence with clusters of pendant, pale orange, green-tipped tubular flowers at the tops of its stout stems. It also thrives in deep shade, but comes from the Eastern Cape Province, where there is no regular dry season, and is less drought tolerant than the other species.

The Australian stream lily, *Helmholtzia glaberrima*, is a distinctively beautiful plant for lightly shaded, moist situations. It produces spikes of pale pink flowers amongst sword-shaped leaves during the summer. Continuing with the theme of narrow, grass-like leaves—the sort of plants that might be used to emphasise qualities of grassiness in combination with forest cabbage trees and climbers like the New Zealand kiekie, *Freycinetia banksii*—we can choose from a number of shade-loving species. The flowers of *Dietes iridioides*, like white irises with deep blue markings, brightened the shadows of the Gouna Forest near Knysna when I was there. This species is one among several forest plants that grow well in shade but flower more freely on the edges of the garden woodland, or in sunlit glades within it. Two other blue and white "irises," from Australia not South Africa, are *Diplarrhena latifolia* and *D. moraea*. Superficially similar, the first is porcelain to the other's plastic, with the finer texture and more clearly drawn, brighter colours that make a mark in the flower border—the latter's less substantial flowers on taller stems look better in informal company. The beautiful *Dietes bicolor*, with flowers like pale primrose butterflies blotched crimson at the bases of their broad tepals, will tolerate shade, but revels in sunshine, and makes a great ornament in any garden—but not for the nervous gardener, whom it terrorises by seeding itself freely and indiscriminately wherever it cares to grow.

Where shadows are deeper, dianellas are better. They grow equally well in sun or shade on soils that are moisture retentive and rich in humus. One of the largest species is *Dianella tasmanica*, with tough, surface-running rhizomatous roots that form spreading clumps. *Dianella nigra* is like a slender phormium with long, arching, tan-flushed leaves. A weed-resistant and easily grown species is *D. caerulea*, with clumps of congested foliage. The star-shaped flowers of dianellas are invariably blue, but some so washed out that, like *D. nigra*, they seem almost white, and appear sparsely for weeks on end, always with a suggestion that next week the display will be better. In a sense this expectation of future promise is rewarded because the brilliantly glossy, deep violet or bright blue berries that gleam in the shadows like enamelled beads are the most attractive feature of these plants. They appear as though all the flowers that have come and gone over the preceding weeks produce their berries together in a grand finale few other plants can match. Forms with variegated foliage include 'Margaret Pringle', a variant of *D. nigra* with cream margins, and 'Blushy', a variegated form of *D. tasmanica* with broad cream margins to leaves that are flushed pink when immature.

The House of Pitmuies near Forfar is on Scotland's cold eastern side, remote from the benign influence of the Gulf Stream, and an enchanting garden presided over by the redoubtable Margaret Ogilvy. Here to my surprise I came across another blue-flowered plant from the Southern Hemisphere, the South African bluebrilliant, *Aristea ecklonii*, unspoilt by weather or reduced by frost. Of fifty or so species in the genus, few are better than *A. major*, with large blue flowers on branching spikes. Aristeas form clumps from woody rhizomes, which disapprove of disturbance and display resentment by re-establishing slowly and flowering frugally for a year or two after being dug up and divided. Seed is a better way to propagate them. Their flowers close soon after midday, and if business takes you away from the garden during the day, you would do better to grow their Australian and South American cousins instead. Orthrosanthus are at least equally beautiful, more amenable to division and replanting, and the flowers of most species remain open for longer. *Orthrosanthus multiflorus* is one of the best, with clusters of bright blue flowers on upright stems above light and graceful foliage. *Orthrosanthus laxus* has tufts of grass-like foliage and open spikes of sky blue flowers on elegant slender stems.

The New Zealand rengarenga, *Arthropodium cirratum*, shares some of the qualities that have made hostas so popular, and is one of the Southern Hemisphere plants I most regret being unable to grow. Its appearance here amongst plants suggested for sheltered, shaded situations may surprise those familiar with its natural preferences—this species grows naturally amongst rocks, on dry clay banks, or sometimes in open scrub close to the sea, and several forms occur on offshore islands in exposed situations. But the rengarenga is partial to shade; perhaps a natural ability to tolerate drought is the clue to its ability to thrive in competition with tree roots for water and nutrients. The flowers are white, although a few manage a suggestion of warmer tones with crimson-flushed buds, or petals in the palest tints of pink. Perhaps one day its Australian relative, the chocolate lily *A. strictum*, will introduce more vibrant lilac and purple tones. Collections like that at the Otari Native Plant Museum in Wellington display some of the variations of *A. cirratum*, including 'Glauca', with glaucous foliage; 'Matapouri Bay', with large flower heads and broad leaves; 'White Cascade', with long, narrow, arching leaves and laxly inclined inflorescences, sometimes with crimson buds; 'White Spire', with more erect, more substantial leaves and shorter, more compact inflorescences, with flower buds most delicately tinted crimson; and 'White Knight', from Poor Knight's Island. This latter cultivar is exceptionally tolerant of drought, wet, sunshine and shade, comes true from seed, and has all the virtues, but unfortunately is even more vulnerable than most to slugs and snails.

The evergreen forests of the south are less friendly to ground-covering perennials than the deciduous forests of the north, and the dead nettles, bugles, epimediums, lungworts, daylilies and hostas that provide invaluable ground cover in northern gardens have few counterparts in the Looking-Glass Garden. But one genus helps to plug this gap. Species of *Plectranthus* growing in parts of Africa, Madagascar, Asia and Australia are mostly shade tolerant (some are shade dependent) broad-leaved perennials that do well in moist, well-drained soils where ample rainfall and frost-free winters combine to provide the conditions they need.

The South African *Plectranthus ciliatus* is probably the best known species, and the one most widely grown in gardens. It roots at the nodes of trailing stems, making excellent, all-investing ground cover. The crimson reverses of its deep green, heavily textured leaves emphasise the shade and shadows of the spaces beneath trees. Like most of its relatives, this species produces its short sprays of purple-blue flowers in autumn, a time when they are particularly appreciated. The prima donna of the genus is the Australian *P. argen-*

tatus. This stylish plant with softly felted, silver leaves and airy spikes of white and lavender-blue flowers impresses at first sight, but is better for lightly shaded situations and for short-term effects rather than tenacious ground-holding. It is easily grown from cuttings, and during the last few years has played a part in the annual displays on the terraces of Powys Castle in East Wales, where its eye-catching combination of silver foliage and open racemes of purple flowers look particularly effective amongst the tender perennials grown there as exotic summer bedding plants. A plant with less immediate eye-appeal but greater reliability as a standby is *P. zuluensis.* It is taller and has soft, pleasantly aromatic foliage and produces a more or less continuous succession of open racemes of pale purple flowers. *Plectranthus ambiguus* 'Manguzuku', from coastal KwaZulu-Natal, develops into a close, ground-hugging cover of shade-tolerant, soft, broad, toothed apple green foliage, beneath spikes of pale purple-blue flowers on short stems in the autumn and winter. *Plectranthus strigosus* 'Albert' is better for more restricted situations: an exceptionally neat, ground-hugging plant with small, deep green leaves embellished by an overall glossy sheen, topped by little spikes of pale flowers. Finally, *P. fruticosus,* from the evergreen forests of the Mist Belt from Knysna in the extreme south of Africa to the border of Zimbabwe, has branching, pyramidal spikes of bluish purple flowers and heart-shaped leaves that are covered with a soft down of white hairs.

CHAPTER 11

Gardens Without Flowers

W HEN PLANTS ceased to be free spirits, opting instead to live rooted to the spot, they encountered a problem: how to have sex without being able to move around to find a partner. Water provided a way for mobile male cells to reach nubile ovules, and for aeons mosses, ferns and similar plants depended on complex life-cycles that made that possible. It was, and is, an uncertain process, limited by the availability of water, and more likely to result in self- than in cross-fertilisation, but until something better turned up it made the benefits of sexual reproduction and gene exchange possible. Pollen was the great invention of the gymnosperms; carried on the wind from one plant to another, it greatly increased opportunities for cycads and later conifers to make matches over considerable distances, so new combinations and qualities rapidly spread amongst whole populations. The gymnosperms started to use animals and birds to distribute their seeds, tempting them with brightly coloured fleshy arils, like those produced by the podocarps. Then, more than a hundred million years ago, angiosperms refined the process by producing conspicuous, brightly coloured, often intricately constructed flowers to attract pollinators. Alliances with birds, animals, insects, snails, the wind and a dozen other agencies led to an astonishing variety of often strikingly ingenious ways to ensure pollination and seed distribution. Such obvious improvements should have consigned less sophisticatedly endowed plants to obsolescence and oblivion.

Previous pages: Tree ferns create unique impressions in gardens. Those shown here growing in a garden near Auckland are typical of the place and the climate—but how long will it be before global warming makes scenes like this commonplace in Northern Hemisphere gardens? Ayrlies, Bev McConnell's garden, Howick, North Island, New Zealand.

But mosses, ferns, cycads and conifers did not go away. Their primitive, fragile and uncertain sexual arrangements do not provide copy for botanists writing volumes about the flowers and the bees, but they suffice, and other qualities have enabled these plants to hang on and survive, often in competition with plants of more advanced design. We expect to find ferns in consistently wet conditions, and in places where rain falls in phenomenal quantities, like the Hoh Valley on Washington's Olympic Peninsula or New Zealand's Fjordland, it is no surprise to see the forest floor, the lower levels of the trees and often the upper levels, too, enveloped in ferns, mosses, liverworts and lichens. In the early stages of their life cycles, ferns are fragile and depend on water for survival, and even then must produce spores by the billion to ensure that one or two land in a place and at a time when they can survive and reproduce. Once in place, however, ferns are extraordinarily enduring and resilient. Other plants become senescent, take sick and wither away, succumb to insects or pathogens, or simply fail to reappear one spring, but polystichums, blechnums and aspleniums seem to go on forever. Unless deliberately destroyed, they will still be around when our children's children are popping up the daisies. By planting ferns as mature individuals, long past their early stages of fragile vulnerability, gardeners can put them in places where they would never grow naturally, allowing us more freedom in the use of these plants.

Fashions for ferns and their associates come and go. When flowers and bright colours are on the up, ferns, tree ferns, mosses, and liverworts slip into obscurity. When texture and form grab our imaginations, we look at these plants anew and are reminded that they are rich in both. A strong refrain in gardening today extols the enduring qualities of shape and substance compared with the ephemeral nature of flowers. We are also learning that the world is warming up around us, and it would take very little global warming to produce conditions favourable to ferns in places where they cannot be grown successfully today.

Ferns

Despite their attractions and the growing sentiment in favour of form and texture, ferns remain minor players in gardens. They were briefly fashionable a century ago, but were recognised as plants apart to be grown in dedicated areas rather than in association with more familiar garden occupants. Today, even in the Southern Hemisphere, where these plants can be seen growing naturally in every continent in ways that should be an inspiration, their presence in gardens is so muted and uncertain that it could fairly be described as trivial. There are exceptions, however, and one of the most notable is to be seen in the recently restored Fernz Fernery in the Domain, a park in the centre of Auckland. During my visit I stood at the bottom (for the garden takes the form of a giant pit) and looked up and around at the masses of ferns on the sides and along the top, some rolling across the ground, some with erupting shuttlecocks, others on short stems emulating the great tree ferns arching above them. Others are climbing ferns like *Lygodium articulatum*, which divides and subdivides repeatedly, eventually forming a tangled net consisting of a single frond that, unravelled, can stretch 100 metres—the longest "leaf" in the world. Everywhere was green; the only flowers to be seen were a few white sprays from some rengarengas. This was a world in which the common colour theme conveyed a tranquillity seldom found in gardens, combined with a luxuriance that is also often lacking, and the variety of forms, textures and shades of colour created as much interest as any garden full of flowers.

The moist forests of Australia and New Zealand present an amazingly diverse assortment of these plants. Some are found clustering on dead stumps or weaving through carpets of mosses and liverworts to form steadily expanding colonies, their foliage often rising only just above the carpet itself; these include *Gleichenia cunninghamii*, with pinnae arranged like the ribs of little lopsided umbrellas at the tops of short stems, and *Grammitis billardierei*, with short, deep green, tongue-like fronds. Other ferns grow epiphytically, hanging from the lower branches of trees. Many spring from more sedentary crowns, arching up and over the plants below them to reinforce the shelter and humidity of the forest canopy high overhead. Still others produce tall, finely divided fronds that overhang, but only lightly shade the ground below them.

The southern shield ferns *Lastreopsis glabella* and *L. hispida* are the epitome of fern foliage, with their finely divided pinnae and light sea green fronds in loosely formed shuttlecocks arising from short rhizomes on the forest floor. The Prince of Wales feather, *Leptopteris superba*, is challenging in gardens, but thrives in cool, wet forests. At its best, it is amongst the most beautiful of all ferns, with ultra-finely divided, forest green, lace-like pinnae on strong, spreading, often almost horizontal fronds that glisten as though charged with water. The erect rhizomes carrying the fronds develop slowly into short trunks.

Some of the lightest and most graceful of all ferns are to be found amongst the maidenhairs, including the widely distributed southern maidenhair, *Adiantum aethiopicum*, a plant that seems in its element in the moist karri forests of southern Western Australia, but which I was surprised to find growing in much more open, drier eucalyptus bush around Lake Eildon in Victoria. I later learnt that, unusual amongst ferns, it has a taste for sunlit sites, provided they are periodically moist—unlike the very similar South African *A. poirettii*, which grows in deep shade in crevices amongst damp rocks in remnants of evergreen forest in the Drakensberg. The giant maidenhair, *A. formosum*, is much more robust than either, but despite the promise of beauty conveyed by its specific name, lacks the delicacy and grace of the other species. It makes a coarse, spreading ground cover in gardens, with fronds arising from branching rhizomes at well-spaced intervals.

The crown fern, *Blechnum discolor*, produces rings of fronds like elegantly constructed pale golden green crowns on stubby trunks formed from the

Colonies of *Leptopteris superba*, Prince of Wales feather, grow amongst the luxuriant mosses, liverworts, filmy ferns and lichens covering the ground and lower levels of the trees in New Zealand's Fjordland. Valley of the Hollyford River, Fjordland, South Island, New Zealand.

erect rhizomes. Another blechnum, kiokio, formerly known as *B. capense* but now an unresolved nomenclatural puzzle, is a vigorous colonising species that is extremely widespread in more sunlit parts of the bush, and easy to grow in gardens. It is a bold plant with large, broadly arching fronds and long pinnae enhanced by wavy margins, its fresh bright green tones often enlivened with touches of crimson.

Hardy, persistent, small and ground covering, few ferns are more serviceable than *Blechnum penna-marina*, unmistakable with its mats of narrow tongue-like fronds rising from creeping rhizomes at ground level, amongst them the short sprays of brown, spore-bearing fertile fronds. Although small, this plant is tough and grows readily in gardens in many situations; in nature this widespread wanderer is as likely to be seen in Tierra del Fuego, south Georgia and the Falkland Islands as in New Zealand or Australia. At the other end of the size scale, the South African mountain water fern, *B. tabulare*, is another easily grown fern, ideal for cool shade in moist places beneath trees. It has considerable presence: a princess when the young fronds appear in spring with immaculately fresh, crimped margins, but a rather severe duchess in maturity when it lapses into a sullen density of dark bronze-green that can be rather depressing unless relieved by its surroundings. Long-established plants develop short trunks. Yet another member of the varied and useful clan of blechnums is *B. fraseri*. This species has none of the dour nature of the last, but resembles a grove of minute tree ferns with deep green, glossy, bipinnate fronds raised on slender, finger-thick trunks. The creeping rhizomes can spread over considerable areas, and it tolerates relatively dry conditions in gardens, but not frost.

One of my favourite ferns is the king fern, *Marattia salicina*. This vigorous, rather magnificent species has deep green, shining, bipinnate fronds that can grow 3 metres high and thrust up in clumps from a large, tuberous, starchy rootstock. The feral pigs, known as Captain Cookers, that infest New Zealand's bush much appreciate these stems and have almost exterminated the plant in the wild. The king fern looks particularly magnificent in frost-free situations, such as at the Pukeiti Rhododendron Trust on the slopes of Mount Taranaki, where soils are moist, deep and fertile; the rhododendrons there provide the shelter and humidity that the fern requires. While being shown round Pieter de Jager's remarkable bushveld garden in Monument

Park in Pretoria, I was introduced to the king fern's rather smaller South African cousin, *M. fraxinea* subsp. *salicifolia*. Known as the tortoise fern for the shape of the base when it reaches maturity, this species has fronds like those of the king fern, though it is less often seen in gardens.

Another large and imposing fern, in an entirely different style, is the Australian bird's nest fern, *Asplenium australasicum*. It grows epiphytically in the crotches of trees, and on rocks, often perching somewhat awkwardly due to the great size of its clusters of long fronds. The fronds form elongated funnels in which water and debris accumulate to nourish the plant. It makes a dramatic impact when imaginatively used in mild, sheltered gardens. The elegant and distinctive *A. polyodon* is often found hanging from the lower branches of trees, with trailing pinnate fronds with toothed margins. The hen and chicken fern, *A. bulbiferum,* has tall, finely divided, slightly overhanging fronds that produce plantlets on their upper surfaces; these plantlets develop into new plants after the old fronds collapse and lie decaying on the ground. A plant that illuminates shaded corners of the moist forests of New Zealand is the aptly named shining spleenwort, *A. oblongifolium,* with upright, open shuttlecocks of broad, pinnate fronds sometimes a metre long. The smooth bright green surfaces of the fronds have a polished gloss and are often flushed with crimson. Although naturally inclined to grow in deeply shaded, moist situations, this species tolerates sunlit settings in gardens that are neither too hot nor too dry; its main drawback is the fondness slugs have for it.

The stag's horn fern, *Platycerium superbum,* and elk horn fern, *P. bifurcatum,* are Australian epiphytes, both so widely grown in gardens and conservatories that they are among the best known of all epiphytic plants. Their papery sterile fronds press tightly against their host to form a great shield-like boss from which the pale green, antler-like fertile fronds emerge. Both species have been over-collected in the wild and are now protected. Although they are rainforest plants, these platyceriums are, like many epiphytes, remarkably tolerant of drought, heat and exposure as well as cool conditions, short of severe frosts. They make excellent garden plants in many parts of the world, including Mediterranea, provided they are placed on their tree hosts in such a way that the overhead canopy shades them in summer, yet allows sunshine to penetrate as the angle of the sun falls in winter.

The highly distinctive form and texture of the elk horn, *Platycerium bifurcatum,* make an impression in any setting. Anne and Tom Stacey's garden, Te Puke, North Island, New Zealand.

Tree Ferns

As gardeners grow to appreciate the forms and shapes of ferns, and as global warming allows such fantasies to be achieved in more northerly latitudes, the appearance of southern Britain, the Pacific Northwest and other such places will be dramatically transformed. Few plants would transform these places more than groves of tree ferns in public squares, rows of them shading cars in supermarket parking lots, or flanking the path to the front doors of suburban homes. The forerunner of the tree-fern invasion will be the smooth tree fern, *Dicksonia antarctica,* and some contend that it would already be here if we were a little more adventurous in our gardening. The specific name displays a rash optimism on the part of the botanist who chose it; nevertheless, the range of this species reaches high into the mountains of south-eastern Australia, immediately below the snow fields, where it grows along creeks and gullies in places where severe frosts and snow are normal for long periods, and plants from these provenances can survive temperatures as low as −10°C (14°F). This is the fern that contributes exotic atmospheres to gardens on the Atlantic fringes of the British Isles, setting the scene on Valentia Island off south-west Ireland, at the Logan Botanic Garden on the Mull of Galloway, and in Inverewe in extreme north-west Scotland. Some specimens at Logan are well over a hundred years old, testimony to their endurance, and about 5 metres high, impressive in itself, but an average growth rate of less than 5 centimetres a year would try most people's patience. *Dicksonia antarctica* grows much more rapidly in more favoured situations, and at Trebah on the southern coast of Cornwall this plant flourished during the garden's period of neglect. Groves of the plant and self-sown seedlings introduce the exotic ambience that is the special prerogative of tree ferns. It may be the least graceful of its kind—with fringes of stubble from the old leaf bases towards the tops of stems like stumpy pillars beneath broad fronds—but at least it is here.

A more graceful species is the rough tree fern, *Cyathea australis,* so-called from the peg-like leaf bases of long dead fronds that persist indefinitely on its stems. It also grows in the eucalypt forests of south-eastern Australia, often in company with *Dicksonia antarctica.* It suffers more from frost but is hardier in other senses, establishing more easily and growing better in gardens subject to drought and exposure. The rough tree fern is adapted to survive the effects of fire, and one of the first hopeful signs of regeneration after fires have passed are the fresh green fronds of this species emerging from the tops of charred stems. The South African *C. dregei* is another fire-adapted toughie, well able to grow in places that are exposed and relatively dry, unlike the more graceful forest tree fern, *C. capensis.* Those who follow South Africa's Garden Route will see *C. capensis* growing in the sheltered, humid, deeply shaded surroundings of the Tsitsikamma Forest, a situation that reflects its need for warmth, shelter and humidity if it is to do well in gardens.

The most widespread tree fern in the forests of New Zealand is wheki, *Dicksonia squarrosa,* and plants growing in cold situations on the high passes that cross from Otago into Fjordland offer possibilities of obtaining hardy stocks. This characterful rather than notably graceful tree has slightly tapering stems, broader towards their crowns, with peg-like leaf bases on their upper halves. The crown is relatively small and has noticeably upright, rather than pendant, shuttlecocks of finely divided fronds. Little groups of two or three stems emerge from almost the same spot from short stolons, and its small size, quick growth and amenable disposition make wheki a good garden plant. John and Susan Wallace use the plant most effectively in their garden near Taumarunui on North Island, where groups of tree fuchsias with whekis form a little glade, thickly underplanted with ferns and woodland plants, that links the garden with a neighbouring stand of native bush. The silver fern, *C. dealbata*, owes its vernacular name to the layer of white wax on the undersurfaces of its fronds, which enables it to do comparatively well in dry situations. The stalks of old fronds hang from the stem as they disintegrate. Unless trimmed by tidy gardeners, the remnants eventually drop off to leave the bases of the stipes sticking out of the main stem like short pegs.

Pat Swain's garden south of Auckland is cut out of a small patch of bush with minimal disturbance of trees or atmosphere. A tall kahiakatea, *Dacrydium dacrydioides*, and a rata, *Metrosideros robustus*, tower above the dense bush below; the rata is in a state of such venerable decay, with shattered upper limbs and crotches stuffed with perching lilies, that it seems incredible that it stays up. Below these trees the dominant theme is provided by the upright columns of nikau palms, *Rhopalostylis sapida*, with their shuttlecock heads. Groups of these trees of different ages establish patterns, all sharing a common form, but with their crowns at different levels, in contrast to the spreading tree-fern fronds of the mamakus, which infill and soften the stiffness of the nikaus. Few plants surpass the tall, graceful, slender mamaku, *Cyathea medullaris*, for sheer presence in the warm, moist, sheltered conditions it needs to grow well. Its black, shiny unfolding croziers on hairy stems, deeply buried amidst inky black stems, make dramatic contrasts with the broadly spreading tops of large fronds, especially in spring when these are a fresh golden green. The fronds fall cleanly from the trunk, leaving patterns like watermarks on the curving stems. These tree ferns are large, not just high but broadly spreading, and fit the scale of Pat Swain's forest garden well; in a smaller space they would be overwhelming, and *C. smithii* might be a better choice. This slender tree fern has distinctive green-gold midribs enhancing the long, fragile-looking fronds; the bases of the scapes are encrusted with curly golden brown scales. Dead fronds droop as they die, forming a skirt that hangs below the shuttlecock top, enfolding the main stem for a large part of its length, rather like the hula palm, *Washingtonia filifera*. Like the palm, this fern is an irresistible temptation to the trimmers and tidiers of the world.

Mosses and Liverworts

New Zealand's Central Otago is a dry, windswept countryside. Russet-red tussock grasses mantle the hillsides from horizon to horizon, and the landscape is dissected by braided rivers in which thin streams of water run between expanses of stones. Sweetbriars grow on dry slopes, and expanses of purple thyme colour the barren ground amongst rocks. This is no place for plants that depend for their survival on the moisture provided by abundant rainfall—but beyond the horizon lies a paradise on earth for mosses, liverworts and others of their kind. Signs of a change can be seen in the beech forests, edged with lancewoods and cabbage trees, on the slopes of the mountains below the Haast Pass to the west, and once over the Pass, the bush towards Thunder Creek Falls fills with broad-leaved evergreens, tree ferns, podocarps and shrubs, as luxuriant as the country a few miles to the

The mosses and liverworts that in Nature form colourful carpets with ferns and astelias are scarcely ever found in cultivation, but with the necessary abundant water and humid atmospheres, they could be used in gardens in many parts of the world. Near Wilmot Pass, Fjordland, South Island, New Zealand.

east is austere. A little farther west and a thousand feet lower down, climbing and epiphytic plants, including kiekies, perching lilies and masses of ferns, festoon trunks and limbs above deep carpets of moss in one of the richest temperate rainforests on earth. As if I might be in need of an explanation for these changes, nature provided me with its own demonstration. On a day when cloudless blue skies prevailed over the inland town of Cromwell, heavy showers towards the Pass were precursors of a continuous downpour on the seaward-facing western slopes. Torrents of rain hid the surrounding scenery, creating a thousand waterfalls rushing in full spate down the sides of the mountains. Ribbons of white water hurtled in narrow plumes of spray from the heights above, drenching the plants on the rocky outcrops of the cliff faces.

This is Westland. It might as appropriately be called Wetland where the trees along the roadside veiled a world dripping with water. Dead stumps, fallen branches, the trunks and lower limbs of trees, and even the extremities of their branches were overlaid by a deep, multicoloured carpet with a rough pile of green, yellow, crimson, brown and grey mosses, lichens, club mosses, liverworts, and filmy and other ferns. To see them was to long to grow them this way in my own garden, setting in train thoughts about how that might be done. Orthodox gardening has no place for these plants. Mosses, liverworts and even lichens—until in today's enlightened era we learnt to regard the latter as indicators, by their absence, of pollution—have all been labelled garden enemies, nuisances or purveyors of undesirable untidiness.

As the cloudbursts during my visit that day reminded me, this luxuriance depends on volumes of rainfall few gardeners experience, and most would not want. Pumps, mist units and all kinds of irrigation and automatic-watering equipment provide the means to the end, however, and where water is available imagination could conjure a wet spot in a small area in the shade of trees where these plants might be grown. That imagination would be a start; the realisation would be more difficult. These communities are alliances between many different plants, each of which contributes to the processes that maintain the humid, shaded, cool moist conditions in which all thrive. Some cover the ground, some rise above it, providing local shelter and humid conditions for others; some act as sponges, some hold water on their surfaces or in their cells, which constantly evaporates to sustain the humid atmosphere. The woodland gardens we have learnt to make in shaded places under trees, even specifically constructed fern gardens, are dry and sterile by comparison.

These mossy carpets are not all they seem. Mosses are present, but more often than not they are outnumbered by superficially similar liverworts in the genus *Lepidozia,* with which they are often confused. The simplest way to distinguish one from the other is to remember that liverworts are broadly two-dimensional, whereas mosses are three-dimensional. There will usually also be numerous club mosses, *Lycopodium,* spreading over the ground or, like *Lycopodium billardierei,* hanging from the branches of trees like bunches of cypress shoots. Other more puzzling objects will be interwoven in the texture of the carpet, looking like old, dry and often rather tattered green, olive-green, russet or grey leaves, broadly subdivided into lobes. These are foliose lichens, plants that also grow on rocks, dead stumps and bark in company with filmy ferns. The latter clothe stumps, emerge amongst mosses and lichens and grow from rocks on the forest floor. Seen for the first time they resemble baby versions of more familiar ferns, but are more delicate, with finely divided, ultra-thin fronds that can survive only in the most sheltered, humid, constantly saturated situations. Many will be *Hymenophyllum* species so saturated with water that they drip constantly, and glisten and gleam as though filled with oil. Others will be the kidney fern, *Trichomanes reniforme,* with distinctive rounded, kidney-shaped fronds on short stems. This widely distributed little fern with deep green, ultra-smooth, glossy fronds is better able to protect itself against desiccation—simply curling up at the edges and waiting for humid times to return—and is not too difficult to grow in suitable situations in a garden.

Conifers

Conifers have played little part in this account, although they grow side by side with broad-leaved evergreens in almost all the forests of the Southern Hemisphere. Just as the pines, firs, spruces, larches and cedars, all cousins within the Pinaceae, epitomise the Northern Hemisphere conifers for me, so their Southern Hemisphere equivalents are the rimus, totaras, yellow-woods, miros and manios in the equally impressive family known as the

Podocarpaceae. The podocarps were long established when Gondwanaland broke up, and members of the family drifted across the planet on the land masses that became Africa, India, Australia, South America and New Zealand. These trees possess the dignity and presence of such an ancient lineage and, like their northern equivalents, impose their character wherever they grow—including gardens. Used thoughtlessly, or as a quick-fix, facile way to create accent plants or contrasts with broad-leaved trees, they overpower their surroundings and create impressions that smother local character and atmosphere. Used imaginatively, and with careful intention, the effects they create can be evocative and powerful.

It could be said that the podocarps are not conifers at all, since they produce no cones, but surround their seeds with fleshy, succulent fruits known as arils, similar to the translucent pink tissues that partially enclose the green seeds of yews. But other conifers of the south are truly cone-bearing, none more so than the Chilean monkey puzzle, *Araucaria araucana*, with giant cones containing mega-versions of pine nuts, and equally enjoyable to eat. The tree has exaggeratedly distinctive leaves, which with its shape (like a giant toffee apple on a stick) give the tree great character. Long ago I was told, or read, that in their native land, the branches of the Chilean monkey puzzle sweep to the ground in graceful curves; I was also told, or read, that to see them growing as they should I must visit Castle Kennedy in south-west Scotland, and view the avenue of monkey puzzles with branches that sweep down to the ground. I dutifully did so, and was duly impressed, and congratulated myself on knowing what a real monkey puzzle tree should look like. Later, in Chile, I discovered that this exotic-looking tree grows in open forests on the slopes and crests of mountains, where they lose their lower branches, just like those to be seen in any suburban garden.

The Norfolk Island pine, *Araucaria heterophylla*, is another truly coniferous southern tree that has exaggerated qualities of texture and form. These gauntly triangular trees, with tiers of branches looking from a distance like the sails and spars of some extraordinary sailing machine, dominate their surroundings wherever they are planted. There should be an indefinite moratorium on any more planting of this tree, which is used as inappropriately, insensitively and almost as ubiquitously in the south as its distant cousin the Leyland cypress (×*Cupressocyparis leylandii*) is in the north.

The cone-bearing kauri, *Agathis australis*, is the king of the New Zealand forests, but like a number of other southern conifers—including the Chilean alerce, *Fitzroya cupressoides*, the Tasmanian Huon pine, *Lagarostrobus franklinii*, and the King Billy pine, *Athrotaxis selaginoides*—it has a reputation for growing slowly in gardens. My encounter with a fully mature kauri in the Durban Botanic Gardens in South Africa suggested that this reputation might be questioned. Not much more than a hundred years old, if that, the specimen's broad columnar trunk and fully formed, compact head of massive branches demonstrated how fast this species can grow under favourable conditions. In New Zealand Graeme Platt, a vigorous proponent of the kauri tree's virtues, grew it in the shelter of ribbonwoods, *Plagianthus regius*, which resulted in such rapid development that the trees outgrew their strength. At the Arboretum of the University of California at Santa Cruz, in conditions far less favourable for a temperate, moisture-loving tree, a couple of kauris have grown so well that they overtop other plants in the immediate vicinity. Unfortunately owls started to use their leaders as convenient lookout posts and repeatedly snapped them off, until the problem was resolved by setting up poles close to and taller than the kauris, which the owls find even more acceptable.

Other cone-bearing gymnosperms from south of the equator include the Australian cypresses, classified as species of *Callitris*, and the she-oaks, species of *Casuarina* and *Allocasuarina*. "Cypress" is an appropriate term, from a gardener's point of view, for trees that look much like the true cypresses, and can often be used for similar purposes in gardens. Some display an exaggeratedly columnar form and can be used to create effects similar to those of the Italian cypresses, *Cupressus sempervirens* 'Stricta'. *Callitris baileyi* has this narrowly upright form, with deep green foliage, and the white cypress pine, *C. glaucophylla*, also grows into a tall vertical column. The South Esk pine, *C. oblonga*, from Tasmania is smaller and more bushily upright, but responds well to clipping, and is more suitable for smaller gardens, especially in cooler conditions. Several Australian cypresses grow naturally close to the sea. The Rottnest cypress, *C. preissii*, is from Rottnest Island in the Indian Ocean, west of Fremantle, Western Australia, which owes its name to the little marsupials found on it, known as quokkas, which early sailors mistook for rats. This attractive and characterful round-topped tree has fresh deep

The giant kauri tree *Agathis australis,* tane mahuta, grows in the Waipoua Forest Sanctuary on North Island, New Zealand. Unlike neighbouring trees of other species, its trunk remains notably free from epiphytes due to the continuous shedding of the outer layers of its bark.

green foliage and distinctive large cones. The Oyster Bay pine, *C. rhomboidea,* is almost equally tolerant of exposure in seaside gardens, and at home too in cool, inland gardens like the Mount Tomah Botanic Garden in the Blue Mountains west of Sydney, where it has been used to make an excellent dense, fine-textured, formal hedge.

The most familiar South African representative of cone-bearing conifers is *Widdringtonia nodiflora.* This small tree, with pale grey sinewy stems and longitudinally striated peeling bark, reminds me of a juniper rather than a cypress, particularly *Juniperus occidentalis,* the rugged, weatherbeaten little tree that is a feature of the sagebrush in central Oregon. The size of *W. nodiflora* makes it a good choice for smaller gardens, especially where a tree is needed to make a strongly individual statement with its form, texture and overall appearance. This tree occurs naturally in isolated groups in a great arc stretching from the Zambezi River to the Cape of Good Hope. Towards the northern limits of its range in moist, well-watered situations, like the gorge of the Pungwe River and the rain-drenched escarpment of the Chimanimani Mountains in Zimbabwe, it grows into a substantial tree, progressively declining in size to the south and west, until in the Western Cape it is no more than a large shrub. I first encountered the much rarer Clanwilliam cypress, *W. cedarbergensis,* at the Garden of St Erth on Simmons Reef in Victoria, where Tommy Garnett had planted seedlings grown from a single cone around the site of an old church to establish a small, sombre grove. This narrowly upright, fine-needled conifer lends itself to the same sort of effects as the evocative columnar forms of the Italian cypress, and perhaps it was memories of those around churches in Italy that inspired its use here. *Widdringtonia cedarbergensis* grows around the Pakhuis Pass in the Cedarberg above the little town of Clanwilliam. The mountains rise like a wall above the plain below, with crests of broken and jagged boulders, amphitheatres of shattered rocks and columns of enormous, fractured blocks, grotesquely fretted and fissured by weathering, balancing precariously one upon another, or lined up to form tattered, shot-torn ramparts, which surely at any moment will collapse thunderingly to the ground below. This chaotic and precarious place makes an appropriate setting for an equally rugged, craggy little tree, so depleted by logging, grazing and fires that its survival once seemed improbable. Recent efforts to plant new seedlings and look after what is left promise to help this species maintain a toehold and perhaps even thrive.

Gardeners are generally accustomed to plants being hermaphrodite, apart from well-known exceptions like hollies, in which we expect to find berries only on the female trees, and ginkgoes, which are strange and outlandish things anyway. Dioecious species are much less unusual in the southern flora and crop up repeatedly in many different families. From the gardener's point of view this has advantages and disadvantages. The South African yellowwoods, *Podocarpus falcatus* and *P. latifolius,* are both dioecious, and the female trees bear round, greenish yellow or purple-blue fruits respectively. They crop only when two or more trees of opposite sexes are gathered together, which can be a disadvantage for those who appreciate the fruits as part of the interest of the plants and as a source of food for birds. Bats also eat the fruits, and gardeners who consider these so-called flying foxes (or flying rats) messy, undesirable creatures, which they would rather not encourage, should grow only male plants. Both of these yellowwoods

Unlike the prevalent cone-bearing conifers of the Northern Hemisphere, female podocarps produce succulent fruits of various kinds, like these plum-like arils of the Outeniqua yellowwood, *Podocarpus falcatus.* Kirstenbosch National Botanical Garden, Western Cape Province, South Africa.

develop eventually into outstanding specimen trees. The Outeniqua yel-lowwood, *P. falcatus,* is heavy limbed, and has flaking, dark elephant grey bark and curving, though only marginally sickle-shaped leaves. Mature true yellowwoods, *P. latifolius,* develop great character and presence with trunks like a topographer's nightmare of knobs, burls and excrescences covered by close-knit, stringy or flaky dark brown bark.

One Chilean species of manio, *Podocarpus salignus,* can be grown in gardens around Dublin, in Cornwall and other similarly cool places. It is a graceful tree with long, narrow leaves like a willow's, and although comparatively hardy, I learnt how vulnerable the young foliage is to spring frosts on a visit to the Speight garden, in a valley below Coronet Peak near Queenstown in New Zealand. A late spring frost had burnt the foliage on a long manio hedge, one of the garden's major features, as though someone had passed along it with a flame gun. The plum pine, *P. elatus,* is a relative from the rainforests of Queensland, and it makes an excellent specimen tree in sheltered situations in places with mild winters, looking particularly attractive when the pale yellow-green new leaves flushed with pink emerge in the spring.

Podocarps are not all large and tree-like. The New Zealand *Podocarpus nivalis,* first encountered in the bleak subalpine scrub that covers the mountain slopes around Arthur's Pass, grows naturally in alpine or similarly harsh environments. It develops as a ground-covering carpet with olive-green needles, rather similar to a whipcord hebe, until the females produce succulent crimson arils towards the tips of their shoots—the fruits provide the mountain parrots, known as keas, with food and a diversion from molesting sheep and removing the trim from parked cars. A closely related species that remains small, though more often as a diminutive tree rather than a spreading carpet, is the mountain plum pine, *P. lawrencei,* from alpine parts of Australia and New Zealand. In exposed places this tree grows like a mat over rocks; in more sheltered situations as a small tree. The aromatic needles are very short and harbour hard little seeds surrounded by bright red succulent arils. A garden form known as 'Purple King', with needles that become blackish crimson as they mature, is upright and shrubby, and eventually forms a small tree. Graham Hutchins of County Park Nurseries in Essex, England, recently bred several new seedlings from crosses made between *P. nivalis* and *P. lawrencei.* These are of particular interest to gardeners in colder parts of the world, and demonstrate the value of taking provenance into account when looking for special qualities, like hardiness. Graham first made collections from nearly thirty populations of *P. nivalis* growing in New Zealand, and three of *P. lawrencei* in Australia. Plants of these species, and their hybrids, are dioecious, and the females produce fruits only when grown in company with males. Cultivars released for sale by County Park Nurseries recognise this, and include two male clones, known as 'Lodestone' and 'Otari', and several females, notable for the colour of their foliage. The females include 'County Park Fire', in which the immature foliage is creamy yellow, changing through pink to green, overlaid with purple in the winter; 'Blaze', with orange-tinted immature foliage turning crimson flushed with bronze in winter; and 'Chocolate Box', with rich brown winter foliage.

Hall's totara, *Podocarpus cunninghamii,* is another plant of the mountains, but it also grows in lowland forests, and like many conifers that carry the label "dwarf," can become big enough in time to dwarf its owners. The true totara, *P. totara,* also grows large eventually, as might be expected of a tree with a life span of eight hundred years or more, though for most of us that time scale is beyond our reckoning. In gardens this comparatively drought resistant, heavily foliaged, dense, dark, round-headed tree makes an attractive, characterful specimen. Selections with golden needles, a weeping form or both are now available for those who enjoy these things. Totara makes an excellent screen or windbreak, and it has a robust vigour about it, quite unlike the more gracefully pendant, but more demanding, rimu, *Dacrydium cupressinum.*

Gardeners often find it difficult to grow other plants beneath established conifers—usually because they go for the wrong plants. Using the right plants, and managing them appropriately, can turn problems into opportunities. This has been achieved most successfully in Felix Jury's enchanted forest at Tikorangi, north of New Plymouth in New Zealand. Sober fact reveals this to be no more than a row of rimu trees, *Dacrydium cupressinum,* planted by Felix's grandfather as a windbreak, but the spaces beneath and around the trees have been planted with the dramatic intensity of a theatrical set. The trailing fronds of the rimus hang like curtains framing a stage set in which different plants and different combinations of plants appeared, disappeared and reappeared as I followed Felix around the garden. The spiky forms of cabbage trees and broad-leaved shrubs around the edges provide contrast and additional shelter for vireyan rhododendrons like the fragrant rose-pink *Rhododendron* 'Silver Shimmer' and the bright red 'Cherry Pie', both raised at Tikorangi. Bromeliads—some on the ground, some on rotting logs, some on the branches of the trees—perch amongst and above hostas, trilliums, azaleas and more vireyan rhododendrons, beneath which little kidney ferns, *Trichomanes reniforme,* and other filmy ferns carpet the ground. The great, glossy deep green leaves of *Monstera deliciosa* scrambling amongst the lower limbs of the rimu trees provided a final touch of drama.

CHAPTER 12

Tropical Drama

C HIC AND minimalist, or rich and opulent? The glossy pictures of other people's houses in lifestyle magazines convey the message that the furnishings in our homes have to be one or the other if we hope to impress neighbours and influence friends. What goes for interior design, also goes for our gardens. Today the tropical look is trendy, and when you decide that your rose beds must go and you cannot bear to live any longer with your stick-in-the-mud, homely old cottage garden, but must be up there with the leaders of style and fashion, you will face a similar choice. Landscape architects assure us that the tropical look is "in," but they cannot agree on what it is. To some it is sparse and spare, a garden of angular shapes, pointed leaves, spiky adornments and plant poses; to others, rich and luxuriant, crammed with vast glossy leaves, exotic plants, extravagances of palms and creepers, sensuous bunches of crimson flowers and strange, soft fragrances. Gardeners who opt for the chic and posed will find their plants amongst those with attitude and individuality, introduced in Chapter Six. But for the opulent and extravagant, read on.

The Hibiscus Coast of KwaZulu-Natal, parts of New Zealand's North Island, coastal areas in Australia around Perth and Sydney, and even Hobart in Tasmania are places where frosts are few or insignificant. Warmth, moisture and humidity, supplemented when necessary by watering, create conditions in which subtropical and even tropical plants can have overwhelming theatrical impact—making traditional garden styles appear restrained, reticent and downright inhibited by comparison. Not for everybody by reason of either taste or circumstances, these plants offer possibilities for exploration, and ideas for new effects that only people dedicated to the most died-in-the-wool orthodoxy

Previous pages: Palms such as *Archontophoenix cunninghamiana* create an unmistakably tropical atmosphere wherever they appear. Their broad fronds provide impressive parasols above tall stems, creating an ideal spot in which to relax while enjoying the garden. Bryan and Gae McDonald's garden, near Auckland, North Island, New Zealand.

284

could entirely resist. Gardeners in other parts of the world, even in Britain, are beginning to discover that they too can indulge in the theatrical and the fantastic—provided they choose their plants imaginatively rather than carefully, and perhaps protect a few key elements from winter frosts.

Who are the performers in this theatrical fantasy? Leading characters are found amongst the palms, unequivocally tropical in appearance and often in origin, and now going through a period of explosive expansion in gardens. Perhaps they would take the female leads in this theatre; if so, some broad-leaved evergreen trees would be their male counterparts, amongst them figs and the Australian umbrella tree. Supporting roles would be filled by trees with pronounced and effective leaf forms, such as the tree ferns and cordylines, as well as by climbers like passion flowers or the Argentine trum-

Here a gravelled area leading to a small pool backed by palms, bromeliads and tropical foliage plants provides the theatre to be viewed from the auditorium of the living room. All is immaculately cared for and manicured, including the spiral patterns formed by the stones of contrasting colour. Bryan and Gae McDonald's garden, near Auckland, North Island, New Zealand.

pet vine. Finally, epiphytes like vireyan rhododendrons and also bromeliads play brilliant cameo roles in this tropical theatre, along with orchids
and numerous vigorous plants offering bold foliage to cover the jungle floor.

Palms

Undoubtedly, the plants that most clearly give a garden title to be called
subtropical are the palms. Once favoured mainly for formal promenades
along avenues or as significant dot plants on a lawn or to make a pretentious
statement on either side of an entrance or vista, palms are popping up where
they were scarcely seen before. Suburban gardens in Auckland, Sydney, Pretoria and elsewhere are filled with the infant forms of multitudes of misplaced palms, put there for the sake of introducing variety or a change of texture. They will grow up into an extraordinary mishmash that will totally

Even a tiny back garden takes on an exotic, tropical air with the broad leaves of colocasias
and the spiky forms of cabbage trees silhouetted against white walls. Christine Crate and Mor-
ris Penny's garden, near Auckland, North Island, New Zealand.

transform the appearance of these places—for good or ill? Used with imagination controlled by well-thought-out intention, palms are amongst the most powerful plants in a landscaper's portfolio. They do not have to be tall and majestic; a little grove of *Phoenix roebelenii* at Lotusland in California, with sunlight filtering through masses of delicately arching fronds, is one of the most evocative sights in the garden. Closely planted cocos palms, *Syagrus romanzoffiana*, make an oasis that is equally effective on a slightly larger scale, and a well-placed group of wild date palms, *P. reclinata*, transforms a garden scene from the mundane to the spectacular with their curving, sinuous stems and broadly spreading feathery heads of fronds.

A few hardy species are now being used adventurously and, to the surprise of many gardeners, successfully in parts of the world that have no claims to tropical or even subtropical titles. The choice becomes much broader in more appropriate sites, but many who plant them, familiar with canary or queen palms, are stuck with the notion that palms are plants that resemble large feather dusters, with single straight stems topped by plumes of broad, finely divided fronds. So they can be, and few palms look more distinguished in this role than the easily grown and broadly tolerant Australian bangalow palm, *Archontophoenix cunninghamiana*. This tree grows rapidly, with strong, elegant, slender stems defined by the rings of the fallen leaf bases. Its clusters of small lilac flowers are followed by large bunches of red fruits, a major source of food for birds. Equally impressive and with greater emphasis on grace, but not so broadly adaptable, is the closely related *A. alexandrae*, a slender feather-leaf palm from moist rainforests in tropical and subtropical parts of north-eastern Australia. This species has a number of different geographical forms, amongst them 'Mount Lewis' with a sometimes rather elusive silver sheen on the undersides of the fronds.

Palms become most interesting, however, when gardeners recognise the variety of their forms and the opportunities they offer for powerful effects in gardens. If your budget is as generous as the one that supported Patrick Watson's fantasies in the gardens of the Palace of the Lost City in South Africa, you too might be tempted to plant a grove of the slow-growing *Hyophorbe lagenicaulis* from the Mascarene Islands in the western Indian Ocean. It creates an inimitable impression, as comic as it is stylish, with the tree's distinctively bottle-shaped stems. Equally effective impressions can be produced with the far less exotic jelly palm, *Butia capitata*, from central southern Brazil, Uruguay and northern Argentina. Several forms of this species are available and widely cultivated in many parts of the world, and it is worth a try even in moderately frosty situations (it can withstand up to six degrees of frost). Named for the edible fruit produced by mature trees, which can be made into jelly, the jelly palm is remarkable for the metallic quality of its steel grey fronds, made all the more characterful by their long, narrow, pointed leaflets. A little grove creates an unforgettable impression, combining sharply defined colour with trailing, needle-pointed foliage, that provides the foundation for distinctively unusual planting schemes. It is reminiscent, on a smaller and more domestically appropriate scale, of the Blue Garden at Lotusland, where light, filtered through the glaucous foliage of Atlantic cedars, combined with the Chilean wine palm, *Jubaea chilensis,* and the Mexican blue palm, *Erythea armata,* creates a theatrically moonlit, ethereally atmospheric woodland glade. Trees of *J. chilensis* survived severe frosts at the Abbey Gardens of Tresco on the Isles of Scilly, and a notable specimen in the Temperate House at the Royal Botanic Gardens, Kew, endured exposure to the winter elements with minimal protection during renovation of the structure.

Several palms with clustered stems can be used to make screens, backgrounds to other plants or as jungly intermissions between one part of a garden and another (like robust bamboos, but without the periodic dereliction that accompanies the post-floral depression of those fickle plants). Their names may reflect their appearance, like the Madagascan golden cane palm, *Chrysalidocarpus lutescens,* sometimes simply called bamboo. The immature stems of the multistemmed clumps of this graceful, small feather palm have bright golden yellow bark. The sealing-wax palm, *Cyrtostachys lakka,* multistemmed and graceful, from Sumatra is even more effective, with brightly glowing orange-red immature stems, but only for warm gardens in sheltered, humid situations. Finally, the kentia palm, *Howea forsteriana,* is familiar for its appearances throughout the world in parlours, palm courts, presidential conventions and anywhere else where the combination of its tolerance of low light, low temperatures and dry atmospheres, its ability to survive for many years in the same container, and its tropically exotic air makes an irreplaceable contribution to pomp and circumstance. It has a reputation for a rather less tolerant attitude in gardens, with a decided preference for temperate, moist, coastal conditions and freedom from even the

This row of slightly askew bottle palms, *Hyophorbe lagenicaulis,* tripping down a steep bank creates a rollicking, slightly comic impression of movement and urgency. The Palace of the Lost City, Pilanesberg, North-West Province, South Africa.

The Chilean wine palm, *Jubaea chilensis*, though now rare in the wild, is widely distributed in gardens, where it grows well. Parque Quinta Normale, Santiago, Chile.

slightest frosts. But as its presence at Lotusland testifies, this species responds to good gardening, aided by careful siting and supplementary watering, when like many palms it will perform well even in comparatively taxing conditions.

A few palms share bamboos' habit of living to flower only once before they die—but on a monumental, almost epic scale. The kosi palm *Raphia australis*, from forests in the hot, steamy swamps of Maputaland where South Africa meets southern Mozambique, is one such palm, with broad, spreading fronds, said to be amongst the largest leaves produced by any plant. When thirty or so years old, these trees produce enormous 3-metre-long inflorescences followed by masses of fruits. Then they die, like the final act of a dark dramatic tragedy, which sentimental gardeners might prefer to ensure takes place when their successors have become responsible for their gardens.

Tropical Trees and Shrubs

During a visit to South Africa, Peter Thomas, who grows anthuriums on his nursery at Holland Farm near Umhlali, took me to see Rosemary Ladlau's garden on the Hibiscus Coast. Rosemary, a talented flower arranger, was away on a tour that involved, amongst other things, doing the flowers at Canterbury Cathedral, and we were met at the garden and taken round by her daughter, Jane Johnson. The garden has a strong structure derived from numerous indigenous trees, a little unusual in a part of the world where so much of the countryside has been cleared to make way for great expanses of sugar cane. Here the trees provide shade and shelter, and a relaxing setting for a brilliant display of tropical plants. Pre-eminent amongst them and close to the house is a magnificent fig, *Ficus lyrata*, its powerful bole filled with fissures and crannies, and a massive head of bold, broad, deep green glossy leaves. This venerable specimen, draped in philodendrons and other creepers, is a harbour for snakes and heaven-knows what else, and big daddy to a great variety of lesser but colourful foliage plants growing in its shade. Foliage effects create the dominant impressions throughout the garden, based on numerous subtropical and tropical evergreen species.

Other figs can be used to provide a tropical impression with their heavy, deep green, entire leaves and massive stems, like the South African wonderboom, *Ficus cordata* ssp. *salicifolia*, or the Australian banana fig, *F. pleuro-*

carpa. These broad-leaved evergreens can play point and counterpoint to the fan-like fronds and slender stems of various palms. Another atmospheric, but overused, tree is the Australian umbrella tree, *Schefflera actinophylla*. Its large clusters of radiating, pendant, glossy green leaves convey an appropriate air of tropical luxuriance. Even more evocatively tropical, the Natal wild banana, *Strelitzia nicolai*, grows rapidly with broad, deep green banana leaves arching from groups of stems. From the same family, and not a true palm, the strikingly architectural traveller's palm, *Ravenala madagascariensis*, provides yet another distinctive form, with broad, paddle-shaped fronds held stiffly in a single plane, like giant fans above short, strong stems. As a grove, with their fronds all orientated in the same direction, this plant creates a unique and slightly disturbing impression of ordered regimentation. The flat crown, *Albizia adianthifolia*, grows in the forests of tropical Africa alongside wild date palms—equally distinctive but entirely different. An ideal plant for hot and humid gardens, it forms a single strong stem supporting arching branches that spread out like a broadly vaulted ceiling to shade the ground below.

The pronounced and effective fronds of tree ferns make these plants prominent players in the tropical garden theatre, especially those that grow rapidly and make their presence felt early, like *Cyathea cooperi* or *C. howeana*. The latter, from subtropical Lord Howe Island off of Australia's eastern coast, has feathery heads of 2-metre-long fronds on tall stems marbled with the traces of pale scars left by the fallen fronds. The forest cordylines, too, support such theatrical scenes, including the broad-leaved palm lily *Cordyline petiolaris*, or the narrower leaved *C. rubra*, both of which produce heads of pale purple flowers followed by glistening red berries.

Crotons, *Codiaeum variegatum*, are useful shrubs for planting below the trees, and most effectively used in this role at the Ladlau garden introduced earlier. The glossy leaves of this species are so shiny and densely coloured that they appear to be lacquered, in combinations of yellow, green, scarlet and crimson. The multicoloured variegated leaves both harmonise and contrast with the broader, softer, foliage of the Fijian *Acalypha wilkesiana*. Cultivars of *A. wilkesiana* contribute pools of densely coloured yellows, scarlets or crimsons, the colours developing most fully in sun. These shrubs do not lend themselves to the modulated contrasts, half-tones and subtle combinations of pastel tints that designers of herbaceous borders and cottage gar-

The leaves of wild croton, *Codiaeum variegatum,* may be broad or narrowly strap-shaped, with colors comprising shades of green, red, yellow, orange and purple. Beverley Estate, Rosemary Ladlau's garden, Umhlali, KwaZulu-Natal, South Africa.

The large, oval leaves of *Acalypha wilkesiana* may be variously coloured bronze, copper, red or crimson, with or without cream or yellow blotches, and serve well as backdrops to other plants. Beverley Estate, Rosemary Ladlau's garden, Umhlali, KwaZulu-Natal, South Africa.

dens look for; they demand much bolder treatment. Broad-leaved perennials creeping amongst the multicoloured crotons and glowing acalyphas in the Ladlau garden create a palimpsest of texture and colour beyond the wildest imaginings of gardeners in cool, grey northern climes.

Climbers and Ground Cover in the Jungle Garden

No jungle is truly jungly without creepers and lianes hanging from the trees. On a grandiose scale, none introduces a more exuberantly exaggerated note than the giant *Solandra grandiflora*. The enormous trumpet-shaped, creamy yellow flowers, stained with crimson in their throats, first impressed me when I met the plant threatening to engulf the verandah of the Duke of Marlborough Hotel in Russell on the shores of the Bay of Islands in northern New Zealand. This may be too big for most purposes; one size down are *Monstera deliciosa* and *Philodendron bipinnatilidum,* both perhaps on the verge of becoming cliché plants, but like the umbrella tree too good to miss — until, hopefully, gardeners' imaginations will conjure up something more original, and even better. Numerous less invasive climbers can be used to add colour and atmosphere, including colourful passion flowers like the red-flowered *Passiflora aurantia* of Queensland, or the pink trumpet vine *Tecomanthe hillii,* all the more valuable for its bright rose-pink and cream flowers produced during the winter. The Argentine trumpet vine, *Clytostoma callistegioides,* is one of a dozen evergreen species from southern Brazil and Argentina. This floriferous and moderately vigorous climber has delicately shaded violet and lilac tubular flowers with flared mouths and unequal lobes. It grows best on moist, well-drained soils, partially shaded at ground level. Finally, *Metrosideros carmineus* is a vigorous, self-clinging creeper with small, deep green leaves that are almost concealed when the heads of crimson-scarlet flowers open.

Epiphytic orchids and vireyan rhododendrons—preferably secured to the trees in their natural manner of growth, perched in the crotches and amongst the branches or growing on the stems of tree ferns—are as essential to the jungle ambience as the climbers. The glowing orange, scarlet, cream or bright rose-pink flowers of the rhododendrons stand out against the glossy greens of evergreen trees and shrubs, while large clumps of the easily grown king orchid, *Dendrobium speciosum,* provide striking displays with their arching racemes of white or rich creamy yellow flowers. The terrestrial white Christmas orchid, *Calanthe triplicata,* is equally beautiful in a coolly elegant way, with glossy green, pleated leaves and heads of flowers on long white stems; as is *Phaius tankervilleae,* with erect spikes of white flowers spiced with ginger, for a moist spot with its roots in shade.

These terrestrial orchids bring us to an innumerable cast of extras to cover the forest floor—and the word *cover* is used deliberately here. The prevailing warmth and humidity that provide the conditions in which this kind of tropical planting thrives are also extremely inviting to weeds. Spaces left unfilled by garden plants are an open invitation to less desirable intruders. Numerous boldly foliaged, vigorous and attractive plants can be used to ensure that our productions are not upstaged by interlopers. These include large plants with big leaves, such as shell ginger, *Alpinia zerumbet* (and a form with brightly variegated leaves, named 'Variegata'), and elephants ears, *Colocasia gigantea.* Many of these plants—as well as dracaenas, marantas, heliconias and nephrolepis ferns—are familiar to temperate gardeners as house plants seen on florists' shelves. Not least of these is the humble spider plant, *Chlorophytum comosum.* So often seen forlornly occupying a shelf in a bathroom, this natural inhabitant of the moist evergreen forests along the coast of KwaZulu-Natal is transformed when used as ground cover

The Argentine trumpet vine, *Clytostoma callistegioides,* produces a long succession of delicately textured violet and lilac tubular flowers. The Regional Botanic Garden at Manurewa, near Auckland, North Island, New Zealand.

amongst other plants, where it will infiltrate gaps and hang on, in deep shade and even during periods of drought, with the same tenacity that enables it to survive neglected on a bathroom shelf. Cultivars with more colourful foliage than the wild form bring light and movement to dark corners of a garden. 'Gold Nugget' is a low-growing, ground-hugging form for particularly shaded situations; 'Mandaianum' is compact with narrow, dark green leaves striped yellow-green; 'Picturatum' has broad yellow stripes down the middles of its leaves; and 'Vittatum' has foliage with white stripes that are broad down the centre and pencil fine towards the margins.

The familiar cottage garden perennials are replaced in tropical climes by plants that are as unashamedly flamboyant as the shrubs and palms beneath which they grow, and Rosemary Ladlau's garden reveals many notable examples. The crimson lake foliage of the Brazilian beef plant *Iresine herbstii* 'Acuminata', or 'Aureo-reticulata' with yellow-veined leaves set off by

Tropical ground cover in the shade of trees can look like the inside of a florist's shop, with the broadly oval leaves of more-or-less familiar house plants forming dense communities luxuriating in constant warmth and humidity. Michael and Jennifer Jackson's garden, Umdloti, KwaZulu-Natal, South Africa.

crimson stems, grow alongside cannas with variegated or purple-flushed leaves topped by spikes of brilliant scarlet, orange or yellow flowers. Various dracaenas supplement and complement the cannas, and grow well in more shaded situations. Other notable plants for such places include the Madagascar native *Dracaena marginata*, which has long narrow leaves with red margins, and the cultivar 'Tricolor', distinguished by the addition of a cream stripe; or *D. fragrans* 'Santa Rosa', in which the deep green leaves have yellow margins with a central lime-green stripe. Marantas from Central and South America spread tenaciously across the ground, even in deep shade, with the veins of their deep green foliage defined and emphasised by subtle overlays of cream and crimson. Many of the cultivated forms are varieties of *Maranta leuconeura*, amongst them var. *erythroneura*, with velvety deep grey-green foliage marked with herring-bone patterns and crimson reverses, and var. *kerchoviana*, with light green leaves marked with brown blotches on either side of the midrib. Erupting amongst them is the broad, upright foliage of *Dieffenbachia seguine*, a vigorous plant from tropical South America, capable of growing to 3 metres. Its deep green leaves are marbled with pale green or

Dense planting like these cannas and iresines, in sunshine or in shade, produces self-sustaining communities that are an essential strategy of survival in gardens where perpetually warm, humid conditions invite rapid colonisation by weeds. Michael and Jennifer Jackson's garden, Umdloti, KwaZulu-Natal, South Africa.

cream between the veins. Available selections include 'Amoena', with creamy white bands and marbling between the veins; 'Rudolph Roehrs' in tones of green; and 'Tropic Marianne', with deep green edges to pale lime-green leaves.

Bromeliads

Like palms and bananas, bromeliads speak of the tropics wherever they are seen, and provide dramatic impact. They were adopted by Roberto Burle Marx as a trademark of his interpretation of the tropical garden. These relatives of the pineapples appear in gardens and in our houses under such names as *Aechmea*, *Billbergia*, *Guzmania*, *Neoregelia*, *Tillandsia* and *Vriesea*. They are plants constructed in an entirely novel and distinctive fashion, with rosettes of often broad, robustly built leaves, which may form a cup to collect water. Other bromeliads from cooler, more temperate, often arid parts of the world, including puyas, dyckias and fascicularias, lack the tropical opulence of those just mentioned. They grow as terrestrials, with closely packed rosettes of long, narrow, sometimes spiny leaves, from which the puyas produce great barrel-shaped compound spikes of strangely coloured lemon-green or blue-green flowers.

The term "tropical opulence" conveys a superficial, misleading impression that these plants grow in conditions of plenty, whereas in fact they are adapted to austerity. Under natural conditions many bromeliads are epiphytes, some in relatively benign situations on tree branches, dead wood and rotting logs; others, technically lithophytes, grow on the austere surfaces of large boulders, often sitting half-baked by the sun's heat day after day. Over the last few years gardeners have begun to warm to these strange plants, and one of my first encounters with them was in Eden Gardens in Auckland. Here they are planted in pockets of soil formed by terracing a steep bank, elsewhere in the garden they grow crowded in a more natural fashion along the gaunt branches of a dead tree arching over a pool of water. I thought then how ill at ease the former looked and how appropriately placed the latter were, and whenever I have seen them since I have never found any reason to alter my belief that these plants look grotesque and out of place when grown as terrestrials, and that their impact in gardens depends on being grown in situations similar to those they inhabit naturally.

Avon Ryan's garden in Whangarei, New Zealand, provided me with one of the most memorable displays of gardening eccentricity that I have en-

Whether growing on the ground or in the air, bromeliads are a simple and effective way to create a tropical ambience in a small space—particularly valuable where there is not room for palms to spread their wings. Avon Ryan's garden, Whangarei, North Island, New Zealand.

countered. A chance visit during a garden festival revealed the delights of bromeliads used in exuberant, extravagant displays that made more careful fashions seen nearby seem positively inhibited. When Avon retired, with no obvious way to occupy his time, his wife's stepmother happened to present him with two bromeliads. These struck such a vital chord that he now gardens as though the Creator never contrived to invent any other kind of plant, and the quarter-acre section around his house is crammed from one end to the other with bromeliads. The front section, enclosed by white painted walls, is entirely filled with bromeliads. They grow in pots on the ground and on shelves; tillandsias, aechmeas and neoregalias cluster on the branches of artificial trees. The effect was dazzling and quite overwhelming, a brighter and more diversely coloured display than I ever imagined could be obtained by exclusive use of these plants. The back section of the garden, equally colourful and eccentric, differed mainly in covering a much larger area. Narrow paths wound between bromeliads massed pot thick in small groups, drifts or edgings of a single kind. A little grove of trees provided shade and shelter for many more covering the ground around a red tele-

Fascicularia bicolor is one of the few bromeliads that does not require frost-free conditions. Even so, it was a surprise to find it growing and thriving in Edinburgh in an enclosure open to the skies, around the Glasshouse Experience. The Royal Botanic Garden, Edinburgh, Scotland.

phone box in endless variations on a single theme. The foliage of these plants ranged from pale yellow to deepest crimson, sometimes tending to a liverish shade, often speckled or blotched with contrasting colours in random patterns, which to the uninitiated are all too inclined to appear as blemishes rather than decoration. Others were rainbow hued, or had longitudinal bands of different colours along the lengths of the leaves; still others, transversely banded, were striped like tigers or speckled like partridges.

Aechmeas include the well-known urn plant *Aechmea fasciata* from southern Brazil. This species has broad leaves banded with different tones of silver and jade-green, and long-lasting spikes of scarlet flowers. It is one of the easiest to grow, provided it has perfect drainage, and water constantly in its cups. Aechmeas with hardish, often colourful leaves do well in shade; those with softer and green leaves prefer sunlit conditions.

The textures and colours of these tillandsias and other bromeliads massed on the trunk and limbs of an artificial tree create a sensational impression that could not be reproduced by any other group of plants. Avon Ryan's garden, Whangarei, North Island, New Zealand.

Billbergias are usually represented by *Billbergia nutans*, with arching olive-green leaves, amongst which bright pink bracts produce pendant spikes of green flowers with violet edges. *Billbergia pyramidalis* has pink and purple flowers enclosed within the rosette of leaves. These easily grown plants are capable of enduring harsh conditions of drought and exposure. Best in full sun, most forms flower in spring, but whereas aechmeas remain colourful for months, billbergias are more likely to last for weeks.

Guzmanias grow most often in rainforests, rather than more open situations. They are less amenable to garden conditions and less tolerant of desiccation and require more care to do well, but their brightly patterned, glossy foliage and exotic looking flowers repay the attention they need. Most species form fairly open rosettes of soft leaves.

Neoregelias are mostly easy to grow in sunshine or in light shade, where the colours of their leaves may be more muted. The cups of the rosettes should be kept constantly filled with water. *Neoregelia spectabilis,* amongst others, produces a ring of small, bright blue flowers in the centre of the rosettes of crimson-flushed leaves. The leaves of some garden varieties, such as *N. meyendorfii* var. *tricolor,* have longitudinal bands of brightly contrasting colours.

Dramatically splendid, tropical-looking foliage is the hallmark of the taros, species of *Alocasia* and *Colocasia*. All need warmth, rain and constantly moist fertile soils to look their best, and since the strikingly opulent appearance of their leaves is the sole reason for growing these plants, there is no point in attempting them unless these conditions can be provided. The biggest and grandest is the well-named elephant's ear, *A. macrorrhiza*, with gigantic, broad, shield-like leaves. The scented taro, *Alocasia odora*, has sweetly fragrant flowers and foliage that dies down in winter, and it is less dependent on constant warmth and moisture. A range of hybrids have been bred specifically for use as ornamentals, emphasising the decorative qualities of their large, bold leaves. The other species involved in the crosses include *A. sanderiana*, notable for its deeply lobed leaves and contrasting silver veins, and *A. ×amazonica*, with lightly glossy, forest green foliage with silver veins and crimson reverses. Amongst the hybrids, 'Portadora' produces clumps of bold, deep green leaves; 'California Shield', clumps of broad, glossy green leaves; and 'Midnight', dark green to almost black leaves and black stems.

Plants in containers allow us to indulge in fantasies and allow imagination to reign, with no more commitment than the time and effort it takes to move pots and pieces around. Bellevue, Vivien Papich's garden, near Wipe, North Island, New Zealand.

PART III

Gardens in Containers

GARDENERS in tune with Nature may pay lip service to the idea that the situations of their gardens and the conditions they provide should be their guiding stars—but all true gardeners strain at these limits, disdaining what grows easily and striving to attain the unattainable. Even in my Shropshire frost pocket I look longingly towards exotic plants from the subtropics, even the tropics, wondering how I might contrive to possess them. Perhaps I could grow them in a conservatory? Maybe plant them in containers and move them under cover in cold weather? If there is one thing I have learnt while going round gardens, it is never to suggest to any owner that their conditions are idyllic. That unleashes descriptions of the horrors they endure from wind, drought, unremitting rain, too much sun, excessive shade, gophers, mole rats, deer, possums, lyre birds, neighbours' cats, their own children, bandicoots, baboons, clay soils, sandy soils, limey soils, mud, dust, floods, volcanic eruptions, lightning strikes or, if imagination fails, civil insurrection. The list of our afflictions is endless, usually amplified by superlatives that make it plain that our particular patch has been designed by Nature to make gardening of any kind an almost insurmountable challenge. How marvellous we all are to carry on in the face of such difficulties!

The fact is that, wherever we live (short of Nirvana), there will always be plants we should like to have but that we cannot or fear to grow in our gardens. Gardeners have always recognised that, and have devised ways to get round it. Tender plants are sheltered in orangeries, greenhouses or conservatories, or grown in containers, so that they can be given the care and attention they need.

Plants from the Southern Hemisphere have something of a reputation for being hard to please when introduced to gardens in the north. Some are born recalcitrant; some have recalcitrance thrust upon them by the grower's lack of familiarity with their needs, rather than any inbuilt intractabilities. Nevertheless, many Looking-Glass plants are susceptible to frost; some must have perfect drainage or are geared to strictly seasonal variations in water availability; others cannot tolerate high nutrient levels or excessive sunlight. It is easier to cater for such special needs by growing them in containers or in greenhouses rather than planting them in the garden. Once their particular quirks, aversions and preferences are recognised, many plants that would never thrive in the free-for-all of the garden become amenable and rewarding in containers.

Customers at my nursery would often ask if a plant they fancied would grow in a container—a reasonable query from someone with a container to fill, but rendered surreal by the fact that the plant they were buying was usually happily doing just that. Where containers are concerned, anything grows, provided it is not killed by kindness, ignorance or neglect. Its destiny is in our hands, and though some plants are more difficult than others to keep alive or encourage to thrive, we are the arbiters of their fate; it is our sins and omissions that determine the results rather than some inborn aversion to being contained on the part of the plant. This is not the place to go into all the variables involved in choosing or mixing composts; learning the skills of watering; deciding how often to apply fertilisers; or unravelling the complexities of plant nutrition. I only have to spend a day at a horticultural trade show to be reminded of those complications. Stand after stand describes why their irrigation system is better than anyone else's, will display the superior benefits of their composts, or advertise the unique virtues of their particular formulations of N-P-K supplemented with obscure additives of unimaginable complexity. Then I come home and continue, as before, to water my motley collection of plants in containers, as and when they seem to need it; I pot them up using the same, pretty well standardised compost that I have used for years; and feed them from time to time with whatever proprietary feed is the flavour of the month with me, or happened to be on the shelves when I went to buy some. Most, though not all, plants seem to do well enough, and as time goes on, occasional disasters, disappointments and failures show me which will not tolerate this casual, slapdash treatment, and teach me that, if I want to grow them, I must offer something a little different, something that recognises their individuality and makes them feel a little special.

Such failures as occur can seldom be traced directly to the variables mentioned in the previous paragraph. Plants that are over- or under-watered do not thrive as they might, but these oversights can usually be corrected long before the plants die; and variations in the composition of the growing medium or its nutrient status will be a matter of life and death only to a minority of faddy, choosy or discriminating plants. Disasters result from negligence of more fundamental kinds that are often in my power to avoid, just because the plants are being grown in containers. Obvious examples are plants that are not frost-hardy. If these are not moved into a greenhouse or other frost-free place, they will be killed during the winter irrespective of compost, feeding or watering—end of story. But not quite the whole story, for some plants that I grow come from places like the Drakensberg, where winters are cold but dry. Left outside, the combination of frost and rain will surely kill them, but when kept dry they can survive quite severe frosts. Aga-

This timber shelter is a simple and economical way to overwinter herbaceous perennials from places with dry winters, like agapanthus, river lilies, watsonias, rhodohypoxis, eucomis and others. Red Lion House, the author's garden, Shropshire, England.

panthus, river lilies *(Hesperantha coccinea)*, dianellas, nerines, pineapple flowers *(Eucomis)* and rhodohypoxis, amongst others, do not need expensive and precious glasshouse space, just overhead shelter from rain in the form of a lean-to timber roof against a wall, open on three sides—the sort of thing that might be built to keep logs dry for the fire, and that is exactly where I put these plants, bringing them out in early spring when the worst frosts are over and just before the plants start to grow again.

Numerous bulbs from Mediterranea retreat underground during the summer after flowering in the spring. Many tolerate moderate but not severe frosts, and grow actively through the winter, when they need ample water, but once they have died down the bulbs must be kept dry during the summer. In my cold garden, moraeas, lachenalias, babianas, bulbinellas, ixias, sparaxis and many other Cape bulbs need winter protection in an unheated greenhouse or frame, and later, after they have flowered, they go back into the frame to be dried out before the summer. Left outside in a cold climate, these plants would fade away within a year or two, at best.

Finally, we return to "Will it grow in a container?"—a question which is more likely to imply suspicion that the plant will soon grow out of the container, than serious doubt that it can grow there at all. But plants do not grow out of their containers, or rather their tops do not, unless the roots have first made their escape into the unrestricted freedom of the soil below. Shoots and leaves depend on roots for their sustenance, and as long as the roots are confined, the growth of the aboveground parts will also be restricted, maintaining a balance between the two. The extreme example of this is the craft of bonsai, by which a grove of trees can be grown in a terracotta tray a few centimetres deep. These bonsaied trees are neither starved of nutrients nor deprived of water; their ambitions are limited by root pruning and confinement, but they continue to be watered and supplied with the nutrients they need to develop, in miniature, their natural growth forms.

A shrub or tree in a container encounters less straightened circumstances but experiences similar though lesser restraints on growth. Starting from a seedling or a rooted cutting, the plant will need to be repotted into successively larger containers, most probably year by year, until eventually it occupies one that holds ten, twenty, fifty or more litres of compost; the ultimate size is limited by the weight and bulk that can be handled if we need to move the container from one place to another. Throughout these transfers, and once in its final quarters, the containerised plant should be provided with water according to its needs and fed with nutrients to support new growth and the production of flowers and fruit—but its eventual size will depend on the size of its container, not how large it would grow unconfined in nature. This physiological balancing act between roots and shoots means that when choosing a plant to grow in a container, we can choose from the whole range of what is available. There is no need to restrict ourselves to the smaller species or to dwarf or compact cultivars, just so long as we make sure that the roots do not escape and assert their right to live free in the soil below.

A few carefully chosen plants in containers can transform the atmosphere of areas close to the house where we sit or party with friends. Bill Armstrong's garden, Glenfield, North Island, New Zealand.

CHAPTER 13

Plants for the Patio

THE VALLEYS in the Hottentots-Holland Mountains around Grabouw in the western Cape are filled with apple orchards. They also
contain one of the most beautiful rose gardens I have ever visited. I was
told about it while planning a trip to South Africa, and my immediate reaction was to give it a miss, with too many recollections of roses arranged
cemetery fashion in coffin-shaped beds filled with the stiff, self-consciously
priggish forms of hybrid teas and modern floribundas. But Barbara and
Peter Knox-Shaw's rose garden is not like that, and when I arrived there,
even though it was still winter and the show was only just beginning, I was
delighted that my initial reluctance had been overcome. Roses grow here in
informal array amongst trees and shrubs, and grassy paths wind amongst
them. They climb over the shrubs and into the trees, hanging in trails above
the paths and clustering head high and higher alongside them. There are old
tea roses from the south of France, Bourbons, hybrid perpetuals and climbers including *Rosa gigantea,* the lesser known parent of the China roses that
transformed our view of these plants in the eighteenth century. The tour of
the garden over, we sat on the stoep and chatted over a drink as darkness
gathered, the air around us fragrant from the roses amongst the trees beyond
the lawn.

Born in Mediterranea, the patio has become the offspring of suburbia—
elsewhere it might be called the terrace, the stoep, the verandah, even the
balcony. It is a place beside the house, an outdoor room, where we sit and
read, or sit and chat, or drink with friends; there may be a corner for a bar-
becue or spar; perhaps it is an adjunct to the swimming pool. It is an ideal
situation for plants in containers, where they are most appreciated and most
easily looked after. It protects us and them from cold winds, the intemper-

ate heat of the sun or the worst effects of cold, and only plants that create positive, even striking impressions over a long time merit a place there. Southern Hemisphere plants like pelargoniums, osteospermums and aloes suit the conditions and furnish agreeable impressions so well that they have become almost indispensable parts of this scene. But many others are equally effective contributors, not least amongst them shrubs from Australia and bulbs and succulents from South Africa. The shrubs are notable for the brilliance of their flowers, the bulbs for the subtleties of their shapes and textures, and the succulents for the enduring nature that enables them to survive long periods of neglect.

Most people start, as I did, with one or two containers to fill: a pair of terracotta pots, a reproduction urn or a clutch of plastic troughs. Kind friends give us these things with no thought that they may be setting us on the slippery slope of one of gardening's many addictions. Years later—when there is scarcely space to sit amongst the throng of plants, and no time to sit because watering, feeding, repotting, trimming and cosseting takes so much of our time—we wryly reflect on the almost forgiven friend whose gift ignited our obsession. Growers of plants in pots may be minimalists who use a few expensive, beautifully designed containers matched by meticulously selected plants with intensely significant shapes. Or they may be maximalists whose plants erupt in every corner, spill out across every surface, hang in trails, drifts and veils from brackets on the walls and hooks from overhead beams, and climb from the ground up the poles of pergolas. Those like myself who enjoy growing plants are seldom minimalists, and face the problem of providing containers in which to grow all the things they cannot do without. Some solve this dilemma by using salvage, anything from painted food cans to old oil drums; others make for the nearest garden centre where they have two choices: pay up, or put up. They can dig deep into their pockets to pay for containers of terracotta, stoneware, fibreglass and other expensive materials, or put up with mass-produced, moulded plastic troughs and pots. So home they go, turn the plants out of the plain black containers in which they bought them, and install them lovingly in hand-thrown clay or machine-pressed plastic, depending on whether purse or prudence ruled the day. A month later the decision scarcely matters, because the foliage and flowers of the plants conceal whatever they are growing in. I am convinced that unless the shapes, forms and textures of the containers are essential parts of the display, simplest and cheapest is best; nothing comes simpler or cheaper than the matte black polypropylene containers in which plants from nurseries and garden centres are sold. They are available in many sizes, they last indefinitely, they cost little, there is no problem mixing and matching one with another, and their dark matte surfaces melt unobtrusively into the shadows beneath the plants.

That brings us to the much more pleasant business of choosing the plants. The first thing we discover is that the Looking-Glass Garden provides a remarkably high proportion of plants that we already are accustomed to growing in containers. The second is that the shapes, forms and textures of numerous plants from the Southern Hemisphere are of just the kind that create distinctive and memorable impressions. The stalwarts that we all know and love include numerous South African daisies, amongst them gazanias, osteospermums, venidiums, arctotis and gerberas. Brilliant colours, bright displays for weeks on end, easily controllable growth and a readiness to be propagated make them perfect home-made plants, provided you do not expect them to greet you for breakfast on the terrace. Several of these are more inclined to lie in till coffee and biscuits at elevenses, when the sun is high and warm in the sky. Massive flower power is provided by petunias from South America in an endless variety of pastel pinks, mauves, violets, white and cream, often accompanied by blue, purple or crimson lobelias from Australia and South Africa, and "geraniums," in particular the regal, ivy-leaved and zonal pelargoniums from South Africa. Mesembs revel in the hottest, brightest situations and are so forgiving of neglectful watering and scant attention to feeding that they are almost indestructible. Species of *Lampranthus, Drosanthemum* and *Delosperma* produce masses of glossy, shimmering daisy heads in eye-catching crimsons, purples, mauves and pinks. More recent additions to the throng include phormiums from New Zealand, plants ranging from barely 30 centimetres high to giants (for suitably giant containers) 3 metres high; also the South African felicias with bright blue or light purple daisies around yellow eyes that flower throughout the summer; and new races of dwarf Peruvian lilies *(Alstroemeria)* and diascias.

The obvious attractions of these plants, supported by massive commercial promotion, have made them the dominant players in the container scene, to be seen in stereotyped displays in the gardens of London, San Francisco, Auckland, Perth and Cape Town. They are bright, they are cheap and cheerful, and the density, brilliance and variety of colours they pack into small spaces are just what we need to pick us up on a low day—but they numb our sense of discrimination. This dazzling flower power is seldom sympathetic or in harmony with its surroundings. It overwhelms its setting, and distracts attention away from architectural, landscape or other features. Other plants from the Southern Hemisphere can be used to enhance the surroundings, create dynamic or restful atmospheres, enliven the garden during otherwise muted seasons, and bring features or points of interest close to places where we sit and relax and enjoy them most. Some create sharply defined impressions that complement architectural features, or have striking sculptural forms that change when seen from different angles or as the light varies through the day—others are so dramatic that they can be deliberately used, if the idea appeals, to impress and astonish your friends. The notably soft foliage or amorphous forms of yet others act as counterpoints, making fewer demands on the onlooker and encouraging a more relaxed atmosphere, an invitation to sit, even to snooze. Nevertheless, it is the flowers that people appreciate and value most, and the longer plants in containers remain colourful, the better—especially when their flowers have interesting qualities apart from size and colour. Interest is where we find it. We may look for flowers or berries that attract birds or butterflies, be enchanted by a plant's aromatic foliage or sweetly fragrant flowers, by its rarity, or by its historical associations. Best of all are those plants that combine a variety of qualities, in which form, colour, texture, flowers, fruits and everything else confer perennial presentability and broadly based attractions.

I have already made the point that anything can be grown in a container, even trees, so there can be no such thing as a short list, or even a long list, of "container" plants, using the term to suggest those that are most amenable to this treatment. The only criteria that need be applied are matching the situation, the time available to care for them, and the effects sought—as in any form of gardening.

Mostly for Flowers

Two tree mallows, *Abutilon vitifolium* and *Alyogyne huegelii,* make fine bold, exceptionally floriferous shrubs with large flowers produced for months on end. The abutilon, a native of Chile, is easily grown from seed, grows rapidly and produces purple, violet, lilac or white flowers precociously and prolifically. Cultivars of the Western Australian *Alyogyne huegelii*, including the striking, vibrant purple-flowered 'Santa Cruz', flower almost continuously in favourable conditions.

The enduring qualities of many aloes, and their tolerance of drought, qualify them as undemanding plants to grow in containers during the summer, when they are appreciated for their sculptural forms; and their vibrantly colourful orange or red tubular flowers are a cheerful prospect to look forward to when winter comes. Two excellent species for containers are *Aloe striata*, the coral aloe, and *A. aristata*, guinea fowl aloe. Some, like *A. saponaria*, look good and have exceptional drought tolerance. Gardeners who are prepared to risk disappointment in search of something special might try *A. polyphylla*, a stemless aloe notable for the perfection of the spiral forms of its rosettes of succulent leaves. In the wild it can be breathtakingly beautiful; in gardens, imperfections are inclined to mar its symmetry. It produces branching spikes of flowers in early spring.

Abutilon vitifolium var. *album* is just as hardy as the species type and offers white flowers for months on end. It is a fast-growing and rewarding plant, especially for those in the early stages of getting a garden going. Powys Castle, Welshpool, Wales.

Banksias can be rewarding shrubs in containers, which can be used to provide the good drainage and watering regimes they require. Amongst many fine forms of *Banksia spinulosa*, 'Birthday Candles' is compact, has attractive foliage and carries numerous blunt cones of lemon-yellow flowers. For something entirely different, *B. blechnifolia* produces clusters of leaves that could be mistaken for the fronds of a fern, until it surprises by producing cylinders of large, yellow and russet flowers deep within the recesses of its fronds. The foliage is held upright in contrast to the plant's prostrate growth form.

For most bulbs, the foliage that accompanies the bright flowers is functional rather than beautiful or interesting, but *Boophone disticha* and *Brunsvigia bosmaniae* challenge that common assessment, adding to their appeal in containers. The former species produces pure white flowers above beautiful fan-shaped foliage with elegantly waved margins. The lipstick pink flowers of *Brunsvigia bosmaniae* radiate from the tops of naked stems in autumn, and are followed in spring by extraordinary, deep green, broad leaves, flat on the surface like pads of some thick, heavily textured plastic.

The Chilean *Buddleja globosa* is too coarse and insufficiently appealing to

The fern-like foliage and large, red cylindrical inflorescences of *Banksia blechnifolia* create a most unusual and striking ensemble. John and Muriel Simmons' garden, Legana, Tasmania, Australia.

merit a container, but its hybrid with *B. davidii*, *B. ×weyeriana*, has whorls of soft apricot flowers that are just as attractive to butterflies as its Chinese parent. A container moderates its growth, reducing it to a size that can easily be accommodated on a patio or terrace, where a plant that brings butterflies close to where we sit is a real asset.

The Australian bottlebrushes make excellent container-grown shrubs, with their cylindrical heads of flowers ranging from brilliant scarlet to shocking pink, above fine foliage that is often flushed with crimson and shines like silk when immature. Their tendency to grow gangly is easily remedied by pruning, and they can be trained, if desired, to form standards. Compact floriferous selections like *Callistemon viminalis* 'Little John' are good choices, but the taller *C. pallidus* 'Mount Oberon', with the added attraction of silver immature foliage and creamy yellow bottlebrushes, for a change, remains compact in a container. These are not shrubs that enjoy austerity, and ample watering and regular feeding produce the best results.

Grasses are seldom seen in containers, but *Chionochloa flavicans*, amongst others, can be effective as a contrast to broad-leaved plants and shrubs. A reluctance to flower unless amply supplied with water and nutrients can be a problem, as with many perennial grasses. They need to be grown in large containers, and when generously treated their broad plumes of creamy white, silky flowers on short strong stems are emphatic enough to make a strong contribution. The rusty foliage and upright spiky forms of *C. rubra* growing in large planters amongst low-growing native shrubs, in the centre of the small town of Te Anau in New Zealand, provided me with a convincing demonstration of the impact this plant can make when imaginatively used in a well-chosen setting.

A great many diascias have appeared on the garden scene over the last two or three decades. They flower profusely from spring till autumn and are so easily and rapidly propagated that, though mostly soft and gutless little plants, they are most useful stand-ins. Formerly almost exclusively coral-pink, the colour range is progressively widening, though still predominantly sugary rather than vibrant.

Patient souls with a taste for suspense and dramatic impact might try *Doryanthes excelsa*, the Australian gymea lily. Its broad leaves create an imposing impression in a container. But even when the plant is grown in good conditions, you can expect to wait perhaps ten years for it to begin producing its magnificent inflorescences of glowing red flowers on stout, pole-like stems.

Lantana camara is a long-established container plant with multicoloured heads of flowers, like verbenas, that develop in succession more or less continuously. Older cultivars can be rampant colonisers and are detested weeds in many parts of the world. Newer hybrids are sterile, and their emasculated condition and innocuous natures enable us to grow them with impunity and enjoy their range of colours and compact shapes. Cultivar names like 'Brasier', 'Cloth of Gold', 'Feston Rose' and 'Snow White' suggest the colours we have to choose from.

Tea trees of many kinds make good container plants, and their habit of flowering during, often throughout, the winter makes them particularly valuable. Widely grown ones include the numerous cultivars of *Leptospermum scoparium*, the New Zealand manuka, with single or double flowers ranging from pure white to deep crimson. These shrubs can be narrowly columnar, broadly rounded, upright, spreading or prostrate. As a change, try selections of the Australian *L. rotundifolium*, such as 'Manning's Choice', which has much larger flowers ranged along its shoots in an attractive shade of crushed strawberry pink.

Another group of shrubs that make a great contribution in mild areas are the leucadendrons, especially the numerous winter-flowering hybrids of the 'Safari Sunset' persuasion. The rather different 'Waterlily', a female selection of *Leucadendron strobilinum*, offers bracts that open green in the spring, change to cream or pale yellow, and eventually become flushed with crimson.

Cultivars of *Leucospermum cordifolium*, now appearing in an endless variety of shades of yellow, flame, scarlet and orange, are dynamic, vibrant and effective shrubs (see Chapter Four for a sampling of such selections). They are often much more successful when grown in containers, where watering and feeding can be controlled more easily than in the garden.

Impeccable drainage, low nutrient status and ample water throughout the growing season reduced to meagre sufficiency during the summer spell health and prosperity for proteas, requirements that are almost impossible to provide in well-endowed gardens, but more easily catered for when the plants are grown in containers. Garden centres now regularly stock numerous species and cultivars, but like rhododendrons, these plants so beguile us with their flowers that we often overlook the many months when they are no more than leaves and shoots; then, proteas all too often are no better than plain, and some are so gawky, dowdy and awkward-looking that they make little repayment for the effort needed to look after them. The king protea, *Protea cynaroides*, is often promoted as the protea with the mostest, even though the broad pink coronet of its flower is closer to a baronet's headgear than the regal crown of a king. It is widespread in the mountains along the southern fringe of Africa, and is one of the hardiest and easiest to grow. Numerous selected forms are available, the reasons for their selection indicated by names such as 'Imperial Pink', 'Imperial Red', 'Scarlet King', 'Silver Monarch' and 'Snow King'. This protea is the national flower of South Africa, and the one with the largest flowers, but its broadly spreading nature develops too readily into a sprawling bush unless cut back hard after flowering. The king's consort, the queen protea, *P. magnifica*, is found in places with cold winters and hot dry summers, and it also flowers between late au-

Hybrids and selections of *Protea neriifolia* are amongst the most amenable garden plants in their genus. Etienne Truter's garden, near Rotorua, North Island, New Zealand.

tumn and spring. But this is a more temperamental plant than the king protea, usually resenting the efforts of those who try to cultivate it, and even when grown successfully can take six years or more to flower from seed. A selection known as 'Pink Diamond', with large reddish pink flowers enclosing an ermine dome of silky white hair tipped with black, is a considerably less demanding lady. The most prolific member of the clan from a gardener's point of view is the black bearded protea, *P. neriifolia*. Its long, narrow bracts range from cream through salmon and rose-pink to deep brick red, each tipped with a fringe of crimson or brown hairs forming a fur-trimmed apex to the flower. Flowers appear from early winter to early spring, and the long grey-green leaves, by no means the least of its attractions, look good at any time. A host of cultivars of *P. neriifolia* have been produced, including 'Silk & Satin', with seductively decadent rose-pink flowers tipped with black fur—opulent and naughty—and 'Frosted Fire', crimson-scarlet with white frosting. The slightly different 'Pink Ice' is a hybrid between *P. neriifolia* and the lime-tolerant *P. susannae*. It is particularly tolerant in cultivation and widely grown for the production of cut flowers. It lacks the fur-tipped bracts of *P. neriifolia*, and with them goes some of the air of the naughty nineties, which is one of the attractions of this group of proteas.

The New Zealand kowhais *Sophora tetraptera* and *S. microphylla* can be grown in containers, where they develop steadily into small trees that are exceptionally beautiful when carrying their clusters of large bright yellow flowers; even when not in flower the tracery of branches and the small, almost fern-like leaves are attractions. Immature plants of *S. microphylla* display a divaricating growth form that provides a talking point. Compact forms like 'Dragon's Gold' or 'Gnome' suggest themselves as more obvious candidates for a container, but these cultivars are shrubs rather than trees.

The arum lily, *Zantedeschia aethiopica*, makes a superb, bold container-grown plant, with its elegant white flowers for months on end amongst broad, deep green leaves, which create splendid effects in their own right. Ample watering and regular feeding are needed to keep arum lilies in growth and bloom. Calla lilies—mostly with spotted foliage and flowers that range in colour from pale cream through deep yellow to apricot, tan and terra-cotta—lack the presence of the arum lily, but provided they are kept dry through the winter, are easily grown and highly effective plants for summer colour.

Mainly for Foliage

Ferns in containers are familiar as house plants or in the conservatory, but are surprisingly seldom seen on the terrace. Most ferns, including *Asplenium bulbiferum* and *Adiantum aethiopicum*, grow well in containers, and many are forgiving of erratic watering and inadequate feeding. Large tree ferns can be grown in quite small containers, and their striking forms and distinctive fronds and trunks make dramatic impressions amongst flowering plants.

For something slightly different from the typical pure white flowers of arum lilies, *Zantedeschia aethiopica* 'Green Tip' is worth a try, with green and white flowers that are more defined and better shaped than the widely grown 'Green Goddess'. Henry Rasmussen's garden, Hylton, KwaZulu-Natal, South Africa.

Most appreciate shaded situations and can be used effectively to fill in spaces and provide contrasting backgrounds to plants with brightly coloured flowers.

Coprosma is a large and varied genus that includes numerous shrubs that merit attention in containers. Their highly polished leaf surfaces, often combined with variegations or tints of copper or crimson, create decorative effects that make greater impact in a container than in the garden. Mirror plants, as these shiny leaved coprosmas are called, that can be guaranteed to make an impact in a container include 'Pride', a broadly growing upright form with extremely glossy, variegated leaves, green with bronzed margins and creamy, lime-green centres; and 'Copper Shine', upright and twiggy with clusters of coriaceous leaves like a butcher's broom *(Ruscus aculeatus)*, brilliantly glossy with bronzed margins. 'Gold Splash', with broad cream margins and a central deep green flash, and 'Painter's Palette', with highly polished crimson, green and cream variegated foliage, are two more that are upright and bushy. 'Kiwi Gold' is prostrate and spreads widely, with small cream-centred leaves with deep green margins. Some coprosmas are amongst the most complexly divaricating of all shrubs, forming extraordinary tangles of twiggy shoots and tiny leaves that can look a mess in the garden, but make a more positive and interesting impression when viewed in a container. Two that would be bound to make an impression—though there may be differences of opinion about whether they are beautiful—are *Coprosma virescens*, a rigidly upright shrub with extraordinary tangled growth of finely drawn copper-coloured shoots and tiny leaves, and *C. rhamnoides*, which takes the form of a tangled ball, dotted with small bright red drupes that turn blackish crimson as they ripen.

The distinctive form and impressive foliage of the New Zealand cabbage tree, *Cordyline australis*, makes it a deservedly popular container plant. The ordinary green and purple forms are becoming almost ubiquitous, used in a stereotyped way dotted about as accent plants amongst flowering annuals. Familiarity should not blind us to the possibilities of using them more imaginatively when large, luxuriant forms like 'Purple Tower' or the spiky and variegated 'Albertii' can be used to create highly theatrical effects.

Several South African restios have considerable potential as container plants as a means of introducing new and different forms that combine par-

Plants with emphatic shapes and forms like *Cordyline australis* 'Purple Tower' are invaluable in containers for the sculptural effects they create. Nymet, Colin and Jean Saunder's garden, Whangarei, North Island, New Zealand.

ticularly effectively with architectural features. *Elegia capensis*, with upright stems like an exotic bamboo embellished with cream and crimson bracts, is outstanding, and becoming more popular. Others with narrow, reed-like foliage or plumes reminiscent of ostrich feathers also offer exciting possibilities. Amongst the smaller species, the gilded inflorescences with a burnished sheen of *Restio festuciformis* cry out to be presented in combination with carefully chosen contrasting forms and textures.

Eucalypts grow rapidly in containers, and with their glaucous foliage and silvery stems can hardly be bettered where attractive plants with a tree form are needed quickly. The varied, often brilliant colours of the juvenile foliage are amongst the eucalypts' greatest attractions. They are so easily grown from seed that groups of one- or two-year-old seedlings can be used to set up stunning displays of foliage, textures and tones.

The short, dense tufts of *Restio festuciformis* could easily be mistaken for some kind of fescue, but one with foliage that has been gilded and burnished so that it shines in the sun with a metallic lustre that no grass possesses. Kirstenbosch National Botanical Garden, Western Cape Province, South Africa.

In gardens in colder parts of the world *Melianthus major* is regularly cut to the ground each winter, so that it never produces flowers and is grown entirely for its deeply divided, bright glaucous leaves, which have a powerful petrochemical smell. The splendid foliage is such an attraction that the plant should be cut back each winter when in a container, to be grown as an excellent, bold foliage plant.

Several species of *Plectranthus* look good in containers, and the soft, silvery, felted foliage and light sprays of violet flowers have made *Plectranthus argentatus* one of the international corpus of plants for containers. It thrives in sunlit positions, but will tolerate light shade.

Principally for Form

The larger aloes, including *Aloe plicatilis* and *A. arborescens,* develop a presence with age that gives them sculptural qualities, in addition to the attractions of their flowers, that are enhanced when grown in containers. These plants are drought resistant and capable of thriving naturally in arid, infertile situations. They are tolerant of neglect, but when treated to more ample conditions respond by growing more rapidly—an important consideration when the sculptural impact of their shapes is the main reason for choosing them.

Several other succulent shrubs also contribute sculptural effects. One of the most widely grown is *Cotyledon orbiculata,* a plant with succulent stems and rounded succulent leaves that occurs naturally in many forms, any of which makes its mark. *Crassula arborescens, Tylecodon paniculatus* or *Cyphostemma juttae,* from the arid countryside of southern Namibia, are similarly sculptural. *Tylecodon paniculatus* is remarkable for the silken texture of its tan skin, or bark, which covers the stems. *Cyphostemma juttae,* a close relative of the grape vine *(Vitis),* is most notable for its decorative bunches of bright red berries, and for its broad cabbage-like leaves, which later drop to reveal the stubby branches and short stout stem covered in layers of peeling white bark. Clusters of green flowers are followed by grape-like berries.

Cycads look impressive in containers, though in common with aciphyllas and cacti, we pay for our visual pleasures when accidental contact reminds us how assertively, seemingly aggressively, prickly these plants are—too much so to be comfortable companions in places where we like to congregate and be sociable. Some cycads, like the Australian *Lepidozamia peroffskyana,* have foliage that is more finely drawn, more graceful and less prickly than others.

The pronounced spiky form of *Richea dracophylla* combines well with architectural features close to the house. It grows moderately rapidly in a container, building up an upright superstructure with long narrow leaves, looking a little like a slender, branching cabbage tree. The distinctive narrowly cone-shaped inflorescences, from which white flowers emerge amongst broad bracts, are attractive, noteworthy and long lasting.

The most widely grown bird-of-paradise is *Strelitzia reginae,* often seen in a container, where its extraordinary flowers inevitably make an impression.

The Australian grass trees are effective living sculptures, and *Xanthorrhoea australis* is a rare treasure—though it takes many years to attain the stature and presence shown here. Mount Annan Botanic Garden, Campbelltown, New South Wales, Australia.

The foliage is not one of its strong points, however, even when quite young, and becomes progressively heavier, dowdier and dishevelled as time goes by. *Strelitzia juncea*, with narrowly rolled stems like long sharp-tipped lances, contributes a great deal more visually and combines well with architectural features.

Provided they are well grown, most Australian grass trees, *Xanthorrhoea*, have the visual impact necessary not merely to attract but to impress as well. The dark trunks, the extremely long attenuated foliage and the strange flower forms—some on tall, spear-like stems rising high above the arching leaves, others with strange knobbly inflorescences like the antennae of giant butterflies—invariably provide talking points and visual excitement wherever they are used.

CHAPTER 14

Gardens Under Glass

MY ARRIVAL at the Royal Botanic Gardens, Kew, during the winter of 1964 happened to coincide with the final days of a trying period in the garden's history, when winters were blighted by long periods of choking, smog-filled, sulphur-laden air. The following year this part of London became a smoke-free zone; domestic fires were converted to smokeless fuels, emissions from local industrial premises were drastically reduced, and the gas works that had loomed menacingly across the Thames for a century or more was closed down. Relief from pollution was immediate. Plants that previously had struggled to survive perked up and began to look healthy, and the gardeners began to dream again of growing the proteas, Cape heaths, banksias and other Southern Hemisphere plants that had enchanted gardeners and thrilled society 150 years earlier. This renaissance acquired tangible form, not long afterwards, when a plant of *Protea cynaroides* growing in the renovated Temperate House produced five flowers—the first time this plant had flowered at Kew since 1826. Plants like this had once fired the imagination of noble lords and newly rich industrialists. Their cultivation led the fashion for elaborate conservatories that enhanced the status of their owners, nurtured a great era of plant collecting, and were amongst the finest achievements of Victorian gardeners. But, since London's expanding urban sprawl had engulfed Kew, Cape heaths and proteas had become almost impossible to grow, and were replaced by plants more tolerant of pollution.

Interest in conservatories had fallen so low during the 1950s and '60s that when Kew's Palm House fell into disrepair, there was talk of pulling it down rather than paying for its restoration. Since then a renaissance of interest in these buildings has sparked innovative approaches to glasshouse

Previous pages: The main part of the Temperate House at Kew was completed in the middle of the nineteenth century, and it has played a major role in the introduction of plants from the Southern Hemisphere. The Royal Botanic Gardens, Kew, England.

330

design and layout, represented by the Princess of Wales Conservatory at Kew, the Glasshouse Experience at the Royal Botanic Garden, Edinburgh, and the South African Botanical Society's Conservatory at Kirstenbosch; and the immediate future holds the promise of yet more significant developments at the newly created National Botanical Garden of Wales, and the inspirationally imaginative conversion of a disused china clay quarry in Cornwall to a world of tropical and subtropical plants known as the Eden Project. On a domestic level, a revival of interest in conservatories has placed them high on the list of indispensable accessories for anyone with social aspirations and commitment to fashionable lifestyles. Meanwhile, the plants that were the mainstays of nineteenth-century conservatories have been almost forgotten. Today's occupants are too often chosen from the subtropical and tropical plants of the forest floor, marketed as house plants by florists and garden centres. Most grow unhappily in the conditions provided by a conservatory, especially those attached to houses, which are neither room nor garden, and in which dry air and lack of shade provide unfriendly conditions for such plants. Discouraged by failures, people limit themselves to modest displays that fall far short of the dreams that inspired these expensive extensions to their homes.

Ferns and club mosses were traditional components of old-style conservatories. They created a relaxed style of background planting that offset the bright colours of flowers, and in a practical fashion helped to humidify the excessively dry atmospheres which are a problem in many of these structures. While in the New Zealand city of New Plymouth, I followed the advice of my host Des Corbett, and visited a remarkable little building designed almost exclusively for these plants: the Pukekura Park Fernery. The Fernery is unobtrusively placed, partially underground, and I made my way into it through a narrow tunnel that opened out into a green atrium surrounded by banks of ferns, club mosses and mosses. I then picked my way through a series of glass-roofed and partially glass-walled structures linked by tunnels and steps, with diffused light filtering down from above to create an atmosphere of subterranean greenery. Ferns grew in leafy banks and burst luxuriantly from beds of selaginellas, lycopodiums and other club mosses, re-creating the lush, unrelievedly green impressions of the forest floor, until in the most secluded, innermost sanctum, orchids, begonias, salpiglossus, and foliage plants provided flashes of colour, like tropical birds, in this world of verdant greenery. As I made my way round, I became aware that I was not alone. The guardian of the grotto, quietly engaged in propagating yet more plants for the display, was keeping a covert eye on me from behind a screen of fern fronds. Although the lack of any means of identifying the plants reduced the garden's value to anyone interested in the names of the ferns, the stylish and effective display appealed to the senses, and illustrated the potential of these plants.

Conservatories take many forms, from the botanical to the purely pleasurable, and none represents the latter more agreeably than the winter garden—forever associated in my mind with seaside resorts like Eastbourne or Weston-super-Mare, where displays of bulbs, annuals and colourful perennials grow under glass to bring a touch of summer into places where resi-

The Botanical Society Conservatory at Kirstenbosch is an inspiring example of the renaissance of interest in conservatories. Kirstenbosch National Botanical Gardens, Western Cape Province, South Africa.

dents in retirement listen to music, gossip or snooze quietly with a good book, and winter- and spring-time visitors take tea. Visits to the Looking-Glass Garden revealed similar displays at the Winter Garden in the Domain in Auckland, and in the curiously eccentric structure that functions as a conservatory at the Royal Tasmanian Botanical Gardens at Hobart. These places are filled with a succession of plants that explode briefly into masses of bright colour. Most are familiar spring and early summer flowers of Northern Hemisphere gardens that create exhilarating impressions of freshness and beauty when muted winter tones predominate outside. Winter gardens are amongst the high points of the gardener's craft, stretching resources and testing skills beyond the capacities of most of us. Their impact depends on skilful timing and the assured ability to produce plants that can be moved into the display area for a few weeks, a month or two at most, when at their peak, before retiring them to resting quarters or throwing them out once their moment has passed. Frames and greenhouses are essential to propagate and bring on plants, and constant care is needed to present them successfully at the unfavourable times of the year, when they make their greatest impact. Most of us have to be content with modest ambitions—a few bowls of bulbs and a handful of winter-flowering plants in containers, particularly welcome when they are fragrant as well as beautiful—and leave the grand displays to the experts.

Even on a small scale, plants in conservatories can give us pleasure out of proportion to the numbers involved and the effort needed to grow them, and numerous Southern Hemisphere representatives can be used to bring colour and atmosphere into our lives during the winter. Bulbous plants are amongst those that make few demands, and freesias, chincherinchees and several of the larger, more colourful lachenalias (especially forms of *Lachenalia aloides*) are part of the corpus of traditional conservatory plants. Others include the South American hippeastrums, often known as amaryllis for their resemblance to the autumn-flowering *Amaryllis belladonna*. The so-called Dutch hybrids, descended from the scarlet-flowered *Hippeastrum reginae* and the white and red *H. vittatum*, produce flowers like giant lilies with broad, flaring, brilliant scarlet, red, orange or white trumpets. These enduring, long-suffering plants put on a monumental display when potted up in the autumn and grown cool through the winter, and with a little feeding, minimal attention and occasional repotting will continue to produce their

The colour and grace of delphiniums and other flowering plants common to orthodox western gardens bring spring and summer into the dead season of the year, but winter-flowering shrubs and bulbs from the Southern Hemisphere would provide more economical, less demanding sources of pleasure for winter gardens. The Winter Garden in the Domain, Auckland, North Island, New Zealand.

great big, flamboyant flowers for years and years. Relatively hardy species with smaller flowers grow naturally in the Chilean Andes, offering exciting prospects for further breeding that could lead to new races of these plants, of special interest to gardeners in Mediterranea and other places with relatively mild winters as well as to conservatory owners.

Clivia miniata thrives in deep shade, and even seems to appreciate a period of benign neglect during its off-season. The artificial, exotic setting of a conservatory provides an ambience in which the large, opulently buxom forms of recently bred cultivars display their charms more effectively than in most gardens. Amaryllis and clivias are so long-lived and capable of survival with such minimal support that they might be called heirloom bulbs. Other equally rewarding, but not quite so undemanding, options include *Veltheimia capensis,* with spotted leaves and upright spikes of pink flowers, for sunlit or shaded situations, and *V. bracteata* var. *rosealba,* with pink and white flowers, which shrinks from bright light and does better in light shade.

Chincherinchees, *Ornithogalum thyrsoides,* grow naturally in the western Cape in South Africa, and are familiar cut flowers, valued for their long-lasting qualities, and imported by the million. When I visited Darling in a year when drought had prematurely ended the spring flower display, the broad bowl-shaped white flowers of the chincherinchees were still fresh and beautiful amongst the burnt-up grasses, long after other things I had come to see had faded from view. It is as enduring and effective in the conservatory as when cut, and a few bulbs potted up in the autumn and grown in a frost-free place through the winter provide six to eight weeks of flower as winter gives way to spring. Some people might be wary of the plant's poisonous nature—a modest bunch is said to be enough to kill a horse—but the millions of flowers sold by florists seem never to have claimed a victim, and horses are usually kept out of conservatories on the same principle that bulls are unwelcome in china shops. Nearly all ornithogalums have white flowers; a notable exception is *Ornithogalum dubium,* also from the Cape, with deep, glowing bright orange flowers. It resents deep planting and should be set with its nose barely below the surface of the compost.

A conservatory should be a place to sit, surrounded by colour and enveloped in warmth and the fragrance of flowers. For me, an essential component of these pleasures is the old-fashioned cherry pie, *Heliotropium arborescens,* from South America. It flowers more or less continuously, producing dense heads of deep purple-blue flowers that fill the air with a pervasive aroma of stewed morello cherries. It should be regularly dead-headed and fed to encourage new growth and the production of yet more flowers. In my memories this perennial is associated with the varied fragrances of the scented-leaved pelargoniums, which exemplify Nature's inclination to indulge from time to time in orgies of experimentation—in this case devising and combining an extraordinary assortment of fragrant essential oils to create a range of subtle and often not-so-subtle scent sensations, with no obvious advantage to the plants that produce them. Pelargoniums with or without aromatic leaves seem equally competent and effective plants, and it is difficult to see how theories about survival of the fittest can be used to rationalise the production of leaves that smell of citrus, spices, camphor, musk and a dozen more on the grounds of economy or utility. 'Lady Plymouth' is one of the easiest and most attractive of the scented pelargoniums, a selection of *Pelargonium graveolens* with brightly variegated leaves and a musky fragrance with sharp overtones. *Pelargonium* 'Citriodorum', 'Citronella' and the variegated 'Peach Cream' smell of lemons; 'Apple Betty' and *P. odoratissimum* of apples; 'Camphor Rose' and 'Lilian Pottinger' of camphor; 'Radula' and 'Old Spice' exude the warm fragrances of spices; and *P. tomentosum* is powerfully imbued with peppermint—to list only a very few amongst a host of definable, indefinable, pungent, sweet, subtle or blatant odours, fragrances and aromas produced by this extraordinary group of easily grown, amenable and eminently satisfactory plants.

During the time when conservatories were out of fashion, I stayed in a hotel in Peebles that possessed what had once been an outstanding example of their kind—by then half-abandoned and verging on dereliction. The bright flowers of a bougainvillea trailed down a wall and twined through the rusting ventilating rods; two plumbagos, *Plumbago auriculata*, once trained to a wall, had fallen forward and their long stems with sky blue flowers spread half-way across the tiled floor; and an African hemp, *Sparmannia africana*, had grown into a flat-headed small tree with broad, soft green leaves and heads of white flowers. These three plants are amongst the best bets for gardeners in search of reliable, attractive plants for a conservatory. Bougainvilleas climb with rampant growth that could only be restrained by persistent use of pruning shears, until a race of relatively compact cultivars came to the relief of the hand that wields the knife, making these colourful plants even more valuable. Their minute flowers are surrounded by showy bracts that range in colour from a cool ivory-white, through every shade of soft or shocking pink, to orange, scarlet, glowing crimson or the natural magenta. The brightest possible sunlit setting is necessary to accommodate the shrieking magenta colour, but growing against a white wall it is one of the most evocative and invigorating sights of the plant world.

The first plumbagos I saw growing naturally in the eastern Cape were shrubby rather than climbing, and I wondered whether they were a different species from the plants I had encountered previously in cultivation. In fact, this flexible shrub remains compact in sunlit, open situations, but happily becomes a scrambler in shadier, more congested conditions, using its neighbours as pathways to the skies. *Plumbago auriculata* flowers for much of the year, is almost hardy—needing the lightest protection from winter

Regal pelargoniums are traditional plants of the conservatory. Able to endure the dry atmospheres and periodic neglect that is the lot of plants in most conservatories, they are rock-hard certainties for those looking for plants to make the most of these often problematical structures. Royal Horticultural Society's Garden, Wisley, Surrey, England.

frosts—and deservedly a most popular old-guard conservatory plant. The African hemp also fits this category, and is one of the most amenable of conservatory plants. It grows naturally in the evergreen forests that overlook the Indian Ocean in South Africa, often in heavily shaded situations; in cultivation it is able to endure shade and neglect in a remarkable way for a plant with such large, soft, seemingly vulnerable leaves.

South Africa might be dubbed the Mother of Conservatories; so many plants from that part of the world play vital roles in conservatory displays, and I have frequently come across wildflowers growing there in associations that reminded me of similar combinations put together by gardeners. The Bloukranz Pass near Storms River on the southern coast cuts through a rugged gorge where great yellowwoods, encrusted with lichens and epiphytes, tower above overhanging crags. The rocky roadside cliffs in the partly sunlit, partly shaded places beneath the trees are shrouded in a luxuriant growth of ferns, arum lilies, and club mosses. Pelargoniums grow in the brighter spaces, and the broad, heavily textured leaves of Cape primroses, *Streptocarpus* spp., nestle amongst mosses in deep, damp, heavily shaded recesses. Similarly luxuriant combinations of greenery and flowers can easily and effectively be reproduced in a conservatory, needing only frost-free conditions during winter to flourish.

Over the last half century, gerberas developed from a relatively obscure wild daisy with flaming vermilion flowers, to a major florist and conservatory plant with hundreds of single- and double-flowered hybrids in every colour, it would seem, but blue. The plant grows naturally around Barberton on the border of South Africa and Swaziland. Plants similar to the wild form still grow in gardens, and I hope will continue to do so. The more delicate proportions of the species give it a grace that has been lost in the solidly textured, stiffly held flowers with immaculately arranged petals of the hybrids. If I were looking for a few plants to brighten winter days in a conservatory, I should be quite happy with the original *Gerbera jamesonii*, a reliable, easily grown perennial that flowers almost continuously in warm situations. Or the orange-scarlet Hilton daisy, *G. aurantiaca*, from KwaZulu-Natal, where a few colonies exist amongst rocky grasslands on the slopes of the Drakensberg. If I needed more variation in colour, I would find it amongst some of the "unimproved" hybrids with *G. kraussii*, which offer slightly larger pink, yellow or orange-scarlet flowers.

The sheltered spaces of gardens in urban and suburban areas, backed up by a glasshouse or conservatory to protect tender plants in winter, are ideal places in which to experiment with Australian, South African and other shrubs that would be borderline or doomed to failure in more exposed situations. An obvious candidate for such experiments, and another plant traditionally grown in conservatories, is mimosa, *Acacia dealbata*, with its fragrant powder-puffs of yellow flowers. It has long been cultivated in the south of France, especially forms with larger, brighter or more densely packed flowers such as 'Le Gaulois', 'Mirandole' and 'Toison d'Or'. The mimosa is likely to be suggested to anyone asking about plants to fill a conservatory, but it grows rapidly into a substantial tree that can be kept within bounds only by constant cutting back, and may be better planted in a sheltered corner of the garden, where frosts occasionally cut it back for you, with the plant returning undaunted from basal shoots. *Acacia retinodes*, also widely used for cut flower production, is more adaptable and has the added advantage of growing well on limey, base-rich soils, so it is valuable as a rootstock for other species (the majority) which prefer soils to be acid. Another easily grown species, tolerant of drought and exposure, is the Sydney golden wattle, *A. longifolia*. It can be kept compact by regular cutting back, and the cylindrical inflorescences of fragrant flowers are produced profusely in the spring even on quite small plants. Gardeners looking for something entirely different might try the bizarre-looking *A. aphylla*, a shrub with almost semi-succulent, blue-green stems that are upright and branching. The plant has potential in its strong sculptural effects, though no specimen I have seen quite fulfilled the promise.

Fragrance can be a very special quality in plants grown in confined spaces or in close proximity to where we sit, and few shrubs scent the air more generously than the Australian boronias, notably *Boronia megastigma*. This is not a particularly good or long-lived garden plant, and must be cut back hard after flowering to keep it compact. Plants that test our skills provide a sense of achievement when grown successfully, and I should love to be able to enjoy the heady fragrance of this plant grown by myself, but have to confess an even greater affection for plants that flourish almost in spite of what I do for them. Provided they have well-drained composts, plenty of air and not too much water during the winter, and are exposed to only light frosts, correas or Australian fuchsias fall in the obliging category. The impressions they create are more subtle and understated than the true fuchsias, and their muted shades of pink, cream, primrose and green, often overlaid with dusky red, once seemed to me too restrained. But these plants have virtues that become more apparent with familiarity, and now I appreciate the gentle qualities of their flowers, and the ways they combine with precisely formed leaves that are often blue-grey or jade-green. Most species flower during winter and into the spring, and though the constant succession seldom amounts to a grand display, it is a prolonged source of pleasure when such things are in short supply. *Correa* 'Carmine Bells' is densely compact, with dusky red, bell-shaped flowers; *C. pulchella* is a popular and easily grown species with pendant, pale pink, bell-shaped flowers; and 'Orange Flame' is a compact form with bright orange bells. Easy to grow, reliable and comparatively hardy, 'Marian's Marvel' has very pale yellow and crimson-shaded, tubular bells. *Correa reflexa* 'Fat Fred' is an easily grown, compact shrub that produces a succession of flowers for several months during the winter.

As discussed in Chapter Four, the discovery of the flora of South Africa by European gardeners led to the revelation that the familiar heathers of west-

Not especially showy, correas like the cultivar 'Fat Fred' are nevertheless some of the most rewarding and undemanding plants anyone could wish to grow. The Arboretum of the University of California at Santa Cruz, California, United States.

ern Europe were only a tiny offshoot of a vast genus, and gardeners have been trying—usually with limited success—to grow Cape heaths in their gardens ever since. The problems still have not been cracked, and gardens where I have seen more than a handful of these plants growing with any sense of conviction that they are thriving—and are likely still to be there if I returned in a couple of years' time—are as rare as hens' teeth. One hundred and seventy years ago, William M'Nab, the superintendent of the Royal Botanic Garden in Edinburgh, grew a collection of Cape heaths that has probably never been equalled. Perhaps his most significant bit of advice is to raise the root ball of the plants a little higher each time they are repotted, so that by maturity it would be two or three inches above the rim of the container. The potting composts he used were very low in nutrients of any sort. He added no supplementary fertilisers, and insisted that perfect drainage and a meagre diet were essential elements in his success—corresponding closely with the conditions of the fynbos where these plants live naturally.

Cape heaths, restios and proteas are the defining trinity of South Africa's fynbos communities, and the Proteaceae are one of the great families of the Looking-Glass Garden, packed with plants that tempt us to grow them in whatever way we can. Conservatories are the only hope of success for gardeners in areas where winters are too cold for these plants, and even in milder and more clement situations these structures may be nearly as essential. Like the Cape heaths, most proteas grow naturally on free-draining, nutrient-impoverished soils subject to summer droughts. They are not well adapted to cope with fertile soils and unfamiliar patterns of rainfall. Few thrive where summer rainfall is high or winter frosts severe, nor do they usually take kindly to intense summer drought, contrary to what might be expected, because although summer rainfall levels are often low in places where proteas grow naturally, the effects are alleviated by mists from the ocean or high atmospheric humidity in montane situations. Nevertheless I have repeatedly seen them for sale in garden centres in Australia, New Zealand, California and even their native South Africa, sometimes in hundreds, where the tiny number found thriving in local gardens is evidence that few of those that are sold survive. In most places South African proteas would grow better in containers and in sheltered accommodations than in the garden, pruned hard immediately after flowering to keep them compact and floriferous and to remove tatty remains of flowers and old foliage.

Protea scolymocephala is not an especially regal or sensuous protea, but has a restrained elegance and subtlety that is just as appealing, especially within the confines of a conservatory. It grows on coastal lowlands and sandy flats close to Cape Town, just where people find it most desirable or easiest to build houses, and the species is severely threatened by such developments. This attractive, low-spreading bush has fine narrow, olive-green leaves flushed with crimson, and flowers made up of cones ringed by parchment-coloured papery bracts, a little like helichrysums.

South of Cape Town, the Cape of Good Hope Nature Reserve is a pleasant day trip. Rolling hills, slashed by outcrops of heavily weathered, shattered rocks, and views across False Bay to Cape Hangklip far away in the distance make up a varied and interesting countryside. The Reserve is reached by running the gauntlet of distinctly unlovable baboons who pose as highwaymen, importuning travellers for food, and threatening unmentionable reprisals on those slow to hand over. Once you are within the reserve, these bandits disappear and plants become the main focus of interest—apart from the chance of seeing ostriches, or groups of gracefully gawky, boldly marked chestnut and white bontebok antelopes. For the first few kilometres the flowers of sunshine conebush, *Leucadendron laureolum*, colour the hillsides bright yellow in spring. Further into the reserve, *L. salignum* is widespread. Here it is a ground-covering, densely compact, flat-topped or hummocked shrub, the males with flowers surrounded by spiky, bright straw-coloured bracts and females with more substantial cones surrounded by broader, brighter bracts. Gardeners who know the widely grown plant often listed as *L. salignum* 'Safari Sunset', with bold heads of flowers surrounded by crimson tulip-shaped bracts on tall upright stems, would not recognise these as the same species. Such suspicions would be partially justified, since this female clone is one of a number of hybrids between forms of *L. salignum* and *L. laureolum*.

These hybrids make excellent conservatory plants. Their bracts start to colour in autumn, strengthening in tone throughout the winter and until well into spring. Some have a naturally upright, rather ungainly stance, but that can be countered by cutting them back hard after flowering to encourage the production of strong shoots for the following year. Variegated sports with pink, green and cream immature foliage that becomes green and cream with maturity have apparently originated independently and include

'Jesters' and 'Safari Sunshine'. Both have bright pink floral bracts with a dark green stripe. Other cultivars include 'Inca Gold', a compact shrub with neat, medium-sized, bright golden bracts tinged with red on crimson stems; and the long-established 'Mrs Stanley', with medium-sized red bracts in autumn intensifying in colour as they age. Gardeners living in colder situations might try 'Julie', a recent introduction that forms a naturally compact shrub with slim, creamy bracts with a bronze-red flush. 'Bell's Sunrise' grows tall and upright in favourable conditions, but remains so low and spreading on poor soils that it can even be used as ground cover; its soft yellow bracts are lightly tinged with red. 'Rewa Gold' is amongst the best known of all culti-vars because of its large, rich golden yellow bracts carrying a tinge of bronze. Showy and long lasting, the bracts have been described as a floral artist's dream. 'Cherry Glow' is compact and floriferous, with small creamy bracts surrounding a cherry red central flower bud that opens to display yellow pet-als. 'Incisum' is an older prostrate form of *L. salignum*. In time it develops a dense, weed-smothering mat that makes an ideal ground cover. Quite large cream-coloured bracts produced during the autumn mature to subtle tones of bronze and orange as spring approaches.

Leucadendron laureolum, one of the aptly named sunshine proteas, colours the mountain-sides around Cape Town during late winter and spring. Cape of Good Hope Nature Reserve, near Cape Town, Western Cape Province, South Africa.

The sunshine conebushes flower during the winter, and few plants are more attractive or create more interest, as demonstrated by the cultivar 'Cloudbank Sunrise' at the Regional Botanic Garden at Manurewa, near Auckland, New Zealand.

Vireyans for the Conservatory

Customers often turned up at my nursery in search of a rhododendron to put in a container to grace their patio or conservatory—and were usually dissuaded from the idea whenever possible. In the first place, we did not sell rhododendrons, so had no interest in promoting them, and tap water in the area contained so much lime that it had lethal effects when used to water them. But more to the point, I have never been persuaded that the brief, one- or two-week display of their flowers compensates for their dull evergreenery during the rest of the year when grown under intensive care, and scrutiny, in a container. That objection does not apply to the vireyans, many of which flower twice or even three times in the course of a year. My first encounter with them in containers was at Keith Thompson's garden outside Auckland, where they were growing in hanging baskets. Since vireyan rhododendrons are naturally epiphytic, a basket full of mossy compost hanging in the air not only seemed to them a home from home, but made it a simple matter for Keith to ensure that they received the alternating cycles of drought and ample water to which these plants respond by coming into flower.

Anyone with a conservatory could grow some vireyans in this way, or, as an alternative, could follow the example seen at the beautifully restored and elegant Turner Glasshouse at the Glasnevin National Botanic Garden in Dublin. Here these epiphytic shrubs are grown on "cork trees" constructed by covering a framework of timber or plastic pipes with strips of cork to provide perching places similar to those on which the plants grow naturally—and which, incidentally, are equally appreciated by bromeliads and orchids, should the urge to mix and match a bit for more varied and interesting effects become pressing. The virtues of vireyans as conservatory plants include a natural inclination to flower during the winter months, and keeping them dry during the autumn reinforces this tendency.

A vast selection of hybrids are available, but when grown in hanging baskets and perched on "cork trees," the smaller, more compact kinds are easier to handle than the taller ones. Two cultivars often recommended for hanging baskets are *Rhododendron* 'Littlest Angel' and 'Wee Annie', the first producing coral-red, broadly tubular flowers with a widely flared mouth, the second similar in leaf and form to a Kurume azalea with clusters of small, bell-shaped, palest pink flowers. Both cultivars are so angelically demure that, although they may be appreciated, they are unlikely to excite much interest. Vireyans appeal to me for their dazzling colours, the silken or satin textures of their petals, and the alternative view they present of rhododendrons. I should prefer to grow a couple of Felix Jury's hybrids: 'Golden Charm', a hardy and most amenable garden vireyan with creamy yellow to rich apricot flowers and outstanding glossy foliage and crimson stems; and 'Red Rover', with flowers that open light red and deepen to a glowing scarlet-crimson, and a spreading growth that makes it ideal for hanging baskets. Other amenable hybrids, too tall for hanging baskets but recommended for conservatories with enough heat to exclude winter chill, are the *R. macgregoriae* hybrid 'Rob's Favourite', which produces a broadly open flower with luscious watermelon pink reflexed petals, and the bright pink 'Alisa Nicole', surely one of the most floriferous of all, producing an almost continuous succession of clusters of tubular flowers. *Rhododendron vitis-idea* and *R. phaeochitum* are two species that provide a new look for rhododendrons. The former has long, asymmetrical tubular scarlet flowers similar to a columnea's. *Rhododendron phaeochitum* is strikingly different, with a dense, glowing tan-coloured indumentum covering the young shoots and undersides of the leaves, amongst which long, tubular, curved, pink flowers are produced in clusters. This shrubby equivalent to the birds-of-paradise comes from New Guinea, a country where vireyans grow amongst dense forests covering high mountain ridges and steep valleys. During the last twenty years or so, enough vireyans have been found to give us a taste of what is there, but many more remain to be discovered and brought into our gardens.

That note of plants waiting to be discovered is an appropriate one on which to end this account of my exploration of the Looking-Glass Garden. This is a garden where so much remains to be discovered. Only a fraction of its plants play a significant part in gardens, and we have scarcely begun to explore ways to use them to create novel effects—or meet the demands of un-

A fine collection of vireyan rhododendrons grows amongst rocks and on artificial trees in the Turner Glasshouse at the Glasnevin National Botanic Garden in Dublin, Ireland.

conventional situations. When we do so, their presence in our gardens will add extra dimensions of interest to our enjoyment of these beautiful, tantalisingly elusive and wilful creations.

Hitherto, all the gardens and places described exist in the real world of the Looking-Glass Garden. They are places that I have visited and you could go to. In the next part of this book we will venture into gardens that exist only in the mind, whose owners, with all their hopes, quandaries and aspirations, are as insubstantial as the stuff that dreams are made of. Yet their problems and opportunities are our problems and opportunities; the plants they use and how they use them could be our plants. We can never meet them, but the ways these folk manage their gardens, and their difficulties and pleasures, hold lessons for us as surely as if we could sit down and chat about them together round their kitchen tables.

Rhododendron 'Cherry Pie', bred by Felix Jury in New Zealand, has large, sumptuously textured, translucent cherry pink flowers. Felix and Mark Jury's garden, Tikorangi, North Island, New Zealand.

PART IV

Through the Looking-Glass in the Northern Hemisphere: Case Studies

Y OU AWAKE one morning resolved to spend the weekend on a garden makeover, but when you arrive at the garden centre you find to your bewilderment that they have never heard of any plant that grows naturally in the Northern Hemisphere. You ask about trees: birches, magnolias, cherries, cypresses or maples—what are they? Your plans for shrubs draw blanks when the garden centre denies any knowledge of camellias, roses, mock oranges, lavenders, rosemaries, or junipers. No delphiniums, hostas, daylilies or lupins will brighten your herbaceous border—not even daffodils and tulips for a little early colour. The rock garden must be made without phloxes, aubrietas, saxifrages, campanulas and almost everything else you had in mind. For on your way to the garden centre you passed through a magic mirror into a world filled with the varied and tempting offerings of the Looking-Glass Garden.

Alice found her way through the looking-glass; we never will. But suppose that unlikely event were to happen—would you look around to see what was available, or sneak home to waste the weekend slumped in front of the television set? This part of my book introduces the plants of the Looking-Glass Garden in a series of theatre sets, complete with characters, drawn from different parts of Western Europe and the Pacific seaboard of the United States. It provides examples of how plants can be used to fit different situations and meet different circumstances, in contexts that are directly applicable to Northern Hemisphere gardens, and in doing so introduces a great many plants that have not, hitherto, received a mention.

Most gardeners could fill their gardens exclusively with Northern Hemi-sphere plants without much effort, and many gardeners grow little else al-ready. But, deprived of roses, daffodils, campanulas and so many other sta-ples, first impressions might suggest that the garden would be a threadbare thing; that to fill it would be a matter of scrimping and denial. The case studies that follow show that nothing could be further from the truth. They demonstrate that the Southern Hemisphere is a treasure-store of plants that are amenable to the conditions and satisfy the aspirations of the owners in situations that cover a wide variety of climates and human needs. If need be, we could as easily compose gardens exclusively with plants from beyond the Looking-Glass as we can using those from north of the equator.

CHAPTER 15

Through the Looking-Glass in California and Mediterranean Europe

Love Amongst the Artichokes

A garden on a private estate of timber houses overlooking Monterey Bay lies in the heart of California's artichoke country. It is in Castroville, a town immortalised in folklore by its claim that by crowning Marilyn Monroe "Artichoke Queen" there in 1949, it launched her into the limelight that led to her career as a film star. The garden belongs to a not-long-married couple who moved from Wisconsin and bought a diner on Route 101 in Salinas. The temperate nature of the coast, with its mild winters, and summers moderated by frequent sea mists, was the attraction that brought them to this part of the world—and they have fallen in love with a place that seems to them almost a tropical paradise, an impression which they attempt to reinforce by the planting of the garden. The side fronting the ocean consists almost entirely of decking partially shaded by a large coast live oak (*Lithocarpus densiflora*), with views to Point Pinos and the bright lights of Monterey at night. The garden covers rather less than 1000 square metres (¼ acre), and the design of the house forms a semi-enclosed courtyard that provides warm, relatively sheltered conditions in which to grow plants.

This couple moved from the extreme continental conditions of Wisconsin to a particularly benign manifestation of a Mediterranean climate, and she embarked on a steep learning curve to adapt her gardening ideas to the new situation. The main problem was trying to work within the physical restrictions of the site. Once planting started, she quickly found that the limited space in the front yard and the enclosed courtyard was not nearly enough to hold all the things that tempted her.

The discovery of Jeff Rosendale's Sierra Azul Nursery and garden in nearby Watsonville was a great step forward. The garden displays plants from Mediterranea, and during a visit with a friend she made copious notes, supervised by a self-possessed, solemn little rough-haired black and tan terrier who left them to it once he was sure they were there with serious intent. After making the mistake of buying plants that quickly outgrew their space, she learnt to concentrate on those that did not grow too big, and also on shrubs that benefited from periodic hard pruning to reduce their size and make space for neighbours. Attempts to reduce routine maintenance included planting ground-covering plants overlying bulbs and beneath shrubs and a scattering of small trees. She finds that the mutual shading effects of several planting layers not only keeps the garden cool, green and pleasant to be in on even the hottest days, but also greatly reduces the rate at which the ground dries out.

The planting around the deck overlooking the ocean is deliberately sparse. A low hedge of *Melaleuca elliptica*, with carmine-red bottlebrushes, is on one side, and the grey-leaved *Arctotis stoechadifolia*, with large cream flowers, carpets the ground around the edges, its surface broken by clumps of Poor Knight's lily, *Xeronema callistemon*, with spectacular heads of scarlet flowers. A few plants of *Salvia africana-lutea* with large russet flowers complete the ensemble.

The main feature in the courtyard is a group of three bottle palms, *Hyophorbe lagenicaulis*, intriguing for their slightly drunken stance. The only other tree here is the narrowly upright shoestring acacia, *Acacia stenophylla*, with long, trailing phyllodes. The middle layer of shrubs includes the Natal plum, *Carissa macrocarpa*, grown for its pure white flowers and edible crimson fruits, and planted along a boundary where its thorns deter unwanted intruders. Amongst the other shrubs are *Leucadendron discolor* 'Flame Tip' and *Leucadendron* 'Red Gem' (like a compact 'Safari Sunset'), both of which are cut back hard after flowering each year. The waist-high, floriferous *Scaevola crassifolia* is valued for its purple-blue flowers, and lemon verbena, *Aloysia triphylla*, is included for the sharp, clear fragrance of its foliage. The pendant, lime-green bells of *Correa reflexa* var. *nummularifolia* bring in hummingbirds during the winter. Several pelargoniums, chosen for their scented foliage, are planted in semi-shaded positions, amongst them *Pelargonium cordifolium*, with large, dark green leaves and lilac flowers; *P. dichondrifolium*, broadly spreading with spicily aromatic leaves; and *P. tomentosum*, with broad, soft foliage smelling strongly of peppermint. A sunnier position was chosen for the chocolate-centred, yellow-margined leaves and bright vermilion flowers of *Pelargonium* 'Vancouver Centennial'. Several bromeliads, there to give the place a tropical look, grow on weathered logs at ground level, including one or two aechmeas and guzmanias, and queen's tears, *Billbergia nutans*, electrifying with its lime-green and blue flowers emerging from pink bracts. The brightly variegated foliage of *Chlorophytum comosum* 'Gold Nugget' and 'Picturatum' reinforce the effect. Mats of the little silver-leaved *Dymondia margaretae* create close ground cover, as do the broadly spreading carpets of *Scaevola aemula* 'Blue Wonder' and *Scaevola* 'Diamond Head', the latter almost continuously in flower above dark green succulent foliage. Changes of height and texture are provided by clumps of *Tulbaghia violacea* 'Silver Lace', with umbels of lavender flowers above narrow silvery foliage. The tall, branching inflorescences of *Verbena bonariensis* bring in the butterflies.

The main feature in the front yard is provided by a pair of fast-growing, broadly spreading tree ferns, *Cyathea cooperi*, and the only other tree is the Australian native frangipani, *Hymenosporum flavum*. Shrubs used for the middle layer include *Chamelaucium uncinatum* 'Purple Pride', with large clusters of bright magenta flowers, and aromatic foliage, cut back annually as the flowers fade; *Kunzea baxteri*, with large orange-vermilion bottlebrushes in winter and spring; and *Leucospermum* 'Veldfire', with flowers like curled scarlet ribbons around orange centres, but just as appreciated for the perennial attractions of its broad, grey-green felted leaves. *Alyogyne huegelii* 'Mood Indigo', with deep lilac flowers, and 'White Swan' are both almost perpetually in flower, and are most forgiving of regular hard cutting back.

A couple of kangaroo paws—*Anigozanthos* 'Red Cross', with velvety crimson flowers, and the orange-tan 'Regal Claw'—form an attractive part of the ground layer and also attract hummingbirds. Ground cover here includes areas covered with spreading colonies of the yellow and orange forms of *Bulbinella fruticosa*, and an edging of the densely grassy leaved *Zephyranthes*

Once regarded as a challenge by gardeners, *Chamelaucium uncinatum* 'Purple Pride' is now more widely grown for its bright magenta flowers. Katandra, Bob O'Neill's garden, Wandin, Victoria, Australia.

rosea, with pink flowers like large, fragile crocuses. The soft, silver foliage and autumn spikes of violet flowers of *Plectranthus argentatus* fill sunlit spaces amongst the shrubs, while mats of *P. coleoides* 'Variegatus', with heavily textured cream and white leaves, suggest dappled sunlight in shadier parts.

Tripping Under the Redwoods

Little River in Mendocino County in northern California is the setting for a garden of nearly half an acre in an affluent housing development set informally amongst redwoods, bishop pines, tanbark oaks and western azaleas. The front yard conforms to the neighbourhood style of mown grass and trees. The backyard is partially enclosed by the house, a studio and other outbuildings on two and a half sides, forming a large rectangle in which precisely laid, broad brick paths form a grid of beds that are floriferous, bountiful, comfortably cosy and cottagey in character; the sort of garden that evolves as old plants succumb and new ones attract the interest of the owner. The layout may be clearly defined and immutable, but the effects created from season to season and from year to year constantly change. The leading light in the garden is a finance facilitator, with an office in Fort Bragg, whose business is mostly done on the local golf courses. His partner is a sculptor, and the creator of what he describes as "native art" carved from redwood. He holds exhibitions of his work on the property from time to time, despite the disapproval and consternation of some of the neighbours.

The climate here has Mediterranean characteristics, but with few of the stresses which that often implies. Summer days are seldom very hot, summer droughts are neither lengthy nor intense, and their effects greatly reduced by sea mists. Winter rainfall is almost invariably high, but frosts are unusual, and minimum temperatures seldom fall more than a few degrees below freezing point. The range of plants that can be grown here is exceptionally broad, and access to specialist nurseries in both Oregon and California makes it relatively easy to take advantage of this plenitude. Visits to the nearby Heritage House Nursery and the Mendocino Coast Botanic Garden provided introductions to some of the plants that could be grown, but the predominance of shrubs in both lessened their value to someone more concerned with the possibilities of perennials. The soil is a fertile, moisture-retentive woodland loam—unsuitable for plants that need a starvation diet to thrive, but ideal for those more accustomed to plenty. The potential problem of high rainfall during the winter was alleviated by digging out some of the beds and refilling them with mixtures of soil, grit, gravel and composted bark to ensure that they drain freely, relying on the hard core packed beneath the brick paths to channel the water away. Native trees provide shelter, some shade and an attractive background, so no more trees were needed, and only a few shrubs. Perennials constitute the major part of the display.

New Zealand tea trees grow exceptionally well in this part of the world, and these were planted to give height where needed, as focal points around which to group perennials, and for their prolonged display of flowers during the winter. Cultivars include *Leptospermum scoparium* 'Apple Blossom' and 'Burgundy', with double pink and crimson flowers, respectively; 'Gaiety Girl', with double rose-pink flowers; 'Helene Strybing', large, single pink and white; the weeping 'Pink Cascade'; and 'Red Ensign', single claret-red with mahogany foliage. 'Manning's Choice' is a too-good-to-resist cultivar of *L. rotundifolium* with large lilac-pink flowers. A few grevilleas are also here, such as 'Pink Pearl', with deep green foliage and pink flowers, and *Grevillea victoriae* 'Murray Valley Queen' for its winter flowers. These are planted with a boronia or two offering fragrant foliage and flowers: the large *Boronia fraseri,* with pungent, delicately fern-like leaves and deep pink flowers, and the much smaller *B. anemonifolia,* with starry white flowers amongst fresh green foliage that smells of turpentine. Salvias account for many of the other shrubby or semi-shrubby plants. Scarlet sage, *Salvia coccinea,* produces bright flowers on knee-high plants; the South African *S. dolomitica* has mounds of silver leaves and lavender-pink flowers; and *S. muirii* is a compact shrub with large, light purple and white flowers. *Salvia guaranitica,* with glossy deep green leaves and deep cobalt blue flowers, is included along with its slate blue form, 'Argentina Skies'. In the early stages of the garden the soft silver-leaved *Helichrysum petiolare* was used as a space filler, but is now banished to the outer edges, where it reveals its capacity to grow as a rampant scrambler with an inclination towards permanent occupation of spaces amongst the bishop pines.

Abandoning the conventional format of broad-leaved perennials relieved by a few clumps of narrow-leaved monocots, the owner decided to rely instead on a predominance of plants with grassy or spiky foliage, creating the impression of a grassy clearing in the forest. The southern flora is rich in these forms, and his collection includes *Agapanthus* 'Storm Cloud', with globular heads of deep violet-purple flowers, and the much smaller blue-flowered 'Queen Anne'. The parrot lily, *Alstroemeria psittacina,* has long stems carrying dusky red, green-tipped flowers. *Clivia miniata* grows in deep, dry shade beneath the redwoods. There are also several flax lilies, particularly the tall *Dianella tasmanica* and its variegated form 'Yellow Stripe', and also blocks of *D. caerulea* used as ground cover in less formal areas. The summer hyacinth, *Galtonia candicans,* was planted by the dozen, until the owner discovered the subtle greeny white *G. viridiflora,* which now largely replaces it. Torch lilies flourish in the well-drained beds, including *Kniphofia* 'Christmas Cheer', with large heads of orange flowers above aloe-like leaves; the very floriferous, waist-high, orange-flowered 'Border Ballet'; and 'Primrose Beauty', with soft yellow flowers above grassy foliage. These are followed later in the year by the tall *Kniphofia rooperi.* Clumps of the Chilean *Libertia formosa,* with its large white flowers, are used repetitively to draw the eye down the length of the garden, and he also grows the more dainty *L. ixioides* from New Zealand. Colonies of *L. peregrinans* quickly established large patches of bright orange leaves around the edges of the garden. Bright blue flowers are provided by *Orthrosanthus multiflorus* and *O. laxus* with more grassy foliage; both have open spikes of sky blue flowers carried on stiffly upright, slender elegant stems. The large spikes of pink flowers of *Watsonia borbonica* and the brilliant white ones of subsp. *ardernei* are appreciated, but warily, due to the inclination of these plants to become rampant colonists. He has used carefully placed aloes in several places, originally with the idea of accentuating impressions of spikiness during the summer, but he now appreciates them at least as much for their brave and cheering colours in winter. He uses mainly the soap aloe, *Aloe saponaria,* with branched clusters of orange flowers in summer; the torch plant, *A. aristata,* with stemless rosettes stippled with white spots; and *A. brevifolia,* another summer flowerer, with leaves suffused with crimson in the winter. *Dyckia brevifolia,* a bromeliad with spiky rosettes of narrow leaves and bell-shaped yellow flowers, also contributes to the effect.

The prolonged flowering periods of many of the broad-leaved perennials came as a pleasant surprise. Peruvian mask flowers like *Alonsoa meridionalis* produce pale pink flowers almost continuously from spring till fall,

Recent developments in plant breeding have produced a number of cultivars of *Clivia miniata* with larger, more substantial flowers than the wild form, and in a variety of colours. Charlie and Mary Muller's garden, Wynberg, Cape Town, Western Cape Province, South Africa.

and *A. warscewiczii* 'Fiery Orange' does equally well. A couple of twinspurs — *Diascia fetcaniensis,* with spreading clumps of dark pink flowers, and *D. integerrima,* with erect stems and coral-pink flowers for months — are useful low fillers. Two South American eryngiums are invaluable for the dramatic effects of their spiky, spiny foliage: *Eryngium agavifolium,* with heads of thimble-sized, silvery green globe thistles raised high in the air, and *E. pandanifolium,* with broader thimbles on shorter stems. The whorls of orange flowers of the South African lion's ear, *Leonotis leonurus,* make a wonderful display in the fall, and the ivory-white 'Harrismith White' is equally attractive. Another plant of more than superficial interest is the dark, wine red—flowered *Lobelia tupa;* the broad, grey leaves of this splendidly sinister-looking plant from Chile were the source of powerful hallucinogens when dried and smoked by the Mapuches. Plants with more innocent appeal, appreciated for their almost perpetual flowering, are the shrublets *Nemesia fruticans,* with vanilla-scented pink flowers, and the white 'Innocence'. Two cultivars of *Phygelius* ×*rectus,* 'Devil's Tears' with dusky crimson flowers and 'Moonraker' with tubular yellow flowers, do well, but a tendency to spread means that they need careful placing. Broad mats of *Osteospermum jucundum* are seldom without at least a sprinkling of pink daisies, and the white *O. ecklonis* is almost as generous.

Beds in more shaded situations contain several cultivars of the New Zealand *Arthropodium cirratum,* as well as the Chilean bridal wreaths *Francoa ramosa,* with long spikes of pure white flowers, and *F. sonchifolia,* with spikes of pink flowers above rosettes of basal leaves. Clumps of the cat's tail *Protasparagus densiflorus* 'Myersii' are used effectively for a change of texture and form, and the acid yellow of the low, shrubby purse flower *Calceolaria integrifolia* 'Golden Nugget' provides bright sparks of colour for months.

The edges of the beds are masked in places with carpeting plants that spread onto the paths. Amongst these are the Kangaroo lobelia, *Dampiera diversifolia,* small and spready with dark blue flowers, and *Laurentia axillaris,* tiny and pretty with minute leaves dotted with starry blue or white flowers. Elsewhere, in damper situations little mats covered with the white flowers of *Pratia angulata* become dotted later with rosy magenta berries, and there is scarcely a month when the ground-covering colonies of the Australian *Viola hederacea* do not have at least some blue and white violets amongst the leaves.

Legacy of a Rich Realtor

A building lot on a private estate east of Lake Casitas in California is buried amongst the foothills of the Los Padres National Forest. The lot belonged to a realtor in the town of Ojai, and was subsequently inherited by his environmentally aware daughter and her boyfriend, who resolved to follow the trend of growing Californian native plants in the garden. This plan was scuppered when an even cleaner, greener friend accused them of ecological sabotage, pointing out that the nursery-grown plants they brought in would interbreed freely with the wildflowers. They would, he said, be Trojan horses, the source of alien and inappropriate genes that could endanger the survival of local populations, possibly even put entire species at risk. Faced with such calamitous effects, they swiftly abandoned further thoughts of natives, and looked around for other ways to make their garden beautiful. Both value their freedom to travel and spend time away with friends, and neither wanted the ties that orthodox gardens would impose.

The situation has a pronounced Mediterranean climate: hot and extremely dry in summer; moist, sometimes wet in winter with temperatures quite frequently falling a degree or two below freezing, and occasionally as low as $-5°C$ ($23°F$). Even in the driest of summers, water percolating down from the mountains through layers of shattered rock below the garden maintains a relatively constant source of moisture within reach of roots. No one has gardened here before, and the ground is free from nutrient residues, particularly phosphates derived from fertilisers, and also from the fungal pathogens associated with cultivated ground.

While casting around, they found Jo O'Connell's Australian Native Plants Nursery at Casitas Springs, and a subsequent visit to the collections of Australian and South African plants at the nearby International Center for Earth Concerns persuaded them that these were the plants they were looking for. The plants lent themselves to extended, freestyle forms of planting rather than arrangements of borders, lawns, walks and other semi-formal features, and being well adapted to the conditions, they were likely to grow satisfactorily without constant care and attention. The absence of pathogens and the low-nutrient status of the ground considerably increased the chances of success. Their interest in these plants was an incentive to travel to places where they occur naturally to find out more about the conditions in which they grow.

Gophers and ground squirrels made short work of bulbs, and these were tried only once. Trees planted for shade and a sense of enclosure include the firewheel tree, *Stenocarpus sinuatus*, which grows well in spite of its rainforest origins; *Eucalyptus caesia*, with large trusses of pinkish red flowers; the South African klapperbos, *Nymania capensis*, remarkable for its masses of decorative rose-pink and green Chinese lanterns; and the South African cabbage tree *Cussonia spicata*, with sinewy stems and broad blue-green leaves. Another South African, the butterspoon, *Cunonia capensis*, is planted in a pocket of moist, fertile soil close to the house, displaying its dense, cylindrical spikes of white flowers and elegant, deep glossy green, pinnate foliage. A hint of formality is introduced by the columnar forms of two Australian cypresses, the blue-green *Callitris glaucophylla* and the deep green *C. baileyi*. A short avenue of fever trees, *Acacia xanthophloea*, with gleaming golden trunks, is planted along the drive, where they benefit from the extra water provided by run-off, and are partially protected from gopher attacks. Other wattles, valued for their rapid growth and nitrogen-fixing ability, include *A. pubescens*, a small tree with feathery pinnate foliage and clusters of fragrant yellow flowers; the mudgee wattle, *A. spectabilis*, with silver bark and masses of chrome yellow flowers amongst brightly glaucous, feathery foliage; and *A. saligna*, with long, curved phyllodes and brilliant yellow bobbles in spring.

Aloes do well here, and *Aloe ferox* is widely planted for the repetitive effect of its powerful stem and top knot of spiky leaves. In search of further character, the couple also tried the kokerboom, *A. dichotoma*, which grows successfully in the drier places. The Australian grass trees *Xanthorrhoea preissii* and the more glaucous *X. quadrangulata* look impressive even as clumps of grass-like leaves, although it will be years before they develop trunks. *Xanthorrhoea minor* produces dense spikes of tiny, aromatic flowers, though this species never forms a trunk, nor does the saw-edged grass tree, *X. macronema*, which has prominent inflorescences resembling drumsticks or robust butterfly antennae.

Numerous members of the protea family are represented, amongst them several banksias. Species with lignotubers—like *Banksia grandis* with yellow candles and *B. menziesii* with creamy red, silver and pale yellow flowers—are cut back hard when they grow too big. Other species without lignotubers are placed where they have space to grow, such as the bright orange flowered *B. ashbyi,* the golden yellow *B. media,* and *B. ericifolia,* with striking rusty orange-red cones of flowers. Isopogons grow well and are valued not only for their thistle-like flower heads but also their fine foliage. *Isopogon anemonifolius* has stiff yellow daisy heads on top of pencil-thin shoots, with leaves reminiscent of flattened tridents. *Isopogon formosus* produces rosy magenta flowers above prickly, much-divided foliage.

The flowers like rose-pink Chinese lanterns of the klapperbos, *Nymania capensis,* are decorative against a blue sky. Karoo National Botanic Garden, Worcester, Western Cape Province, South Africa.

Prospects for proteas and leucospermums were uncertain due to their susceptibility to frost, and the generally more hardy leucadendrons were a better bet. *Leucadendron* 'Cloudbank Jenny', with tulip-like yellow bracts and red centres, 'Pisa', with creamy bracts and silvery foliage, and 'Wilsons Wonder', with variegated foliage, can all be seen here. *Phylica plumosa*, with feathery heads of very pale straw-coloured flowers, was planted once, and thereafter sowed itself. Dryandras, like the isopogons, are planted partially for the sake of their foliage. *Dryandra formosa* has narrow, deeply divided, fernlike leaves and golden yellow flowers, *D. quercifolia* has deeply lobed leaves, and *D. drummondii* produces ground-hugging clumps of upright, deeply divided ferny foliage, with the immature leaves densely covered with cinnamon velvet.

Phylica plumosa grows fast and easily in cultivation, often self-seeding freely, and though not likely to be long-lived, it is a good choice when rapid effects are needed. Kirstenbosch National Botanical Garden, Western Cape Province, South Africa.

Numbered among the smaller shrubs are several boronias, including the red boronia, *Boronia heterophylla*, with masses of sparky rosy cerise flowers and aromatic foliage; *B. denticulata*, with pale lilac-rose flowers ranged along angled stems amongst greyish green foliage; and *B. anemonifolia*, with starry white flowers amongst small, fresh green leaves that smell like turpentine. Emu bushes grow well in the drier parts of the garden, particularly *Eremophila maculata*, most of which bear crimson tubular flowers, but some are peach coloured or almost yellow. Also doing well are *Eremophila divaricata*, with mauve flowers and fine grey foliage, and the lavender flowers of *E. bowmanii* look particularly attractive amongst its silver-grey foliage.

Following advice, the owners tried the South African wild rosemary, *Eriocephalus africanus*, with small, grey, soft, aromatic leaves, but they were not impressed by its clusters of somewhat dirty ivory-white flowers, nor did they much like the woolly seed heads that followed. They found *Sutherlandia frutescens* much more appealing. This shrub with silvery grey leaves has bold clusters of bright red flowers followed by inflated bladder-like fruits amongst fine pinnate foliage. Another good shrub, also from the pea family and with bright red flowers, is the Western Australian cockies tongues, *Templetonia retusa*.

Sunshine and Cactus on the Riviera

This garden in Bordighera on the Italian Riviera is almost overlooked by the decrepit Hotel Angst, the jagged metal letters on its roof still forlornly spelling out its name long after the departure of the last of its illustrious guests. It was bought by the wife of a former cabinet minister in preparation for the retirement of her husband, forced to resign his portfolio, who opted to quit rather than risk deselection at the next election. For him, it is a peaceful place, away from former colleagues, where he can write his memoirs; for her, it is an escape at last from the social formalities of London, and from the hassle of importunate constituents and the media. Both were excited by their new acquisition and by the possibilities of growing proteas, cycads, bougainvilleas and other exotic plants. Friends told them that they "simply must go to La Mortola." They did and made notes about many of the Southern Hemisphere trees and shrubs growing there—but came away depressed and saddened by the sight of a great garden in decline. A visit to Le Jardin Exotique in Monte Carlo opened their eyes to the possibilities of doing exciting things with aloes, cereus and other succulents. She joined the Mediterranean Garden Society, and found visits to the gardens of other members sociable, enjoyable and informative.

Summer on the Riviera is a time of heat and drought, when shade and water are essential to the enjoyment of the garden. Winters normally include lengthy mild periods when the sun shines and it is a pleasure to be outside. The garden, covering about a tenth of a hectare ($1/4$ acre), is in a favoured site, sheltered from winter's cold winds from the north and east. The soil is fertile and in good order, though unsuitable for calcifuge plants, and the garden is adequately supplied with water, supplemented by the storage of rain water from the roofs in an underground cistern.

The garden is designed as a series of rooms, or *chartreuses,* separated, secluded and sheltered by stone walls and evergreen hedges. In order to cre-

ate distinctively different ambiences from one room to the next, a high proportion of the plants in each one share particular qualities, such as form, colour or texture. Shaded, sheltered situations in several parts of the garden
provide attractive, cool places to sit in summer, as well as sunlit arbours in
winter; and water trickling in rills, or splashing in pools from fountains,
plays important roles in several of these spaces. Additional trees were
planted, using several wattles to offset heavily foliaged trees with their pinnate, fern-like phyllodes; the wattles were grafted on to *Acacia retinodes* rootstocks to enable them to grow on the base-rich soil. The climate is suitable
for proteas and other South African fynbos plants, but the fertile, base-rich
soil is not to their liking. This problem is solved partly by growing lime-tolerant kinds, and by planting others in deep beds of scoria and road metal
brought in from outside. No base fertiliser was added to the beds, and plants
are fed sparingly with light top-dressings of sulphate of ammonia. The proteas are sprayed with water frequently during the summer, but watered with
rainwater from the cistern only when absolutely necessary to prevent the
beds from drying out.

Australian brachychitons are included amongst the trees for their brilliant
displays of scarlet flowers. The flame kurrajong, *Brachychiton acerifolius,* can
be quite a sight, but in some years no flowers appear at all, or only a single
branch produces flowers. The red velvety balls of *B. bidwillii* and small bell-
shaped flowers of *B. australis* are more reliable. *Brachychiton rupestris* was
also planted, less for its small yellowish flowers than for its characterful
swollen trunk.

They obtained several proteas, which they were assured were lime tolerant and would grow on their soil, including *Protea obtusifolia,* with full,
rounded heads of rich crimson or ivory-white bracts, and *P. susannae,* with
mahogany-red bracts, but foliage that the wife thought smelt disgustingly
obnoxious. A close relative, *Leucospermum patersonii,* also chosen for its lime
tolerance, produces bright orange pincushions during spring and early summer, and is well on the way to developing into a small tree. Finally, they are
pleased with one of the sunshine conebushes, *Leucadendron meridianum,*
not only for the bright yellow bracts of its flowers but also for its persistent
female cones covered with silver hairs.

These successes encouraged them to try other members of the family that
are less lime tolerant, growing them in the specially made-up beds described

earlier, including several of the hybrids between *Leucadendron salignum* and *L. laureolum,* arising from crosses first made in New Zealand by Jean and Wallace Stevens; the success of 'Safari Sunset' fully justified its reputation as a splendid and amenable garden plant. *Leucadendron strobilinum* is also doing well, but their silver tree, *L. argenteum,* was a disappointment.

Another rewarding group from the protea family are the grevilleas, which also flower mainly during winter and spring. *Grevillea* 'Copper Crest' with pink flowers and bronze foliage, 'Jubilee' with terminal clusters of bright red and yellow flowers, and other Austraflora hybrids are hits. *Grevillea longifolia* is grown commercially in the area to provide foliage for florists, and several are planted here; and they also like its red toothbrush flowers. The spider-web grevillea, *G. thelemanniana,* with soft grey-green leaves and rich red toothbrushes from autumn till spring, is used as ground cover and to trail over low walls, and three or four Poorinda hybrids, including the pink-flowered 'Halo' and the claret-coloured 'Royal Mantle', also help to keep the weeds down.

The flame kurrajong, *Brachychiton acerifolius,* is magnificently spectacular when its bare branches are covered with scarlet flowers. The Royal Botanic Gardens, Sydney, New South Wales, Australia.

After visiting the Kirstenbosch National Botanical Gardens during a trip to South Africa, the owners of this Mediterranean garden introduced restios as a dominant theme in one of the "chartreuses," with mixed results. They are delighted with the imposingly tall stems of *Cannomois virgata* topped by fine plumes of light green foliage, and with the tan-coloured bracts of *Elegia racemosa*. After a slow start, dakriet, *Chondropetalum tectorum*, has grown into a characterful, stiffly upright mass of dull bronze or olive-green narrowly cylindrical stems relieved by bands of slightly lighter tints. The description of the feathery foliage and dark bronze, satiny sheened inflorescences of *Thamnochortus cinereus* sounded good, but the owners did not care for the inflorescences, and the appearance of its dead foliage is dispiritingly squalid. The Australian tassel-cord rush, *Restio tetraphyllus*, is amongst the best of the restios in the collection. It steadily develops into broad, chest-high clumps of reed-like stems banded pale and dark green with ultra-fine feathery foliage. There is also a nice dwarf form, subsp. *meiostachys*, about half the height and width of the type.

Elsewhere they planted succulent or spiky plants, including several puyas, which entranced them with their barrel-like inflorescences of almost luminous flowers. *Puya chilensis* offers massive, lofty heads of lime-green flowers, and *P. alpestris* has electric blue-green tubular flowers above dense rosettes of silver-green foliage. Several species of cactus accentuate the effect, including the Chilean *Eulychnia acida*, with multiple, spiny columnar stems; *Oreocereus celsianus*, with hairy columns of cylindrical spiny stems, from northern Argentina; and for a change of shape, a couple of barrel cacti from the same country, *Echinopsis bruchii* and *E. kuehnrichii*. Several cactus-like euphorbias go well with the true cacti, including *Euphorbia mammilaris*, with congested clusters of small, warty, spiny columns, and *E. caput-medusae*, which grows like nests of little writhing spiny serpents.

Wine and Roses in Provence

This garden covers about 1.5 hectares (3.75 acres) around a Provençal *mas* between La Garde-Freinet and the Mediterranean Sea. It is set almost within sight of the sea amongst open woodland of pines, cork oaks and mimosas, with cistus, tree heaths and brooms growing beneath the trees on well-drained, sandy soil. Nearly 1 hectare (2.5 acres) is a vineyard; the rest shows no sign of ever having been gardened. The owner, an Australian ophthalmic surgeon with a fashionable private practise, owned the place for years as a weekend and holiday home for the family. He semi-retired after a divorce from his French wife, who returned to Marseilles; their children were at University or in the early stages of professional careers elsewhere, and he moved in to be conveniently close to his companion in dalliance, a sassy Port Grimaud widow, intending to "civilise" the place. He is a keen sailor with a boat in a smart marina near St Tropez, really not much interested in the garden, apart from the vineyard, which provides the wherewithal to play the *vigneron*—it is just within the designated Côtes de Provence—and practise his conviction that God created "Ozzies" to teach the French how to make wine. He loves entertaining, and regards the garden as a setting for pleasant days in the company of friends.

Short visits on holiday had left him with little appreciation of the true conditions here. He was appalled by the ferocity and chill of the mistral, not only in winter when he had expected it, but in spring too. The heat and drought of summer, idyllic during short visits on holiday, also proved unexpectedly hard to live with as a day-to-day experience. His never more than half-hearted enthusiasm for gardening wilted even more when exposed to the realities of the climate, to the temptation to go sailing, to the impossibility of finding anyone reliable who would garden for him for the peanuts he was prepared to pay, and to the discovery that keeping extensive displays of plants alive in the well-drained sandy soil during the summer would require hundreds of thousands of litres of water, to be paid for drop by drop.

After wrestling intermittently, frustratingly and ill-temperedly with his problems, he reluctantly bowed to the inevitable and sought help from a friend of a friend who was a landscape architect. It was not hard to persuade him to abandon ambitious plans, and confine serious gardening to the area closest to the house, merging the boundaries of the surrounding woodland with the garden (while taking care to preserve a clear area as a fire break). A swimming pool constructed close to the house became the central feature of the garden, forming part of a terrace, sheltered in the angle of a newly built wall and the house itself. Additional shelter was provided by constructing a semi-glazed garden room and hot tub as an extension to the house at the head of the pool. A pergola was erected parallel to the pool on the third side to produce a long shaded arbour to retreat to in the summer. Plants are used sparingly—some in beds, others in large containers around the pool—and much of the garden's interest lies in the combinations of stone, brick, tile and tessera used to make the walls, paths and other surfaces, chosen with great care to create interesting patterns, forms and motifs.

The Australian coast tea tree, *Leptospermum laevigatum,* grows along the exposed side of the pergola to form a wind-excluding screen. It was first planted in the lea of a temporary wattle fence until it became established. The side closest to the pool is planted with a number of different climbers, amongst which are several of Alister Clark's roses—honorary rather than actual Southern Hemisphere plants. On learning that the owner was an Antipodean, a local nurseryman persuaded him to buy a collection of roses said to be descendants of hybrids Clark had exchanged many years previously with Sir Cecil Hanbury at La Mortola on the Italian Riviera. Like those of Father George Schoener near Santa Barbara with whom he exchanged seeds, these hybrids were derived from *Rosa gigantea,* and bred by Clark to thrive in the heat and drought of a Melbourne summer, and to flower for exceptionally long periods starting early in spring. The nurseryman's plants were not reliably named, but a particularly long-flowering, peach-coloured semi-double is believed to be 'Sunlit', and a pink form with an equally prolonged season is most probably the climbing sport of the well-known 'Lorraine Lee'. A vigorous climber with distinctive scarlet flowers shadowed with deep velvety crimson labelled 'Black Boy' is probably true to name, and another vigorous climber with rather short-lived masses of pink flowers in spring is identified as 'Jessie Clark', named by Alister after a niece.

Fast-growing, small pioneer trees reinforce the shelter from the pergola around the pool. These include the multistemmed, shrubby *Psoralea pinnata,* as well as several wattles: *Acacia podalyriifolia,* with outstandingly bright silvery phyllodes; the Port Lincoln wattle, *A. iteaphylla,* tall and multistemmed with an inclination to weep, particularly attractive in spring when the immature phyllodes become flushed with pink; and the black wattle, *A. mearnsii,* with ferny, bipinnate foliage and pale yellow flowers during late spring. The two New Zealand kowhais are in slightly more sheltered positions. *Sophora microphylla* is a twiggy, divaricating shrub with wiry interlacing branches and sparse leaves when juvenile, before eventually acquiring tree form, and *S. tetraptera* develops more rapidly into a small, spreading tree. Masses of pale mauve-pink flowers are produced throughout the spring by the South African keurboom, *Virgilia divaricata.*

Drought-resistant, undemanding plants are used close to the house and around the pool, planted in small beds and large containers. The evergreen, spring-flowering agapanthus hybrids derived from *Agapanthus praecox* are located in the shelter of the pergola, where they are protected from occasional frosts, and the deciduous descendants of *A. campanulatus* are in more exposed positions. Additionally, the purple-leaved form of the hop bush, *Dodonaea viscosa* 'Purpurea', grows here, and the New Zealand Marlborough rock daisy, *Pachystegia insignis,* contributes its notably presentable leathery leaves, with a soft sheen, and long-lasting heads of pure white flowers. Arum lilies, *Zantedeschia aethiopica,* provide magnificent broad foliage in the winter followed by numerous elegant white flowers in spring before dying down for the summer. Variously coloured kinds of Jersey lily, *Nerine sarniensis,* are a blaze of colour in early autumn. Other plants with distinctive shapes and textures are used to create atmosphere, including large specimens of *Aloe plicatilis* placed in the more sheltered corners and valued for the sculptural effects of their sinewy stems bearing fans of blue-green foliage. Two tree ferns were chosen for their relative tolerance of drought: the Australian rough tree fern, *Cyathea australis,* which now grows well enough after initial difficulties during establishment, and the New Zealand silver fern, *C. dealbata.*

The Marlborough rock daisy, *Pachystegia insignis,* has attractive leathery leaves and flowers that look good in bud and in bloom. Guy Bowden's garden, Tutukaka, North Island, New Zealand.

Artist's Pad in a French Hill Town

A tiny whitewashed house, one in a row in the hill town of Cabris in Provence, consists of a paved yard of about 100 square metres (120 square yards)—reached from the house by a short flight of stone steps from the kitchen door or through an archway between the house and one of the neighbours—and a slightly raised narrow strip of ground, bounded by a high wall at the far end. The owner, waking on the morning of her fortieth birthday with a feeling that life was passing her by, gave up her secure but mundane job as an investment consultant for a large French bank and exchanged her two-bedroom apartment, monthly salary and eventual pension for this tiny place and a small nest egg, supplemented by occasional sales of pictures to tourists. She lives there with her four cats, and claims to have no time for, and less than no interest in, gardening. Nevertheless, she has inherited, picked up and variously acquired a collection of attractive pots and other containers, which she has filled with plants to decorate the yard.

This garden just happened—almost in spite of its owner—and little more needed to be done. The main concerns were that the courtyard became unbearably hot during the summer, and the white walls created bright, unrelieved glare. The plants in the containers had been assembled haphazardly, and increased variety and more selective grouping was needed to make them more vital and attractive.

The owner had painted and drawn pots and plants in the yard a number of times. The replanning process started by making trial drawings in which she introduced new features or layouts as a means of visualising possible changes. A rough pole pergola was constructed against the wall of the house to provide a shaded place to sit, chat, have a meal or a glass of wine; and the strip of ground at the bottom of the garden was planted with densely foliaged evergreens to provide a restful, glare-free background. Her search for plants led to encounters with euphorbias, and to the recognition that these are succulents with attitude. She was immediately attracted to the combination of their assertive, emphatic natures and their diversity of sculptural forms and textures. She made a good intention—carried out well enough to avert a direct transit to Hell—to feed most of the plants in the containers at the beginning of each month from January to July, using a proprietary liquid feed, and following the instructions on the label.

Her first euphorbia, donated by a friend as a Christmas present, was the crown of thorns, *Euphorbia milii,* ferociously thorny but with spectacular red bracts round its small flowers. The winters here are a little too cold for this plant, and it loses its leaves, but survives if kept dry in a sheltered place. Others include *E. virosa,* which grows into an upright, urn-shaped bush with numerous, succulent, ridged, cylindrical stems; and the so-called weeping form of *E. ingens,* more like a thick, green, spiny boa constrictor than a plant. Another favourite is the elephant bush, *E. dregeana,* with numerous, slender, ascending columnar green stems, which looks particularly satisfying against the white stone walls of the house.

In this part of the world pergolas are almost inevitably covered with roses and vines, but the owner of this garden was determined to break new ground. She settled for the blue-flowered *Plumbago auriculata,* a couple of bower plants *Pandorea jasminoides*—one with trusses of sumptuously textured white flowers, the other with pink flowers with crimson throats—and the pink-flowered form of the Australian bluebell creeper, *Sollya heterophylla.* Only the last proved to be a mistake, as its washed-out pink flowers made little impression, and it was later replaced with its blue-flowered counterpart.

Heavily foliaged shrubs are planted at the bottom of the garden to reduce glare, including the Australian water gum, *Tristaniopsis laurina,* which is notably drought tolerant in spite of its vernacular name. Several New Zealand pseudopanaxes serve a similar function, including *Pseudopanax* 'Adiantifolius' with deeply lobed, glossy green leaves, and the variegated 'Gold Splash'. Two other variegated plants that combine glare relief with visual interest are *Schefflera* 'Hong Kong Bicolour' and the parapara *Pisonia umbellifera* 'Variegata', with broad green, cream and white leaves, which forms a dense and substantial wall-covering twining through a trellis.

The floral display in pots and containers relies on tender perennials of various kinds, including several osteospermums: 'Buttermilk', with yellow petals around crimson centres; 'Whirligig', with white and metallic blue, spoon-shaped petals, and its counterpart 'Pink Whirls'; 'Blue Streak', white with sparkling blue centres; 'Silver Sparkler', white flowers amongst cream and green variegated leaves; and the fine chrome yellow 'Zulu'. Blue flowers are provided by felicias, such as the variegated forms of *Felicia amelloides* and *F. amoena,* appreciated for their prolonged flowering periods.

Her collection of fragrant-foliaged pelargoniums includes *Pelargonium* 'Brunswick', with rose-pink flowers and deeply lobed, toothed leaves pungently laced with camphor; 'Citronella', upright and twiggy with trilobed, sharply lemony leaves and lilac flowers; 'Lara', rose-pink flowers and deeply subdivided, narrowly lobed aromatic foliage; 'Radula', with finely subdivided, narrowly lobed leaves and a musky pelargonial fragrance enlivened by sharper undertones; and 'Sweet Mimosa', with pale pink flowers, deeply lobed leaves and a strong pelargonial aroma with a hint of lemon. The delicately pretty 'Roller's Satinique' has medium-sized, bright rose-pink flowers with deep pink honey guides, and its small, greyish, deeply lobed foliage has a sharp camphor fragrance. The mauve-flowered 'Mabel Grey' smells of lemons with more than a hint of eucalyptus. 'Kewense' is a vigorous, rangy plant with long internodes and bountiful clusters of narrow cerise-pink flowers, and *P. fulgidum* is scarcely fragrant, but notable for its small, bright scarlet flowers and soft, deeply lobed leaves.

B&B with Marmite on the Costa del Sol

A garden west of Estepona in southern Spain, originally part of a small farm, was an impulse purchase by a British couple looking forward to an idyllic retirement picking oranges, pickling olives and selling the fruits of their labours to local hotels. Rosy impressions of the climate, gained during winter holidays escaping from the wet and cold of home, had not prepared them for the problems of working in the heat of the Spanish summer. Their accountant also pointed out that even their least optimistic forecasts greatly overestimated the rewards they could hope to receive from selling oranges and pickled olives, and advised them to find a tenant for part of their property. They did, and retained a little over 750 square metres (900 square yards) around the house as a garden. This played a part in their plans to run the house as a B&B, providing evening meals for tourists, and the garden was a major contributor to the atmosphere of the establishment. They are close enough to Gibraltar for shopping expeditions to the Safeway Supermarket, establishing a lifeline for supplies of pork pies, sliced bread, fish fingers, marmite and other familiar indispensables.

A trip to the gardens of the Generalife in Granada organized by "Friends in Retirement" filled their thoughts with plans for fountains, pools and the sound of running water, with a shady, gravelled space close by where they and their guests could relax and play an occasional games of *boule* or what-ever the local equivalent may be. The closeness of the house to a main road was a mixed blessing, good for passing business but bad for peace and quiet, and it was essential to create a more secluded atmosphere. The space around the house, previously a melon field, was wholly exposed to the sun, not too big a disadvantage in winter, when much of their business was done, but un-bearably uncomfortable in the heat of summer.

The hot, dry conditions during summer, moderate, sometimes heavy, winter rainfall and siliceous neutral soil favour plants from Western Aus-tralia and the South African Cape, making it easy to find plants that look good during the winter and early spring. Proposals for swimming pools and fountains died an early death when their solicitor pointed out that al-most all the water rights on the property had been transferred to the tenant. The garden and its planting had to be economically and carefully planned following water-wise principles. They used a high proportion of plants nat-urally adapted to cope with hot, dry conditions, grouping those which de-pend on regular supplies of water together in beds close to the house where they have most impact, and mulching newly planted trees and shrubs with deep layers of stones to conserve water. A long curving pergola was con-structed and covered with climbing plants to provide shade and shelter, and a screen of fast-growing trees was planted along the roadside. Elsewhere, palms provide much of the exotic atmosphere that their guests expect and appreciate.

The first plant chosen for the roadside screen was *Eucalyptus ficifolia*, se-duced by its scarlet-crimson flowers. This tree was quickly joined by several young specimens of *Corymbia citriodora* with brilliant silver bark and lemon-scented foliage. Other eucalypts with colourful flowers were added later, in-cluding a red-flowered form of *E. nutans*, a multistemmed mallee with bur-nished light golden tan bark, and *E. eremophila*, another mallee with smooth, battleship grey bark and clusters of bright yellow flowers from horn-shaped buds. The owners of this garden looked for something differ-ent and distinctive to plant on either side of the entrance, and eventually chose the variegated form of Brisbane box, *Lophostemon confertus* 'Variegata', with cream centres to broad green leaves. Although they grew rapidly, the eu-calypts made an insubstantial screen and had to be reinforced with more densely foliaged plants, including the bushy, deep green, glossy Rottnest cypress, *Callitris preissii*, and the more grey leaved but equally dense honey myrtle *Melaleuca lanceolata*, which produces white bottlebrushes in spring.

Small groups of willow peppermints, *Agonis flexuosa*, and karrees, *Rhus lancea*, provide shade within the garden The pergola is planted with fast-growing, densely foliaged climbers like the coral vine, *Kennedia coccinea*, with masses of bright red flowers, and *K. nigricans*, remarkable for its insect-like black and yellow flowers. Another rapid shade provider is the Cape honeysuckle, *Tecomaria capensis*, which was ideal during the first few years but later needed constant cutting back to curb its vigour. Bougainvilleas with magenta, pink or scarlet flowers provide masses of flamboyant colour, set off by the blue-flowered *Petrea volubilis*, a characteristic plant of Southern Hemisphere gardens, though not originating in that part of the world. Another blue-flowered plant that scrambles rather than climbs amongst its neighbours is *Hardenbergia comptoniana*. *Protasparagus setaceus* is also included, valued for the way its twining stems weave through the other climbers, so that its light, ferny foliage brightens even the darkest recesses. Another South African, *Jasminum multipartitum*, is grown for the sake of its strongly fragrant, large, starry white flowers and the quality of its deep green, glossy foliage.

The palms are a long-term project, but even when still quite small the blue fronds and spiky appearance of *Trithrinax campestris* from the Argentine pampas creates the right sort of impression. This palm is backed up with a couple of clumps of the multistemmed *Phoenix reclinata* and a row of the cocos palm, *Syagrus romanzoffiana*, along the drive. A pair of Australian bangalow palms, *Archontophoenix cunninghamiana*, will one day add distinction to the main entrance, and the slow-growing, little *Livistona muelleri* is another promising Australian.

The search for drought-resistant plants started with the obvious mesembs. They planted numerous brilliantly coloured drosanthemums and lampranthus, and the annual Livingstone daisy, *Dorotheanthus bellidiformis*, enjoying them for their spectacular display when in flower, but finding their appearance afterwards dispiriting. A friend pointed out that the garden would look more interesting if it included plants with more defined shapes and textures, suggesting they put in some succulent shrubs. A couple of *Aloe ferox* and a specimen plant of the tree *A. barberae* convinced them she was right. They added several kinds of *Crassula ovata*, including 'Blue Bird' and

'Coral', as well as the tall *C. arborescens,* with its thick fleshy trunk and succulent rounded leaves outlined in crimson and covered with a silvery bloom. *Cotyledon orbiculata* contributes heads of hanging orange flowers. They were thrilled to find plants of the ultra-sculptural *Cyphostemma juttae,* which to their amazement proceeded to produce small crops of scarlet grape-like berries.

More colour was needed, and supplied by bulbs. Ixias and sparaxis serve well, and their generally yellow, orange and cream flowers combine nicely with the purples and violets of babianas; white chincherinchees, *Ornithogalum thyrsoides,* cool things down a bit. Finally, they came across a nursery with a good list of watsonias and, thrilled by the bright colours and spikes of flowers like compact gladioli, planted several species from the Cape, including the early flowering, bright red *Watsonia aletroides,* pink *W. amabilis* and orange *W. coccinea.*

Cyphostemma juttae brings highly distinctive sculptural effects into a garden. Karoo National Botanic Garden, Worcester, Western Cape Province, South Africa.

CHAPTER 16

Through the Looking-Glass in the Pacific Northwest and Britain

Chance of Life in a Cool Retreat

On a tract of logged-over forest overlooking Grays Bay in Wahkiakum County in Washington State, on the north shore of the Columbia River's broad estuary, a small house is tucked away amongst forest dotted with boggy hollows illuminated by the yellow hoods of skunk cabbages in spring, and brightened by tall flag irises in summer. The house's owner, formerly an officer on the *Victoria Clipper* ferry service from Seattle to Vancouver Island, was forced to hang up her sea boots after being diagnosed with multiple sclerosis. Ignoring advice to stay conveniently close to "civilised" facilities like supermarkets and an airport, she and her husband bought this place. The prevailing garden style in the neighbourhood consists of closely mown lawns and stilted arrangements of meticulously spaced, narrowly vertical or columnar little conifers in rows and curves following the line of the drive, the edge of a lawn or the boundary fence. Such detailed, finicky forms of gardening require prolonged or precise manipulation of tools, repeated changes of posture or lengthy periods spent kneeling or bending over—unacceptable physical demands that had to be avoided—and the main need was for broad, easily graded paths to make the garden accessible on foot or in a wheelchair. In addition, she wanted something more in sympathy with the surrounding countryside. In doing so, she devised a garden that gives endless pleasure and positive encouragement without making oppressive demands on time, agility or strength.

The markedly oceanic climate here has very wet and cool, rather than cold, winters. High temperatures during summer are unusual, and rainfall, although barely a quarter of winter levels, is sufficient to prevent serious drought. The natural vegetation is luxuriant mixed broadleaf and conifer forest, where big leaf maples, rhododendrons and madrones grow amongst hemlock and Douglas fir above woodland perennials, ferns and carpets of moss. In developing the garden, great care was taken to avoid unnecessary disturbance of the forest soil's profile and vegetation, including the moss carpets. Existing plants were destroyed only when space was needed to insert perennials, shrubs and trees as unintrusively and naturally as possible. The prevailing moist atmosphere and relatively mild winters have affinities with conditions in southern Chile, New Zealand and western Tasmania, and many of the plants chosen for the garden grow naturally in those places.

Additional shelter was planted on the seaward side of the garden, with the dense apple green leaves of *Griselinia littoralis* providing the backbone. This is supplemented with *Escallonia rubra* var. *macrantha*, bearing rosy red flowers and large, glossy green, aromatic leaves, and with several daisy bushes, including *Olearia odorata*, tall and spreading with numerous sweetly scented white flowers, *O. ilicifolia*, a multistemmed small tree also with fragrant white flowers, and *O. macrodonta*, with broad, grey-green, spiny foliage. The grey-leaved woolly tea tree *Leptospermum lanigerum* is planted close to the estuary in the more exposed situations.

Ornamental trees and large shrubs planted within the shelter of the forest include two azaras chosen for the intense fragrance of their yellow flowers as winter gives way to spring: *Azara microphylla*, with tiny dark leaves, and *A. petiolaris*, with comparatively large leaves. *Crinodendron hookerianum* does well, and so many were planted that this species' hanging crimson lanterns have become something of a feature in the garden. Another successful inclusion is *Drimys winteri*, which produces great glossy deep green leaves, not unlike those of magnolias, and clusters of white flowers with conspicuous yellow stamens. They also planted several embothriums, first *Embothrium coccineum* 'Inca Flame', but after being warned that this cultivar was not very hardy, they added the narrower, semi-deciduous 'Lanceolatum' as insurance—both survived and make a brave show with dense masses of scarlet flowers. Eucryphias were a natural choice for this maritime climate, and the Chilean *Eucryphia cordifolia*, in particular, makes an outstanding contribution with its broad leathery foliage and pure white bowl-shaped flowers. A grove of the Tasmanian leatherwood, *E. lucida*, rapidly developed into large shrubs, some with white and some with pink flowers. Another tree with beautiful, virginal white flowers like clustered cherry blossoms is the deciduous *Hoheria lyallii*.

Several of the southern myrtles were planted, much the most satisfactory being *Luma apiculata*, with its dense, dark, small leaves and warm cinnamon bark, mottled with ivory when peeling. The golden-leaved sport 'Glanleam Gold' was tried, but seemed out of place in this setting, as did the variously variegated forms of the New Zealand natural hybrid *Lophomyrtus* ×*ralphii*. Instead, one of its parents, *L. bullata*, was tried, but it too failed to make an impression, even when its leaves become suffused with crimson. Two outside chances from New Zealand were the northern rata *Metrosideros robustus* and the southern *M. umbellatus*. The first failed to survive, but the second, although cut to the ground by a harder than usual frost, threw up strong shoots from the base and did well. Two southern beeches look good here: the red beech, *Nothofagus fusca*, with translucent crimson leaves like stained glass in spring, planted in sheltered places, and the tougher but less distinctive silver beech, *N. menziesii*, in more open situations.

The Chilean *Gunnera tinctoria* is the little brother of the so-called giant rhubarb, *Gunnera manicata*, and a more appropriate size for smaller gardens. Parque Nacional Alerce Andino, Puerto Montt, Chile.

One mistake the owners came to regret was an attempt to replace *Gaultheria shallon* with its Chilean analogue, *G. mucronata*. This shrub began to spread rather too enthusiastically, and the artificial-looking clusters of large white or rosy magenta berries and the untidy growth habit failed to please. Much more successful was the introduction of the Chilean bamboo *Chusquea culeou* 'Tenuis', with clusters of short leaves towards the ends of erect branches, looking like clumps of little palm trees. *Gunnera tinctoria* is planted around some of the boggy parts, where its large leaves complement those of the skunk cabbage.

The woods are full of ferns, and these provide another key theme in the garden. Several Southern Hemisphere species supplement the natives, including the little *Blechnum penna-marina*, which quickly forms colonies of close-set, densely ground-covering mats of tiny fronds. Large clumps of the dark *B. tabulare* make an imposing, if rather sombre presence in damp, shaded, sheltered places; *B. wattsii* is a more cheerful prospect, forming patches of broad, crimson-flushed foliage from spreading rhizomes. The crown fern, *B. discolor,* is harder to please but one of the most rewarding with shuttlecocks of pale, gleaming fronds. The southern mother shield fern, *Polystichum proliferum,* supplements the native *P. munitum,* as does *P. vestitum,* less graceful, but a sturdy, characterful plant with dark green, glossy, bipinnate fronds, with the added bonus of being deer resistant.

Planting to Make Life More Interesting
South-west of Portland in Oregon, a garden of about ¼ hectare (⅔ acre) near Sherwood overlooks the Willamette River Valley. It lies on the slopes of a hill down which cold air drains to the valley below, and temperatures seldom fall below −5°C (23°F), and only very occasionally down to −10°C (14°F). The owner is a furniture maker and designer, closer to forty than thirty, with two small children (the boyfriend departed soon after the birth of the second) and slender resources; commissioned sales of furniture just about keep things going. She realised that the garden's old-fashioned, orthodox layout was taking up too much of her time and provided little space for the children to play, and that she had to choose between a radical transformation or a move. To change was cheaper and more appealing than to move.

Total rainfall here during the year would seem adequate, but its uneven distribution, with more than three-quarters falling during the winter months, means that summers can be very dry. Although by no means part of Mediterranea, the site has climatic characteristics that suit many plants from those places, while also providing amenable conditions for those adapted to cool-temperate oceanic and even semi-continental conditions.

Robust, self-maintaining styles of planting that would look attractive and interesting with minimum attention were a primary consideration for the new garden. The original orthodox layout of lawns, flower borders and a large veggie garden was replaced by bold groups of evergreen and deciduous trees and shrubs, several with variegated or silver foliage to relieve any impression of sombre greenery. These woody plants provide settings for perennial and other plants with varied textures and forms, particularly resilient kinds that would not be easily damaged by the children's activities. A silted-up pool at the bottom of the garden was cleaned out, becoming a focal point and the means of linking groups of grasses, sedges and similar plants to create a sense of unity throughout the garden.

The clumps of evergreen trees include both green and variegated forms of *Pittosporum tenuifolium* and *P. eugenioides*. *Crinodendron patagua*, with pale off-white, bell-shaped flowers, and *Lomatia myricoides*, with creamy white flowers in the leaf axils, were also planted. Hummingbirds are attracted to the sombre, inconspicuous flowers of the New Zealand tree fuchsia, *Fuchsia excorticata*, and later other birds to its reddish crimson berries. The weeping *Maytenus boaria* 'Green Showers', a particularly graceful tree, was planted a little apart from others, where its form could be appreciated. The Tasmanian waratah, *Telopea truncata*, is also included, not altogether successfully, for the sake of its striking scarlet flowers, and the silver foliage of several eucalypts provide effective contrast, notably *Eucalyptus glaucescens* and *E. dalhousiae*. The small, upright *E. moorei* brightens a rather infertile, dry, sunny bank.

Water hawthorn, *Aponogeton distachyos*, is planted in the pool, instead of the conventional water lilies. It partially covers the surface with its elongated leaves and heads of fragrant white flowers; the fleshy green seed pods that follow are not merely edible, but are enjoyable when cooked in a stew. The margins of the pond are planted with bulrushes, *Typha muelleri*; clumps of the sedge *Carex secta*, with great mop heads raised on short trunks; and *Zantedeschia aethiopica* 'Goliath', with broad, ivory-white, rather reflexed spathes. *Nertera granadensis*, planted where the ground remains permanently moist, produces masses of tiny, round, cherry red drupes amongst groups of river lilies, *Hesperantha coccinea*, including 'Oregon Sunset' with coral-red flowers in the fall. In hope, rather than expectation, the Tasmanian button grass, *Gymnoschoenus sphaerocephalus*, was planted for the sake of its bright tan foliage and hemispherical inflorescences, but it turned out to

The weeping form of *Maytenus boaria,* known as 'Green Showers', makes a most graceful garden tree, and can survive quite severe frosts. The Valentine garden, Montecito, California.

be a vain hope. Two New Zealand pampas grasses provide links between the pool and other parts of the garden: *Cortaderia fulvida* in the damper parts, and the even larger toe-toe, *C. richardii*, where the ground is better drained, both in places where the knife-edged leaves would be out of the way of children's hands. Phormiums are used to establish similar links, with erect forms concentrated in the damper areas nearer the pool, amongst them *Phormium* 'Variegatum', with understated colour contrasts; the tall 'Rainbow', with olive-green leaves margined with pink when young; and 'Maori Chief', with crimson edgings. Cultivars with more laxly arching foliage are placed in drier parts further afield, including 'Maori Maiden', with rose-red to creamy yellow leaves margined with green; 'Dazzler', deep maroon, striped scarlet; 'Yellow Wave'; and the imposing, deep crimson 'Dark Delight'.

Astelia banksii is used to maintain the grassy theme with its narrow, silver-filigreed leaves and panicles of crimson-black berries on the female plants. Several sedges, mostly planted in dryish situations, are valued for their warm foliage tones, including the arching tufts of yellow-green leaves of *Carex comans,* the rusty brown *C. flagellifera,* and the bright orange *C. testacea.* A few large torch lilies grow in well-drained sites just above the pool, in the hope of attracting hummingbirds. *Kniphofia* 'Alcazar' produces rosy salmon flowers, 'Shenandoah' has tubular yellow flowers emerging from orange buds, and 'Springtime' displays paler flowers from coral-red buds in late summer, despite its name. *Kniphofia caulescens,* with swirling, broad, blue-green foliage, continues the theme amongst the phormiums further from the pool.

Numerous shrubs, many of them from Chile, New Zealand and south-eastern Australia, are used to contrast with the grass-like forms and reinforce the clusters of trees. *Brachyglottis repanda* 'Purpurea', known to the children's merriment as Bushman's loo paper, has large crimson leaves, and the kaka beak, *Clianthus puniceus,* displays hanging clusters of vivid scarlet flowers. *Fuchsia procumbens* 'Variegata' is planted as ground cover in a few places, producing tiny purple and green, upward-facing, orange-tipped flowers amongst little heart-shaped leaves, followed by large red berries. One of the most extraordinary of the shrubs, and one with a spiny nature that needs to be approached with caution, is the Chilean *Colletia paradoxa*. It is much appreciated by the children for its sections of angular flattened stems, which look like little aeroplanes when snapped off the bush, and by the owner for its strange appearance and clusters of white flowers. *Desfontainea spinosa* is another Chilean native that grows well, producing leaves like holly, and tubular orange flowers—another plant for the hummingbirds. *Drimys lanceolata* is a modestly attractive little bush, really only noticed when its copper-coloured young leaves emerge in spring. Grevilleas were amongst the first Australian shrubs attempted, which are appreciated because the deer leave them alone, and one or two rice bushes also proved successful. *Pimelea nivea* grows well with rounded clusters of pure white flowers atop long, grey felted stems, and the ground-hugging alpine rice flower, *P. alpina*, has branches crowded with tiny, stemless blue-green leaves dotted with heads of pink flowers emerging from crimson buds. *Hebe salicifolia* is used for large clumps of dense cover, and several cultivars of *H. speciosa* for their long spikes of bright purple and crimson flowers. Amongst the other hebes are several of the Wiri series from New Zealand, bred by Jack Hobbs at the Regional Botanic Gardens near Auckland. These include the compact 'Wiri Dawn' and the taller 'Wiri Gem', both with rose-pink flowers, and the white 'Wiri Mist'. One of the best is the vigorous, upright 'Wiri Prince', with long racemes of deep purple flowers. Finally, the owner planted a few mint bushes for the sake of their aromatic foliage and attractive flowers: *Prostanthera incisa* 'Variegata', a large, round-profiled shrub with masses of soft purple flowers and variegated foliage, and the taller *P. lasianthos,* with quite large white flowers with purple and yellow markings in their throats.

Alpines in a Frigid Zone

This small garden on a windswept ridge near Otley in the north of England is only 200 square metres (230 square yards). The owners, an actuarial assistant in the Bradford Wool Exchange and his wife, are both in their thirties; there are no plans for children. She is not interested in gardening. He had tried, but she was unimpressed by her husband's attempts, derisively referring to him as "the man in charge of Kew Gardens" when friends called. A visit to the Harrogate Flower Show turned him on to alpines; he joined the Alpine Garden Society and even used his holidays one year to go to "Southern Alpines '96," an international meeting organised by the New Zealand Alpine Garden Society in Christchurch. His wife finds his new obsession thoroughly irritating, regarding it as another daft idea and a waste of money—a view reinforced when she accompanied him to Christchurch, which she thought a dull place compared to Bodrum in Turkey, where she had planned to spend her fortnight in the sun. She told him that what the garden needed was some of those nice golden fir trees that nearly everyone else on the road used to make hedges, and a bit of grass for her to sunbathe on.

The main challenges in this garden—apart from the opposed temperaments of its owners—are exposure to cold winds and the heavy clay loam soil, which drains very slowly and lies cold and waterlogged most of the winter. The builders of the estate irresponsibly failed to lay drains to rectify the latter, and nothing could be done at this late stage. Previous attempts to follow orthodox forms of gardening had been defeated by the unfavourable conditions. The wife's suggestion for a lawn was impractical due to the state of the ground, and a screen of the leyland cypress 'Castlewellan Gold' would have been a sadly hackneyed and unsuitable way to provide shelter. Nevertheless, far apart though the attitudes of the two owners may have seemed, there were ways to combine her need for sheltered space in which to sunbathe with his plans for a more interesting garden.

Initial plans for a rock garden were abandoned in favour of raised beds after the garden-maker saw examples at the Northern Horticultural Society's Harlow Carr Gardens in Harrogate. He provided shelter for the garden by planting shrubs and small trees on a broad raised bank along the most exposed boundaries, reinforcing the effect by the positioning of the alpine house and an extension of one of the side walls to make a warm and secluded sunbathing area. Elsewhere the level of the garden was raised by covering the surface of the soil with a 15-centimetre (6-inch) layer of scalps (a mixture of quarry dust and stone fragments up to 7.5 centimetres long, available from quarries supplying roadstone), on which the surface features of the garden were constructed. Paving was laid over the scalps around the greenhouse and raised beds to make a comfortable, secure, all-weather surface. An area on the far side of the greenhouse, reserved for cold frames and standing-out ground for pots, was covered with a light topping of fine gravel. A couple of the raised beds and containers close to the house were filled with annuals and bulbs or low-growing floriferous perennials for spring and summer colour.

The raised beds and the spaces in the paving provide homes for numerous alpines. Acaenas with no barbs on their burrs are used for ground cover, amongst them the small *Acaena glabra*, bearing glossy olive-green leaves with glaucous reverses, and *A. microphylla*, which forms broad, close-set mats with a range of bronze, dove grey or soft purple tones, and a few plants of the taller cultivar 'Pewter Carpet'. Several of the barbed species are planted on raised beds where the burrs cannot cling to passing feet, including *A. caesiiglauca*, with mats of blue-grey foliage studded with tan-coloured burrs, and the widely grown cultivars *A. microphylla* 'Copper Carpet' and 'Blue Haze', the latter a form of *A. saccaticupula* with dove grey foliage and burrs carried well above the mats of leaves.

Several smaller aciphyllas are included on the raised beds for textural contrast. The most successful are the New Zealand *Aciphylla montana*, with tufts of spiky olive-green leaves with a hint of burnished bronze, and *A. pinnatifida*, which has well-marked yellow central stripes and is easily propagated by division. The Australian snow aciphylla, *A. glacialis,* is a big hit, with its stiff, finely divided leaves like miniature palm fronds above loose, cushiony tufts. The raised beds also provide good conditions in which to make the most of the diversity of colour and texture to be found amongst

Containers can be used to grow collections of plants that might not grow in the garden itself—like these New Zealand alpines. This composition of wahlenbergias, helichrysums and grasses has an aesthetic appeal that is worth more than a second look. Fernglen, Muriel Fisher's garden, Birkenhead, North Island, New Zealand.

hebes. *Hebe cupressoides* 'Boughton Dome' contributes close-set, bun-shaped mounds of tiny, samphire-like, grey-green shoots. *Hebe buchananii* 'Minor' grows as a spreading, ground-hugging shrublet with short, upright, finely twiggy shoots and tiny leaves ranked along their lengths. The upright, olive-green, whipcord shoots of *H. lycopodioides* look more like a club moss than a shrubby veronica, and the more vigorous *H. ochracea* develops into an irregularly flat-topped shrub with bright tan-coloured whipcord shoots.

The creator of this garden first encountered the southern clematis when he bought *Clematis* ×*cartmannii* 'Joe' at a plant sale, and was so intrigued by its low-arching branches, finely divided foliage and white flowers that he made a point of finding one of its parents, *C. marmoraria*. This species is so floriferous that its domed cushion of leaves is almost hidden by the white flowers. His discovery of a shrub that grew as a cushion so captivated him that he made a little collection of the many Southern Hemisphere "alpines" that adopt this form. Amongst the first acquisitions were South American species of oxalis, starting with several named clones of pink- or white-flowered *Oxalis enneaphylla*, and then some of the more striking forms of *O. laciniata* with quite deep violet-blue or blue-veined flowers. *Oxalis nahuelhuapiensis*, with deep yellow flowers above green cushions, was also tried, but did not grow well—but, as his wife said, what can you expect with a name like that?

Other cushions in the collection, mostly grown in the frames and alpine house, include *Celmisia argentea*, which produces mats that eventually grow to the size of dinner plates, composed of silver leaves studded with small white flowers, a little like an androsace. The coarser, looser and broader spreading *C. sessiliflora* also appears here. The owner tried *C. prorepens*, with its mats of viscous green leaves beneath white daisies on short sticky stems, but found that it is a martyr to aphids. One plant that even intrigued his wife was the New Zealand edelweiss, *Leucogenes leontopodium*, a convincing version of the real thing with white flannel flowers above rosettes of pewter leaves covered with silver hairs. Rash optimism prompted him to try one of the vegetable sheep, *Raoulia eximia*, but it died a slow death. He did better with golden scabweed, *R. australis*, a good mini-carpeter for bulbs in a raised bed; *R. haastii*, the green mat daisy; and *R. grandiflora*, with conspicuous white everlasting daisies on glistening mats of silvery blue foliage. Hummocks of *Bolax gummifera* from Tierra del Fuego, with its rosettes of green leaves, grow in crevices in the paving, and the carpets of slightly succulent leaves of Maori musk, *Mimulus repens,* topped with large, lilac monkey flowers are pleasing as well. The tiny cushions of minute green leaves studded with white flowers of *Chionohebe pulvinaris* were attempted outdoors but failed to thrive, though the plant does well in the alpine house, as does the very similar *Phyllachne colensoi.* Both need composts that provide perfectly drained conditions without ever drying out in summer.

A tiny shrub that does well in this garden is one of the dragon trees, *Dracophyllum minimum,* with mossy-looking but almost rock hard tufts of tiny leaves harbouring minute, white bell flowers. Another successful alpine shrub from Tasmania is the cushion riceflower, *Pimelea pygmaea,* with tightly congested foliage beneath a scatter of white flowers. The owner was delighted to find several cushion plants that produced colourful fruit. The first to come his way was *Nertera granadensis,* with mats of bright green foliage dotted with orange ball-bearings. *Cyathodes dealbata* produced fleshy crimson berries on loose mats of interlacing stems, and several plants of *Coprosma petriei* surprised with their variously coloured translucent green, pale blue or crimson drupes on loosely knit mats of twiggy stems. Finally, he was intrigued to discover *Dacrydium laxifolium.* Credited as the smallest pine in the world, this species forms a ground-hugging network of fine stems and small needles studded with fleshy arils like little yew berries.

A Touch of the Tropics

A small house optimistically described by estate agents as "a cottage on the edge of the fashionable Cotswolds" is in reality a plain, early 1930s house in an overgrown village in the upper Thames Valley. It is occupied by a software designer, who works for a multinational company in Swindon, his wife and two small children, and his mother, who is the owner. The back garden, measuring about 250 square metres (300 square yards), had been shared amicably by mother and son—he doing the work, and she telling him what to do—but following a holiday abroad he returned with fancy ideas about exotic plants. Such notions appalled the mother, who was fearful of the comments from friends and neighbours about such a very un-English garden. She could imagine only too clearly their description of it as—horror of horrors—vulgar, and their condemnation of her as not "one of us."

The previous garden was tritely unimaginative and cheerless, and the son's rebellious stirrings stemmed from the realisation that a garden can be a creative and stimulating outlet for imagination. He grasped the fact that—irrespective of convention and what other people might say—this was his patch, and he could do whatever he liked with it. (Actually it was his mother's patch, and she held a different view of its destiny, but in principle he was right.) Shelter was needed to make the garden a more pleasant place to be in, turning it into an asset rather than a chore to be attended to, but otherwise it was not a bad site for his dream. The well-drained, infertile nature of the light sandy loam soil and the garden's southern aspect favoured appropriate plants, and cold air drained into the valley below, so that severe frosts were few and far between.

The disagreements over the garden were resolved when mother spent a winter with relatives in South Africa, and son took the opportunity to make radical changes. The new garden is designed around a patio and a fountain in a raised basin feeding a long, narrow pool, flanked by paving and plants in large containers. Raised beds on either side are contained by low, white-painted walls topped by terracotta tiles, and filled with topsoil mainly derived from mother's precious lawn. Shade is provided by a pergola of roughly squared wood supported on columns made from concrete pipes painted a sandy yellow colour, and a screen of trees is planted on either side of the garden. Carefully chosen plants are used sparingly for maximum effect, including a preponderance with spiky, silver or aromatic foliage. Some less hardy, mood-inducing plants grown in containers are overwintered in a lean-to greenhouse. Mother eventually was reconciled to the new garden, aided by peace offerings in the form of cut foliage of eucalypts and griselinias, bottlebrush and calla flowers, which greatly increased her standing amongst her friends in the flower-arranging society.

Eucalypts form the backbone of the shelter belts. These include the very hardy *Eucalyptus archeri*; *E. glaucescens* for its bright silver foliage; the spinning gum, *E. perriniana*, for its distinctive round leaves deeply flushed dove grey when immature; and *E. subcrenulata*, which has deep apple green foliage not unlike a griselinia's in texture and colour. All are periodically cut back hard to restrain exuberant growth and ensure a continuation of their attractive juvenile foliage. Towards the lower end of the garden, eucalypts are replaced by griselinias mixed with hardy wattles: *Acacia pravissima*, with small, triangular phyllodes; the mountain hickory wattle, *A. obliquinervia*, with large phyllodes; and a high-altitude provenance of the ferny leaved *A. dealbata* subsp. *subalpina*, with white down on the young shoots and clusters of fragrant flowers.

A number of large shrubs provide secondary shelter within the garden, amongst them the light violet flowered *Abutilon* ×*suntense* and *Abutilon* 'Violetta', with deep violet-purple flowers. Bottlebrushes are used for the exotic appearance of their inflorescences, such as the scarlet-flowered *Callistemon citrinus* 'Splendens' and the creamy yellow *C. sieberi*. Assurances of their hardiness encouraged him to try some honey myrtles, specifically *Melaleuca decussata*, with pinky purple bottlebrushes in spring and summer and peeling bark, and *M. elliptica*, with striking blue-green foliage and red bottlebrushes. The garden's "tropical" look depends heavily on numerous grassy or spiky forms centred around a group of green cabbage trees, *Cordyline australis*, in association with two variegated but more dubiously hardy forms: 'Torbay Dazzler', with striped green and cream leaves, and 'Torbay Red', so named for its central red stripe. These are underplanted with such phormiums as the tall and spiky 'Copper Beauty', with burnished foliage, and 'Purpureum', with purple, along with the smaller 'Maori Maiden' (leaves with pale pink centres and a cream outer stripe) and 'Maori Sunrise' (red, pink and bronze stripes). The arching foliage of the purple *Phormium* 'Dark Delight' and the yellow and green 'Yellow Wave' introduce a softer touch. These link visually with the grasses *Cortaderia selloana* 'Gold Band', with yellow-variegated foliage, and 'Silver Stripe', with white and green striped leaves. The bright silver foliage of *Astelia chathamica* maintains the grassy theme in its distinctive eye-catching fashion. Clumps of two other plants, chosen for their unusual appearance, play parts in this association: *Elegia capensis*, which is overwintered under cover, and the Chilean bamboo *Chusquea culeou*, with whorls of short, spiky leaves on upright stems.

The pergola was quickly covered with the Chilean potato vine *Solanum crispum* 'Glasnevin' interplanted with seedlings of *Eccremocarpus scaber* bearing orange, yellow or crimson flowers. Summer colour is provided by a number of plants in large containers, notably *Agapanthus* 'Rosewarne', a strain with extra-large heads of purple-blue flowers, and 'White Ice', with dense heads of white flowers. The tall, raised pineapple heads of *Eucomis pole-evansii* and the shorter ones of *E. comosa* both look good for many weeks each summer. Large containers are also planted with a mixture of *Helichry-*

sum petiolare 'Limelight' or 'Variegatum' with the tall pink *Pelargonium frute-torum* 'The Boar'. The bright pink flowers of *Nerine bowdenii* at the base of low walls produce a final fling of colour in the autumn, often overlapping with the last flowers of pots filled with the bold-spotted leaves of hybrid calla lilies, including *Zantedeschia* 'Mango', with copper-red flowers streaked with apricot, 'Treasure', peach flushed red, and 'Black Magic', yellow with a black eye. These are kept dry through the winter in a timber shelter, and are held in their containers for three or even four years before being divided and re-potted.

Finally, he tried several major feature plants, with varying success. The jelly palm, *Butia capitata*, and the tree fern *Dicksonia antarctica* survive by being covered on cold nights during the winter. *Aloe striatula*, with its orange-yellow flowers above spiky fleshy rosettes of leaves in early summer, succeeds in pots overwintered in the greenhouse. The bromeliads *Fascicu-laria bicolor* and *Puya berteroniana*, the hardiest of its kind, were perhaps a lit-tle too adventuresome, as neither are growing well enough to make quite the hoped-for impact.

Wedding Present for the Bride

This bungalow directly fronting the sea between Weymouth and Swanage on the south coast of England has fine views overlooking the Channel and Portland Bill to the west. The owner, a local government officer, has lived in the house for nearly twenty years, and his attempts to grow the roses, del-phiniums and other plants that he had so enjoyed in his previous garden in the suburbs of Gloucester were defeated by the robust seaside conditions. For fifteen years the garden was a dog run rather than a place for plants. Then, to his great surprise, he found himself, on the point of retirement, about to get married for the first time. His bride-to-be accepted his proposal on condition that something be done about the garden, and he arranged for it to have a radical face-lift as a present to his bride.

The garden face-lift was a generous but rash impulse. His ignorance of gardening was equalled only by that of the self-styled "landscaper" he en-trusted with the work. Neither saw much point in consulting the wife-to-be. The 1000-square-metre (¼-acre) site poses formidable problems, balanced by equally substantial and stimulating opportunities. Problems stem from the exposure to gales and salt spray, which are further complicated by the

The jelly palm, *Butia capitata,* is a promising palm for those seeking tropical effects in chilly gardens. Dick Endt's garden, Landsendt, near Auckland, North Island, New Zealand.

need to retain the views from the low windows of the bungalow, ruling out dense screens of trees. The clay loam soil, with flints above limestone giving way to pebbles near the sea, plays a minor rather than major role in this context. The site's compensations include the mild winters, during which snow or lengthy periods of frost are most unusual, and temperatures below −5°C (23°F) almost unheard of. High sunshine levels, even during the winter, are an added bonus.

The couple's relationship plunged into crisis following her discovery of his intentions. The rapid exit of the landscaper helped to resolve the conflict, along with an explanation that "doing something about the garden" meant her taking it in hand. Trees were planted behind the house, away from the sea to lift incoming winds, and shrubs were carefully placed as screens within the garden itself, using plants highly tolerant of exposure to salt-laden winds. Ideas were gathered from visits to gardens in similar situations, including the nearby Abbotsbury, where acid soils complicated comparisons, and further afield, at Coleton Fishacre in Devon and Lamorran House in Cornwall. A visit to the Ventnor Botanic Garden on the Isle of Wight was also inspirational, and tempted experiments with a number of plants of doubtful hardiness—a surprising number of which survived. Local garden centres contained few of the plants needed, but an expedition to Burncoose Nurseries near Redruth in Cornwall and Trevena Cross Nursery near Penzance helped to fill the gaps.

The shelter belt behind the house is intended to lift, rather than filter, the force of the wind, and is constructed from densely foliaged trees and shrubs like *Pittosporum tenuifolium* and *Griselinia littoralis* interplanted with *P. crassifolium, Coprosma repens* (including the cultivar 'Pink Splendour', in which the shiny green leaves become suffused with pink in cold weather), and *Pseudopanax laetus,* which was afflicted by cold and exposure until the other trees provided it with some protection. In the garden between the house and the sea, hedges or carefully placed screens divide up the garden and form sheltered enclosures in which to grow other plants. The screening plants include *Corokia* ×*virgata* 'Frosted Chocolate'; *Escallonia* 'Red Hedge', with fresh deep apple green, glossy leaves and masses of small red flowers; *Escallonia* 'Iveyi', with deep green glossy leaves and pure white flowers; *Fuchsia magellanica* 'Thompsonii' and *Fuchsia* 'Riccartonii'; *Leptospermum macro-*

carpum, with fresh green foliage, like a myrtle, and pale pink flowers in spring; and *Olearia traversii* and *O. avicennifolia*, both with fragrant white flowers.

Shrubs and small trees, several chosen for their bright flowers, are planted where they reinforce shelter and contribute colour and interesting textural contrasts. *Acacia baileyana* grows in a relatively sheltered spot by the house, and *Banksia integrifolia* was included in optimistic anticipation of the character it develops with age. Others are the *Callistemon citrinus* cultivars 'Burning Bush' and 'Mauve Mist', two floriferous, moderately compact bottle-brushes; small clumps of *Dodonaea viscosa* 'Purpurea' in exposed places closest to the sea; and several New Zealand tea trees, including *Leptospermum scoparium* 'Coral Candy', with semi-double, bright rose-pink flowers frosted with white, the double white 'Snow Flurry', and 'Red Damask', with crimson flowers and bronze foliage. A few long shots were planted in the hope that they would be spared severe frosts during their first few years, amongst them *Grevillea* 'Canberra Gem', which produces small trusses of cerise-red flowers for most of the year, *G. alpina* 'Olympic Flame', with orange spider flowers, and the more reliably hardy *G. juniperina* forma *sulphurea*. *Hakea laurina*, an outside chance, has flowers like pale sea urchins. Some smaller daisy bushes were particularly successful: *Olearia phlogopappa* with panicles of lilac or mauve flowers, *O. semidentata* with large lilac daisies amongst narrow grey-green foliage, and *Olearia* 'Zennoriensis' with striking sharply toothed, silver-backed leaves. Several correas grace sheltered enclosures, including *Correa* 'Mannii', a *C. reflexa* hybrid with small leaves and tubular red flowers with reflexed tips, and *C. backhouseana*, which has a greenish tinge to its ivory bells. She finds that the main problem with these Australian fuchsias is that even a light frost, early in the winter, kills most of the flower buds, leading to a disappointing display when they should be at their best. Small shrubs appreciated for their aromatic, heath-like foliage are *Coleonema pulchellum* and its golden yellow selection 'Sunset Gold'. In very sheltered situations close to the house, two leucadendrons—a red form of *Leucadendron salignum* with claret-coloured bracts, said to be hardier than the type, and *L. tinctum* with yellow bracts flushed with crimson—are growing in containers, as are 'Tahiti' and the variegated 'Gold Finger', compact selections of *Metrosideros kermadecensis*.

Clumps of phormiums with exposure-proof qualities derived from *Phormium cookianum*, like 'Cream Delight' and 'Green Dwarf', are planted with the narrow-leaved *Astelia nervosa*. These grow amongst carpets of Hottentot figs: *Carpobrotus muirii* with magenta flowers, *C. edulis* with yellow, and the white-flowered *C. sauerae* closest to the sea, their banana-shaped leaves complementing the linear lines of the phormiums and astelias.

Montbretias were amongst the few flowers that survived in the original garden, and reducing their numbers was something of a problem. They have been replaced with crocosmia hybrids, which grow exceptionally well and provide much of the late summer colour. *Crocosmia ×crocosmiiflora* 'His Majesty' has large, overblown, somewhat floppy flowers; the soft apricot flowers of 'Lady Hamilton' are almost as large and more shapely. Several of Alan Bloom's Bressingham hybrids, notably 'Firebird', 'Ember Glow' and 'Blaze', provide outstanding intensely orange and scarlet flowers. Mesembs are also at home here, creating a colourful spring feature in the better drained parts of the garden. *Delosperma floribunda*, with mauve-pink flowers above mats of fleshy leaves, and ground-covering species such as *D. nubigenum*, with bright yellow flowers, *D. ashtonii*, with tiny white daisies, and *D. lavisiae*, with bright magenta ones, quickly established themselves.

Plastic Plants for the Patio

A townhouse recently constructed in the grounds of a large Victorian villa in Twickenham in south-west London is backed by a small garden of about 150 square metres (175 square yards). High walls and surrounding houses shelter the site. The owners are a young married couple, at work all day and she for much of most weekends—he as an accountant and she as the manager of a large leisure complex. This is their first house and garden, and television programmes on Friday evenings accounted for most of their slender knowledge of gardening—generating plenty of ideas, mostly wildly impractical. Neither has time for nor relishes housework, whether in house or garden, and they agreed that lawns were out, but rather felt that water gardens were in. They needed a place to sit and relax when at home alone or with friends, an outdoor room rather than a garden, furnished with plants that looked attractive without much attention. This is a garden to match the needs of its owners: just the right size, warm, sheltered and secluded, and a potentially attractive setting for outdoor living.

Years of inadequate gardening, and recent disturbance during building activities, left the soil on the site impoverished, and had destroyed its structure. Although in poor condition, the free-draining, infertile soil provided quite a good medium in which to grow many plants appropriate to the needs of the owners. It was agreed that the greater part should be covered with hard surfaces, or used for the water feature. It became a standing joke that if the husband had his way the plants would be made of moulded plastic. As far as possible, the plants chosen had similar easy-care properties.

The focal point of the garden is a bowl formed from several large, rounded boulders, from which water spills into a narrow channel leading to a tiny shaded pool overhung by another giant boulder. Most of the remaining area is covered by a coarse mosaic of stone paving, old brick pavers and gravel, except for a few beds containing a screen of plants around the boundary, and raised beds edged by broad copings that invite people to perch on them. A few key specimen plants are used to create atmosphere, supplemented by little groups with brightly coloured flowers. There is neither space nor inclination to raise many colourful flowers on site, and they are brought in each spring, and thrown out in the autumn. Plants are mostly grown in raised beds above and beyond the trample zone of errant feet; containers are avoided due to their frequent watering needs. In order to provide a firm base for the paving, topsoil was removed down to a depth of 15 centimetres (6 inches) and replaced by hard core and sand; the topsoil was then mixed with composted bark and grit in the proportions of 5:2:2 to make a planting compost to fill the raised beds.

Atmosphere is provided by three smooth tree ferns, *Dicksonia antarctica*, with 2-metre- (6-foot-) long trunks, seemingly expensive but worth every penny for the impression they create. Amongst the small trees used to provide a sense of enclosure, *Azara microphylla* is especially appreciated for its vanilla fragrance in early spring, which the husband finds indistinguishable from his wife's favourite perfume. The weeping form of *Hoheria sexstylosa* provides a glorious display of delicate white flowers in autumn. Several forms of *Pittosporum tenuifolium* present an authentically plastic appearance that is particularly appropriate, and none excels 'Silver Sheen' in this respect, with its wiry black stems and pale green leaves, remarkable for the absence of veining, shading or other variations in tone. The other pittosporum selections are 'Irene Paterson', with variegated green and white foliage; 'Deborah's Gold', with deep green margins around yellow-green centres; and 'James Stirling', with small grey-green leaves and wiry black stems. Several evergreen climbers weave amongst these small trees and brighten them with their flowers, including *Billardiera longifolia*, with pendant yellow tubular bells followed by deep blue fruits the shape of slightly deflated footballs, and *Berberidopsis corallina*, with clusters of sealing-wax red flowers.

In the little water garden a couple of large fairy's fishing rods, *Dierama pulcherrimum*, are growing by the bowl at its head, and the dwarf arum lilies *Zantedeschia aethiopica* 'Apple Court Babe' and 'Childsiana' are along the rill. The variegated 'Pershore Fantasia' was also planted but quickly reverted to plain green. A group of early flowering *Hesperantha coccinea* cultivars provide autumn colour at one end of the pool, including the long-flowering, deep red 'Major'; 'Fenland Daybreak' and 'Professor Barnard', both with pale rose-pink flowers; and 'Tambara', almost white with the faintest flush of pink.

Diascias and fuchsias play major roles in the floral display, between them providing flowers from spring till late autumn. The diascias, renewed each spring, vary from year to year. At first almost all had coral-red flowers, like

Hoheria sexstylosa is a graceful evergreen tree that becomes completely covered with white flowers in autumn. The Royal Botanic Garden, Edinburgh, Scotland.

'Ruby Field', a hardier, free-flowering selection of *Diascia barberae,* and 'Forge Cottage', a vigorous, free-flowering form of *D. rigescens.* More recently a much broader variety has included the racemes of large, yellowish pink or apricot flowers of *Diascia* 'Blackthorn Apricot', the pale pink 'Appleby Apple Blossom' and the strange grey-blue tones of 'Blue Bonnet'. Several low-grow-ing carpeters have also contributed to the display: 'Hector's Hardy', with short racemes of deep pink flowers, 'Joyce's Choice', peach or apricot flow-ers, and the deep mauve-purple 'Twinkle'. 'Coral Belle', 'Ice Cracker' and 'Ap-pleby Apricot' are planted to trail over the edge of the raised beds.

The fuchsias chosen are hardy enough to remain outdoors all winter— and in most years here they are not even cut back to the ground. Amongst these are the broad-petalled, rose-pink *Fuchsia* 'Beacon Rosa'; 'Mrs Popple' and 'Brutus', both with large crimson and purple flowers; 'Alice Hoffmann', pink and white; 'Display', two-tone pink; and 'Lena', with large, blowsy flow-ers with violet sepals and white flushed pink petals. A small speciality here is the seldom seen prostrate cultivar 'Caledonia', not unlike the popular 'Marinka', but hardy and with longer, narrower flowers. Taking advantage of

The river lily *Hesperantha coccinea* 'Major' has its deep red flowers long into autumn. Red Lion House, the author's garden, Shropshire, England.

the foliage's tendency to remain colourful even in deep shade, *F. magellanica* 'Aurea' and 'Variegata' are used to brighten up corners overshadowed by walls or trees. Busy Lizzies, or *Impatiens* cultivars, add more colour and excitement in similarly shaded situations; for several years the owners stuck with the well-known Super Elfin series, but recently have been tempted by the larger flowers and more varied colours of the newer Tempo series. In the last year or two they have discovered the Princess Hybrids of *Alstroemeria*, bred by van Staaveren, and are won over by the plants' compact growth covered with masses of flowers, seemingly for months on end.

Renewal in the Garden

The garden of a house in a rural setting on the outskirts of Cardiff belongs to a Committee Sessions Secretary in the Welsh Assembly. His wife left him and his two teenaged sons several years ago to live with one of his oldest friends. The garden surrounds a substantial Victorian house, previously owned by a well-known plantswoman and writer of books about gardening. It is about ²/₅ hectare (1 acre), and has been opened to the public several times a year for many years, becoming something of an embarrassment to its present owner, who felt it reflected a diminishing inheritance from the past rather than actual circumstances. During the 1980s several trees collapsed in a series of gales, leaving the garden rather exposed. At first the owner mourned their loss as the final blow in a series of disasters, starting with his wife's desertion, but now realises that their departure opened the way for the radical changes that have made the garden easier to look after and much more interesting. For the first time in years, gardening has become an exciting and stimulating challenge, rather than a series of endless chores struggling to maintain what often seemed more like someone else's garden.

Located in a mild climate, the garden overlies heavy, silty clay. During the tenure of the new owner, the soil became increasingly intractable due to neglect—including the overzealous tidying up and burning of fallen leaves and other compostable material—resulting in increased plant losses and unnecessary problems when cultivating and weeding. The loss of dominant, overshadowing mature trees led to infiltration by grasses and other weeds in some places, but also made it easier to find spaces in which to establish new plants. The garden contained remnants of a once fine collection of plants, which were used as sources of cuttings and divisions for replanting.

A Chilean friend of the owner's sons at University was delighted to encounter several familiar plants during a short stay at the house. She found many *liutos,* a large *canelo,* several *notros* and numerous *chilcos* growing in the garden—translated, these turned out to be alstroemerias, a drimys, embothriums and various fuchsias. With a little encouragement from her, these gave the owner the idea of using plants from Chile as a dominant theme in a part of the garden. The first step was to renew the trees that had sheltered the garden, then to renovate the borders in succession, lifting perennial plants in July and August and potting up divisions to be overwintered in frames before replanting them in large groups between shrubs and trees. Once the perennial plants were safely out of the way, weeds between the remaining shrubs and trees were killed with glyphosate sprays, and heavy dressings of farmyard manure were spread over the ground to be assimilated through the winter. The more compliant shrubs were cut back to ground level to facilitate herbicide application and access to the beds, as well as to rejuvenate the plants. The owner's rekindled interest in the garden gave him the enthusiasm to embark on new projects—a renewal not limited to the garden. For the first time since his wife's departure, he has found himself a girlfriend—the Chilean student, much to his sons' discomfiture!

Several deciduous southern beeches were included in the new shelter planting, amongst them the fast-growing rauli, *Nothofagus alpina,* with broad leaves much like a true beech's that fall amidst a fiery display of colours in autumn, and roble, *N. obliqua,* with smaller, broadly ovate foliage. The smaller-leaved nire, *N. antarctica,* was less successful, and the slow but steady growth of the evergreen coihue, *N. dombeyi,* made it of little immediate value as shelter. Another tree intended more for future effect than present usefulness was the monkey puzzle, *Araucaria araucana,* planted as a grove of seven trees just inside the entrance gates to greet visitors in an original fashion.

The orange and yellow flowers of the invasive *Alstroemeria aurea* were a rather too ubiquitous feature of the old garden, and herbicides had to be employed to control its spread. It was partially replaced with seedlings of the more varied Ligtu Hybrids, and also with bold clumps of several cultivars from New Zealand, including *Alstroemeria* 'Fireglow', 'Pink Dream', 'Red Baron' and 'Violet Butterfly', with fuller flowers and better defined markings than the ligtus. Two old stagers from the previous garden are *Berberis darwinii* and *Buddleja globosa*, both with orange flowers, and they are supplemented by numerous other Chilean shrubs. The larger ones, used as supplementary shelter, include *Azara lanceolata*, with fragrant yellow flowers in spring, and the summer-flowering *A. serrata*, with broader leaves; the gracefully beautiful *Eucryphia glutinosa*, with pinnate foliage, masses of white flowers and good autumn colour, and the more columnar *Eucryphia* 'Nymansay'. Arrayan, *Luma apiculata*, also provides useful secondary shelter, as does a group of chaquihue, *Crinodendron hookerianum*, with glowing cerise Chinese lanterns. Though too slow growing to be effective in the early stages of the garden, avellano, *Gevuina avellana*, is included for its clusters of white flowers followed in warm years by red fruits, and tineo, *Weinmannia trichosperma*, another tree with attractive pinnate leaves, is notable for its clusters of small white bottlebrushes.

Of the numerous smaller shrubs around the garden, the escallonias are some of the most colourful and endurable. Outstanding amongst these are the pink and white flowers of *Escallonia* 'Apple Blossom', the pink 'Peach

Many alstroemerias grow in the Chilean Andes. Many are not reliably hardy in cold gardens, but as gardening develops a life of its own in places with milder climates, the attractions and value of the genus in gardens is becoming more appreciated. Rosalie's Retreat, Rosalie McCullough's garden, Waiotira, North Island, New Zealand.

Blossom', and several Slieve Donard seedlings, notably 'Beauty' with red flowers and aromatic foliage and 'Radiance' with clusters of rose-red, chalice-shaped flowers and exceptionally large, glossy dark green leaves. Pelu, *Sophora microphylla*, better known as a New Zealand small tree, might appear out of place here, but it also grows naturally in the Chilean Lake District. Other rather smaller shrubs, also with yellow flowers, include *Cestrum parqui*, which fills the garden with fragrance at night, and *Vestia foetida*, with clusters of narrow tubular blooms. Rounding out the selection are *Fabiana imbricata*, much like a heather with narrow spikes of small, tubular, purple-lilac flowers; *Grindelia chiloensis*, with broad, deep yellow daisy flowers in late summer and autumn, opening from rounded buds overlaid with a sticky latex; and the attractively demure *Jovellana violacea*, with lopsided violet cups dotted with crimson and yellow. Cool, semi-shaded situations provide homes for the brilliant vermilion flowers of botellita, *Mitraria coccinea*, sprawling on the ground or climbing up into a neighbour. Coicopihue, *Philesia magellanica*, has equally attention-attracting large, tubular, plum-purple flowers on a hummocked, dark-leaved little shrub.

After several unsuccessful attempts, the owner of this Chilean-themed garden finally managed to persuade estrellita, *Asteranthera ovata*, to cling to a moss-covered dead log, spangling it with its crimson flowers. To his great delight, another cool, shaded corner provided a place where several copihues, *Lapageria rosea*, could decorate neighbouring shrubs with their large pendant bells, both the plum-crimson and pure white forms. The climbing mutisias were also tried, with mixed success. He was disappointed not to be able to grow the brilliant orange *Mutisia decurrens*, but it needs a sunnier situation and more freely drained soil than he can provide. However, two species with pink daisy flowers do well climbing into and over other shrubs: the vigorously straggly *M. ilicifolia* and the more compact and attractive *M. oligodon*. Following a visit to Chile he returned with small plants of the giant fern *Lophosora quadripinnata* in the hope that one day he would stand beneath its tall, gracefully arching fronds. He is still waiting.

Hardiness Zones of Looking-Glass Plants

The United States Department of Agriculture's Hardiness Zones are based on minimum winter temperatures. These zone ratings are useful as a guide, but should be used with caution. Winter conditions, in particular rainfall patterns, as well as the presence of shelter and the nature of the soil, strongly influence prospects of survival in a given hardiness zone. For many readers, the most significant hardiness zones will be 8, 9 and 10. Zone 8 covers areas in cool temperate parts of the world, including much of the United Kingdom and some heavily populated parts of the oceanic states of the United States. Zone 10 often applies to places with Mediterranean climates, subject to slight frosts during the winter. The performance of *Fuchsia magellanica* can provide a helpfully practical indication of the zone status of a garden: gardens where this species is regularly cut to the ground in winter are likely to match Zone 8; those where the plant is seldom or never severely reduced by frost and remains almost evergreen will be close to Zone 10; and an intermediate performance indicates conditions akin to Zone 9. In small, sheltered gardens and in many unusual situations the performance of this plant is likely to be a more accurate indication of what might be grown than perusal of hardiness zone maps.

AVERAGE ANNUAL MINIMUM TEMPERATURE		
Temperature (°C)	Zone	Temperature (°F)
−45.6 and Below	1	Below −50
−45.5 to −40.0	2	−50 to −40
−40.0 to −34.5	3	−40 to −30
−34.4 to −28.9	4	−30 to −20
−28.8 to −23.4	5	−20 to −10
−23.3 to −17.8	6	−10 to 0
−17.7 to −12.3	7	0 to 10
−12.2 to −6.7	8	10 to 20
−6.6 to −1.2	9	20 to 30
−1.1 to 4.4	10	30 to 40
4.5 and Above	11	40 and Above

Abutilon ×*suntense*, Zone 8
Abutilon vitifolium, Zone 8
Abutilon vitifolium var. *album*, Zone 8
Acacia baileyana, Zone 8
Acacia caven, Zone 9
Acacia cultiformis, Zone 8
Acacia dealbata, Zone 8
Acacia harpophylla, Zone 9
Acacia iteaphylla, Zone 8
Acacia karroo, Zone 9
Acacia leprosa, Zone 8
Acacia longifolia, Zone 9
Acacia mearnsii, Zone 8
Acacia podalyriifolia, Zone 9
Acacia pravissima, Zone 8
Acacia pubescens, Zone 9
Acacia retinodes, Zone 8
Acacia saligna, Zone 9
Acacia sieberiana var. *woodii*, Zone 9
Acacia spectabilis, Zone 9
Acacia stenophylla, Zone 9
Acacia xanthophloea, Zone 9
Acaena caesiiglauca, Zone 6
Acaena glabra, Zone 6
Acaena microphylla, Zone 6
Acaena microphylla 'Copper Carpet',
  Zone 7
Acaena microphylla 'Pewter Carpet',
  Zone 7
Acalypha wilkesiana, Zone 10
Aciphylla aurea, Zone 7
Aciphylla montana, Zone 7
Acmadenia heterophylla, Zone 9
Actinodium cunninghamii, Zone 9
Adenandra obtusata, Zone 10
Adiantum aethiopicum, Zone 9
Adiantum formosum, Zone 9
Adiantum poirettii, Zone 9
Aechmea fasciata, Zone 10
Agapanthus africanus, Zone 9
Agapanthus 'Baby Blue', Zone 9
Agapanthus campanulatus, Zone 7
Agapanthus 'Castle of Mey', Zone 7

Agapanthus 'Headbourne Hybrids',
  Zone 7
Agapanthus inapertus subsp. *pendulus*,
  Zone 8
Agapanthus praecox, Zone 9
Agathis australis, Zone 9
Agathosma apiculata, Zone 9
Agathosma ciliata, Zone 9
Agathosma collina, Zone 9
Agathosma crenulata, Zone 9
Agathosma ovata, Zone 9
Agathosma serpyllacea, Zone 9
Agonis flexuosa, Zone 9
Alberta magna, Zone 10
Albizia adianthifolia, Zone 9
Allocasuarina torulosa, Zone 8
Allocasuarina verticillata, Zone 8
Alocasia ×*amazonica*, Zone 10
Alocasia macrorrhiza, Zone 10
Alocasia odora, Zone 10
Alocasia sanderiana, Zone 10
Aloe arborescens, Zone 9
Aloe aristata, Zone 9
Aloe barberae, Zone 9
Aloe brevifolia, Zone 9
Aloe dichotoma, Zone 9
Aloe ferox, Zone 9
Aloe melanacantha, Zone 9
Aloe pillansii, Zone 9
Aloe plicatilis, Zone 9
Aloe polyphylla, Zone 9
Aloe saponaria, Zone 9
Aloe striata, Zone 9
Aloe striatula, Zone 9
Aloe variegata, Zone 9
Alonsoa meridionalis, Zone 10
Alonsoa warscewiczii 'Fiery Orange',
  Zone 10
Aloysia triphylla, Zone 8
Alpinia zerumbet, Zone 10
Alstroemeria aurea, Zone 7
Alstroemeria Ligtu Hybrids, Zone 7
Alstroemeria psittacina, Zone 8

Alyogyne hakeifolia, Zone 10
Alyogyne huegelii, Zone 10
Amomyrtus luma, Zone 9
Androcymbium ciliolatum, Zone 9
Angophora costata, Zone 9
Anigozanthos 'Dawn', Zone 9
Anigozanthos flavidus, Zone 9
Anigozanthos 'Heritage', Zone 9
Anigozanthos 'Illusion', Zone 9
Anigozanthos humilis, Zone 9
Anigozanthos manglesii, Zone 9
Anigozanthos 'Pearl', Zone 9
Anigozanthos 'Radiance', Zone 9
Anigozanthos 'Regal Claw', Zone 9
Anigozanthos rufus, Zone 9
Anigozanthos 'Twilight', Zone 9
Anigozanthos viridis, Zone 9
Aponogeton distachyos, Zone 8
Araucaria araucana, Zone 8
Araucaria heterophylla, Zone 10
Archontophoenix alexandrae, Zone 10
Archontophoenix cunninghamiana, Zone 9
Arctotheca calendula, Zone 8
Arctotheca populifolia, Zone 9
Arctotis acaulis, Zone 9
Arctotis fastuosa, Zone 9
Arctotis hirsuta, Zone 9
Arctotis stoechadifolia, Zone 9
Aristea ecklonii, Zone 9
Aristea major, Zone 8
Arthropodium cirratum, Zone 8
Asplenium australasicum, Zone 10
Azara lanceolata, Zone 8
Azara microphylla, Zone 7
Azara petiolaris, Zone 8
Azara serrata, Zone 8

Banksia ericifolia, Zone 8
Banksia grandis, Zone 9
Banksia integrifolia, Zone 9
Banksia marginata, Zone 8
Banksia media, Zone 9
Banksia menziesii, Zone 9

Banksia ornata, Zone 9
Banksia repens, Zone 9
Banksia speciosa, Zone 9
Banksia spinulosa 'Birthday Candles',
    Zone 9
Berberidopsis corallina, Zone 8
Berberis darwinii, Zone 7
Berzelia lanuginosa, Zone 9
Berzelia squarrosa, Zone 9
Billardiera longifolia, Zone 8
Billbergia nutans, Zone 10
Billbergia pyramidalis, Zone 10
Blechnum discolor, Zone 8
Blechnum fraseri, Zone 8
Blechnum penna-marina, Zone 7
Blechnum tabulare, Zone 9
Blechnum wattsii, Zone 8
Bolax gummifera, Zone 7
Bolusanthus speciosus, Zone 9
Boophone disticha, Zone 10
Boronia anemonifolia, Zone 9
Boronia citriodora, Zone 9
Boronia denticulata, Zone 9
Boronia fraseri, Zone 9
Boronia heterophylla, Zone 9
Boronia megastigma, Zone 9
Brachychiton acerifolius, Zone 9
Brachychiton australis, Zone 10
Brachychiton bidwillii, Zone 10
Brachychiton rupestris, Zone 9
Brachyglottis repanda 'Purpurea', Zone 9
Brunia lanata, Zone 9
Brunsvigia bosmaniae, Zone 9
Buddleja globosa, Zone 7
Buddleja salviifolia, Zone 8
Buddleja ×*weyeriana*, Zone 7
Bulbinella fruticosa, Zone 8
Butia capitata, Zone 8

Calanthe triplicata, Zone 10
Calceolaria integrifolia 'Golden Nugget',
    Zone 8
Callistemon citrinus, Zone 8

Callistemon citrinus 'Anzac', Zone 8
Callistemon citrinus 'Mauve Mist', Zone 8
Callistemon citrinus 'Splendens', Zone 8
Callistemon pallidus, Zone 9
Callistemon salignus, Zone 9
Callistemon sieberi, Zone 8
Callistemon speciosus, Zone 9
Callistemon viminalis, Zone 9
Callistemon viridiflorus, Zone 9
Callitris baileyi, Zone 10
Callitris glaucophylla, Zone 9
Callitris oblonga, Zone 9
Callitris preissii, Zone 10
Callitris rhomboidea, Zone 8
Calodendrum capense, Zone 9
Carex comans, Zone 6
Carex buchananii, Zone 7
Carex flagellifera, Zone 6
Carex secta, Zone 7
Carex testacea, Zone 7
Carissa macrocarpa, Zone 9
Carissa macrocarpa 'Emerald Carpet',
   Zone 9
Carissa macrocarpa 'Horizontalis', Zone 9
Carpobrotus edulis, Zone 8
Carpobrotus muirii, Zone 9
Carpobrotus sauerae, Zone 9
Celmisia allanii, Zone 7
Celmisia argentea, Zone 7
Celmisia asteliifolia, Zone 6
Celmisia gracilenta, Zone 7
Celmisia holosericea, Zone 7
Celmisia prorepens, Zone 7
Celmisia semicordata, Zone 7
Cephalophyllum alstonii, Zone 8
Ceratopetalum apetalum, Zone 9
Cestrum parqui, Zone 9
Chamelaucium uncinatum, Zone 10
Chasmanthe aethiopica, Zone 9
Chasmanthe floribunda, Zone 9
Cheiridopsis cigarettifera, Zone 9
Chionochloa conspicua, Zone 7
Chionochloa rubra, Zone 7

Chlorophytum comosum 'Gold Nugget',
   Zone 9
Chondropetalum tectorum, Zone 8
Chrysalidocarpus lutescens, Zone 10
Chrysanthemoides monilifera, Zone 9
Chusquea culeou, Zone 7
Clematis aristata, Zone 8
Clematis gentianoides, Zone 9
Clematis hookeriana, Zone 8
Clematis marmoraria, Zone 8
Clematis paniculata, Zone 6
Clianthus puniceus, Zone 8
Clivia miniata, Zone 10
Clivia nobilis, Zone 10
Clytostoma callistegioides, Zone 9
Codiaeum variegatum, Zone 11
Coleonema album, Zone 9
Coleonema pulchellum, Zone 9
Colletia paradoxa, Zone 7
Colocasia gigantea, Zone 10
Conicosia pugioniformis, Zone 9
Coprosma acerosa, Zone 8
Coprosma crassifolia, Zone 9
Coprosma petriei, Zone 7
Coprosma repens, Zone 9
Cordyline australis, Zone 8
Cordyline banksii, Zone 9
Cordyline indivisa, Zone 9
Cordyline petiolaris, Zone 10
Cordyline pumilio, Zone 9
Cordyline rubra, Zone 10
Corokia ×*virgata*, Zone 8
Correa aemula 'Mt Lofty', Zone 9
Correa alba, Zone 9
Correa backhouseana, Zone 8
Correa 'Mannii', Zone 9
Correa pulchella, Zone 9
Correa reflexa, Zone 9
Cortaderia fulvida, Zone 8
Cortaderia jubata, Zone 8
Cortaderia richardii, Zone 8
Cortaderia selloana, Zone 6
Cortaderia selloana 'Gold Band', Zone 6

Corynocarpus laevigatus, Zone 9
Cotula lineariloba, Zone 9
Cotyledon orbiculata, Zone 9
Crassula arborescens, Zone 9
Crassula ovata, Zone 9
Crassula ovata 'Coral', Zone 9
Crinodendron hookerianum, Zone 8
Crinodendron patagua, Zone 8
Crocosmia aurea, Zone 8
Crocosmia ×*crocosmiiflora* 'Blaze', Zone 7
Crocosmia masoniorum, Zone 8
Cunonia capensis, Zone 9
Cussonia paniculata, Zone 9
Cussonia spicata, Zone 8
Cyanella alba, Zone 9
Cyathea australis, Zone 9
Cyathea capensis, Zone 9
Cyathea cooperi, Zone 10
Cyathea dealbata, Zone 9
Cyathea dregei, Zone 9
Cyathea howeana, Zone 9
Cyathea medullaris, Zone 9
Cyathea smithii, Zone 9
Cyathodes dealbata, Zone 9
Cynodon transvaalensis, Zone 8
Cyphostemma juttae, Zone 9
Cyrtostachys renda, Zone 12

Dacrydium cupressinum, Zone 8
Dampiera diversifolia, Zone 9
Dampiera linearis, Zone 9
Daviesia horrida, Zone 9
Daviesia ulicifolia, Zone 9
Delosperma ashtonii, Zone 9
Delosperma floribunda, Zone 9
Delosperma lavisiae, Zone 9
Delosperma nubigenum, Zone 8
Dendrobium speciosum, Zone 9
Desfontainea spinosa, Zone 8
Dianella caerulea, Zone 9
Dianella nigra, Zone 9
Dianella tasmanica, Zone 8
Diascia barberae 'Ruby Field', Zone 8

Diascia fetcaniensis, Zone 8
Diascia integerrima, Zone 8
Diascia rigescens 'Forge Cottage', Zone 8
Dicksonia antarctica, Zone 8
Dicksonia fibrosa, Zone 8
Dicksonia squarrosa, Zone 8
Dieffenbachia seguine, Zone 10
Dierama pulcherrimum, Zone 8
Dietes bicolor, Zone 9
Dietes grandiflora, Zone 9
Dietes iridioides, Zone 8
Dimorphotheca sinuata, Zone 8
Diplarrhena latifolia, Zone 7
Diplarrhena moraea, Zone 8
Dodonaea viscosa, Zone 8
Dorotheanthus bellidiformis, Zone 9
Doryanthes excelsa, Zone 9
Doryanthes palmeri, Zone 9
Dracaena fragrans 'Santa Rosa', Zone 10
Dracaena marginata, Zone 10
Drimys lanceolata, Zone 8
Drimys winteri, Zone 8
Drosanthemum speciosum, Zone 9
Dryandra drummondii, Zone 9
Dryandra formosa, Zone 9
Dryandra quercifolia, Zone 9
Duvernoia adhatodoides, Zone 9
Dyckia brevifolia, Zone 9
Dymondia margaretae, Zone 8

Eccremocarpus scaber, Zone 8
Elegia capensis, Zone 9
Embothrium coccineum, Zone 8
Encephalartos altensteinii, Zone 10
Encephalartos friderici-guilielmi, Zone 9
Encephalartos horridus, Zone 9
Encephalartos humilis, Zone 9
Encephalartos lehmannii, Zone 9
Encephalartos transvenosus, Zone 10
Eremophila maculata, Zone 9
Erica cerinthoides, Zone 9
Erica coccinea, Zone 9
Erica patersonia, Zone 10

Erica perspicua, Zone 9
Erica plukenetii, Zone 10
Erica sessiliflora, Zone 9
Eriocephalus africanus, Zone 9
Eryngium agavifolium, Zone 9
Eryngium pandanifolium, Zone 8
Escallonia 'Apple Blossom', Zone 7
Escallonia 'Iveyi', Zone 8
Escallonia rubra var. *macrantha*, Zone 8
Eucalyptus archeri, Zone 8
Eucalyptus caesia, Zone 9
Eucalyptus calophylla, Zone 9
Eucalyptus coccifera, Zone 8
Eucalyptus cornuta, Zone 9
Eucalyptus dalrympleana, Zone 8
Eucalyptus debeuzevillei, Zone 8
Eucalyptus delegatensis, Zone 9
Eucalyptus diversicolor, Zone 9
Eucalyptus eremophila, Zone 9
Eucalyptus ficifolia, Zone 9
Eucalyptus gomphocephala, Zone 9
Eucalyptus gunnii, Zone 7
Eucalyptus lehmannii, Zone 9
Eucalyptus macrandra, Zone 8
Eucalyptus nicholii, Zone 8
Eucalyptus obliqua, Zone 9
Eucalyptus pauciflora, Zone 7
Eucalyptus perriniana, Zone 8
Eucalyptus regnans, Zone 9
Eucalyptus risdonii, Zone 8
Eucalyptus salmonophloia, Zone 9
Eucalyptus sideroxylon, Zone 9
Eucalyptus sieberi, Zone 9
Eucalyptus subcrenulata, Zone 9
Eucalyptus tetragona, Zone 9
Eucalyptus tetraptera, Zone 10
Eucalyptus torquata, Zone 9
Eucalyptus viminalis, Zone 9
Eucalyptus woodwardii, Zone 9
Eucomis bicolor, Zone 8
Eucomis comosa, Zone 8
Eucomis pole-evansii, Zone 9
Eucryphia cordifolia, Zone 9

Eucryphia glutinosa, Zone 8
Eucryphia lucida, Zone 8
Eucryphia milliganii, Zone 8
Eucryphia ×*nymansensis* 'Nymansay',
    Zone 8
Eulychnia acida, Zone 9
Euphorbia caerulescens, Zone 9
Euphorbia dregeana, Zone 7
Euphorbia esculenta, Zone 8
Euphorbia ingens, Zone 9
Euphorbia mammilaris, Zone 7
Euphorbia milii, Zone 10
Euphorbia tuberculata, Zone 9
Euphorbia virosa, Zone 7
Euryops acraeus, Zone 8
Euryops pectinatus, Zone 9
Euryops virgineus, Zone 9

Fabiana imbricata, Zone 8
Fascicularia bicolor, Zone 8
Felicia amelloides, Zone 9
Felicia amoena, Zone 9
Felicia bergeriana, Zone 9
Felicia echinata, Zone 9
Ficus lyrata, Zone 10
Ficus macrophylla, Zone 10
Ficus rubiginosa, Zone 10
Ficus sur, Zone 10
Fitzroya cupressoides, Zone 8
Francoa ramosa, Zone 7
Francoa sonchifolia, Zone 7
Freycinetia banksii, Zone 10
Fuchsia 'Alice Hoffmann', Zone 8
Fuchsia 'Beacon Rosa', Zone 8
Fuchsia 'Brutus', Zone 8
Fuchsia 'Display', Zone 9
Fuchsia excorticata, Zone 8
Fuchsia 'Lena', Zone 8
Fuchsia magellanica, Zone 7
Fuchsia 'Marinka', Zone 9
Fuchsia 'Mrs Popple', Zone 8
Fuchsia procumbens 'Variegata', Zone 9
Fuchsia 'Riccartonii', Zone 7

Galtonia candicans, Zone 6
Galtonia viridiflora, Zone 8
Gaultheria mucronata, Zone 7
Gerbera jamesonii, Zone 8
Gevuina avellana, Zone 9
Gibbaeum pubescens, Zone 9
Gladiolus scullyi, Zone 9
Gladiolus tristis, Zone 7
Grevillea alpina, Zone 8
Grevillea australis, Zone 8
Grevillea banksii, Zone 9
Grevillea 'Canberra Gem', Zone 7
Grevillea hilliana, Zone 9
Grevillea johnsonii, Zone 8
Grevillea juniperina forma sulphurea,
    Zone 8
Grevillea laurifolia, Zone 9
Grevillea longifolia, Zone 9
Grevillea robusta, Zone 8
Grevillea 'Robyn Gordon', Zone 9
Grevillea rosmarinifolia, Zone 8
Grevillea thelemanniana, Zone 8
Grevillea victoriae, Zone 7
Grevillea wilsonae, Zone 9
Greyia sutherlandii, Zone 9
Grindelia chiloensis, Zone 6
Griselina littoralis, Zone 8
Griselinia lucida, Zone 8
Gunnera hamiltonii, Zone 8
Gunnera magellanica, Zone 7
Gunnera manicata, Zone 8
Gunnera tinctoria, Zone 6
Guzmannia, Zone 10

Hakea gibbosa, Zone 9
Hakea laurina, Zone 9
Hakea lissosperma, Zone 9
Hakea salicifolia, Zone 8
Hakea suaveolens, Zone 9
Hakea victoriae, Zone 9
Halleria lucida, Zone 8
Hardenbergia comptoniana, Zone 9
Hardenbergia violacea, Zone 9

Harpephyllum caffrum, Zone 10
Hebe buchananii 'Minor', Zone 7
Hebe cupressoides 'Boughton Dome',
    Zone 7
Hebe lycopodioides, Zone 7
Hebe ochracea, Zone 6
Hebe salicifolia, Zone 7
Hebe speciosa, Zone 9
Hebe stricta, Zone 9
Hebe 'Wiri Dawn', Zone 8
Hebe 'Wiri Gem', Zone 8
Hebe 'Wiri Mist', Zone 8
Hedycarya arborea, Zone 10
Helichrysum petiolare, Zone 9
Helichrysum petiolare 'Limelight', Zone 9
Helichrysum petiolare 'Variegatum', Zone 9
Heliophila coronopifolia, Zone 9
Heliotropium arborescens, Zone 9
Hesperantha coccinea, Zone 7
Hibbertia scandens, Zone 9
Hoheria lyallii, Zone 7
Hoheria sexstylosa, Zone 7
Howea forsteriana, Zone 10
Hymenosporum flavum, Zone 9
Hyophorbe lagenicaulis, Zone 11
Hypocalymma cordifolium 'Golden Veil',
    Zone 9
Hypocalymma robustum, Zone 9

Ilex mitis, Zone 8
Iresine herbstii 'Acuminata', Zone 10
Isopogon anemonifolius, Zone 9
Isopogon formosus, Zone 9
Ixia maculata, Zone 9
Ixia paniculata, Zone 9
Ixia viridiflora, Zone 9

Jovellana violacea, Zone 9
Jubaea chilensis, Zone 8

Kennedia coccinea, Zone 10
Kennedia rubicunda, Zone 9
Kiggelaria africana, Zone 9

Kingia australis, Zone 9
Knightia excelsa, Zone 9
Kniphofia caulescens, Zone 7
Kniphofia galpinii, Zone 7
Kniphofia porphyrantha, Zone 7
Kniphofia rooperi, Zone 7
Kniphofia uvaria, Zone 6
Kunzea baxteri, Zone 9
Kunzea ericoides, Zone 8
Kunzea pomifera, Zone 9

Lachenalia aloides, Zone 9
Lachenalia bulbifera, Zone 9
Lachenalia matthewsii, Zone 9
Lachenalia mutabilis, Zone 9
Lachenalia reflexa, Zone 9
Lagarostrobus franklinii, Zone 8
Lampranthus aureus, Zone 9
Lampranthus blandus, Zone 9
Lampranthus spectabilis, Zone 9
Lantana camara, Zone 9
Lapageria rosea, Zone 9
Lastreopsis glabella, Zone 10
Lastreopsis hispida, Zone 10
Leonotis leonurus, Zone 9
Lepidozamia peroffskyana, Zone 10
Leptopteris superba, Zone 10
Leptospermum laevigatum, Zone 9
Leptospermum lanigerum, Zone 8
Leptospermum rotundifolium, Zone 9
Leptospermum scopulorum, Zone 8
Leptospermum squarrosum, Zone 9
Leschenaultia biloba, Zone 10
Leschenaultia formosa, Zone 9
Leucadendron argenteum, Zone 9
Leucadendron discolor 'Flame Tip', Zone 9
Leucadendron laureolum, Zone 9
Leucadendron 'Safari Sunset', Zone 9
Leucadendron 'Safari Sunshine', Zone 9
Leucadendron salignum, Zone 9
Leucadendron strobilinum, Zone 9
Leucadendron strobilinum 'Waterlily',
    Zone 9

Leucadendron tinctum, Zone 9
Leucogenes leontopodium, Zone 7
Leucophyta brownii, Zone 9
Leucospermum cordifolium, Zone 9
Leucospermum oleifolium, Zone 9
Leucospermum reflexum, Zone 9
Libertia formosa, Zone 8
Libertia ixioides, Zone 8
Libertia peregrinans, Zone 8
Lilium formosanum, Zone 6
Livistona muelleri, Zone 10
Lobelia tupa, Zone 8
Lomandra longifolia, Zone 9
Lomatia myricoides, Zone 8
Lophomyrtus bullata, Zone 8
Lophomyrtus ×*ralphii*, Zone 8
Lophostemon confertus 'Variegata', Zone
    10
Luma apiculata, Zone 8
Lygodium articulatum, Zone 10

Mackaya bella, Zone 9
Macropiper excelsum, Zone 10
Macrozamia communis, Zone 9
Maranta leuconeura, Zone 11
Massonia angustifolia, Zone 9
Massonia depressa, Zone 9
Maytenus boaria, Zone 8
Melaleuca decussata, Zone 9
Melaleuca elliptica, Zone 9
Melaleuca ericifolia, Zone 9
Melaleuca erubescens, Zone 9
Melaleuca fulgens, Zone 9
Melaleuca heugelii, Zone 9
Melaleuca lanceolata, Zone 9
Melaleuca leucadendra, Zone 10
Melaleuca quinquenervia, Zone 10
Melianthus major, Zone 9
Melicope ternata, Zone 10
Melicytus ramiflorus, Zone 9
Meryta sinclairii, Zone 10
Metrosideros carmineus, Zone 9
Metrosideros excelsus, Zone 10

Metrosideros kermadecensis 'Gold Finger', Zone 10
Metrosideros robustus, Zone 9
Metrosideros umbellatus, Zone 8
Mimetes cucullatus, Zone 9
Mimetes fimbrifolius, Zone 9
Mitraria coccinea, Zone 9
Monstera deliciosa, Zone 10
Moraea alpina, Zone 8
Moraea aristata, Zone 9
Moraea ciliata, Zone 9
Moraea fugax, Zone 9
Moraea neopavonia, Zone 9
Moraea serpentina, Zone 9
Mutisia decurrens, Zone 8
Mutisia ilicifolia, Zone 9
Mutisia oligodon, Zone 9
Myoporum insulare, Zone 9
Myoporum laetum, Zone 9
Myoporum parvifolium, Zone 9
Myosotidium hortensia, Zone 8

Nemesia caerulea, Zone 8
Nemesia strumosa, Zone 9
Nemesia versicolor, Zone 9
Neoregalia spectabilis, Zone 10
Nerine bowdenii, Zone 8
Nerine filifolia, Zone 9
Nerine masonorum, Zone 9
Nerine sarniensis, Zone 9
Nertera granadensis, Zone 8
Nothofagus alpina, Zone 7
Nothofagus antarctica, Zone 7
Nothofagus betuloides, Zone 7
Nothofagus cunninghamii, Zone 8
Nothofagus dombeyi, Zone 8
Nothofagus fusca, Zone 7
Nothofagus menziesii, Zone 7
Nothofagus moorei, Zone 9
Nothofagus nitida, Zone 7
Nothofagus obliqua, Zone 8
Nothofagus pumilio, Zone 7
Nothofagus solandri, Zone 7

Nothofagus solandri var. *cliffortioides*, Zone 7
Nuytsia floribunda, Zone 9

Olearia avicennifolia, Zone 8
Olearia frostii, Zone 8
Olearia ilicifolia, Zone 8
Olearia macrodonta, Zone 7
Olearia odorata, Zone 8
Olearia paniculata, Zone 9
Olearia phlogopappa, Zone 8
Olearia semidentata, Zone 8
Olearia traversii, Zone 8
Olearia virgata, Zone 7
Oreocallis pinnata, Zone 9
Oreocereus celsianus, Zone 9
Ornithogalum dubium, Zone 9
Ornithogalum thyrsoides, Zone 9
Orthrosanthus multiflorus, Zone 9
Oscularia caulescens, Zone 9
Osteospermum 'Blue Streak', Zone 8
Osteospermum 'Buttermilk', Zone 8
Osteospermum ecklonis, Zone 8
Osteospermum hyoseroides, Zone 9
Osteospermum jucundum, Zone 8
Oxalis enneaphylla, Zone 6
Oxalis laciniata, Zone 8
Oxalis obtusa, Zone 9
Oxalis pes-caprae, Zone 7
Oxalis purpurea, Zone 8
Oxylobium ellipticum, Zone 9

Pachypodium lamerei, Zone 9
Pachypodium namaquanum, Zone 9
Pachystegia insignis, Zone 8
Pandorea jasminoides, Zone 9
Pandorea jasminoides 'Pink Magic', Zone 9
Pandorea pandorana, Zone 9
Passiflora aurantia, Zone 10
Pelargonium cordifolium, Zone 10
Pelargonium dichondrifolium, Zone 10
Pelargonium fulgidum, Zone 10
Pelargonium graveolens, Zone 9

Pelargonium incrassatum, Zone 10
Pelargonium inquinans, Zone 10
Pelargonium 'Lady Plymouth', Zone 8
Pelargonium 'Mabel Grey', Zone 8
Pelargonium odoratissimum, Zone 10
Pelargonium peltatum, Zone 9
Pelargonium 'Pretty Lady', Zone 9
Pelargonium 'Scarlet Unique', Zone 9
Pelargonium 'Splendide', Zone 9
Pelargonium tomentosum, Zone 10
Pelargonium tricolor, Zone 9
Pelargonium zonale, Zone 9
Pennisetum clandestinum, Zone 9
Petrea volubilis, Zone 10
Phaenocoma prolifera, Zone 9
Phaius tankervilleae, Zone 10
Philesia magellanica, Zone 9
Philodendron bipinnatifidum, Zone 10
Phoenix reclinata, Zone 10
Phoenix roebelenii, Zone 10
Phormium cookianum, Zone 8
Phormium 'Dark Delight', Zone 8
Phormium 'Dazzler', Zone 8
Phormium 'Maori Chief', Zone 8
Phormium 'Maori Maiden', Zone 8
Phormium 'Purpureum', Zone 8
Phormium 'Sundowner', Zone 8
Phormium tenax, Zone 8
Phormium 'Variegatum', Zone 8
Phygelius ×rectus 'Devil's Tears', Zone 8
Phygelius ×rectus 'Moonraker', Zone 8
Phylica plumosa, Zone 9
Pimelea ferruginea, Zone 9
Pimelea nivea, Zone 9
Pimelea rosea, Zone 9
Pisonia umbellifera 'Variegata', Zone 10
Pittosporum cornifolium, Zone 9
Pittosporum crassifolium, Zone 8
Pittosporum eugenioides, Zone 9
Pittosporum tenuifolium, Zone 8
Pittosporum tobira, Zone 9
Pittosporum umbellatum, Zone 9

Pittosporum viridiflorum, Zone 9
Plagianthus regius, Zone 7
Platycerium bifurcatum, Zone 9
Platycerium superbum, Zone 10
Plectranthus argentatus, Zone 10
Plectranthus ciliatus, Zone 9
Plectranthus ecklonii, Zone 9
Plectranthus fruticosus, Zone 10
Plectranthus madagascariensis, Zone 10
Plectranthus verticillatus, Zone 10
Plumbago auriculata, Zone 9
Poa labillardieri, Zone 8
Podalyria calyptrata, Zone 9
Podalyria sericea, Zone 9
Podocarpus elatus, Zone 9
Podocarpus latifolius, Zone 9
Podocarpus lawrencei, Zone 7
Podocarpus nivalis, Zone 7
Podocarpus salignus, Zone 8
Podocarpus totara, Zone 9
Polygala myrtifolia 'Grandiflora', Zone 9
Polygala virgata, Zone 9
Polystichum proliferum, Zone 5
Polystichum vestitum, Zone 7
Portulacaria afra, Zone 9
Pratia angulata, Zone 7
Prostanthera cuneata, Zone 8
Prostanthera lasianthos, Zone 8
Prostanthera ovalifolia, Zone 9
Prostanthera rotundifolia, Zone 9
Protea cynaroides, Zone 9
Protea mundi, Zone 9
Protea neriifolia, Zone 9
Protea obtusifolia, Zone 9
Protea scolymocephala, Zone 9
Protea susannae, Zone 9
Pseudopanax lessonii, Zone 9
Pseudopanax arboreus, Zone 9
Pseudopanax ferox, Zone 9
Pseudopanax laetus, Zone 9
Psoralea pinnata, Zone 9
Puya alpestris, Zone 9

Puya berteroniana, Zone 9
Puya chilensis, Zone 9

Ranunculus lyallii, Zone 7
Raoulia australis, Zone 7
Raoulia eximia, Zone 7
Raoulia haastii, Zone 7
Ravenala madagascariensis, Zone 11
Restio tetraphyllus, Zone 9
Rhododendron javanicum, Zone 10
Rhododendron lochiae, Zone 10
Rhodohypoxis baurii var. *baurii*, Zone 8
Rhopalostylis sapida, Zone 10
Rhus lancea, Zone 9
Richea dracophylla, Zone 8
Richea pandanifolia, Zone 8
Romulea hirta, Zone 9
Romulea rosea, Zone 8
Romulea sabulosa, Zone 9
Ruschia macowanii, Zone 10

Salvia africana-lutea, Zone 9
Salvia coccinea, Zone 8
Salvia dolomitica, Zone 9
Salvia guaranitica, Zone 9
Salvia guaranitica 'Argentina Skies', Zone 9
Santalum acuminatum, Zone 9
Scaevola aemula 'Blue Wonder', Zone 9
Scaevola crassifolia, Zone 10
Scaevola 'Diamond Head', Zone 9
Schefflera actinophylla, Zone 10
Schefflera digitata, Zone 9
Scleranthus uniflorus, Zone 7
Sclerocarya birrea subsp. *caffra*, Zone 10
Senecio elegans, Zone 9
Senecio magellanica, Zone 8
Serruria florida, Zone 9
Solandra grandiflora, Zone 10
Solanum crispum, Zone 8
Solanum crispum 'Glasnevin', Zone 8
Sollya heterophylla, Zone 9
Sophora microphylla, Zone 8

Sophora tetraptera, Zone 8
Stangeria eriopus, Zone 9
Stenocarpus sinuatus, Zone 9
Stenotaphrum secundatum, Zone 9
Strelitzia juncea, Zone 9
Strelitzia nicolai, Zone 10
Strelitzia reginae, Zone 9
Strelitzia reginae 'Mandela's Gold', Zone 9
Sutherlandia frutescens, Zone 9
Syagrus romanzoffiana, Zone 10

Tecomaria capensis, Zone 9
Telopea oreades, Zone 9
Telopea 'Shady Lady' series, Zone 9
Telopea speciosissima, Zone 9
Telopea truncata, Zone 9
Telopea 'Wirrimbirra White', Zone 9
Templetonia retusa, Zone 10
Tetratheca ciliare, Zone 9
Thunbergia alata, Zone 9
Toona ciliata, Zone 9
Trichomanes reniforme, Zone 9
Tristaniopsis laurina, Zone 10
Trithrinax campestris, Zone 10
Tulbaghia violacea 'Silver Lace', Zone 7
Tylecodon paniculatus, Zone 9

Veltheimia bracteata var. *rosealba*, Zone 9
Veltheimia capensis, Zone 9
Verbena bonariensis, Zone 7
Verticordia chrysantha, Zone 10
Verticordia grandis, Zone 10
Vestia foetida, Zone 8
Viola hederacea, Zone 8
Virgilia divaricata, Zone 9
Virgilia oroboides, Zone 9
Vitex lucens, Zone 9

Watsonia aletroides, Zone 9
Watsonia borbonica, Zone 8
Watsonia borbonica subsp. *ardernei*,
    Zone 8

Watsonia coccinea, Zone 9
Weinmannia trichosperma, Zone 9
Welwitschia mirabilis, Zone 9
Westringia angustifolia, Zone 10
Westringia fruticosa, Zone 9
Westringia fruticosa 'Morning Light',
    Zone 9
Westringia glabra, Zone 9
Wiborgia monoptera, Zone 9
Widdringtonia cedarbergensis, Zone 9
Widdringtonia nodiflora, Zone 9

Xanthorrhoea arborea, Zone 10
Xanthorrhoea australis, Zone 9
Xanthorrhoea preissii, Zone 10
Xanthorrhoea quadrangulata, Zone 10
Xeronema callistemon, Zone 10

Zantedeschia aethiopica, Zone 8
Zantedeschia 'Crowborough', Zone 7
Zantedeschia 'Green Goddess', Zone 8
Zantedeschia 'Mango', Zone 8
Zantedeschia rehmannii, Zone 8
Zoysia tenuifolia, Zone 10

South Africa

— International boundary
—·—·— Province boundary
★ National capital
⊙ Province capital *

| Railroad
Expressway
Road

0   100   200   300 Kilometers
0   100   200   300 Miles
Lambert Conformal Conic Projection, SP 6S/30S

NAMIBIA

BOTSWANA

ZIMBABWE

MOZAMBIQUE

Maun
Bulawayo
Masvingo
Plumtree
Francistown
Rutenga
Makgadikgadi
(salt pans)
Selebi-Pikwe
Beitbridge
Chicualacuala
Mahalapye
Messina

NORTHERN
PROVINCE
Pietersburg
(Polokwone)
Chokwe
Gaborone
Nylstroom
Xai-Xai
Lobatse
Nelspruit
Rustenburg
Kalkrand
Mariental
Tshabong
Mmabatho
Pretoria
Witbank
Mbabane
Maputo
NORTH-
WEST
Johannesburg
GAUTENG
MPUMALANGA
Bethanien
Keetmanshoop
Vryburg
Klerksdorp
Vereeniging
SWAZILAND
Seeheim
Hotazel
Standerton
Sishen
Kroonstad
KWAZULU-
NATAL
Golela
Karasburg
Bethlehem
Ladysmith
Ulundi
Upington
FREE
STATE
Richards Bay
Port Nolloth
Springbok
Kimberley
Bloemfontein
Maseru
LESOTHO
Pietermaritzburg *
NORTHERN
CAPE
Mefeteng
Durban
De Aar
Kokstad
Port Shepstone
Calvinia
Victoria West
Middelburg
Umtata
SOUTH
ATLANTIC
OCEAN
Vanrhynsdorp
Queenstown
EASTERN CAPE
INDIAN
OCEAN
Beaufort
West
Bisho
Saldanha
East London
WESTERN
CAPE
Worcester
Cape Town
Swellendam
Mosselbaai
Port Elizabeth
Cape of
Good Hope
Cape Agulhas
INDIAN OCEAN

*Province boundaries are subject to change under
provisions of the South African Constitution.*

* *The KwaZulu-Natal provincial legislature has not
yet chosen its provincial capital. Press reports
indicate that capital will be either Pietermaritzburg
or Ulundi. Final province capitals are to be
determined.*

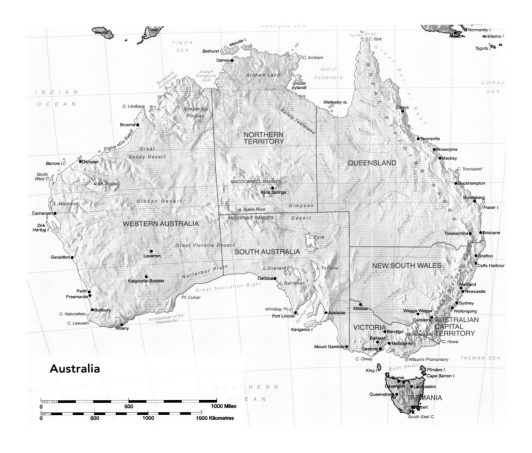

Australia

| 0 | | | | | 500 | | | | 1000 Miles |
| 0 | | | 500 | | | 1000 | | | 1500 Kilometres |

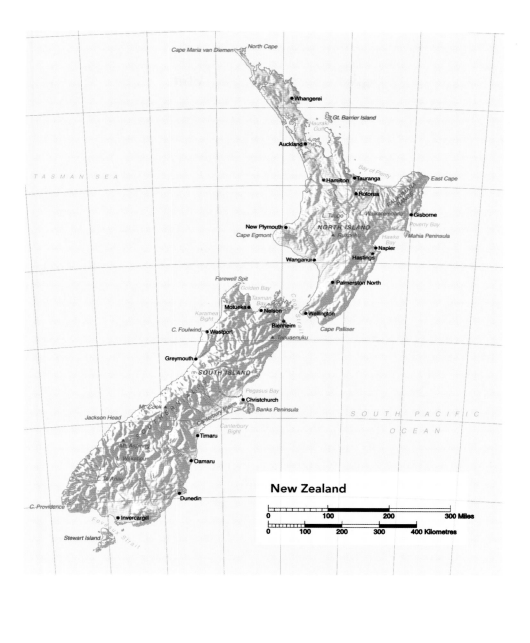

New Zealand

Bibliography

An overview of the plants of the Southern Hemisphere reveals more than six hundred genera of interest to gardeners. The space available in the *Looking-Glass Garden* is sufficient to say a few words about a thousand species and cultivars, providing only a fleeting introduction to what is there. Long lists of species and detailed descriptions of plants are redundant in an age when so much has been published already. Excellent reference books on particular groups of plants are relatively easy to locate and readily available. A number of books on more general, less specific topics are listed here.

GENERAL

A–Z Encyclopaedia of Garden Plants (The Royal Horticultural Society, London). Descriptions of about 15,000 cultivars and species, with some 6000 illustrations.

Botanica: The Illustrated A–Z of Over 10,000 Garden Plants (Random House, Milsons Point, New South Wales). Short descriptions and small illustrations of a very large number of plants, including many from the Southern Hemisphere.

AUSTRALIA

The Austraflora A–Z of Australian Plants, by Bill Molyneux and Sue Forrester (Reed Books, Australia). A source of concise lists of tabulated information on a wide range of plants.

Australian Plants: A Guide to their Cultivation in Europe, by Thomas Ross and Jeffrey Irons (privately published). A stimulating review of the possibilities Australian plants offer gardeners in Europe, both in Mediterranean and cooler regions, that should inspire more gardeners to try their luck.

Australian Plants for the Garden, by Thistle Y. Harris (Angus and Robertson, Sydney and London). Information on growing Australian plants with brief descriptions of a large number of species.

Australian Rainforest Plants, by Nan & Hugh Nicholson, in four parts (Terania Rainforest Publishing, The Channon, New South Wales). Well-illustrated descriptions of numerous rainforest trees, shrubs, climbers and ferns.

Australia's Western Wildflowers, by M.K. Morcombe (privately published). A popular, well-illustrated introduction to the plants of the region.

419

Collins Field Guide to the Wild Flowers of South-East Australia by Jean Galbraith (published by Collins, Sydney and London). A comprehensive guide to the wildflowers of the region with very abbreviated botanical descriptions.

Creating an Australian Garden, by John Hunt (Kangaroo Press, Kenthurst, New South Wales). Provides information on plants in cultivation and descriptions of the mound-and-channel method of growing them.

Encyclopaedia of Australian Plants Suitable for Cultivation, W.R. Elliot and D.L. Jones, in seven volumes plus supplements (Lothian Books, Port Melbourne, Victoria). A comprehensive and invaluable resource for anyone interested in the possibilities of Australian plants in gardens.

Key Guide to Australian Palms, Ferns and Allies, by Leonard Cronin (Reed Books, Australia). Illustrations and comprehensive descriptions of a selected list of palms and ferns. Also *Key Guide to Australian Trees* and *Key Guide to Australian Wildflowers.*

The Kuranga Handbook of Australian Plants, by Gwen Elliot, Rodger Elliot, Evan Clucas and Leanne Weston (Lothian Books, Melbourne). Lists concise, tabulated details of some 1300 plants suitable for gardens.

Wildflowers of Western Australia, by C.A. Gardner (St George Books, Perth, Western Australia).

CHILE

Arboles Natives de Chile–Chilean Trees: Identification Guide, by Claudio Donoso Zegers (Marisa Cuneo Ediciones, Valdivia). An illustrated pocket guide in Spanish and English to some of the more notable Chilean trees, with distribution maps.

Bosques de Chile, by Jurgen Rottman (Ingenieria de Gestion, Santiago). Description of the plants and other attributes of the Chilean Forests, in Spanish and English.

Flora of Tierra del Fuego, by David Moore (Anthony Nelson, Oswestry, United Kingdom). Comprehensive botanical flora of the area with descriptions, line drawings and distribution maps.

Flora Silvestre de Chile–Zona Central, by Adriana Hoffman (Fundacion Claudio Gay, Santiago). A field guide with brief descriptions and coloured illustrations of the wildflowers in parts of Chile centred on Santiago. Also *Flora Silvestre de Chile–Zona Sud,* covering the country around and south of Puerto Montt.

NEW ZEALAND

The Cultivation of New Zealand Plants, by Lawrie Metcalfe (Godwit Press, Auckland). A guide to the cultivation of numerous native herbaceous plants, ferns, ornamental grasses and small shrubs.

The Cultivation of New Zealand Trees and Shrubs, by Lawrie Metcalf (Reed, Wellington). Companion volume to the preceding book, dealing with woody plants.

Ferns of New Zealand, by Susan Firth, Martyn Firth and Elizabeth Firth (Hodder and Stoughton, Auckland). Illustrated descriptions of numerous New Zealand ferns, with information about their cultivation.

Gardening with New Zealand Plants, Shrubs & Trees, by Muriel Fisher, E. Satchell and Janet Watkins (Collins, Auckland). An introduction to the cultural needs of numerous native plants.

Native New Zealand Flowering Plants, by J.T. Salmon (Reed, Auckland). An illustrated guide to the trees, shrubs, herbaceous plants and grasses of New Zealand in relation to their natural habitats, with short descriptions.

The Native Trees of New Zealand, by J.T. Salmon (Reed, Wellington). A comprehensive, finely illustrated guide to the trees, including many of the larger shrubby species.

New Zealand Native Plants for your Garden, by Julian Matthews (Viking Pacific, Auckland). Descriptions of the garden uses of a number of popular native New Zealand plants, with illustrations.

The Subtropical Garden in New Zealand, by Gil Hanley (Godwit Publishing, Auckland). A well-illustrated account of trees, shrubs, palms and other plants used to create subtropical effects in gardens.

SOUTH AFRICA

Beautiful Gardens of South Africa, by Nancy Gardiner (Struik Timmins Publishers, Cape Town). Descriptions of a number of selected gardens from all parts of the country, with numerous fine photographs.

A Field Guide to the Wild Flowers of KwaZulu-Natal and the Eastern Region, by Elsa Pooley (Natal Flora Publications Trust, Durban). A comprehensive guide to the wildflowers of the region, with concise descriptions of characteristics and habitats.

Fynbos–South Africa's Unique Floral Kingdom, by Richard Cowling and Dave Richardson (Fernwood Press, Vlaeberg, South Africa). Excellent, authoritative account of the plants and circumstances of the fynbos.

Namaqualand–South African Wildflower Guide, No. 1, by Annelise le Roux and Ted Schelpe (Botanical Society of South Africa). This is one in a series of illustrated, popular guides to the flowers of South Africa, rather reduced in value by the excessively abbreviated descriptions of the plants and their attributes. Others are: *Outeniqua, Tsitsikama and Eastern Little Karoo, No.2; Cape Peninsula, No 3; Transvaal, Lowveld and Escarpment, No. 4; Hottentots-Holland to Hermanus, No.5; Karoo, No. 6; West Coast, No. 7; Southern Overberg, No. 8;* and *Nieuwoudtville, Bokkeveld Plateau and Hantam, No. 9.*

Gardening with Indigenous Plants, by Kristo Pienaar (Struik Publishers, Cape Town). Brightly illustrated account of some of the more easily cultivated South African plants, with information about their care in cultivation.

South African Flowers for the Garden, by Sima Eliovson (Howard Timmins, Cape Town). This book and *Flowering Shrubs and Trees for South African Gardens* by the same author provide wide-ranging guides to the cultivation of South African plants in gardens.

Index